Articles of Association for Charities and Not for Profit Organisations: Guidance and Precedents

Articles of Association for Charities and Not for Profit Organisations: Guidance and Precedents

Richard C. Bishop MA DipFA

Bloomsbury Professional
LONDON • DUBLIN • EDINBURGH • NEW YORK • NEW DELHI • SYDNEY

BLOOMSBURY PROFESSIONAL

Bloomsbury Publishing Plc

50 Bedford Square, London, WC1B 3DP, UK

1385 Broadway, New York, NY 10018, USA

29 Earlsfort Terrace, Dublin 2, Ireland

BLOOMSBURY and the Diana logo are trademarks of Bloomsbury Publishing Plc

First published in Great Britain 2021

British Library Cataloguing-in-Publication Data

A catalogue record for this book is available from the British Library.

ISBN: HB: 978 1 52651 620 6
ePDF: 978 1 52651 622 0
ePub: 978 1 52651 621 3

Typeset by Compuscript Ltd, Shannon
Printed and bound by CPI Group (UK) Ltd, Croydon, CR0 4YY

MIX
Paper from responsible sources
FSC® C013604
FSC www.fsc.org

To find out more about our authors and books visit www.bloomsburyprofessional.com. Here you will find extracts, author information, details of forthcoming events and the option to sign up for our newsletters

Downloadable Precedents

The precedents for this edition are available to download electronically from https://bloomsburyprofessionallaw.com/articlescharities.

They are password-protected and the password is JB9FR5.

They can be downloaded individually or in totality.

If you have any problems downloading the precedents or have any questions, please contact Bloomsbury Professional customer services on 01444 416119 or by email at customerservices@bloomsburyprofessional.com.

For a Licence agreement relating to the use of this Data, please see overleaf at p vi.

Licence Agreement

The Data on https://bloomsburyprofessionallaw.com/articlescharities is © Bloomsbury Professional 2021.

Bloomsbury Professional ('the Publishers') grant you a non-exclusive and non-transferable licence to use the Data from https://bloomsburyprofessionallaw.com/articlescharities.

You may download, copy or print the Data from https://bloomsburyprofessionallaw.com/articlescharities for private use or use in the ordinary course of your business but you may not make any profit from the use of the Data other than would ordinarily be made in the course of your business. You may not sell the Data under any circumstances or make or sell any copy or reproduction of it. You may not copy or print out any part of the Software for any purpose or make any modifications to the Software.

If you have any queries about the use of the Data from https://bloomsburyprofessionallaw.com/articlescharities, please contact customer services at Bloomsbury Professional: customerservices@bloomsburyprofessional.com.

Foreword

Becoming a Trustee of a charity, especially one that is aligned with personal beliefs and values, brings with it both a sense of enormous enthusiasm and great responsibility. My first appointment as a Trustee of a charity was in 2015 when I was asked to join the Board at The Museum of Carpet, in part to help the organisation to move forward with its longer-term strategy – the museum having opened just a couple of years previously with support from the Heritage Lottery Fund.

More recently, as Chair of the Elvaston Castle and Gardens Trust, I have had the opportunity to lead a charitable trust through the first few years of a major £35m regeneration project creating a vibrant new visitor hub at the core of the historic estate and country park. This is phase one of a ten-year plan to regenerate and revitalise the estate to ensure it has a long-term and financially secure future.

The charitable sector has always been an important part of my career. My first job working for The National Trust, and much of my career since has been spent working within the UK tourism industry, within sectors that are dominated by charitable organisations: museums; heritage centres; historic houses; zoos and many others. These are organisations whose remits are usually focussed on conservation, education (through public access) and community participation. Of course, I recognise that my experiences barely scratch the surface of the breadth of activities undertaken by charities – from health and social care to education and animal welfare.

Many of the UKs biggest heritage attractions operate as charitable trusts – and research suggests that many of their visitors are unaware that owners of important historical buildings choose the charity route to secure the long-term future of the country's important historical assets. Indeed, my early contribution to the restoration at Elvaston was spent, with others, developing the most appropriate model for a single management body to operate the estate – a charity with a separate trading arm provides that balance. While other structures were considered, it was clear that being a charity brings with it some important messaging for potential supporters – not least a recognition that we are independent, regulated by the Charity Commission and can be held to account for failures in our duties as Trustees.

The creation of a charity comes with responsibilities that should not be underestimated. Agreeing the charitable objects does not just define the focus of the charity, it defines the work that the charity can claim as its charitable activities. The many benefits of being a charity – collecting Gift Aid and attracting grants and funding, for example, are limited to the work covered by those objects – another reason to also consider the development of a commercial trading arm that can generate revenue from other sources – usually as a Not-For-Profit business.

Trustees, who are almost without exception, volunteers, come from all walks of life. It is important to recognise the work the charity will be undertaking and to create a Board that brings together all the skills that are needed. Many charities struggle because their boards are made up of similar individuals, or those who are passionate about the cause but less knowledgeable about the practicalities and requirements of operating a charity. Carrying out skills audits and ensuring that the right structure exists (Chair, Vice-Chair, Treasurer) is critical to success. I have always sought to create Boards that reflect the responsibilities of the organisation.

This means recruiting individuals who share common values but come from a range of backgrounds where, together, they can make informed decisions (or at least know the right questions to ask of experts and staff) around human resources, legal requirements, financial management and operational management as well as sector specific expertise. At Elvaston we have worked hard to ensure that we have expertise around tourism, events and heritage (which is the 'core business') and that we also have Trustees with specialist knowledge gained in other sectors – at Elvaston our Trustees come from a range of backgrounds including manufacturing, engineering, architectural consultancy, education, tourism, events, logistics and supply chain, financial services, legal services, project management and organisational development. We have a shared passion for the project and have worked hard to review and audit skills to fill gaps and diversify our expertise.

We also recognise the shared responsibilities that we have for the correct management of the charity, we continually evaluate risk. We regularly review our constitution. We have created sub-committee structures to reflect these responsibilities and we ensure that we regularly report on our financial activities. We have appointed a company secretary; we minute our meetings, and we vote on critical decisions. We are a team united by a common passion and an understanding of our responsibilities.

While compliance and procedure are not the most exciting aspect of managing a charity, doing it properly allows us to focus on delivering our charitable objects knowing we are 'doing the right thing'. I look forward to the publication of this book as it will help us further reflect on our practices to ensure that we are scrupulous in the dissemination of our charitable responsibilities.

Dr Peter Robinson
PhD, MA, PGCert, BA (Hons), F.Inst.TT, FTMI, FTS, PFHEA
Head of The Centre for Tourism and Hospitality Management
Chair of the Elvaston Castle and Gardens Trust

Preface

How to use this text

Chapter 1: Not for Profit Companies: England and Wales

The initial chapter provides an overview of the articles of association.

Chapter 2: Analysis of the Model Articles for Private Companies Limited by Guarantee

Chapter 2 provides analysis of the new model articles[1] prescribed by the Companies Act 2006. It should be noted the new model articles are not suitable if the company aspires to incorporate as a company and register as a charity in the UK.

Chapter 3: Analysis of the Model Articles of Association for a Charitable Company (GD1)

Chapter 3 outlines the regulatory prescribed model articles of association[2] for charities based in England or Wales.[3] The structures available to set up a charity are rather complex and include:

- Charitable companies
- Charitable incorporated organisations
- Unincorporated companies
- Trusts
- NHS charities
- Armed forces charities

This text focuses on charitable companies,[4] therefore we have provided analysis of the Charity Commission prescribed articles of association, these are commonly referred to as (GD1).[5]

1 Schedule 2 Regulation 3 Model articles for private companies limited by guarantee.

2 https://assets.publishing.service.gov.uk/government/uploads/system/uploads/attachment_data/file/586363/GD1_articles_of_association.pdf.

3 Registration is mandatory with the Charity Commission if the charity is based in England or Wales and has over £5,000 income per year.

4 The new model articles described in Chapter 2 are not fit for purpose as the Charity Commission prescribes their own model articles of association.

5 Charities are obligated to dual register and incorporate with Companies House and register with the Charity Commission.

Chapter 4: Analysis of the Model Articles of Association for a Right to Manage Company

Chapter 4 discuses the prescribed articles of association[6] for right to manage companies.

Chapter 5: Analysis of the Model Articles of Association for a Community Interest Company

The term 'not for profit' in the corporate setting can be ambiguous, as the term has no legal significance. The community interest company, a company incorporated by shares or guarantee, includes an 'asset lock' in the articles of association. In addition, dividends payments may be restricted to another asset locked body or capped.

For organisations whose main objective is to project an image of encompassing the not for profit philosophy, the CIC is the closest body corporate obtainable.

Chapter 6: Analysis of the Model Articles for a Company and Trust with Employee Ownership

The UK government is very keen to promote the employee ownership (EO) model.[7] Not all EO companies are strictly incorporated to follow the strategic approach of not for profit, nonetheless, companies must, by definition, use the EO philosophy, which arguably produces a company focused on its employees and customers with a diminished emphasis on profits.

The text provides analysis and commentary on the employees' trust and the employee company articles of association.

Precedents

The text provides four long form precedents, along with boilerplate provisions:

- Not for profit company
- Membership organisation
- Charitable company
- Museum

6 The RTM Companies (Model Articles) (England) Regulations 2009, SI 2009/2767.
7 Sharing Success: the Nuttall Review of Employee Ownership (4 July 2012).

If you require help or guidance in using the precedents, please contact the author: richard@richardbishop.co.uk.

Please note, I cannot guarantee a formal reply, however I will endeavour to help and advise where possible.

For my wife Jackie and my parents Alan and Irene

Note to the Reader

This text discusses the main articles of association for charities and non-profit organisations and provides outline, long form precedents for each. For clarity, the text focuses on articles of association that are prescribed by law or statutory instrument in the charity and not for profit sectors.

Articles of Association for Charities and Not for Profit Organisations: Guidance and Precedents is the second book written, following the first, *Articles of Association: Guidance and Precedents*. It is acknowledged by the author the content of certain chapters does reiterate parts of the text from book 1, this is inevitable given the crossover of the subject matter.

Articles of Association for Charities and Not for Profit Organisations: Guidance and Precedents is the second book I've written on the subject of company and charity constitutions. Although both texts are credited to myself, alone, it would not have been possible to publish either without the considerable assistance of the team at Bloomsbury Professional.

The encouragement and advice from Andy Hill has been invaluable, along with Claire Banyard who copy edited both books. Claire's input and advice has been pivotal in publishing both texts, I thank both Andy and Claire for their efforts in supporting my publishing career.

Sharon Heaton has provided outstanding support in both the design and online marketing of both books, along with my office manager Amanda Chambers who spends her time printing drafts and helping with the initial edit, both deserve credit for their help and assistance.

Contents

Table of Statutes

[All references are to paragraph numbers]

Table of Statutory Instruments

[All references are to paragraph numbers]

R

Table of Cases

[*All references are to paragraph numbers*]

Chapter 1 Not for Profit Companies: England and Wales

What is a not for profit company?

1.1

The term 'not for profit' (NFP) is typically used in the UK to define an organisation that is established for the purpose of furthering its objects,[1] without the prerequisite to make a surplus profit and distribute dividends to shareholders.

It is common practice for the articles of association[2] of a company limited by guarantee to include objects clauses, which unambiguously identify the objects of the company, its focus and any restrictions to the company's activities.

Private companies limited by guarantee have directors and members, this contrasts with a private company limited by shares, which by definition has directors and members who are shareholders. Incorporating by either model, the company may still claim to be a NFP company. In the UK the private limited company limited by guarantee is utilised more often for a NFP company.

What is the benefit of incorporating?

1.2

Individuals who operate in the NFP or charity sector who employ the trust or unincorporated model, may leave themselves open to liability. This may comprise of personal legal liability or debts incurred in running the charity.

To overcome this problem, those wishing to form an organisation focused on charitable acts or to operate in the NFP sector, typically incorporate. The main advantage achieved is the company is legally separate from the individuals who

1 The company objects are the range and scope of activities which the company may undertake. Companies formed prior to 1 October 2009 specifically restricted company activities by the inclusion of a clause in the memorandum of association. Under the Companies Act 2006, objects are unrestricted unless the articles of association state otherwise.

2 Or memorandum of association for companies incorporated prior to 1 October 2009.

run it, and maintains separate finances from the members. The members act as guarantors to a limited monetary amount, the 'guaranteed amount'.[3]

It should be noted that particular community organisations[4] may incorporate as a company and fail to meet charity status and be liable for taxes on the same basis as any limited company by guarantee.

Incorporating a company limited by guarantee

1.3

Companies incorporated to operate in the NFP or charity sector will not issue shares and therefore the company will not have shareholders to hold the directors to account. Instead, the company has guarantors who agree to pay a nominal amount if the company is wound up, typically the guarantee amount is £1 as set out in the articles of association. The individuals who acts as guarantors on incorporation subscribe to the memorandum of association and are referred to as the founding members.

How is the members' liability agreed?

1.4

The members' liability is detailed in the new model articles,[5] Part 1 Interpretation and limitation of liability, section 2 liability of members.

Limited liability

1.5

Article 2 of Schedule 2 of the 2008 Regulations states:

> 'Liability of members
>
> 2. The liability of each member is limited to £1, being the amount that each member undertakes to contribute to the assets of the company in the event of its being wound up while he is a member or within one year after he ceases to be a member, for—
>
> (a) payment of the company's debts and liabilities contracted before he ceases to be a member,

3 See www.gov.uk/limited-company-formation.

4 Charities Act 2011, s 6(1) (Registered sports clubs). 'A registered sports club established for charitable purposes is to be treated as not being so established, and accordingly cannot be a charity.'

5 Companies (Model Articles) Regulations 2008, SI 2008/3229, Schedule 2 Model articles for private companies limited by guarantee.

(b) payment of the costs, charges and expenses of winding up, and

(c) adjustment of the rights of the contributories among themselves.'

Membership of the company limited by guarantee

1.6

The articles of association and its provisions provide the process of admitting new members to the company. Once the company is formed by the guarantors and the directors have been appointed, new members may request to join the company. The process for application and termination is specified in articles 21 and 22 of the new model articles:[6]

'Part 3 Members

Becoming and ceasing to be a member

Applications for membership

21. No person shall become a member of the company unless—

(a) that person has completed an application for membership in a form approved by the directors, and

(b) the directors have approved the application.

Termination of membership

22.—(1) A member may withdraw from membership of the company by giving 7 days' notice to the company in writing.

(2) Membership is not transferable.

(3) A person's membership terminates when that person dies or ceases to exist.'

Can I change the membership articles?

1.7

The provisions in articles 21 and 22 can be adapted to include various classes of membership, together with bespoke provisions to address the specific requirements of company.

6 Companies (Model Articles) Regulations 2008, SI 2008/3229, Schedule 2 Model articles for private companies limited by guarantee.

Members' register

1.8

The members must appoint at least one director to manage the company, generally the guarantor members would appoint themselves directors. The company is required to keep a register of members which must include: the member's name and address, the date membership commenced and in the case of a member withdrawing from membership the date membership ceased.[7]

It should be noted, the directors are bound by the rules and regulations of the Companies Act 2006, in particular they must abide by the general duties of directors.[8]

Private limited companies by guarantee: the benefit of no shareholder actions

1.9

Private companies limited by shares may need to consider the potential for minority shareholders seeking redress through the courts to enforce compliance with the articles of association if they consider the majority has acted in its own favour. In particular, potential shareholder actions may include: the winding up of the company and fair price valuations of the minority shareholding on transfer or death. It is good practice to draft unambiguous provisions in the articles of association to offset potential actions by the minority.

A considerable advantage of the company limited by guarantee is that on the basis no shareholdings are issued, the company is simpler to manage without the potential for shareholder actions against the company.

Which articles do private limited companies by guarantee use?

1.10

For NFP companies that incorporate under the Companies Act 2006 without registering with the Charity Commission, the default articles applied are the Schedule 2 Regulation 3 Model articles for private companies limited by guarantee.

7 Companies Act 2006, s 113 (Register of members).
8 Companies Act 2006, Pt 10, Ch 2 (General duties of directors).

For companies incorporated under previous Companies Acts, generally the Companies Act 1985, the constitution will consist of the memorandum of association and Table C.[9]

Charities that are also companies (GD1)

1.11

A charity may incorporate with Companies House as a company limited by guarantee and register with the Charity Commission, the advantage for the organisation is the generous government exemption from most direct taxes.

The Charity Commission provides default articles of association (GD1)[10] that meet the requirements of both the Companies Act 2006 and the Charities Act 2011 and are discussed in Chapter 3.

What are the articles of association?

1.12

The company articles of association are the internal policies, rules and procedures that the directors and members must follow when making decisions concerning the company.

Members delegate all powers to the directors,[11] who in turn make decisions at board meetings. Members will require assurance that any decision making by the directors follows an agreed procedure. In addition, they provide an aide-memoire for the directors of the main statutory regulations imposed by the relevant Companies Act the company was incorporated under.

The legality of the articles of association

1.13

The articles of association constitute a contract between the members and the company and between each individual member.[12] The provisions of

9 The Companies (Tables A to F) Regulations 1985, SI 1985/805, see www.legislation.gov.uk/uksi/1985/805/pdfs/uksi_19850805_en.pdf.

10 See assets.publishing.service.gov.uk/government/uploads/system/uploads/attachment_data/file/586363/GD1_articles_of_association.pdf.

11 Model articles, article 3 'Directors' general authority': '3.Subject to the articles, the directors are responsible for the management of the company's business, for which purpose they may exercise all the powers of the company.'

12 *Wood v Odessa Waterworks Co* (1889) 42 Ch D 636.

the company's constitution are covenants which bind the company and its members.[13]

What provisions should the articles of association contain?

1.14

The articles should detail members' rights, for example rights to attend meetings, to appoint and dismiss directors and members, and rights on voting, together with more complex areas of the Companies Act 2006.

Are the articles legally binding?

1.15

If detailed in the articles of association, any rights or agreements are enforceable in law (*Postgate & Denby (Agencies), Re*).[14] Before drafting detailed provisions and procedures, care must be taken to ensure they are for the benefit of the company and referring back to the directors' duties they promote the success of the company.

The courts' overall view on the articles of association is they ought to produce unambiguous outcomes and reasonable business efficacy. In *Holmes v Lord Keyes*[15] per Jenkins LJ:

> 'the articles of association of the company should be regarded as a business document and should be construed so as to give them reasonable business efficacy where a construction tending to that result is admissible on the language of the articles, in preference to a result which would or might prove unworkable'.

Restrictive articles of association that may fetter the directors' powers or conflict with the Companies Act 2006 could be deemed void and more often than not make running the company more problematic.

How do I draft the articles of association for a company?

1.16

The articles are complex legal documents, therefore the government of the day acknowledged when passing legislation concerning company law that the

13 Companies Act 2006, s 33 (Effect of company's constitution).
14 [1987] BCLC 8.
15 [1959] Ch 199.

drafting of such documents is typically beyond the remit of a company director or charity trustee.

All Companies Acts of Parliament provide model articles of association, prescribed by the Secretary of State or by statutory instrument. The most recent are:

- The Companies (Tables A to F) Regulations 1985, SI 1985/805, Table A.[16] Memorandum and articles of association. For private companies without share capital incorporated under the Companies Act 1985, Table C will apply.
- Companies Act 2006. Schedule 2 Regulation 3 Model articles for private companies limited by guarantee.[17]

Table A is the name given to the prescribed format for articles of association of a company limited by shares under the Companies Act 1985 and earlier legislation. When a company incorporates, it was not required to file bespoke articles, the relevant company legislation[18] provided standard articles, often referred to as model articles.

The first prescribed format, made in the Joint Stock Companies Act 1856, was called 'Table B', because it was preceded by a form of memorandum of association called 'Form A'. The articles were first called 'Table A' in the Companies Act 1862.

Constitutional documents – before 1 October 2009

1.17

Companies formed prior to 1 October 2009[19] were legally required to draft a memorandum of association and articles of association. The memorandum was an important constitutional document that stated the company name, powers, registered office, the company objects[20] and its liability. The memorandum prevails over the articles under any circumstances of ambiguity between the two documents.[21]

Companies that have not updated their articles of association under the Companies Act 2006 must abide by the memorandum, however the provisions

16 The Companies (Tables A to F) Regulations 1985, SI 1985/805.
17 Companies Act 2006, s 19 (Power of Secretary of State to prescribe model articles).
18 Articles were brought into force by statutory instrument.
19 Companies formed after 1 October 2006 will fall under the Companies Act 2006, Chapter 2 Articles of association.
20 Company objects state the purpose of the company, powers and the range of trading activities. The company is restricted to its powers and stated objects.
21 *Guinness v Land Corp of Ireland* (1882) 22 Ch D 349.

will be deemed to form part of the articles of association as legally they are now one document.[22]

Constitutional documents – after 1 October 2009

1.18

As regards companies formed after 1 October 2009, the company's constitution excludes the memorandum, see section 17:

> 'A company's constitution
>
> Unless the context otherwise requires, references in the Companies Acts to a company's constitution include—
>
> (a) the company's articles, and
>
> (b) any resolutions and agreements to which Chapter 3 applies (see section 29).'

The Companies Act 2006 still uses the term 'memorandum of association', the document is not constitutional and simply states the members wish to form a company and agree to become members and in the case of companies with share capital the member agrees to take at least one share.

The memorandum is still important as it forms part of the required registration process, as discussed, and by virtue of section 17 it is not constitutional and the majority of the elements of the pre-1 October 2009 memorandum are dealt with in additional documents and the registration process.

Amending the articles of association

Company

1.19

Along with providing the rules on how a company is run and governed the company constitution binds contractually the company and its members, therefore the provisions should be discussed and agreed by all parties involved in the company. The articles are amendable by passing a special resolution,[23] it should be noted in the case of a company that is a charity section 21(2)(a) will apply.[24]

22 Companies Act 2006, s 28 (Existing companies: provisions of memorandum treated as provisions of articles).

23 Companies Act 2006, s 21 (Amendment of articles) '(1) A company may amend its articles by special resolution'.

24 Companies Act 2006, s 21 (Amendment of articles) '(2) In the case of a company that is a charity, this is subject to (a) in England and Wales, sections 197 and 198 of the Charities Act 2011'.

The company may use the prescribed articles under the Act under which it was incorporated or it may draft its own.

All articles of association are subject to the Companies Act under which they are formed, the company is in addition constricted by case law (rules made by judges' decisions in court). Consequently, the articles may not contain provisions that are against the law. The company has complete freedom to draft bespoke articles and develop rules to suit the individual company and the requirements of the members.

Charity and restrictions on alteration of objects

1.20

A company that is a charity is free to amend its articles of association under section 21 of the Companies Act. Sections 197 and 198 of the Charities Act 2011 stipulate any regulated alteration must be approved by the Commission, regulated activities include: changing the charitable purposes of the company, the process on winding up and alteration to the rules concerning directors' benefits. Written consent is required before the passing of a special resolution to make any alterations to the articles that include regulated activities. A draft resolution must be submitted online to the Commission[25] before convening a general meeting of the company.

The section applies to all charitable companies:[26]

> '198 Alteration of objects by companies and Commission's consent
>
> (1) Any regulated alteration by a charitable company—
>
> (a) requires the prior written consent of the Commission, and
>
> (b) is ineffective if such consent has not been obtained.
>
> (2) The following are regulated alterations—
>
> (a) an amendment of the company's articles of association adding, removing or altering a statement of the company's objects,
>
> (b) any alteration of any provision of its articles of association directing the application of property of the company on its dissolution, and
>
> (c) any alteration of any provision of its articles of association where the alteration would provide authorisation for any benefit to be obtained by directors or members of the company or persons connected with them.'

25 How to make changes to your charity's governing documents: see https://www.gov.uk/guidance/how-to-make-changes-to-your-charitys-governing-document.

26 Charities Act 2011, s 198 applies to companies incorporated prior to 1 October 2009 whose members may require alteration to the memorandum of association.

Post-1 October 2009 model articles – the position today

1.21

In terms of the company constitution today, the members only need to concern themselves with the articles of association, as discussed they have complete freedom to draft provisions to meet the requirements of the company on the basis they do not fetter Acts of Parliament or case law.

It should be noted that the articles cannot compel members to commit unlawful acts. The memorandum of association is a non-constitutional document, its requirements under the Companies Act 2006 are defined by statutory instrument[27] and are primarily used as part of the registration process.[28] The company's objects are not restricted (unless the members wish to restrict them), any provisions concerning objects would be drafted in the articles.

The Companies (Model Articles) Regulations 2008 prescribe three types of model articles, private companies limited by shares, private companies limited by guarantee and public companies.[29] The new model articles simplified and reduced the legalistic language of the previous articles and attempted to reflect the updated Companies Act 2006. The department for business innovation and skills[30] at the time of drafting the new model articles focused on 'think small first', therefore the articles for private companies are designed for small companies.

For any company formed after 1 October 2009 the new model articles will automatically apply by 'default application', unless the articles are clear that the default articles should not apply. For companies who follow the default application process, they are not required to register articles. The company may override the default application by three methods: totally exclude (stating the model articles do not apply), exclude provisions of the Companies Act 2006, or state the model articles apply with clearly drafted modifications.

The ability to use these methods is useful for medium sized limited companies limited by shares who may wish to adopt the articles by default but include some of the provisions from the public limited default articles, for example a company could include article 44 (power to pay commissions), which broadly is unlikely to affect most small private limited companies. Overall this reduces the need to draft complete bespoke articles and therefore eradicates expensive legal advice.

27 The Companies (Registration) Regulations 2008, SI 2008/3014.

28 Form (1N01 Application to register a company) contains much of the information previously detailed in the pre-1 October 2009 memorandum.

29 The Companies (Model Articles) Regulations 2008, SI 2008/3229.

30 Replaced by the Department for Business, Energy and Industrial Strategy.

Key points

1.22

- For NFP companies incorporating today who will not register with the Charity Commission, the default articles of association are: Schedule 2 Regulation 3 Model articles for private companies limited by guarantee.[31]
- Under the Companies Act 1985 the articles of association were brought about by statutory instrument, therefore long form model articles are created by using Table A[32] – Regulations for management of a company limited by shares, which is then adapted by Table C,[33] described in the same statutory instrument.[34]
- Companies incorporated under the Companies Act 1985 (and previous Companies Acts) will, in addition to the articles of association, hold a memorandum of association, which is still binding on the company.[35]
- Companies who incorporated as private limited companies by guarantee, prior to 1 October 2009 who have not updated their articles of association, generally will use Table C.
- A charity may incorporate as a company under the Companies Act 2006 and register as a charity with the Charity Commission. The company is then required to use the Charity Commission prescribed articles of association (GD1).
- The articles of association form a binding contract between the company and its members and the members themselves as a group. The articles may be enforced in law.

Guide to the new model articles

1.23

Chapter 2 of this book provides analysis of the model articles for private companies limited by guarantee.

31 See www.gov.uk/government/publications/model-articles-for-private-companies-limited-by-guarantee.

32 The Companies (Tables A to F) Regulations 1985, SI 1985/805, Table A, Regulations for a management of company limited by shares.

33 The Companies (Tables A to F) Regulations 1985, SI 1985/805, Table C, A company limited by guarantee and not having a share capital, Articles of association.

34 See Table C, Appendix 2.

35 Companies Act 1985, Memorandum of association. Separate document to the articles of association and contains the name of the company, registered office address and the objects of the company.

1.24

The articles of association for private limited companies are specifically drafted for small companies with the minimum number of rules which directly correspond to the Companies Act 2006. The Act is 700 pages long with 1,300 sections, which until the Corporation Tax Act 2009 held the legislative UK record for being the longest Act in the history of British Parliament. The model articles are a condensed synopsis covering the main legislation the members should consider when making decisions.

Although the Companies Act has been in force for over a decade it is worthwhile covering the main areas that a company should consider when amending the new model articles or updating from when incorporated under previous Companies Acts. The new model articles can broadly be assigned under three sub-headings:

(1) Articles amended by the removal of statutory duties.

(2) Articles applied in conjunction with the Companies Act 2006.

(3) Articles which provide guidance that allows for freedom to amend.

Articles that are amended by the removal of statutory duties

Annual general meetings (AGM)

1.25

A private company limited by shares or guarantee is not required to hold an annual general meeting (AGM). Companies incorporated under previous Acts may have articles detailing the requirement for an AGM, therefore members will expect the company to hold one.

The Companies Act 2006 does not override the articles of previous acts, therefore the members would be required to pass a special resolution to agree to remove the AGM article and update from Table A to the new model articles.

Conversely if members of a company incorporated after 1 October 2009 require the company to hold an AGM the articles would require adaptation following a special resolution agreeing the amendment.

Company secretary

1.26

A private company is no longer required to have a company secretary, as with the new rules on AGMs, the existing articles should be reviewed and amendments made to suit the members' requirements. If a company incorporated after 1 October 2009 requires a company secretary then the articles should be adapted to reflect this.

Articles which provide guidance with freedom to amend

1.27

Article 53 provides power to the company to provide company directors with insurance, the article is a new addition and did appear in the previous Table A. The insurance is optional, therefore the article could be removed completely, in doing so it would not upset any provisions in the Companies Act or case law.

> '53. Insurance
>
> (1) The directors may decide to purchase and maintain insurance, at the expense of the company, for the benefit of any relevant director in respect of any relevant loss.
>
> (2) In this article—
>
> (a) a "relevant director" means any director or former director of the company or an associated company,
>
> (b) a "relevant loss" means any loss or liability which has been or may be incurred by a relevant director in connection with that director's duties or powers in relation to the company, any associated company or any pension fund or employees' share scheme of the company or associated company, and
>
> (c) companies are associated if one is a subsidiary of the other or both are subsidiaries of the same body corporate.'

Housekeeping on drafting bespoke articles

1.28

The following should be noted before attempting modification. The articles must be in a single document with consecutively numbered paragraphs.[36] A special resolution is required to amend the articles[37] with the exception of determining the terms and conditions of share redemptions where it is possible to amend the articles by ordinary resolution.[38] Any article that conflicts with the memorandum or established law is void and unenforceable.[39]

36 Companies Act 2006, s 18(3).

37 Companies Act 2006, s 21(1).

38 Companies Act 2006, s 685 (Terms and manner of redemption) '(2) A resolution under subsection (1)(b) may be an ordinary resolution, even though it amends the company's articles.'

39 *Welton v Saffery* [1895–99] All ER Rep 567. Lord Macnaghten: 'It is familiar law that no article can be valid or binding upon the shareholders, which is in conflict with the memorandum or with the general law.'

In *Welton v Saffery*[40] the articles contained an *ultra vires* provision authorising the company to issue shares at a discount.

Key drafting points Companies Act 1985 updating to Companies Act 2006

1.29

A company incorporated prior to 1 October 2009 under any of the relevant Companies Acts is not required to update their constitutional documents to the requirements of the Companies Act 2006.

Memorandum of association

1.30

For companies incorporated before 1 October 2009, the memorandum remains an important constitutional document that is automatically deemed to now form part of the articles of association by section 28 of the Companies Act 2006:

> 'Existing companies: provisions of memorandum treated as provisions of articles
>
> (1) Provisions that immediately before the commencement of this Part were contained in a company's memorandum but are not provisions of the kind mentioned in section 8 (provisions of new-style memorandum) are to be treated after the commencement of this Part as provisions of the company's articles.
>
> (2) This applies not only to substantive provisions but also to provision for entrenchment (as defined in section 22).
>
> (3) The provisions of this Part about provision for entrenchment apply to such provision as they apply to provision made on the company's formation, except that the duty under section 23(1)(a) to give notice to the registrar does not apply.'

Incorporation of the memorandum requires no action from the company, for limited liability companies the liability of members is now covered in the articles of association, see Part 1 section 2. The objects clauses in the memorandum[41] which may restrict the company's powers can be removed by special resolution,[42] updating the Table A articles may present an opportunity to lessen any restrictions on the company's scope of activities or means of operation.

40 *Welton v Saffery* [1897] AC 299.

41 Objects clause describes the purpose of the company and the activities it may undertake or not undertake. A company acting outside their stated objects is *ultra vires*.

42 Special resolution requires at least 75% of the votes cast by shareholders.

Updating the articles of association

1.31

When company law is amended by a new Act the company's articles of association remain bound to the Companies Act under which the company was incorporated. If the members of the company wish to update the constitutional documents to fall under a prevailing Act, for example, a company incorporated in 1989 under the Companies Act 1985 to the Companies Act 2006, they must amend their articles.

The amendment requires 75% of the eligible voting members to agree and pass a special resolution,[43] charities are subject to the Charity Commission rules and in addition may be required to seek approval for any constitutional changes.[44]

Key points

1.32

- A company must have articles of association.[45]
- The articles must contain a provision detailing the limits of any liability.
- Articles must be in a single document with numbered paragraphs.
- A company on formation will automatically adopt the model articles on formation, unless it decides otherwise.
- Companies incorporated using Table A will not automatically be upgraded to the new articles under the Companies Act 2006. The memorandum will be 'automatically deemed' to form part of the companies' articles of association.
- The memorandum is still utilised as part of the registration process, it is not a constitutional document from companies incorporated after 1 October 2009.
- Companies incorporated under the Companies Act 2006 objects are unlimited and without restriction unless they choose to restrict them.
- Existing companies incorporated before 1 October 2009 can update to the new articles by passing a special resolution.[46]

43 Companies Act 2006, s 21 (Amendment of articles) '(1) A company may amend its articles by special resolution.'
44 Charities Act 2011, ss 197 and 198.
45 Companies Act 2006, s 18(1).
46 Subject to additional Companies House/registrar filing requirements.

- Companies by special resolution are able to amend the articles of association.[47]
- When amending or adopting articles first consider company and case law. The article may be voidable.
- Articles cannot contain provisions that would cause the company or its directors to act outside of the law.
- Amending articles falls broadly into three categories:
  - (a) Amended by changes in law.
  - (b) Amended in conjunction with the Companies Act 2006.
  - (c) Guidance only, that allow for freedom to amend.

Charities

Forms of company

1.33

Chapter 3 of this book provides analysis of the prescribed articles for a charitable company (GD1).

1.34

The Charities Act 2011 recognises two types of company, the charitable company as defined by section 193[48] and the Charitable Incorporated Organisation (CIO) defined by section 205.[49] The constitution for a charitable company is stipulated by the Companies Act 2006;[50] in contrast the constitution for a CIO is defined by the Charites Act 2011.[51]

Charitable Incorporated Organisation

1.35

The CIO is an alternative legal form for a charity. Legally it is a corporate body, without the requirement to incorporate under the Companies Act 2006. The considerable advantage of the CIO versus a charitable company is that the Companies House reporting and accounting requirement are negated,

47 Companies Act 2006, s 21(1).
48 Charities Act 2011, s 193 (Meaning of 'charitable company') 'In this Act "charitable company" means a charity which is a company.'
49 Charities Act 2011, s 205(1) 'A CIO is a body corporate.'
50 Companies Act 2006, s 18 (Articles of association).
51 Charities Act 2011, s 206 (Constitution).

together with the onerous company regulations. The company retains its own legal identity and therefore the directors' liability is limited[52] if the CIO is wound up.

The Charities Act 2011 specifies what the CIO constitution must state.[53] Section 206 allows the Charity Commission to specify its own regulations as to the form and contents of the CIO constitution.[54]

The CIO constitution must contain:

- its name;[55]
- its purpose;[56]
- its address[57] in England and Wales;[58]
- the liability of members on winding up or if the members have no liability;[59]
- who may become a member and the process of becoming a member;[60]
- the appointment of one or more trustees and any conditions of eligibility;[61] and
- how property is to be distributed on the dissolution of the CIO.[62]

Charity Commission model governing documents

1.36

The Charity Commission provides a range of model governing documents which are discussed in the next section. It should be noted in the corporate sphere the company articles of association were simplified by the Companies Act 2006[63] and on incorporation a company may adopt model articles[64] without any amendment.[65]

52 'Constitution of a CIO whose only voting members are its charity trustees', Clause 8 – Liability of members – The constitution must state whether members of the CIO either have no liability or liable to contribute to a maximum amount.
53 Charities Act 2011, s 206.
54 Charities Act 2011, s 206(5).
55 Charities Act 2011, s 206(1).
56 Charities Act 2011, s 206(1).
57 The principal office of the CIO must be in England or Wales, written in English or in Welsh if located in Wales.
58 Charities Act 2011, s 206(1).
59 Charities Act 2011, s 206(1).
60 Charities Act 2011, s 206(2).
61 Charities Act 2011, s 206(2).
62 Charities Act 2011, s 206(2).
63 Companies Act 2006, Part 3, Chapter 2 Articles of association.
64 Companies Act 2006, s 19 (Power of Secretary of State to prescribe model articles).
65 Charity Commission Guidance, 'How to write your charity's governing document (CC22b)'.

Charities are required by the Charity Commission to add specific provisions into the model constitutions and articles, in particular the charity objects which are particular to each individual charity.

Additional information

1.37

The articles must contain:[66]

- the charity's name;
- its objects and purpose;
- the powers available to the company;
- who can be a trustee, how they are appointed, how long they can hold office and if they can be reappointed;
- how many meetings are needed, how they are arranged, how a chair is appointed, how votes are made and counted (including minimum numbers for this);
- who can be a member, age restrictions, how to end someone's membership, how membership meetings are called;
- how trustees must not benefit from the charity (excluding reasonable expenses) without Commission approval or unless it is authorised in the governing document;
- how the trustees can change the charity's governing document, when Commission approval is needed, how amendments are recorded; and
- if the charity can be closed, what happens to any remaining assets (charitable assets can only be used for charitable purposes).

Charity purposes: its objects

1.38

The articles of a non-charitable company incorporated under the Companies Act 2006 are not required to have objects. Companies incorporated under previous Companies Acts were required to include an objects clause in the Memorandums of Association describing the purpose of the company and the activities it was authorised to undertake. Acting outside of the company objects is *ultra vires*.

66 Charitable Companies: Model Articles of Association (GD1) 2014 revised 2017.

Charitable articles must restrict the company's activities to specifically furthering the charitable objects. The charity's objects are defined by identifying the charity's purpose and what it is set up to achieve.

Charities in England and Wales are set up with the singular function of achieving their charitable purpose. The purpose must fall within the description of purposes described in section 3 of the Charities Act 2011[67] and benefit the public.[68] The Charity Commission provides guidance on writing a charity's purpose.[69]

Governing documents

1.39

In 2018–19 roughly 60% of applications submitted to the Charity Commission resulted in registration; 40% of applications failed based on incorrect information being submitted or failure to follow up requests by the Commission for further information.[70] It could be speculated a great many applications fail due to inaccurate governing documents.

The Charity Commission suggests employing the relevant Charity Commission's model governing documents to reference the contents and form the basis of the constitution. The Commission provides the following templates.

Charity Commission

1.40

For companies incorporating under the Companies Act 2006:

- Model articles of association for a charitable company.

Charitable Incorporated Organisation (CIO)

1.41

- Model constitution for CIO with voting members other than its charity trustees ('Association' model).

67 Charities Act 2011, s 3(1) (Descriptions of purposes).

68 Charities Act 2011, s 4 (The public benefit requirement) '(1) In this Act "the public benefit requirement" means the requirement in section 2(1)(b) that a purpose falling within section 3(1) must be for the public benefit if it is to be a charitable purpose.'

69 Charity Commission Guidance, 'How to write your charity's governing document (CC22b)'.

70 Charity Commission Annual Report 2018–2019.

- Model constitution for a CIO whose only voting members are its charity trustees ('Foundation' model).

It should be noted the CIO is not a company as defined by any Companies Act and the organisation is not required to register with Companies House.

Additional constitutions

1.42

In addition the Commission provides the following model governing documents:[71]

- Model memorandum of association for a charitable company not having a share capital.
- Model trust deed for a charitable trust.
- Model constitution for a small charity.
- Model constitution for an unincorporated charity.

NHS charities[72]

1.43

- NHS charities: model declaration of trust for an NHS special purpose charity (2007 version) – model C.[73]
- NHS charities: supplemental deed for general purpose charities comprising unrestricted funds but whose objects are more narrowly defined than the statutory remit – model G.[74]

Armed Forces charities[75]

1.44

- Constitution for Membership Service Funds – no managing trustee.
- Constitution for Membership Service Funds – with managing trustee.

71 Charity Commission Guidance, 'Setting up a charity: model governing documents'.

72 NHS charities: model trust deeds, see www.gov.uk/government/publications/nhs-charities-model-trust-deeds.

73 Model C, for use where an NHS Trust or Primary Care Trust or other NHS body acts as sole corporate trustee.

74 Model G, for use by a general purpose NHS charity with more narrowly defined objects.

75 Charities supporting the armed forces: model governing documents, see www.gov.uk/government/publications/charities-supporting-the-armed-forces-model-governing-documents.

- Trust Deed/Standard Governing Document Non Membership – no managing trustee.
- Trust Deed/Standard Governing Document Non Membership – with managing trustee.

Key points

1.45

- A charity may incorporate as a company. Dual registration is required with Companies House and the Charity Commission.
- A charitable company is subject to dual legislation: the Companies Act 2006 and the Charities Act 2011.
- The model articles for a private company limited by guarantee are not fit for purpose if registering with the Charity Commission and will require the inclusion of additional information required by the Commission (see additional information above).
- The model articles provided by the Commission can be adapted to provide specific bespoke clauses and rules particular to the charity.
- The alternative to the onerous responsibilities of dual registration is to use a CIO, providing the trustees a body corporate with a separate legal identity and the provision of no or limited liability.
- CIO utilises a constitution as opposed to the articles of association of a company incorporated under a Companies Act.
- The contents and format of the CIO constitution is provided legislatively, in addition, the Commission is free to make rules on its subject matter. The CIO constitution is prescribed and cannot be adapted, modified or replaced, as is the case with the articles of association of a non-charitable company.
- The Charity Commission expects those registering as a charity to use the model governing documents.

RTM companies

Right to manage companies

1.46

Chapter 4 of this book provides analysis of the prescribed articles of association for a right to manage company.

1.47

Right to manage (RTM) companies[76] are private companies limited by guarantee enabling long leaseholders in blocks of flats to take over the management of their building irrespective of any fault on the part of their landlord. Leaseholders must form a company to exercise their management functions.[77]

Introduction

1.48

The Commonhold and Leasehold Reform Act 2002 provided legislation for tenants of flats to take over the management of the property. A full discussion of the qualifying rules to acquire and manage property[78] is beyond the scope of this text, which is focused on the analysis of the prescribed articles of association and the relevant legislation.

Commonhold and Leasehold Reform Act 2002

1.49

Sections 73 and 74[79] form the central legislation for RTM companies, describing what constitutes an RTM company and provisions for the adoption of articles of association.

Section 73

1.50

The right to manage a property must be set up using a right to manage company,[80] it cannot be initiated by an individual or partnership. The RTM must be incorporated at Companies House and take the form of a private company limited by guarantee,[81] its objects must include the acquisition and right to manage the proposed property.[82]

76 All RTM companies are private companies limited by guarantee.

77 Explanatory memorandum to The RTM Companies (Model Articles) (England) Regulations 2009, SI 2009/2767.

78 Commonhold and Leasehold Reform Act 2002, Chapter 1 Right to manage.

79 Commonhold and Leasehold Reform Act 2002.

80 Commonhold and Leasehold Reform Act 2002, s 71(1).

81 Commonhold and Leasehold Reform Act 2002, s 73(2)(a).

82 Commonhold and Leasehold Reform Act 2002, s 73(2)(b).

Section 74

1.51

The legislation allowed for an appropriate national authority[83] to make regulations concerning the form and content of the articles of an RTM company.[84] The default provisions are applied by statutory instrument[85] and came into force on 9 November 2009. The RTM articles cover the provisions for taking up membership, voting rights and governance.

Background to the legislation

1.52

The RTM Companies (Model Articles) (England) Regulations 2009[86] revoked and replaced the transitional provisions under the Companies Acts 1985 and 1989.[87]

When introduced, the Companies Act 2006 made changes to the constitutional documents of companies, the 2009 Regulations reflected the appropriate changes. The 2006 Act abolished requirements for a company to restrict its objects and retain a separate memorandum of association. It should be noted, the 2009 Regulations restrict the objects of the company to RTM functions only.[88]

The drafting of the prescribed articles of association for a RTM company is based on the Companies (Model Articles) Regulations 2008, which are designed to be more focused on the needs of smaller companies. The additional provisions concentrated on membership, insurance and inspection of documents.

Transitional arrangements

1.53

For companies incorporated under previous Companies Acts, their memorandum and articles are prescribed by the RTM Companies (Memorandum and Articles of Association) (England) Regulations 2003.[89]

83 Commonhold and Leasehold Reform Act 2002, s 74(2). The 'appropriate national authority' in respect of England is the Secretary of State and, in respect of Wales, is the Welsh Ministers.

84 Powers conferred by the Commonhold and Leasehold Reform Act 2002, s 74(2), (4) and (6) and s 178(1).

85 The RTM Companies (Model Articles) (England) Regulations 2009, SI 2009/2767.

86 SI 2009/2767. The instrument applies to England.

87 RTM Companies (Memorandum and Articles of Association) (England) Regulations 2003 (SI 2003/2120).

88 Companies Act 2006, s 31 (Statement of company's objects) '(1) Unless a company's articles specifically restrict the objects of the company, its objects are unrestricted.'

89 SI 2003/2120. The memorandum and articles of association prescribed for RTM companies, under the Companies Acts 1985 and 1989, were based upon the Table C format made under the 1985 Companies Act. See The Companies (Table A to F) Regulations 1985.

The new 2009 Regulations[90] revoked the previous instrument, subject to transitional provisions.[91] RTM companies incorporated before 9 November 2009 were able to use the old articles, until their abolition in 30 September 2010.[92] Existing RTM companies were required to update their articles at the end of the transitional period.

Key benefits

1.54

The prescribed articles of association (2009 Regulations) were drafted with simplicity in mind and focused on the needs of smaller companies. Following the introduction of the Companies Act 2006, RTM companies incorporated after implementation benefited from being able to adopt the simpler constitutional documents rather than those existing before that date.

RTM articles – adaptation and modification

1.55

It should be noted the RTM articles prescribed by the 2009 Regulations or the 2003 Regulations cannot be altered or bespoke provisions included. Article 2 'the name of the company' and article 3 'the registered office' are the two exceptions, where information will be required to be entered into the articles of association.

Key points

1.56

- The Commonhold and Leasehold Reform Act 2002 articles of association are stipulated by statutory instrument. RTM companies do not exist in Scotland or Northern Ireland.
- All companies in England who incorporated prior to 1 October 2009 used the memorandum and articles of association under the 2003 Regulations.
- The articles of association SI 2003/2120 were abolished on 30 September 2010 and updated to comply with the changes under the Companies Act 2006.

90 The RTM Companies (Model Articles) (England) Regulations 2009, SI 2009/2767.
91 The RTM Companies (Model Articles) (England) Regulations 2009, SI 2009/2767, p 1, para 4.3.
92 Companies were free to adopt the new articles before this date if they chose.

- Companies incorporated prior to 1 October 2009 were required to update to the new RTM articles of association regulations 2009.
- The members of the right to manage company should be familiar with the RTM articles: their contents, powers and restrictions.

CICs

Community interest companies

1.57

Chapter 5 of this book provides:

- Analysis of the prescribed articles of association for a community interest company (CIC Limited by Guarantee. Schedule 1 large membership).
- Analysis of the prescribed articles of association for a community interest company (CIC limited by shares. Schedule 2 large membership).

1.58

Community interest companies (CIC)[93] are overseen by the Office of the regulator of community interest companies (ORCIC) which is responsible for the effective regulation and provision of information to support the growth of community interest companies in the UK.

Legislation

1.59

The principal legislation concerning CIC is as follows:

- The Companies Act 2006.[94]
- The Companies (Audit, Investigations and Community Enterprise) Act 2004.[95]
- The Community Interest Company Regulations 2005.[96]

93 Community Interest Companies (CICs) were first established in the UK in 2005.

94 The Companies Act 2006 (Consequential Amendments etc) Order 2008, SI 2008/948 contains consequential amendments relating to the CIC report. The Companies Act 2006 (Consequential Amendments, Transitional Provisions and Savings) Order 2009, SI 2009/1941 contains consequential amendments to bring the CIC legislation in line with Company legislation.

95 Part 2 and Schedules 3–7. Provisions relating to the appointment of the Regulator of Community Interest Companies came into force on 1 January 2005 and the remaining provisions relating to CICs came into force on 1 July 2005.

96 Provisions relating to CICs. The Community Interest Company Regulations 2005, SI 2005/1788 came into force on 1 July 2005.

CIC overview

1.60

The CIC concept is very popular, with over 18,000 established companies in the UK on public record increasing by 20% each year.[97] A CIC is a limited company, created to conduct business activities for the benefit of the community as opposed to bottom line profitability.[98] Public limited companies, provident societies, private companies limited by shares and guarantee may convert to the CIC format.

Main points

1.61

A full discussion on the rules and regulations for establishing and running a CIC are beyond this text, which concentrates only on the analysis of the model articles of association, provided by the regulator. A condensed overview of the main points concerning CIC are provided below:

- CIC are a type of limited company incorporated or converted for the purpose of social enterprise.
- CIC are a useful vehicle for enterprises of all sizes from a small community care project to a large organisation providing international fair trade type distribution systems for the benefit of overseas producers.
- CIC are a legal form for holding property not local assets such as community halls.
- CIC must meet the community interest test.
- Once a company is a CIC it cannot become an ordinary company.[99]
- There are limitations on the payment of dividends.
- A CIC will not have any special tax status.
- Political parties[100] and pressure groups, or companies owned or controlled by them, cannot become CICs.
- A charity cannot be established as a CIC,[101] a charity may utilise a CIC as a subsidiary.

97 Community Interest Companies, 'Annual Report' 2019/2020.
98 They are not strictly NFP, and CICs can deliver returns to investors.
99 Winding up a CIC involves dissolving the company or converting to a charity.
100 Community Interest Company Regulations 2005, SI 2005/1788, Part 2 The community interest test and excluded companies.
101 Companies (Audit, Investigations and Community Enterprise) Act 2004, s 26 (Community interest companies).

- A CIC's name must end in either CIC or community interest company and not limited or ltd.
- The directors can be paid or unpaid and have the same rights and duties as any other directors.
- A CIC operates in the same way as any other company.

Legal structures

Company limited by guarantee without a share capital

1.62

A CIC is a special type of company incorporated by guarantee which exists to benefit the community. To ensure the company is perceived as NFP and will not distribute profits to its members or employees, the CIC model articles incorporate asset lock provisions. Registering a CIC with Companies House automatically makes an application to the community interest regulator.

Private and public company limited by shares

1.63

Members wishing to form a CIC with share capital with the ability to pay dividends must ensure that they adopt the appropriate form of articles of association.

Overview: CIC constitutional documents

1.64

The four main elements that differentiate the articles of association of a CIC from a traditional company incorporated under the Companies Act 2006[102] are:

- Asset-locked body provision must be included in the articles of association.
- Alteration of the objects clause is required.
- Specific articles require amendment subject to the type of company converted or incorporated.

102 Or any previous Companies Acts: eg the Companies Act 1985.

- Existing companies will be required to change the existing company name.

Asset lock

1.65

The 'asset lock' is designed to ensure the assets[103] of the CIC are used for the benefit of the community. This asset lock is permanent and cannot be reversed. The company may adopt asset lock rules that impose more stringent requirements, in addition to the prescribed provisions.

The asset lock provides confidence to both members and investors (those providing funds for the company) that the assets of the company will be used for the benefit of the community and not unjustifiably benefit the CIC's directors, members or employees.

The assets of the company may be transferred in limited circumstances with the permission of the regulator,[104] provisions to this effect must be included in a CIC's articles.

Dividend and performance-related interest cap

1.66

The calculation and rules on the dividend cap are beyond this text, broadly after 1 October 2014, 65% of the CICs profits must be reinvested back into the company. The CIC may encounter borrowing, where the interest payable is linked to the performance of the CIC. This may provide the ability to pay uncapped interest and possibly fetter the dividend cap rules. Any performance related interest is capped at 20% after 1 October 2014.

Company limited by shares: Schedule 2

1.67

Under Schedule 2, the company may pay dividends (subject to the Companies Act 2006) to another specified and approved asset-locked body. The dividend cap is not applicable.

103 Defined by the Office of the Regulator of Community Interest Companies as: profits or other surpluses generated by its activities.

104 Full market value so that the CIC retains the value of the assets transferred to another asset-locked body (a CIC or charity, a registered society or non-UK based equivalent) which is specified in the CIC's articles of association, to another asset-locked body with the consent of the Regulator; or it is made for the benefit of the community.

Company limited by shares: Schedule 3

1.68

Under Schedule 3, the company may pay dividends[105] (subject to the Companies Act 2006), to those who are not approved asset-locked bodies or private investors, however the dividend payable is capped.

Purchase of own shares

1.69

The Regulations[106] prevent the redemption and purchase of shares, unless the amount to be paid by the company in respect of any such share does not exceed the paid up value of the share.[107] The CIC, is additionally, restricted on the distribution of assets to its members by reducing the company's share capital, unless the reduction is to reduce liabilities or does not exceed the paid up value of their shareholdings.[108]

CIC articles of association

1.70

The ORCIC provides model articles for various types of company. The company articles of association, in addition to any requirements of the Companies Act 2006, must comply with the requirements of the:

- Companies (Audit, Investigations and Community Enterprise) Act 2004.
- Community Interest Company Regulations 2005.

You cannot use limited company model articles if you are setting up a community interest company.

Legislative provisions

1.71

- A company limited by guarantee without a share capital must include the provisions in Schedule 1.

105 Any dividend paid is subject to the Companies Act 2006, the company's articles of association and the CIC legislation.
106 Community Interest Company Regulations 2005, SI 2005/1788.
107 Community Interest Company Regulations 2005, SI 2005/1788, reg 24 (Redemption and purchase of shares).
108 Community Interest Company Regulations 2005, SI 2005/1788, reg 25 (Reduction of share capital).

- A company limited by shares must include either the provisions in Schedule 2[109] or the provisions in Schedule 3.[110]

See Appendix D (Schedule 2) and Appendix E (Schedule 3).

Object statement

1.72

Section 31 allows a company to operate without any restriction on its objects.[111] The ORCIC require (on incorporation or conversion) for the company objects to be restricted to meet the community interest test. If the object statement requires amendment, new articles will need to be submitted to Companies House[112] who will seek approval from the ORCIC before taking effect.

Model articles of association[113]

1.73

The ORCIC provides the following model articles of association for non-profit companies limited by guarantee and shares.[114]

Private company limited by guarantee

1.74

Company limited by guarantee with a small membership.

Assumptions:

- All the directors are also members.
- The directors will make the decisions concerning the company.

109 A company which adopts the Schedule 2 provisions will only be able to pay dividends, and otherwise transfer assets for less than full consideration, to other asset-locked bodies or otherwise for the benefit of the community.
110 A company which adopts Schedule 3 is able to pay dividends (subject to the dividend cap) to shareholders who are not asset-locked bodies.
111 Companies Act 2006, s 31 (Statement of company's objects).
112 Requires the passing of a special resolution.
113 See www.gov.uk/government/publications/community-interest-companies-constitutions.
114 The ORCIC provides model articles for private limited companies limited by share for schedule 2 and schedule 3. It should be noted the regulator does not provide model articles for public limited companies.

Company limited by guarantee with a large membership.

Assumptions:

- More members than directors.
- Members will be more involved with decision making.
- Increased formality in decision making over and above the new model articles.[115]

Private company limited by shares[116]

1.75

CIC model constitution: company limited by shares private schedule 2 with a small membership – articles of association:

- Aimed at private companies limited by shares.
- The directors are members of the company and all of whose members are directors of the company.
- It assumes that the directors will take most important decisions as directors rather than as members.

CIC model constitution: company limited by shares private schedule 2 with a large membership – articles of association:

- Is aimed at private companies limited by shares, which have more members than they have directors.
- Assumes that the members will delegate most of the decision making within the company to the directors.
- Allows, subject to certain procedural safeguards, for relatively informal decision making by directors (including by email).
- The company is only permitted to pay dividends to specified asset-locked bodies, or other asset-locked bodies with the consent of the Regulator.

115 Schedule 2 Regulation 3 Model articles for private companies limited by guarantee.

116 The ORCIC in addition provides two further constitutions: CIC model constitution: company limited by shares private schedule 3 with a small membership – articles of association and CIC model constitution: company limited by shares private schedule 3 with a large membership – articles of association. Both articles of association are not analysed here on the basis they may pay capped dividend payments to shareholders and therefore by definition are NFP.

EOC

Employee ownership companies

1.76

Chapter 6 of this book provides:

- Analysis of the model articles of association of a company with employee ownership.
- Analysis of the model articles of association of the trustee company (a guarantee company).

1.77

Employee ownership is typically defined as all employees hold a significant and meaningful stake in the business, and there are no set rules on the percentage of share capital issued to employees. The model documentation forms the foundation[117] for the majority of employee-owned companies and was provided in response to the Nuttall Review 2012.[118]

Direct and indirect employee ownership

1.78

Employee ownership has two forms: direct, where the employees' company shareholdings are held collectively through a tax advantaged share plan wrapper, or indirectly via an employee share trust, referred to as the trust model. Companies may combine the two models, typically the indirect trust may hold shares from leavers which have been purchased by the trust, or the trust may hold shares or sale to new employees. A full discussion on the mechanisms of establishing employee ownership companies is beyond this text, further information is available from the Employee Ownership Association.[119]

117 The model documentation is flexible enough to enable whatever level of employee ownership a business desires. Although the model documentation is not specifically designed for businesses that wish to give employees a controlling interest, it could be readily adapted for this purpose.

118 The Nuttall Review of Employee Ownership (July 2012).

119 The Employee Ownership Association (EOA) (see http://employeeownership.co.uk/) is the voice of employee-owned business in the UK – most UK businesses that become employee owned are helped to do so by the EOA.

Assumptions

1.79

The model articles of association assume:

- An employee-owned trust (EOT) will be established by incorporating a private company limited by guarantee (the trustee company).
- Corporate trustees will be appointed (as opposed to individuals).
- The trustee company will require bespoke articles of association.
- The trust will appoint directors in accordance with the trust deed and the articles of association.
- The trustee directors must only ever deal with the shares and other assets held in the trust 'in the best interests of the beneficiaries'.
- The trust is governed by the terms of the trust deed as well as the rules of English trust law.
- The trust company plays no part in managing the company (with the exception that an employee director may sit on the board).
- The beneficiaries of the trust company do not include any employees.
- The articles shall specify the number of trustees and the requirement for the appointment of an independent trustee.[120]
- The members of the company shall vest control to the directors.

Example – Hudson Green Energy Limited

1.80

Hudson Green Energy Limited was established in 1997 with three directors who hold 40%, 40% and 20%. The directors have decided to convert the operation into an employee-owned company.

The three directors agree to sell, over time, their shareholdings to a trust company, Hudson Employee Trust Limited (HETL), a private limited company limited by guarantee, incorporated for the purpose of acquiring shares in the company for the benefit of the employees. HETL will appoint directors, the

120 An independent trustee director is an individual who is familiar with the company and its business but is 'independent' of the company. The role of an independent trustee director is partly to ensure that the affairs of the trust are properly conducted. See the Department for Business Innovation and Skills, Model documentation for a company with employee ownership, p 6.

trustee directors, who have full[121] responsibility for the affairs of the trust. The articles may specify the number of trustee directors, it should be noted an independent trustee director will be required.

The directors' strategy is to sell all their shares, therefore the Hudson Trust will acquire full control of the company.

Who controls Hudson Green Energy Limited?

The members vest control to the directors in the articles of association, the directors must abide by the directors' duties specified in the Companies Act 2006.[122] The directors must act in the way they consider, in good faith, would be most likely to promote the success of the company for the benefit of its members as a whole,[123] this principle cannot be restricted by the company constitution.

The employees can be involved in the decision making and retain some control over the directors' powers by establishing an employees' council, the principles and rules of which are included in the Hudson trust articles of association. The trust may appoint one employee director, the individual determined by the employee council.

The company constitution[124] consists of:

- Hudson Green Energy Limited – articles of association.
- Hudson Employee Trust Limited – articles of association.

It should be noted, the execution and transfer to employee ownership is complex, this text concentrates on the analysis of the articles of association only. Legal advice would be required to understand how the company articles and the trust deeds[125] operate together in addition to tax considerations.

121 Under the terms of the trust, the trustee directors (acting on behalf of the trustee) have an overriding duty to deal with the trust property. See the Department for Business Innovation and Skills, Model documentation for a company with employee ownership, p 6.
122 Companies Act 2006, Part 10, Chapter 2 General duties of directors.
123 Companies Act 2006, s 172 (Duty to promote the success of the company).
124 In addition a formal trust deed is drafted. The deed specifies the powers of the trust, removal and appointment of trustees, perpetuity periods and the beneficiaries.
125 The law relating to trusts is different under Scots law as compared to the law of England & Wales. It is important therefore that the model trust deed, which is governed by the law of England & Wales, is adapted where appropriate in the circumstances.

Chapter 2 Analysis of the Model Articles for Private Companies Limited by Guarantee

Interchangeable terms

2.1

The analysis of the private limited company limited by guarantee provides a holistic overview of the provisions. The terms 'directors', 'director trustees' and 'trustees' are interchangeable throughout the various articles of association considered in the text.

Members

2.2

Members can be defined as: employees, members of the association or club, members of the company (initial individuals providing funds) or corporate members (charity or other bodys corporate). For example:

Article 3. Directors' general authority

3.—Subject to the articles, the directors are responsible for the management of the company's business, for which purpose they may exercise all the powers of the company.

May appear in charity articles of association as:

Article 3. Trustees general authority

3.—Subject to the articles, the trustees are responsible for the management of the company's business, for which purpose they may exercise all the powers of the company.

It should be noted, directors may be called trustees,[1] the term member has wide remit throughout the various articles of association consider in this text.[2]

Previous provisions

2.3

Where applicable the analysis provides the previous provisions for companies incorporated under the Companies Act 1985, who may not have updated to the new model articles.

Part 1 Interpretation and limitation of liability

Article 1 Defined terms

2.4

1. In the articles, unless the context requires otherwise—

"articles" means the company's articles of association;

"bankruptcy" includes individual insolvency proceedings in a jurisdiction other than England and Wales or Northern Ireland which have an effect similar to that of bankruptcy;

"chairman" has the meaning given in article 12;

"chairman of the meeting" has the meaning given in article 25;

"Companies Acts" means the Companies Acts (as defined in section 2 of the Companies Act 2006), in so far as they apply to the company;

"director" means a director of the company, and includes any person occupying the position of director, by whatever name called;

"document" includes, unless otherwise specified, any document sent or supplied in electronic form;

"electronic form" has the meaning given in section 1168 of the Companies Act 2006;

"member" has the meaning given in section 112 of the Companies Act 2006;

1 Regardless of the term used, if the company is incorporated, the trustees are directors and must abide by the relevant company the company was duly incorporated under.

2 Companies Act 2006, s 250 (Director) – in the Companies Acts 'director' includes any person occupying the position of director, by whatever name called.

"ordinary resolution" has the meaning given in section 282 of the Companies Act 2006;

"participate", in relation to a directors' meeting, has the meaning given in article 10;

"proxy notice" has the meaning given in article 31;

"special resolution" has the meaning given in section 283 of the Companies Act 2006;

"subsidiary" has the meaning given in section 1159 of the Companies Act 2006; and

"writing" means the representation or reproduction of words, symbols or other information in a visible form by any method or combination of methods, whether sent or supplied in electronic form or otherwise.

Unless the context otherwise requires, other words or expressions contained in these articles bear the same meaning as in the Companies Act 2006 as in force on the date when these articles become binding on the company.

Article 1 Previous provisions

Table A 1985: Regulation 1

The definition of 'the holder'[3] is omitted from Table A 1985.

Article 2 Liability of members

2.5

2. The liability of each member is limited to £1, being the amount that each member undertakes to contribute to the assets of the company in the event of its being wound up while he is a member or within one year after he ceases to be a member, for—

(a) payment of the company's debts and liabilities contracted before he ceases to be a member,

(b) payment of the costs, charges and expenses of winding up, and

(c) adjustment of the rights of the contributories among themselves.

3 The Companies (Tables A to F) Regulations 1985, SI 1985/805, Table C, A company limited by guarantee and not having a share capital, Articles of association, para 2.

Article 2 Analysis

Article 2 provides the statement of guarantee, the provisions text is derived from section 11 of the Companies Act 2006.[4] Companies limited by guarantee must comply with the article as defined by the act. Removal, omission or adaption of article 2 would breach the Companies Act 2006, in contrast if article 2 for private companies limited by shares is omitted the result is only the loss of liability for the members.

The amount of liability is a specified amount, detailed in the article. The Companies Act 2006 does not specify a minimum or maximum liability, therefore the directors are free to choose any amount they desire.[5]

Article 2 Previous provisions

There is no corresponding provision in Table A 1985. The provisions previously appeared in the memorandum.

Part 2 Directors – Directors' powers and responsibilities

Article 3 Directors' general authority

2.6

3.—Subject to the articles, the directors are responsible for the management of the company's business, for which purpose they may exercise all the powers of the company.

Article 3 Analysis

Article 3 provides that all power lies with the board of directors, or more accurately the managing director powers are an implied delegation by the board.[6] The term 'all powers' requires the directors to act within the confines of the company constitution and they may only be exercised for the purpose they are granted. In English company law, a company is not bound by a decision of its directors made otherwise than bona fide in the best interests of the company.[7]

The company's articles may also restrict directors' duties, however they must not fetter the statutory obligations of the directors' duties specified in sections 170 to 177[8] of the Companies Act 2006.

4 Companies Act 2006, s 11 (Statement of guarantee).
5 Companies Act 2006, s 11(3)(a).
6 *Hely-Hutchinson v Brayhead Ltd* [1968] 1 QB 549.
7 Esso Petroleum Co Ltd v Texaco Ltd and others – [1999] All ER (D) 1122.
8 Companies Act 2006, Ch 2 (General duties of directors).

Directors' powers and responsibilities

Part 2 of the model articles[9] defines the directors' powers and responsibilities under the following sections:

3. Directors' general authority

4. Members' reserve power

5. Directors may delegate

6. Committees

It should be noted, in practice it is common to replace Part 2 sections 3–6 with bespoke precedents under the headings 'objects and powers'.

Article 3 Previous provisions

Table A 1985: Regulation 70

70. Subject to the provisions of the Act, the memorandum and the articles and to any directions given by special resolution, the business of the company shall be managed by the directors who may exercise all the powers of the company. No alteration of the memorandum or articles and no such direction shall invalidate any prior act of the directors which would have been valid if that alteration had not been made or that direction had not been given. The powers given by this regulation shall not be limited by any special power given to the directors by the articles and a meeting of directors at which a quorum is present may exercise all powers exercisable by the directors.

Article 4 Members' reserve power

2.7

4.—(1) The members may, by special resolution, direct the directors to take, or refrain from taking, specified action.

(2) No such special resolution invalidates anything which the directors have done before the passing of the resolution.

Article 4 Analysis

Article 4(1) gives an overriding power to the members in a general meeting by special resolution, in principle the members hold a veto over the directors' authority.

9 Schedule 2 Regulation 3 Model articles for private companies limited by guarantee.

In order for a company to operate successfully the members are obligated to delegate the responsibility of management to the directors. They may decide to reaffirm their authority in relation to a specific matter.

The members cannot alter the directors' powers in any way that is unlawful or in contradiction of the Companies Act 2006. The general duties of directors outlined in sections 170–181[10] cannot be fettered by the powers provided in article 4(1).

Article 4(2) is important for the continuity of decisions made by the directors as it preserves any contracts or commitments the directors have entered into on behalf of the company, prior to the passing of any special resolution. This does not however prevent directors from breaching any contract or the members requesting them to do so.

Article 4 Previous provisions

Table A 1985: Regulation 70

70. Subject to the provisions of the Act, the memorandum and the articles and to any directions given by special resolution, the business of the company shall be managed by the directors who may exercise all the powers of the company. No alteration of the memorandum or articles and no such direction shall invalidate any prior act of the directors which would have been valid if that alteration had not been made or that direction had not been given. The powers given by this regulation shall not be limited by any special power given to the directors by the articles and a meeting of directors at which a quorum is present may exercise all powers exercisable by the directors.

Article 5 Directors may delegate

2.8

5.—(1) Subject to the articles, the directors may delegate any of the powers which are conferred on them under the articles—

(a) to such person or committee;

(b) by such means (including by power of attorney);

(c) to such an extent;

(d) in relation to such matters or territories; and

(e) on such terms and conditions;

as they think fit.

10 Companies Act 2006, Ch 2 (General duties of directors).

(2) If the directors so specify, any such delegation may authorise further delegation of the directors' powers by any person to whom they are delegated.

(3) The directors may revoke any delegation in whole or part, or alter its terms and conditions.

Article 5 Analysis

Article 5 reflects how modern companies are run, for example the board may delegate the company's borrowing requirements to a finance committee, who in turn delegate the responsibility to the chief financial officer, who in turn delegates the key tasks to their staff.

The directors may 'delegate any of their powers to committees consisting of such member or members of their body as they think fit', that delegation may be to one director (*Fireproof Doors Ltd, Re*).[11]

The 2007 consultation paper commented on the range of powers as the provision in article 5(1) provides a relatively free hand on the powers of delegation. It should be noted the scope of delegation is controlled by the powers in the articles, therefore those delegated to have no special authority unless provided by specific provisions in the articles (*Harold Holdsworth & Co (Wakefield) Ltd v Caddies*).[12]

Article 5 Previous provisions

Table A 1985: Regulations 71 and 72

71. The directors may, by power of attorney or otherwise, appoint any person to be the agent of the company for such purposes and on such conditions as they determine, including authority for the agent to delegate all or any of his powers.

72. The directors may delegate any of their powers to any committee consisting of one or more directors. They may also delegate to any managing director or any director holding any other executive office such of their powers as they consider desirable to be exercised by him. Any such delegation may be made subject to any conditions the directors may impose, and either collaterally with or to the exclusion of their own powers and may be revoked or altered. Subject to any such conditions, the proceedings of a committee with two or more members shall be governed by the articles regulating the proceedings of directors so far as they are capable of applying.

11 [1916–17[All ER Rep 931; [1916] 2 Ch 142.
12 [1955] 1 ALL ER 725.

Article 6 Committees

2.9

6.—(1) Committees to which the directors delegate any of their powers must follow procedures which are based as far as they are applicable on those provisions of the articles which govern the taking of decisions by directors.

(2) The directors may make rules of procedure for all or any committees, which prevail over rules derived from the articles if they are not consistent with them.

Article 6 Analysis

Previous versions of the articles have all included provisions on how committees operate.

A committee can be a group or an individual.[13] Article 6 does not specify how a committee may be formed, company boards may wish to only delegate to committees consisting of directors for certain matters or external members only for a particular issue. The directors can adapt the articles and make specific procedures for each committee.

The board may specify the delegation of powers for a limited period of time or certain reporting procedures or rules to be followed before final implementation of any decision the committee makes.

It should be noted the company cannot form a committee and delegate all its powers to that committee and exclude directors. In *Great Western Railway Co v Rushout*,[14] it was found the forming of a General Purposes Committee to the exclusion of the directors appointed by the Great Western Railway Company (and all the powers of the directors were delegated to and exercised by that Committee) was illegal, and excluded the voice of the minority.

Article 6 Previous provisions

Table A 1985: Regulation 72

72. The directors may delegate any of their powers to any committee consisting of one or more directors. They may also delegate to any managing director or any director holding any other executive office such of their powers as they consider desirable to be exercised by him. Any such delegation may be made subject to any conditions the directors may impose, and either collaterally with or to the exclusion of their own powers and may be revoked or altered. Subject to any such conditions, the proceedings of a committee with two or more members shall be governed by the articles regulating the proceedings of directors so far as they are capable of applying.

13 *Fireproof Doors Ltd, Re* [1916–17[All ER Rep 931; [1916] 2 Ch 142.
14 *Great Western Railway Co v Rushout* (1852) 64 ER 1121.

Decision-making by directors

Article 7 Directors to take decisions collectively

2.10

7.—(1) The general rule about decision-making by directors is that any decision of the directors must be either a majority decision at a meeting or a decision taken in accordance with article 8.

(2) If—

(a) the company only has one director, and

(b) no provision of the articles requires it to have more than one director,

the general rule does not apply, and the director may take decisions without regard to any of the provisions of the articles relating to directors' decision-making.

Article 7 Analysis

Article 7 stipulates the general rule that decision making by directors must be passed by a majority decision.[15] Article 7(2) provides an exclusion for companies with a single director whereby the rules for decision making in the articles do not apply, therefore accordingly the sole director is free to make decisions as they see fit.

Article 7 Previous provisions

Table A 1985: Regulation 88

88. Subject to the provisions of the articles, the directors may regulate their proceedings as they think fit. A director may, and the secretary at the request of a director shall, call a meeting of the directors. It shall not be necessary to give notice of a meeting to a director who is absent from the United Kingdom. Questions arising at a meeting shall be decided by a majority of votes. In the case of an equality of votes, the chairman shall have a second or casting vote. A director who is also an alternate director shall be entitled in the absence of his appointor to a separate vote on behalf of his appointor in addition to his own vote.

15 Companies Act 2006, s 282 (Ordinary resolutions) '(1). An ordinary resolution of the members (or of a class of members) of a company means a resolution that is passed by a simple majority.'

Article 8 Unanimous decisions

2.11

8.—(1) A decision of the directors is taken in accordance with this article when all eligible directors indicate to each other by any means that they share a common view on a matter.

(2) Such a decision may take the form of a resolution in writing, copies of which have been signed by each eligible director or to which each eligible director has otherwise indicated agreement in writing.

(3) References in this article to eligible directors are to directors who would have been entitled to vote on the matter had it been proposed as a resolution at a directors' meeting.

(4) A decision may not be taken in accordance with this article if the eligible directors would not have formed a quorum at such a meeting.

Article 8 Analysis

Article 8 adds new additions to the new model articles which acknowledge the increased use of technology in decision making by directors. The 'by any means' described in article 8(1) may include: mobile telephone, text, email and teleconferencing, this allows a board of directors to make decisions without the need for written resolutions or calling a formal meeting.

Care ought to be taken with the phrase in article 8(1) 'indicate to each other' which implies that all directors have sight of the same information on which the decision is based. For example, the directors should read any email chain in full.

In 2019 sharing technology is certainly fit for purpose in order to speed up decision making, especially in small companies with possibly two or three directors.

Article 8 Previous provisions

Table A 1985: Regulations 88 and 93

88. Subject to the provisions of the articles, the directors may regulate their proceedings as they think fit. A director may, and the secretary at the request of a director shall, call a meeting of the directors. It shall not be necessary to give notice of a meeting to a director who is absent from the United Kingdom. Questions arising at a meeting shall be decided by a majority

of votes. In the case of an equality of votes, the chairman shall have a second or casting vote. A director who is also an alternate director shall be entitled in the absence of his appointor to a separate vote on behalf of his appointor in addition to his own vote.

93. A resolution in writing signed by all the directors entitled to receive notice of a meeting of directors or of a committee of directors shall be as valid and effectual as it if had been passed at a meeting of directors or (as the case may be) a committee of directors duly convened and held and may consist of several documents in the like form each signed by one or more directors; but a resolution signed by an alternate director need not also be signed by his appointor and, if it is signed by a director who has appointed an alternate director, it need not be signed by the alternate director in that capacity.

Article 9 Calling a directors' meeting

2.12

9.—(1) Any director may call a directors' meeting by giving notice of the meeting to the directors or by authorising the company secretary (if any) to give such notice.

(2) Notice of any directors' meeting must indicate—

(a) its proposed date and time;

(b) where it is to take place; and

(c) if it is anticipated that directors participating in the meeting will not be in the same place, how it is proposed that they should communicate with each other during the meeting.

(3) Notice of a directors' meeting must be given to each director, but need not be in writing.

(4) Notice of a directors' meeting need not be given to directors who waive their entitlement to notice of that meeting, by giving notice to that effect to the company not more than 7 days after the date on which the meeting is held. Where such notice is given after the meeting has been held, that does not affect the validity of the meeting, or of any business conducted at it.

Article 9 Analysis

Article 9 modernises the previous regulation 88 of Table A 1985 which stipulated a director absent from the United Kingdom would not require notification of a meeting. The change reflects the advent of modern communication techniques where it is possible to hold a directors meeting remotely. If it is envisaged any directors may not attend personally article 9(2)(c) stipulates the method of communication (for example Skype) ought to be proposed and agreed. It is established common law that notices need not be in writing, article 9(3) reflects this position.

If the company has not appointed a company secretary article 9(1) can be amended as below:

9.—(1) Any director may call a directors' meeting by giving notice of the meeting to the directors.

Article 9 Previous provisions

Table A 1985: Regulation 88

88. Subject to the provisions of the articles, the directors may regulate their proceedings as they think fit. A director may, and the secretary at the request of a director shall, call a meeting of the directors. It shall not be necessary to give notice of a meeting to a director who is absent from the United Kingdom. Questions arising at a meeting shall be decided by a majority of votes. In the case of an equality of votes, the chairman shall have a second or casting vote. A director who is also an alternate director shall be entitled in the absence of his appointor to a separate vote on behalf of his appointor in addition to his own vote.

Article 10 Participation in directors' meetings

2.13

10.—(1) Subject to the articles, directors participate in a directors' meeting, or part of a directors' meeting, when—

(a) the meeting has been called and takes place in accordance with the articles, and

(b) they can each communicate to the others any information or opinions they have on any particular item of the business of the meeting.

(2) In determining whether directors are participating in a directors' meeting, it is irrelevant where any director is or how they communicate with each other.

(3) If all the directors participating in a meeting are not in the same place, they may decide that the meeting is to be treated as taking place wherever any of them is.

Article 10 Analysis

Article 10, which is a new provision, is drafted to complement the intention of directors to facilitate the use of video-conference calls to facilitate decision making. Case law has established the main principles for calling a board meeting, in particular that a reasonable notice period for any proposed meeting ought to be given to directors (*Browne v La Trinidad*).[16]

The law fails to define what is considered as 'reasonable', the court has considered the manipulation of the company decision making process by calling meetings under short notice in the hope of excluding fellow directors (*Homer District Consolidated Gold Mines, Re*).[17]

Article 10 is a new addition to the articles which expressly allows for meetings to be held with directors in different locations.[18]

It is important to consider article 9(2)(c) if a board meeting is to be called when it is known certain directors will not attend in person, the method of communication of the proposed meeting needs to be established and conveyed to each director prior to the meeting.

As the intention of articles 9 and 10 is to allow directors to attend meetings from different locations in the world using technology, the previous provision under regulation 88 of Table A 1985 meant it was not necessary to notify any director of a proposed meeting if they were outside of the UK.

Article 10 Previous provisions

There is no corresponding provision in Table A 1985.

Article 11 Quorum for directors' meetings

2.14

11.—(1) At a directors' meeting, unless a quorum is participating, no proposal is to be voted on, except a proposal to call another meeting.

(2) The quorum for directors' meetings may be fixed from time to time by a decision of the directors, but it must never be less than two, and unless otherwise fixed it is two.

(3) If the total number of directors for the time being is less than the quorum required, the directors must not take any decision other than a decision—

(a) to appoint further directors, or

(b) to call a general meeting so as to enable the members to appoint further directors.

16 (1887) 37 Ch D 1 (CA).
17 (1988) 39 Ch D 546 (CA).
18 See article 10(2) '… it is irrelevant where any director is or how they communicate with each other'.

Article 11 Analysis

A quorum is the minimum number of directors required to vote at a meeting. Case law provides any decisions made at an inquorate board meeting is deemed void, the directors may not fetter the law to overcome a specific problem, even for the good of the company. (*North Eastern Insurance Co Ltd, Re*).[19]

It is established law, in accordance with the articles of association, in this case article 14, that on the occurrence of the director attending a meeting whom could be considered conflicted, they are duly counted in determining the quorum and may vote on the matter.

Directors hold a general duty to exercise their power to vote in good faith in the interests of the company (see *Colin Gwyer & Associates Ltd v London Wharf (Limehouse) Ltd*).[20]

Article 11(3) provides for the appointment of further directors if a quorum cannot be formed. Article 11(2) fixes the minimum quorum at two and appears at odds with section 154 of the Companies Act 2006 which states a private company must have at least one director. By virtue of Article 7(2), sole directors may ignore the requirements for 'directors to take decisions collectively'.

It is obvious article 7 and article 11 are conflicted, the former acknowledging alignment with section 154 of the Companies Act 2006, conversely the latter appearing to insist a private company must have at least two directors to form a quorum.

To provide clarity article 11 may be amended in two forms, precedent AA allows the directors to adjourn a meeting if a quorum cannot be formed and the option to fix the quorum at more than two directors. Precedent AA states the voting rights of the quorum clearly.

Article 11 states clearly that sole directors will not be required to form a quorum and they alone will make all the decisions of the company, for an investor into a private company with a sole director is unambiguous concerning who will have decision making powers.

Article 11 Previous provisions

Table A 1985: Regulations 89 and 90

89. The quorum for the transaction of the business of the directors may be fixed by the directors and unless so fixed at any other number shall be two. A person who holds office only as an alternate director shall, if his appointor is not present, be counted in the quorum.

19 [1919] 1 Ch 198.
20 [2002] EWHC 2748 (Ch); [2002] All ER (D) 226 (Dec).

> 90. The continuing directors or a sole continuing director may act notwithstanding any vacancies in their number, but, if the number of directors is less than the number fixed as the quorum, the continuing directors or director may act only for the purpose of filling vacancies or of calling a general meeting.

Article 12 Chairing of directors' meetings

2.15

12.—(1) The directors may appoint a director to chair their meetings.

(2) The person so appointed for the time being is known as the chairman.

(3) The directors may terminate the chairman's appointment at any time.

(4) If the chairman is not participating in a directors' meeting within ten minutes of the time at which it was to start, the participating directors must appoint one of themselves to chair it.

> *Article 12 Analysis*
>
> The article allows the board of directors to appoint a chairman, this power is vested in the directors alone, the members cannot interfere with the process (*Clarke v Workman*).[21]
>
> A director who is under discussion and being proposed for removal is entitled at that meeting to be appointed as chair, it is established law[22] the chair is not required to be neutral and may cast his or her vote as he or she sees fit (*Might SA v Redbus Interhouse Plc*).[23]
>
> It is the duty of a chairman to preserve order,[24] conduct proceedings regularly, and take care that the sense of the meeting is properly ascertained with regard to any question before it. It should be noted the chair's powers

21 [1920] 1 IR 107.

22 Lindsay J, 'But it is to be borne in mind that I am not considering the sharpest form of conflict when a man is considering his own position as a director. What I am considering is simply the position of the chairman and the conduct of the meeting. That, as it seems to me, is a much less conflicted position than that of a director whose personal appointment is sought to be ended as such.' *Might SA v Redbus Interhouse Plc* [2003] EWHC 3514 (Ch).

23 [2003] EWHC 3514 (Ch).

24 'Unquestionably it is the duty of the chairman, and his function, to preserve order, and to take care that the proceedings are conducted in a proper manner, and that the sense of the meeting is properly ascertained with regard to any question which is properly before the meeting:' *National Dwellings Society v Sykes* [1894] 3 Ch 159 at para 162, per Chitty J.

are limited to preserving order, the chair is prohibited from deciding matters at their own pleasure (*National Dwellings Society v Sykes*).[25]

Article 12 Previous provisions

Table A 1985: Regulation 88

88. Subject to the provisions of the articles, the directors may regulate their proceedings as they think fit. A director may, and the secretary at the request of a director shall, call a meeting of the directors. It shall not be necessary to give notice of a meeting to a director who is absent from the United Kingdom. Questions arising at a meeting shall be decided by a majority of votes. In the case of an equality of votes, the chairman shall have a second or casting vote. A director who is also an alternate director shall be entitled in the absence of his appointor to a separate vote on behalf of his appointor in addition to his own vote.

Article 13 Casting vote

2.16

13.—(1) If the numbers of votes for and against a proposal are equal, the chairman or other director chairing the meeting has a casting vote.

(2) But this does not apply if, in accordance with the articles, the chairman or other director is not to be counted as participating in the decision-making process for quorum or voting purposes.

Article 13 Analysis

The appointment of the chairman allows for a casting vote (article 13(1)) in directors meetings, the option is useful to prevent potential deadlocks. It should be noted the chairman appointed is free to act as they see fit with no requirement for impartiality.[26]

Another matter for the chair is there is no obligation to either abstain or to vote in favor of the status quo or vote at a meeting where perhaps the chair had indicated or possibly agreed an opinion on matter prior to the meeting, for example they were against the motion and subsequently used a casting to vote to pass the motion.[27]

25 [1894] 3 Ch 159.

26 See *Might SA v Redbus Interhouse Plc* [2003] EWHC 3514 (Ch).

27 Bingham LJ, 'Those agreements, desirable though they no doubt were, simply cannot be interpreted as constituting any promise or representation to the voters of **Bradford** that the Lord Mayor would or would not use his casting vote in any particular manner.' See *R v Bradford City Council Ex p Wilson* [1990] 2 QB 375.

Article 13 Previous provisions

Table A 1985: Regulation 88

88. Subject to the provisions of the articles, the directors may regulate their proceedings as they think fit. A director may, and the secretary at the request of a director shall, call a meeting of the directors. It shall not be necessary to give notice of a meeting to a director who is absent from the United Kingdom. Questions arising at a meeting shall be decided by a majority of votes. In the case of an equality of votes, the chairman shall have a second or casting vote. A director who is also an alternate director shall be entitled in the absence of his appointor to a separate vote on behalf of his appointor in addition to his own vote.

Article 14 Conflicts of interest

2.17

14.—(1) If a proposed decision of the directors is concerned with an actual or proposed transaction or arrangement with the company in which a director is interested, that director is not to be counted as participating in the decision-making process for quorum or voting purposes.

(2) But if paragraph (3) applies, a director who is interested in an actual or proposed transaction or arrangement with the company is to be counted as participating in the decision-making process for quorum and voting purposes.

(3) This paragraph applies when—

(a) the company by ordinary resolution disapplies the provision of the articles which would otherwise prevent a director from being counted as participating in the decision-making process;

(b) the director's interest cannot reasonably be regarded as likely to give rise to a conflict of interest; or

(c) the director's conflict of interest arises from a permitted cause.

(4) For the purposes of this article, the following are permitted causes—

(a) a guarantee given, or to be given, by or to a director in respect of an obligation incurred by or on behalf of the company or any of its subsidiaries;

(b) subscription, or an agreement to subscribe, for securities of the company or any of its subsidiaries, or to underwrite, sub-underwrite, or guarantee subscription for any such securities; and

(c) arrangements pursuant to which benefits are made available to employees and directors or former employees and directors of the company or any of its subsidiaries which do not provide special benefits for directors or former directors.

(5) For the purposes of this article, references to proposed decisions and decision-making processes include any directors' meeting or part of a directors' meeting.

(6) Subject to paragraph (7), if a question arises at a meeting of directors or of a committee of directors as to the right of a director to participate in the meeting (or part of the meeting) for voting or quorum purposes, the question may, before the conclusion of the meeting, be referred to the chairman whose ruling in relation to any director other than the chairman is to be final and conclusive.

(7) If any question as to the right to participate in the meeting (or part of the meeting) should arise in respect of the chairman, the question is to be decided by a decision of the directors at that meeting, for which purpose the chairman is not to be counted as participating in the meeting (or that part of the meeting) for voting or quorum purposes.

Article 14 Analysis

On 1 October 2008 a new duty was placed on company directors to avoid conflicts of interests in the company. Section 175[28] of the Companies Act 2006 requires directors to avoid conflicts of interest, the provisions replaced the previous equitable obligations that any director must account for any profit made personally in conflict with their own duty to the company.[29]

As regards transactional conflicts of interest, section 177[30] requires directors to disclose any interest in a proposed transaction or arrangement with the company which is a separate duty to disclosing any interest in an existing transaction or arrangement with the company.

The court's view on the conflicts a director may encounter is first and foremost that the appointed director must demonstrate allegiance to the company. The principle does not concern itself with proving fraud or corruption. The basic premise in the words of Upjohn LJ, is the company is entitled 'to the undivided loyalty of its directors' (*Boulting v Association of Cinematograph, Television and Allied Technicians*).[31]

28 Companies Act 2006, s 175 (Duty to avoid conflicts of interest) '(1) A director of a company must avoid a situation in which he has, or can have, a direct or indirect interest that conflicts, or possibly may conflict, with the interests of the company.'

29 The case *Boardman v Phipps* [1967] 2 AC 46 provides the court's view on duty.

30 Companies Act 2006, s 177 (Duty to declare interest in proposed transaction or arrangement) '(1) If a director of a company is in any way, directly or indirectly, interested in a proposed transaction or arrangement with the company, he must declare the nature and extent of that interest to the other directors.'

31 [1963] 2 QB.

Situational or transactional conflicts do not depend on fraud, or absence of bona fides, (*Regal (Hastings) Ltd v Gulliver*),[32] the majority of conflicts may arise through business opportunities or joint ventures. If any director were to enrich himself instead of the company he is liable for breach of duty, regardless of the fact that he acted in good faith.

A common conflict concerns a business opportunity presented to the board of directors which is dismissed by the company, subsequently if any board member obtains the opportunity for himself he will be liable to the company. The fact the company rejected the opportunity is of no consequence (*Foster Bryant Surveying Ltd v Bryant*).[33]

Regardless of all matters concerning any conflicted director he or she must vote and make decisions based solely on the success of the company.[34]

Transitional rules on conflicts of interest

For private companies incorporated before 1 October 2008 the board are required to pass an ordinary resolution to authorise any conflicts or they may amend the articles of association. The duties under section 175[35] apply to conflicts of interest that arise after 1 October 2008, therefore as regards companies incorporated under previous Companies Acts the law which applied will continue to pertain to any situation concerning conflicts of interest.[36]

Article 14 Previous provisions

Table A 1985: Regulations 94, 95, 96 and 98

Table A is modified. In paragraph (c) of regulation 94 the words 'shares, debentures, or other securities' are replaced with 'debentures'.[37]

94. Save as otherwise provided by the articles, a director shall not vote at a meeting of directors or of a committee of directors on any resolution concerning a matter in which he has, directly or indirectly, an interest or duty which is material and which conflicts or may conflict with the interests of the company unless his interest or duty arises only because the case falls within one or more of the following paragraphs—

(a) the resolution relates to the giving to him of a guarantee, security, or indemnity in respect of money lent to, or an obligation incurred by him for the benefit of, the company or any of its subsidiaries;

32 [1967] 2 AC 134.

33 [2007] EWCA Civ 200.

34 See *Colin Gwyer & Associates Ltd v London Wharf (Limehouse) Ltd* [2002] EWHC 2748 (Ch); [2002] All ER (D) 226 (Dec).

35 The Companies Act 2006 (Commencement No. 5, Transitional Provisions and Savings) Order 2007, SI 2007/3495, Part 3, reg 47(1) 'Section 175 of the Companies Act 2006 (duty to avoid conflicts of interest) applies where the situation described in subsection (1) of that section arises on or after 1st October 2008.'

36 The Companies Act 2006 (Commencement No. 5, Transitional Provisions and Savings) Order 2007, SI 2007/3495, Part 3, reg 47(2) 'The law that applied before that date continues to apply to such a situation that arose before that date.'

37 The Companies (Tables A to F) Regulations 1985, SI 1985/805, Table C, A company limited by guarantee and not having a share capital, Articles of association, para 10.

(b) the resolution relates to the giving to a third party of a guarantee, security, or indemnity in respect of an obligation of the company or any of its subsidiaries for which the director has assumed responsibility in whole or part and whether alone or jointly with others under a guarantee or indemnity or by the giving of security;

(c) his interest arises by virtue of his subscribing or agreeing to subscribe for any **debentures** of the company or any of its subsidiaries, or by virtue of his being, or intending to become, a participant in the underwriting or sub-underwriting of an offer of any such **debentures** by the company or any of its subsidiaries for subscription, purchase or exchange;

(d) the resolution relates in any way to a retirement benefits scheme which has been approved, or is conditional upon approval, by the Board of Inland Revenue for taxation purposes.

For the purposes of this regulation, an interest of a person who is, for any purpose of the Act (excluding any statutory modification thereof not in force when this regulation becomes binding on the company), connected with a director shall be treated as an interest of the director and, in relation to an alternate director, an interest of his appointor shall be treated as an interest of the alternate director without prejudice to any interest which the alternate director has otherwise.

95. A director shall not be counted in the quorum present at a meeting in relation to a resolution on which he is not entitled to vote.

96. The company may by ordinary resolution suspend or relax to any extent, either generally or in respect of any particular matter, any provision of the articles prohibiting a director from voting at a meeting of directors or of a committee of directors.

98. If a question arises at a meeting of directors or of a committee of directors as to the right of a director to vote, the question may, before the conclusion of the meeting, be referred to the chairman of the meeting and his ruling in relation to any director other than himself shall be final and conclusive.

Article 15 Records of decisions to be kept

2.18

15. The directors must ensure that the company keeps a record, in writing, for at least 10 years from the date of the decision recorded, of every unanimous or majority decision taken by the directors.

Article 15 Analysis

This article reinstates section 248[38] that every company must keep all proceedings at meetings of the directors of the company for at least 10 years. Failure to adhere is punishable by a fine and the articles may not fetter the act.

Any failure to keep records on a decision, does not invalidate the decision,[39] however an offence is committed by every officer of the company who is in default.[40]

Article 15 Previous provisions

Table A 1985: Regulation 100

Table A is modified. In paragraph (b) of regulation 100 the words 'of the holders of any class of shares in the company'[41] are omitted.

100. The directors shall cause minutes to be made in books kept for the purpose—

(a) of all appointments of officers made by the directors; and

(b) of all proceedings at meetings of the company, and of the directors, and of committees of directors, including the names of the directors present at each such meeting.

Article 16 Directors' discretion to make further rules

2.19

16. Subject to the articles, the directors may make any rule which they think fit about how they take decisions, and about how such rules are to be recorded or communicated to directors.

Article 16 Analysis

Article 16 is a new provision intended to provide clear guidance that directors are able to adapt the articles of association for any particular circumstance. The provision expressly states 'subject to the articles',

38 Companies Act 2006, s 248 (Minutes of directors' meetings) '(1) Every company must cause minutes of all proceedings at meetings of its directors to be recorded.'

39 *North Hallenbeagle Mining Co, Re* (1866–67) LR 2 Ch App 321.

40 Companies Act 2006, s 248(3) (Minutes of directors' meetings).

41 The Companies (Tables A to F) Regulations 1985, SI 1985/805, Table C, A company limited by guarantee and not having a share capital, Articles of association, para 11.

in principle the directors have no scope to cause conflicting rules or amendments. When considering further rules section 171[42] affirms directors must act for the company with full consideration of its constitution.

Article 16 Previous provisions

Table A 1985: Regulation 88

88. Subject to the provisions of the articles, the directors may regulate their proceedings as they think fit. A director may, and the secretary at the request of a director shall, call a meeting of the directors. It shall not be necessary to give notice of a meeting to a director who is absent from the United Kingdom. Questions arising at a meeting shall be decided by a majority of votes. In the case of an equality of votes, the chairman shall have a second or casting vote. A director who is also an alternate director shall be entitled in the absence of his appointor to a separate vote on behalf of his appointor in addition to his own vote.

Appointments of directors

Article 17 Methods of appointing directors

2.20

17.—(1) Any person who is willing to act as a director, and is permitted by law to do so, may be appointed to be a director—

(a) by ordinary resolution, or

(b) by a decision of the directors.

(2) In any case where, as a result of death, the company has no members and no directors, the personal representatives of the last member to have died have the right, by notice in writing, to appoint a person to be a director.

(3) For the purposes of paragraph (2), where 2 or more members die in circumstances rendering it uncertain who was the last to die, a younger member is deemed to have survived an older member.

Article 17 Analysis

The provision outlines the methods of appointing a director and combines regulations 78 and 79 of Table A. The previous requirements to fix a maximum number of directors and re-appointment or retire by rotation have been removed.

42 Companies Act 2006.

Although not specified, 'a person who is willing to act' must have reached the age of 16 and not be an undischarged bankrupt. There is no maximum number of directors allowed for a company, section 154[43] requires a minimum of one for a private company.

In smaller limited companies, appointing directors without due process set out in article 17 may occur for reasons of expediency. The courts' view is any director not appointed in accordance with articles is considered invalid (*Sierra Leone Telecommunications Co Ltd v Barclays Bank plc*).[44]

Article 17 Previous provisions

Table A 1985: Regulations 78 and 79

78. Subject as aforesaid, the company may by ordinary resolution appoint a person who is willing to act to be a director either to fill a vacancy or as an additional director and may also determine the rotation in which any additional directors are to retire.

79. The directors may appoint a person who is willing to act to be a director, either to fill a vacancy or as an additional director, provided that the appointment does not cause the number of directors to exceed any number fixed by or in accordance with the articles as the maximum number of directors. A director so appointed shall hold office only until the next following annual general meeting and shall not be taken into account in determining the directors who are to retire by rotation at the meeting. If not reappointed at such annual general meeting, he shall vacate office at the conclusion thereof.

Article 18 Termination of director's appointment

2.21

18. A person ceases to be a director as soon as—

(a) that person ceases to be a director by virtue of any provision of the Companies Act 2006 or is prohibited from being a director by law;

(b) a bankruptcy order is made against that person;

(c) a composition is made with that person's creditors generally in satisfaction of that person's debts;

43 Companies Act 2006, s 154 (Companies required to have directors) '(1) A private company must have at least one director. (2) A public company must have at least two directors.'

44 [1998] 2 All ER 821.

(d) a registered medical practitioner who is treating that person gives a written opinion to the company stating that that person has become physically or mentally incapable of acting as a director and may remain so for more than three months;

(e) [paragraph omitted pursuant to The Mental Health (Discrimination) Act 2013]

(f) notification is received by the company from the director that the director is resigning from office, and such resignation has taken effect in accordance with its terms.

Article 18 Analysis

Article 18 specifies the factors that would automatically terminate a director's appointment. The main omission from the previous Table A (1985) is the failure to attend directors meetings for six consecutive months, resulting in termination.

Article 18(e) is now omitted with the introduction of The Mental Health (Discrimination) Act 2013. The Act's main objective is to remove discrimination for mental health reasons and eradicate the stigma associated with mental illness. The Act resulted in company directors having increased safeguarding from being removed as a company director on the basis of mental health.

Companies formed prior to 28 April 2013 (who have not updated their articles) ought to consider amending them to include the new legislation.

Article 18 Previous provisions

Table A 1985: Regulation 81

81. The office of a director shall be vacated if—

(a) he ceases to be a director by virtue of any provision of the Act or he becomes prohibited by law from being a director; or

(b) he becomes bankrupt or makes any arrangement or composition with his creditors generally; or

(c) he is, or may be, suffering from mental disorder and either—

 (i) he is admitted to hospital in pursuance of an application for admission for treatment under the Mental Health Act 1983 or, in Scotland, an application for admission under the Mental Health (Scotland) Act 1960, or

 (ii) an order is made by a court having jurisdiction (whether in the United Kingdom or elsewhere) in matters concerning mental disorder for his detention or for the appointment of a receiver, curator bonis or other person to exercise powers with respect to his property or affairs; or

(d) he resigns his office by notice to the company; or

(e) he shall for more than six consecutive months have been absent without permission of the directors from meetings of directors held during that period and the directors resolve that his office be vacated.

Article 19 Directors' remuneration

2.22

19.—(1) Directors may undertake any services for the company that the directors decide.

(2) Directors are entitled to such remuneration as the directors determine—

(a) for their services to the company as directors, and

(b) for any other service which they undertake for the company.

(3) Subject to the articles, a director's remuneration may—

(a) take any form, and

(b) include any arrangements in connection with the payment of a pension, allowance or gratuity, or any death, sickness or disability benefits, to or in respect of that director.

(4) Unless the directors decide otherwise, directors' remuneration accrues from day to day.

(5) Unless the directors decide otherwise, directors are not accountable to the company for any remuneration which they receive as directors or other officers or employees of the company's subsidiaries or of any other body corporate in which the company is interested.

Article 19 Analysis

The main change from the previous Table A is the directors are able to set their own renumeration without involvement from the shareholders and they can act (and be remunerated) as both employees and executives.

It should be noted section 1214 of the Companies Act 2006[45] specifies an independence requirement for auditors, article 19(1) allows 'any services', and officers and employees of the company are specifically barred from acting as auditors.[46]

Duomatic principle

Article 19(2) reflects the courts view[47] that directors are not required to formally approve, by resolution, any payments in a general meeting of the company. The directors must evidence they have applied their minds to the question of whether the drawings should be approved – the so called *Duomatic* principle.[48] In *Deakin v Faulding*[49] Hart J confirmed the same principle shall apply to bonus payments.[50]

Article 19 Previous provisions

Table A 1985: Regulations 82, 84, 87

82. The directors shall be entitled to such remuneration as the company may by ordinary resolution determine and, unless the resolution provides otherwise, the remuneration shall be deemed to accrue from day to day.

84. Subject to the provisions of the Act, the directors may appoint one or more of their number to the office of managing director or to any other executive office under the company and may enter into an agreement or arrangement with any director for his employment by the company or for the provision by him of any services outside the scope of the ordinary duties of a director. Any such appointment, agreement or arrangement may be made upon such terms as the directors determine and they may remunerate any such director for his services as they think fit. Any appointment of a director to an executive office shall terminate if he ceases to be a director but without prejudice to any claim to damages for breach of the contract of service between the director and the company. A managing director and a director holding any other executive office shall not be subject to retirement by rotation.

87. The directors may provide benefits, whether by the payment of gratuities or pensions or by insurance or otherwise, for any director who has held but no longer holds any executive office or employment with the company or with any body corporate which is or has been a subsidiary of the company

45 Companies Act 2006.

46 Companies Act 2006, s 1214 (Independence requirement) '(1) A person may not act as statutory auditor of an audited person if one or more of subsections (2), (3) and (4) apply to him.'

47 *Duomatic* principle.

48 *Duomatic Ltd, Re* [1969] 1 All ER 161.

49 *Deakin v Faulding* (2001) 98(35) LSG 32; [2001] All ER (D) 463 (Jul).

50 Hart J, 'In my judgment, therefore, the Deakins are entitled to retain the bonuses as a result of the application of the *Duomatic* principle'. *Deakin v Faulding* (2001) 98(35) LSG 32; [2001] All ER (D) 463 (Jul).

or a predecessor in business of the company or of any such subsidiary, and for any member of his family (including a spouse and a former spouse) or any person who is or was dependent on him, and may (as well before as after he ceases to hold such office or employment) contribute to any fund and pay premiums for the purchase or provision of any such benefit.

Article 20 Directors' expenses

2.23

20. The company may pay any reasonable expenses[51] which the directors properly incur in connection with their attendance at:

(a) meetings of directors or committees of directors,

(b) general meetings, or

(c) separate meetings of the holders of debentures of the company,

or otherwise in connection with the exercise of their powers and the discharge of their responsibilities in relation to the company.

Article 20 Analysis

Article 20 takes a broad approach to the payment of expenses and improves upon the previous Table A (1985) regulations that allowed for travelling and other expenses only. The article is somewhat implicit stating 'may pay' and 'reasonable expenses', it must be assumed that which expenses will be paid and the definition of reasonable are matters are for the board of directors to decide.

The provision is to some extent conflicted with article 23 that promoted the use of technology to attend meetings. A director who resides 200 miles from head office who wishes to attend in person for every meeting would incur reasonable expenses in doing so – in contrast with a director who may only attend by conference call would cost the company far less in expenses.

It may be appropriate (as many companies do) to expand on this general article and detail directors expenses by employing internal procedures and documents. The articles of association are public documents, it could be expected companies would not want their directors' expenses to be public knowledge, therefore, editing the article to include more detailed expense data ought to be avoided.

51 An express provision is required in the articles of association.

Article 20 Previous provisions

Table A 1985: Regulation 83

83. The directors may be paid all travelling, hotel, and other expenses properly incurred by them in connection with their attendance at meetings of directors or committees of directors or general meetings or separate meetings of the holders of **any class of shares** or of debentures of the company or otherwise in connection with the discharge of their duties.

Part 3 Members – Becoming and ceasing to be a member

Article 21 Applications for membership

2.24

21. No person shall become a member of the company unless—

(a) that person has completed an application for membership in a form approved by the directors, and

(b) the directors have approved the application.

Article 21 Analysis

The subscribers to the memorandum of association of the company and such other persons as are admitted to membership in accordance with the articles shall be members of the company.

No person shall be admitted a member of the company unless he is approved by the directors. Every person who wishes to become a member shall deliver to the company an application for membership in such form as the directors require executed by him.

Article 21 Previous provisions

Table A 1985: Regulation 3

Table A is modified. Paragraph 3 is inserted.[52]

3. The subscribers to the memorandum of association of the company and such other persons as are admitted to membership in accordance with the articles shall be members of the company. No person shall be admitted

52 The Companies (Tables A to F) Regulations 1985, SI 1985/805, Table C, A company limited by guarantee and not having a share capital, see https://www.legislation.gov.uk/uksi/1985/805/pdfs/uksi_19850805_en.pdf.

a member of the company unless he is approved by the directors. Every person who wishes to become a member shall deliver to the company an application for membership in such form as the directors require executed by him.

Article 22 Termination of membership

2.25

22.—(1) A member may withdraw from membership of the company by giving 7 days' notice to the company in writing.

(2) Membership is not transferable.

(3) A person's membership terminates when that person dies or ceases to exist.

Article 22 Analysis

A member may at any time withdraw from the company by giving at least seven clear days' notice to the company. Membership shall not be transferable and shall cease on death.

Article 22 Previous provisions

Table A 1985: Regulation 4

Table A is modified. Regulation (Paragraph) 4 is inserted.[53]

4. A member may at any time withdraw from the company by giving at least seven clear days' notice to the company. Membership shall not be transferable and shall cease on death.

Organisation of general meetings

Article 23 Attendance and speaking at general meetings

2.26

23.—(1) A person is able to exercise the right to speak at a general meeting when that person is in a position to communicate to all those attending the meeting, during the meeting, any information or opinions which that person has on the business of the meeting.

53 The Companies (Tables A to F) Regulations 1985, SI 1985/805, Table C, A company limited by guarantee and not having a share capital, Articles of association, para 4.

(2) A person is able to exercise the right to vote at a general meeting when—

(a) that person is able to vote, during the meeting, on resolutions put to the vote at the meeting, and

(b) that person's vote can be taken into account in determining whether or not such resolutions are passed at the same time as the votes of all the other persons attending the meeting.

(3) The directors may make whatever arrangements they consider appropriate to enable those attending a general meeting to exercise their rights to speak or vote at it.

(4) In determining attendance at a general meeting, it is immaterial whether any two or more members attending it are in the same place as each other.

(5) Two or more persons who are not in the same place as each other attend a general meeting if their circumstances are such that if they have (or were to have) rights to speak and vote at that meeting, they are (or would be) able to exercise them.

Article 23 Analysis

Article 23, a new provision, builds on the general assumption that modern companies require the board of directors to have flexibility in how they conduct meetings. Broadly, with the advent of technology it is envisaged that the board will not always be present in a room at the same location. Article 23(3) allows for directors who may have disabilities that may impede formal communication.

Article 23 Previous provisions

There is no corresponding provision in Table A 1985.

Article 24 Quorum for general meetings

2.27

24. No business other than the appointment of the chairman of the meeting is to be transacted at a general meeting if the persons attending it do not constitute a quorum.

Article 24 Analysis

Article 24 outlines the requirements for two directors to form a valid quorum, it should be noted the company may alter the provisions in the articles to specify how a quorum is to be formed. Section 318(2) of the Companies Act 2006 allows the articles to override this specific section of the act.

The persons who constitute the quorum are not limited to its members. Section 318 of the Companies Act 2006 stipulates 'qualifying person' which means a member, a person appointed by proxy or a corporate representative (as defined in section 323 of the Companies Act 2006). If the meeting is inquorate it must be adjourned. If a company has only one member, then their attendance at a meeting is a quorum (Companies Act 2006, s 318(1)).

Article 24 Previous provisions

Table A 1985: Regulation 40

40. No business shall be transacted at any meeting unless a quorum is present. Two persons entitled to vote upon the business to be transacted, each being a member or a proxy for a member or a duly authorised representative of a corporation, shall be a quorum.

Article 25 Chairing general meetings

2.28

25.—(1) If the directors have appointed a chairman, the chairman shall chair general meetings if present and willing to do so.

(2) If the directors have not appointed a chairman, or if the chairman is unwilling to chair the meeting or is not present within ten minutes of the time at which a meeting was due to start—

(a) the directors present, or

(b) (if no directors are present), the meeting,

must appoint a director or member to chair the meeting, and the appointment of the chairman of the meeting must be the first business of the meeting.

(3) The person chairing a meeting in accordance with this article is referred to as "the chairman of the meeting".

Article 25 Analysis

Article 25 confers the provisions in the Companies Act[54] which allow the company to appoint a chairman.[55] It is allowable under the Act to draft provisions in the company constitution that state who may or may not be chairman.[56]

The powers conferred by the constitution are vested in the directors alone, the shareholders (or members) cannot interfere with the process of appointing a chairman (*Clarke v Workman*).[57]

Article 25 Previous provisions

Table A 1985: Regulations 42, 43

42. The chairman, if any, of the board of directors or in his absence some other director nominated by the directors shall preside as chairman of the meeting, but if neither the chairman nor such other director (if any) be present within fifteen minutes after the time appointed for holding the meeting and willing to act, the directors present shall elect one of their number to be chairman and, if there is only one director present and willing to act, he shall be chairman.

43. If no director is willing to act as chairman, or if no director is present within fifteen minutes after the time appointed for holding the meeting, the members present and entitled to vote shall choose one of their number to be chairman.

Article 26 Attendance and speaking by directors and non-members

2.29

26.—(1) Directors may attend and speak at general meetings, whether or not they are members.

(2) The chairman of the meeting may permit other persons who are not members of the company to attend and speak at a general meeting.

Article 26 Analysis

The provision in this article allows for accountants, solicitors or other professionals to speak at general meetings.

54 Companies Act 2006.

55 Companies Act 2006, s 319 (Chairman of meeting) '(1) A member may be elected to be the chairman of a general meeting by a resolution of the company passed at the meeting.'

56 Companies Act, s 319(2) 'Subsection (1) is subject to any provision of the company's articles that states who may or may not be chairman.'

57 [1920] 1 IR 107.

Article 26 Previous provisions

Table A 1985: Regulation 44

Table A is modified. The words 'and at any separate meeting of the holders of any class of shares in the company' are omitted from regulation 44.[58]

44. A director shall, notwithstanding that he is not a member, be entitled to attend and speak at any general meeting.

Article 27 Adjournment

2.30

27.—(1) If the persons attending a general meeting within half an hour of the time at which the meeting was due to start do not constitute a quorum, or if during a meeting a quorum ceases to be present, the chairman of the meeting must adjourn it.

(2) The chairman of the meeting may adjourn a general meeting at which a quorum is present if—

(a) the meeting consents to an adjournment, or

(b) it appears to the chairman of the meeting that an adjournment is necessary to protect the safety of any person attending the meeting or ensure that the business of the meeting is conducted in an orderly manner.

(3) The chairman of the meeting must adjourn a general meeting if directed to do so by the meeting.

(4) When adjourning a general meeting, the chairman of the meeting must—

(a) either specify the time and place to which it is adjourned or state that it is to continue at a time and place to be fixed by the directors, and

(b) have regard to any directions as to the time and place of any adjournment which have been given by the meeting.

(5) If the continuation of an adjourned meeting is to take place more than 14 days after it was adjourned, the company must give at least 7 clear days' notice of it (that is, excluding the day of the adjourned meeting and the day on which the notice is given)—

(a) to the same persons to whom notice of the company's general meetings is required to be given, and

58 The Companies (Tables A to F) Regulations 1985, SI 1985/805, Table C, A company limited by guarantee and not having a share capital, Articles of association, para 6.

(b) containing the same information which such notice is required to contain.

(6) No business may be transacted at an adjourned general meeting which could not properly have been transacted at the meeting if the adjournment had not taken place.

Article 27 Analysis

With the exception of section 332,[59] the Companies Act 2006 says very little on the issue of adjournment of meetings, therefore, article 27 is based on common law principles. If considering an adjournment, the chairman ought not to act alone (even with powers conferred by the articles), instead he should gain consent or direction from the members present.

The decision to adjourn ought to be decided on the facts at hand and the urgency of the matter (*Byng v London Life Association Ltd*).[60] Article 27(1) allows for automatic adjournment in the event a meeting fails to form a quorum, the Companies Act 2006 requires two qualifying persons (unless the company has only one member).[61]

Disorderly meetings are addressed in article 27(2), the chairman has residual common law power of adjournment, generally the powers are vested in the meeting as per article 27(3).

It should be noted if the chairman has instigated the disorder by his actions any adjournment is deemed invalid, concerning disorderly meetings (without violence) any adjournment ought to be short, with all efforts made to restore order (*John v Rees and Others*).[62]

Article 27(4)–27(5) outlines the requirement of seven days' notice of the adjourned meeting which is to take place 14 days after the adjournment.

Article 27 Previous provisions

Table A 1985: Regulations 41, 45

41. If such a quorum is not present within half an hour from the time appointed for the meeting, or if during a meeting such a quorum ceases to be present, the meeting shall stand adjourned to the same day in the next week at the same time and place or to such time and place as the directors may determine.

45. The chairman may, with the consent of a meeting at which a quorum is present (and shall if so directed by the meeting), adjourn the meeting from

59 Companies Act 2006, s 332 (Resolution passed at adjourned meeting). 'Where a resolution is passed at an adjourned meeting of a company, the resolution is for all purposes to be treated as having been passed on the date on which it was in fact passed, and is not to be deemed passed on any earlier date.'

60 [1990] Ch 170.

61 Companies Act 2006, s 318 (Quorum at meeting).

62 [1969] 2 All ER 274.

time to time and from place to place, but no business shall be transacted at an adjourned meeting other than business which might properly have been transacted at the meeting had the adjournment not taken place. When a meeting is adjourned for fourteen days or more, at least seven clear days' notice shall be given specifying the time and place of the adjourned meeting and the general nature of the business to be transacted. Otherwise it shall not be necessary to give any such notice.

Voting at general meetings

Article 28 Voting: general

2.31

28. A resolution put to the vote of a general meeting must be decided on a show of hands unless a poll is duly demanded in accordance with the articles.

Article 28 Analysis

The rules on voting are provided by section 284[63] of the Companies Act 2006, which outlines that each member has one vote in the case of a written resolution, show of hands or poll. The company is free to assign voting rights[64] as it sees fit to any share classes the company may have created, article 28 would require adaptation if different share classes held unique voting rights.

Article 28 Previous provisions

Table A 1985: Regulation 46

Table A is modified. Paragraph (d) of regulation 46 is omitted: 'by a member or members holding shares conferring a right to vote at the meeting being shares on which an aggregate sum has been paid up equal to not less than one-tenth of the total sum paid up on all the shares conferring that right'.[65]

46. A resolution put to the vote of a meeting shall be decided on a show of hands unless before, or on the declaration of the result of, the show of hands a poll is duly demanded. Subject to the provisions of the Act, a poll may be demanded—

(a) by the chairman; or

(b) by at least two members having the right to vote at the meeting; or

63 Companies Act 2006, s 284 (Votes: general rules).

64 Companies Act 2006, s 284(4) 'The provisions of this section have effect subject to any provision of the company's articles.'

65 The Companies (Tables A to F) Regulations 1985, SI 1985/805, Table C, A company limited by guarantee and not having a share capital, Articles of association, para 7.

(c) by a member or members representing not less than one-tenth of the total voting rights of all the members having the right to vote at the meeting; or

and a demand by a person as proxy for a member shall be the same as a demand by the member.

Article 29 Errors and disputes

2.32

29.—(1) No objection may be raised to the qualification of any person voting at a general meeting except at the meeting or adjourned meeting at which the vote objected to is tendered, and every vote not disallowed at the meeting is valid.

(2) Any such objection must be referred to the chairman of the meeting whose decision is final.

Article 29 Analysis

Article 29 allows the chairman a decisive final decision on entitlement to vote at general meetings. Objections on the validity to vote must be raised at the meeting or adjourned meeting. Adapting the article may lead to disputes without the powers of a final decision vested in the chairman.

Article 29 Previous provisions

Table A 1985: Regulation 58

58. No objection shall be raised to the qualification of any voter except at the meeting or adjourned meeting at which the vote objected to is tendered, and every vote not disallowed at the meeting shall be valid. Any objection made in due time shall be referred to the chairman whose decision shall be final and conclusive.

Article 30 Poll votes

2.33

30.—(1) A poll on a resolution may be demanded—

(a) in advance of the general meeting where it is to be put to the vote, or

(b) at a general meeting, either before a show of hands on that resolution or immediately after the result of a show of hands on that resolution is declared.

(2) A poll may be demanded by—

(a) the chairman of the meeting;

(b) the directors;

(c) two or more persons having the right to vote on the resolution; or

(d) a person or persons representing not less than one tenth of the total voting rights of all the members having the right to vote on the resolution.

(3) A demand for a poll may be withdrawn if—

(a) the poll has not yet been taken, and

(b) the chairman of the meeting consents to the withdrawal.

(4) Polls must be taken immediately and in such manner as the chairman of the meeting directs.

Article 30 Analysis

The general position outlined in article 30 is that votes at general meetings are decided on a show of hands. If the vote is unclear or possibly disputed, then a poll may be called.

Article 30 summarises the rules and describes who has the right to demand a poll. The foundations of the provisions are founded on section 321[66] and therefore members are provided statutory rights to call a poll, regardless of the company's constitution.

Any latitude for adapting the articles is somewhat curtailed by the provisions in the Act, which without ambiguity state that any provisions that exclude rights to demand a poll are void, with the exception of electing a chairman or adjournment of a meeting.[67]

Article 30 Previous provisions

Table A 1985: Regulations 46, 48, 49, 51

Table A is modified. Paragraph (d) of regulation 46 is omitted: 'by a member or members holding shares conferring a right to vote at the meeting being shares on which an aggregate sum has been paid up equal to not less than one-tenth of the total sum paid up on all the shares conferring that right'.[68]

66 Companies Act 2006, s 321 (Right to demand a poll).

67 Companies Act 2006, s 321(1).

68 The Companies (Tables A to F) Regulations 1985, SI 1985/805, Table C, A company limited by guarantee and not having a share capital, Articles of association, para 7.

46. A resolution put to the vote of a meeting shall be decided on a show of hands unless before, or on the declaration of the result of, the show of hands a poll is duly demanded. Subject to the provisions of the Act, a poll may be demanded—

(a) by the chairman; or

(b) by at least two members having the right to vote at the meeting; or

(c) by a member or members representing not less than one-tenth of the total voting rights of all the members having the right to vote at the meeting; or

and a demand by a person as proxy for a member shall be the same as a demand by the member.

48. The demand for a poll may, before the poll is taken, be withdrawn but only with the consent of the chairman and a demand so withdrawn shall not be taken to have invalidated the result of a show of hands declared before the demand was made.

49. A poll shall be taken as the chairman directs and he may appoint scrutineers (who need not be members) and fix a time and place for declaring the result of the poll. The result of the poll shall be deemed to be the resolution of the meeting at which the poll was demanded.

51. A poll demanded on the election of a chairman or on a question of adjournment shall be taken forthwith. A poll demanded on any other question shall be taken either forthwith or at such time and place as the chairman directs not being more than thirty days after the poll is demanded. The demand for a poll shall not prevent the continuance of a meeting for the transaction of any business other than the question on which the poll was demanded. If a poll is demanded before the declaration of the result of a show of hands and the demand is duly withdrawn, the meeting shall continue as if the demand had not been made.

Article 31 Content of proxy notices

2.34

31.—(1) Proxies may only validly be appointed by a notice in writing (a "proxy notice") which—

(a) states the name and address of the member appointing the proxy;

(b) identifies the person appointed to be that member's proxy and the general meeting in relation to which that person is appointed;

(c) is signed by or on behalf of the member appointing the proxy, or is authenticated in such manner as the directors may determine; and

(d) is delivered to the company in accordance with the articles and any instructions contained in the notice of the general meeting to which they relate.

(2) The company may require proxy notices to be delivered in a particular form, and may specify different forms for different purposes.

(3) Proxy notices may specify how the proxy appointed under them is to vote (or that the proxy is to abstain from voting) on one or more resolutions.

(4) Unless a proxy notice indicates otherwise, it must be treated as—

(a) allowing the person appointed under it as a proxy discretion as to how to vote on any ancillary or procedural resolutions put to the meeting, and

(b) appointing that person as a proxy in relation to any adjournment of the general meeting to which it relates as well as the meeting itself.

Article 31 Analysis

A proxy may attend and vote at general meetings in place of a member of the company. The Companies Act 2006 provides statutory rights to appoint proxies by virtue of the provisions defined in sections 324–331.

Article 31 Previous provisions

Table A 1985: Regulations 60, 61

60. The appointment of a proxy shall be executed by or on behalf of the appointor and shall be in the following form (or in a form as near thereto as circumstances allow or in any other form which is usual or which the directors may approve)—

> "........... PLC/Limited .... I/We, ..., of ...., being a member/members of the above-named company, hereby appoint .... of ...., or failing him, ... of ...., as my/our proxy to vote in my/our name[s] and on my/our behalf at the annual/any other general meeting of the company to be held on .... 19 ...., and at any adjournment thereof. Signed on .... 19 ....".

61. Where it is desired to afford members an opportunity of instructing the proxy how he shall act the appointment of a proxy shall be in the following

form (or in a form as near thereto as circumstances allow or in any other form which is usual or which the directors may approve)—

"..................... PLC/Limited .... I/We, ..., of ...., being a member/members of the above-named company, hereby appoint .... of ...., or failing him .... of ...., as my/our proxy to vote in my/our name[s] and on my/our behalf at the annual/any other general meeting of the company, to be held on .... 19 ...., and at any adjournment thereof. This form is to be used in respect of the resolutions mentioned below as follows: Resolution No. 1 *for *against Resolution No. 2 *for *against. *Strike out whichever is not desired. Unless otherwise instructed, the proxy may vote as he thinks fit or abstain from voting. Signed this .... day of .... 19 ....".

Article 32 Delivery of proxy notices

2.35

32.—(1) A person who is entitled to attend, speak or vote (either on a show of hands or on a poll) at a general meeting remains so entitled in respect of that meeting or any adjournment of it, even though a valid proxy notice has been delivered to the company by or on behalf of that person.

(2) An appointment under a proxy notice may be revoked by delivering to the company a notice in writing given by or on behalf of the person by whom or on whose behalf the proxy notice was given.

(3) A notice revoking a proxy appointment only takes effect if it is delivered before the start of the meeting or adjourned meeting to which it relates.

(4) If a proxy notice is not executed by the person appointing the proxy, it must be accompanied by written evidence of the authority of the person who executed it to execute it on the appointor's behalf.

Article 32 Analysis

Article 32 is somewhat mistitled as it describes the revocation of proxy notices and the procedures thereof.

Article 32(1) reiterates statutory rights under the Act.[69] Article 32(2) again mirrors the Companies Act,[70] requiring written submissions to enable

69 Companies Act 2006, s 330(2).

70 Companies Act 2006, s 330 (Notice required of termination of proxy's authority). '(A1) In the case of a traded company the termination of the authority of a person to act as proxy must be notified to the company in writing.'

revocation. It should be noted in accordance with section 330(6) the articles cannot be modified to reduce the timeframes for delivery of any notice of termination to below the statutory 48 hours for meetings.[71]

The articles may be adapted to nominate a specific person that notices ought to be given to,[72] which replaces the relatively vague description of 'company' in the article above.

Article 32 Previous provisions

Table A 1985: Regulations 62, 63

62. The appointment of a proxy and any authority under which it is executed or a copy of such authority certified notarially or in some other way approved by the directors may—

(a) in the case of an instrument in writing be deposited at the office or at such other place within the United kingdom as is specified in the notice convening the meeting or in any instrument of proxy sent out by the company in relation to the meeting not less than 48 hours before the time for holding the meeting or adjourned meeting at which the person named in the instrument proposes to vote; or

(aa) in the case of an appointment contained in an electronic communication, where an address has been specified for the purpose of receiving electronic communications—

- (i) in the notice convening the meeting, or
- (ii) in any instrument of proxy sent out by the company in relation to the meeting, or
- (iii) in any invitation contained in an electronic communication to appoint a proxy issued by the company in relation to the meeting, be received at such address not less than 48 hours before the time for holding the meeting or adjourned meeting at which the person named in the appointment proposes to vote;

(b) in the case of a poll taken more than 48 hours after it is demanded, be deposited or received as aforesaid after the poll has been demanded and not less than 24 hours before the time appointed for the taking of the poll; or

71 Companies Act 2006, s 330(6) '(2) Any provision of the company's articles is void in so far as it would have the effect of requiring any such appointment or document to be received by the company or another person earlier than the following time—

(a) in the case of a meeting or adjourned meeting, 48 hours before the time for holding the meeting or adjourned meeting;

(b) in the case of a poll taken more than 48 hours after it was demanded, 24 hours before the time appointed for the taking of the poll;'.

72 Companies Act 2006, s 330(4).

(c) where the poll is not taken forthwith but is taken not more than 48 hours after it was demanded, be delivered at the meeting at which the poll was demanded to the chairman or to the secretary or to any director; and an appointment of proxy which is not deposited, delivered or received in a manner so permitted shall be invalid. In this regulation and the next, "address", in relation to electronic communications, includes any number or address used for the purposes of such communications.

63. A vote given or poll demanded by proxy or by the duly authorised representative of a corporation shall be valid notwithstanding the previous determination of the authority of the person voting or demanding a poll unless notice of the determination was received by the company at the office or at such other place at which the instrument of proxy was duly deposited or, where the appointment of the proxy was contained in an electronic communication, at the address at which such appointment was duly received before the commencement of the meeting or adjourned meeting at which the vote is given or the poll demanded or (in the case of a poll taken otherwise than on the same day as the meeting or adjourned meeting) the time appointed for taking the poll.

Article 33 Amendments to resolutions

2.36

33.—(1) An ordinary resolution to be proposed at a general meeting may be amended by ordinary resolution if—

(a) notice of the proposed amendment is given to the company in writing by a person entitled to vote at the general meeting at which it is to be proposed not less than 48 hours before the meeting is to take place (or such later time as the chairman of the meeting may determine), and

(b) the proposed amendment does not, in the reasonable opinion of the chairman of the meeting, materially alter the scope of the resolution.

(2) A special resolution to be proposed at a general meeting may be amended by ordinary resolution, if—

(a) the chairman of the meeting proposes the amendment at the general meeting at which the resolution is to be proposed, and

(b) the amendment does not go beyond what is necessary to correct a grammatical or other non-substantive error in the resolution.

(3) If the chairman of the meeting, acting in good faith, wrongly decides that an amendment to a resolution is out of order, the chairman's error does not invalidate the vote on that resolution.

Article 33 Analysis

Article 33 is governed by common law principles, which provide guidance for amending resolutions at general meetings. In *Betts & Co Ltd v Macnaghten*[73] the court decided amendments can be made with some latitude to the original resolution proposed, as the notice must simply state the general nature of the business, this is reiterated in the Companies Act 2006.[74]

In addition, on the basis an amendment is within the scope of the notice of the meeting, substantive changes are allowable. For example: a notice to appoint one new director, John Smith, does not prevent an amendment to appoint Jane Smith in his place. Article 33(1)(b) aligns to the common law and provides direction to the chairman.

Article 33(3) is drafted with the court's decision in mind (*Henderson v Bank of Australasia*),[75] any error in good faith does not invalidate the result of the vote on the resolution, however if the chairman acts improperly and refuses to accept an amendment the vote on the resolution is void.

Article 33 Previous provisions

There is no corresponding provision in Table A 1985.

Part 4 Administrative arrangements

Article 34 Means of communication to be used

2.37

34.—(1) Subject to the articles, anything sent or supplied by or to the company under the articles may be sent or supplied in any way in which the Companies Act 2006 provides for documents or information which are authorised or required by any provision of that Act to be sent or supplied by or to the company.

(2) Subject to the articles, any notice or document to be sent or supplied to a director in connection with the taking of decisions by directors may also be

73 [1910] 1 Ch 430.

74 Companies Act 2006, s 311(2) (Contents of notices of meetings). '(2) Notice of a general meeting of a company must state the general nature of the business to be dealt with at the meeting.'

75 (1888) 40 Ch D 170.

sent or supplied by the means by which that director has asked to be sent or supplied with such notices or documents for the time being.

(3) A director may agree with the company that notices or documents sent to that director in a particular way are to be deemed to have been received within a specified time of their being sent, and for the specified time to be less than 48 hours.

Article 34 Analysis

The Companies Act 2006 provides detailed provisions on the sending or supplying of documents or information.[76] Article 34(1) allows for technological advancements and does not restrict the methods in which a company may send documents.

It should be noted if documents are sent electronically, members are entitled to receive the same information in hard copy without charge,[77] it is an offence if the company fails to comply with the member's request.

Article 34(2) allows the company to agree with directors the method of delivery in relation to documents and information when making decisions, this may encompass text messages, WhatsApp, or private messaging on social media. Article 34(3) allows the company to specify 'deemed delivery' time scales, section 1147[78] of the Companies Act 2006 specifies a standard 48 hours for electronic, post and website. The company may amend its articles to lessen the statutory 48 hours by virtue of section 1147.[79]

Article 34 Previous provisions

Table A 1985: Regulations 111, 112

Table A is modified. In regulation 112 the second sentence 'In the case of joint holders of a share, all notices shall be given to the joint holder whose name stands first in the register of members in respect of the joint holding and notice so given shall be sufficient notice to all the joint holders.' is omitted.[80]

111. Any notice to be given to or by any person pursuant to the articles (other than a notice calling a meeting of the directors) shall be in writing or shall be given using electronic communications to an address for the time being notified for that purpose to the person giving the notice. In this regulation, "address", in relation to electronic communications, includes any number or address used for the purposes of such communications.

76 Companies Act 2006, ss 1143–1148 (Sending or supplying documents or information).

77 Companies Act 2006, s 1145(1–5).

78 Companies Act 2006, s 1147 (Deemed delivery of documents and information).

79 Companies Act 2006, s 1147. '(6)(a) in its application to documents or information sent or supplied by a company to its members, any contrary provision of the company's articles;'.

80 The Companies (Tables A to F) Regulations 1985, SI 1985/805, Table C, A company limited by guarantee and not having a share capital, Articles of association, para 12.

112. The company may give any notice to a member either personally or by sending it by post in a prepaid envelope addressed to the member at his registered address or by leaving it at that address or by giving it using electronic communications to an address for the time being notified to the company by the member. A member whose registered address is not within the United Kingdom and who gives to the company an address within the United Kingdom at which notices may be given to him, or an address to which notices may be sent using electronic communications, shall be entitled to have notices given to him at that address, but otherwise no such member shall be entitled to receive any notice from the company. In this regulation and the next, "address", in relation to electronic communications, includes any number or address used for the purposes of such communications.

Article 35 Company seals

2.38

35.—(1) Any common seal may only be used by the authority of the directors.

(2) The directors may decide by what means and in what form any common seal is to be used.

(3) Unless otherwise decided by the directors, if the company has a common seal and it is affixed to a document, the document must also be signed by at least one authorised person in the presence of a witness who attests the signature.

(4) For the purposes of this article, an authorised person is—

(a) any director of the company;

(b) the company secretary (if any); or

(c) any person authorised by the directors for the purpose of signing documents to which the common seal is applied.

Article 35 Analysis

The Companies Act 2006 provides provisions for the execution of documents[81] which allows execution by affixing the company's common seal. Companies tend to execute documents using authorised signatories.[82]

81 Companies Act 2006, s 44 (Execution of Documents). '(1) Under the law of England and Wales or Northern Ireland a document is executed by a company—

(a) by the affixing of its common seal, or
(b) by signature in accordance with the following provisions.'

82 Companies Act 2006, s 44(2).

The Act allows, by virtue of section 45(1),[83] that a company is not required to execute documents by common seal, for clarity the article should be removed if execution by signatory is the preferred method of the company.

Article 35 Previous provisions

Table A 1985: Regulation 101

101. The seal shall only be used by the authority of the directors or of a committee of directors authorised by the directors. The directors may determine who shall sign any instrument to which the seal is affixed and unless otherwise so determined it shall be signed by a director and by the secretary or by a second director.

Article 36 No right to inspect accounts and other records

2.39

36. Except as provided by law or authorised by the directors or an ordinary resolution of the company, no person is entitled to inspect any of the company's accounting or other records or documents merely by virtue of being a member.

Article 36 Analysis

Article 36 precludes members' interference with the running of a company by requiring detailed accounting data or documents. Members hold certain rights conferred under the Companies Act 2006 to inspect and require copies of certain documents.[84]

Investors may require further provisions (by adapting or editing article 36) allowing access to detailed company or financial information, to which under the Companies Act 2006[85] they would have no entitlement. Generally, these issues are dealt with by employing a shareholder agreement, as the details remain private, unlike the articles which are public record.

Companies house provides information freely to members for inspection and covers the majority of requirements under the Act.

83 Companies Act 2006, s 45(1) (A company may have a common seal, but need not have one).
84 Companies Act 2006, s 116 (Rights to inspect and require copies).
85 Companies Act 2006.

Article 36 Previous provisions

Table A 1985: Regulation 109

109. No member shall (as such) have any right of inspecting any accounting records or other book or document of the company except as conferred by statute or authorised by the directors or by ordinary resolution of the company.

Article 37 Provision for employees on cessation of business

2.40

37. The directors may decide to make provision for the benefit of persons employed or formerly employed by the company or any of its subsidiaries (other than a director or former director or shadow director) in connection with the cessation or transfer to any person of the whole or part of the undertaking of the company or that subsidiary.

Article 37 Analysis

This article aligns with section 247(6)[86] of the Companies Act 2006 which provides powers to make provision for the benefit of existing or former employees on winding up or sale. The directors must abide by the general rule of promoting the success of the company when considering making any provisions for benefits.[87] The article is subject to any further provisions detailed in the company's constitution, these take precedent and must be complied with.[88]

Payments must be authorised by resolution and paid from profits before winding up. Directors, existing or former, do not qualify as 'persons employed or formerly employed by the company' as described in the article.

Article 37 Previous provisions

There is no corresponding provision in Table A 1985.

86 Companies Act 2006.
87 Companies Act 2006, s 172.
88 Companies Act 2006, s 247(6).

Directors' indemnity and insurance

Article 38 Indemnity

2.41

38.—(1) Subject to paragraph (2), a relevant director of the company or an associated company may be indemnified out of the company's assets against—

(a) any liability incurred by that director in connection with any negligence, default, breach of duty or breach of trust in relation to the company or an associated company,

(b) any liability incurred by that director in connection with the activities of the company or an associated company in its capacity as a trustee of an occupational pension scheme (as defined in section 235(6) of the Companies Act 2006),

(c) any other liability incurred by that director as an officer of the company or an associated company.

(2) This article does not authorise any indemnity which would be prohibited or rendered void by any provision of the Companies Acts or by any other provision of law.

(3) In this article—

(a) companies are associated if one is a subsidiary of the other or both are subsidiaries of the same body corporate, and

(b) a "relevant director" means any director or former director of the company or an associated company.

Article 39 Insurance

2.42

39.—(1) The directors may decide to purchase and maintain insurance, at the expense of the company, for the benefit of any relevant director in respect of any relevant loss.

(2) In this article—

(a) a "relevant director" means any director or former director of the company or an associated company,

(b) a "relevant loss" means any loss or liability which has been or may be incurred by a relevant director in connection with that director's duties or powers in relation to the company, any associated company or any pension fund or employees' share scheme of the company or associated company, and

(c) companies are associated if one is a subsidiary of the other or both are subsidiaries of the same body corporate.

Articles 38 and 39 Analysis

Companies are able to provide indemnities for directors and adapt article 38 as they see fit. Article 38(1) outlines the company may pay for the insurance.

English company law prohibits waivers or indemnification by contract or by means of the company's constitution. Section 232(1) of the Companies Act 2006 affirms the rule of company law that introducing any provision that may waive liability, or indemnify any director into the company's constitution, is void.

In accordance with section 232(2) and section 233 and by contravention of any of the provisions, the company may indemnify the director for negligence, default, breach of duty or breach of trust. It ought to be noted that Directors and officers liability insurers are unlikely to cover 'negligence, default, breach of duty or breach of trust in relation to the company or an associated company' as defined in the indemnity article if any dishonesty has taken place.

It could be argued the article is improperly drafted, the government review initially omitted articles 38 and 39, stating the raft of variations concerning indemnification was too wide and companies ought to consider drafting special provisions to suit their circumstances. The latter approach would appear the better option.

If the company fails to cover a director employing D&O insurance and subsequently they are required to defend themselves from any criminal or civil proceedings in connection with any alleged negligence, default, breach of duty or breach of trust, the company without shareholder consent may make funds available to cover any legal expenditure. The loan is repayable to the company if the director is convicted or any judgment is made against him.[89]

Article 38 Previous provisions

Table A 1985: Regulation 118

118. Subject to the provisions of the Act but without prejudice to any indemnity to which a director may otherwise be entitled, every director or other officer or auditor of the company shall be indemnified out of the assets of the company against any liability incurred by him in defending any

89 Companies Act 2006, s 205(2)(a).

proceedings, whether civil or criminal, in which judgment is given in his favour or in which he is acquitted or in connection with any application in which relief is granted to him by the court from liability for negligence, default, breach of duty or breach of trust in relation to the affairs of the company.

Article 39 Previous provisions

There is no corresponding provision in Table A 1985.

Chapter 3 Analysis of the Model Articles of Association for a Charitable Company (GD1)

Introduction

3.1

The following chapter provides analysis and commentary of the prescribed articles of association for a charity that incorporates as a company under the Companies Act 2006.

COMPANY NOT HAVING A SHARE CAPITAL

Articles of Association for a Charitable Company

Article 1

3.2

1 The company's name is [insert company name]

(and in this document it is called the 'charity').

> *Article 1 Analysis*
>
> The company is not restrained in selecting a name.[1] The Charity Commission may give a direction[2] to change the name, on the basis it is already registered or is too similar to a registered name[3] or may mislead the public to the true nature of the charitable company's purposes.[4]

1 For further guidance on the Charity Commission rules on the charity name see 'How to choose a charity name', available at https://www.gov.uk/guidance/how-to-choose-a-charity-name.
2 Charities Act 2011, s 42 (Power to require name to be changed).
3 Charities Act 2011, s 42(2)(a) (Power to require name to be changed).
4 Charities Act 2011, s 42(2)(b) (Power to require name to be changed).

Any proposed company name must in addition comply with the requirements of the Companies Act 2006. A company may not register a name that is currently registered in the index of company names.[5]

Article 2 Interpretation

3.3

2 In the articles:

> 'address' means a postal address or, for the purposes of electronic communication, a fax number, an e-mail or postal address or a telephone number for receiving text messages in each case registered with the charity;
>
> 'the articles' means the charity's articles of association;
>
> 'the charity' means the company intended to be regulated by the articles;
>
> 'clear days' in relation to the period of a notice means a period excluding:
>
> - the day when the notice is given or deemed to be given; and
> - the day for which it is given or on which it is to take effect;
>
> 'the Commission' means the Charity Commission for England and Wales;
>
> 'Companies Acts' means the Companies Acts (as defined in section 2 of the Companies Act 2006) insofar as they apply to the charity;
>
> 'the directors' means the directors of the charity. The directors are charity trustees as defined by section 177 of the Charities Act 2011;
>
> 'document' includes, unless otherwise specified, any document sent or supplied in electronic form;
>
> 'electronic form' has the meaning given in section 1168 of the Companies Act 2006;
>
> 'the memorandum' means the charity's memorandum of association;
>
> 'officers' includes the directors and the secretary (if any);
>
> 'the seal' means the common seal of the charity if it has one;
>
> 'secretary' means any person appointed to perform the duties of the secretary of the charity;
>
> 'the United Kingdom' means Great Britain and Northern Ireland; and

5 Companies Act 2006, s 66 (Name not to be the same as another in the index).

words importing one gender shall include all genders, and the singular includes the plural and vice versa.

Unless the context otherwise requires words or expressions contained in the articles have the same meaning as in the Companies Acts but excluding any statutory modification not in force when this constitution becomes binding on the charity.

Apart from the exception mentioned in the previous paragraph a reference to an Act of Parliament includes any statutory modification or re-enactment of it for the time being in force.

Article 3 Liability of members

3.4

3 The liability of the members is limited to a sum not exceeding £10, being the amount that each member undertakes to contribute to the assets of the charity in the event of its being wound up while he, she or it is a member or within one year after he, she or it ceases to be a member, for:

(1) payment of the charity's debts and liabilities incurred before he, she or it ceases to be a member;

(2) payment of the costs, charges and expenses of winding up; and

(3) adjustment of the rights of the contributories among themselves

> *Article 3 Analysis*
>
> See analysis of article 2 in **2.5**.

Article 4 Objects

3.5

4 The charity's objects ('Objects') are specifically restricted to the following:

[Nothing in the articles shall authorise an application of the property of the charity for purposes which are not charitable in accordance with section 7 of the Charities and Trustee Investment (Scotland) Act 2005 and/or section 2 of the Charities Act (Northern Ireland) 2008.]

Article 4 Analysis

A charitable company's[6] articles of association must restrict the company to act only to further the charitable objects. Objects must be articulated in charitable terms, for example: the prevention or relief of poverty, the advancement of education or the advancement of religion.[7]

The company may amend its articles by special resolution,[8] in the case of a company that is a charity section 21 of the Companies Act 2006 is subject to sections 197 and 198 of the Charities Act 2011. Any proposed alteration of the objects requires the prior written consent of the Charity Commission.[9]

Article 5 Powers

3.6

5 The charity has power to do anything which is calculated to further its Object(s) or is conducive or incidental to doing so. In particular, the charity has power:

(1) to raise funds. In doing so, the charity must not undertake any taxable permanent trading activity and must comply with any relevant statutory regulations;

(2) to buy, take on lease or in exchange, hire or otherwise acquire any property and to maintain and equip it for use;

(3) to sell, lease or otherwise dispose of all or any part of the property belonging to the charity. In exercising this power, the charity must comply as appropriate with sections 117 and 122 of the Charities Act 2011.

(4) to borrow money and to charge the whole or any part of the property belonging to the charity as security for repayment of the money borrowed or as security for a grant or the discharge of an obligation. The charity must comply as appropriate with sections 124–126 of the Charities Act 2011 if it wishes to mortgage land;

6 To be a charity in England and Wales, everything it is set up to achieve must be charitable. This means each of its purposes must: fall within one or more 'descriptions of charitable purposes' for the public benefit (see Charity Commission Guidance CC22b 'How to write your charity's governing document').

7 Charities Act 2011, s 3 (Description of Purposes).

8 Companies Act 2006, s 21 (Amendment of articles). '(1) A company may amend its articles by special resolution.'

9 Charities Act 2011, s 198 (Alteration of objects by companies and Commission's consent). '(1) Any regulated alteration by a charitable company – (a) requires the prior written consent of the Commission, and (b) is ineffective if such consent has not been obtained.'

(5) to co-operate with other charities, voluntary bodies and statutory authorities and to exchange information and advice with them;

(6) to establish or support any charitable trusts, associations or institutions formed for any of the charitable purposes included in the Objects;

(7) to acquire, merge with or to enter into any partnership or joint venture arrangement with any other charity;

(8) to set aside income as a reserve against future expenditure but only in accordance with a written policy about reserves;

(9) to employ and remunerate such staff as are necessary for carrying out the work of the charity. The charity may employ or remunerate a director only to the extent it is permitted to do so by article 7 and provided it complies with the conditions in that article;

(10) to:

(a) deposit or invest funds;

(b) employ a professional fund-manager; and

(c) arrange for the investments or other property of the charity to be held in the name of a nominee; in the same manner and subject to the same conditions as the trustees of a trust are permitted to do by the Trustee Act 2000;

(11) to provide indemnity insurance for the directors in accordance with, and subject to the conditions in, section 189 of the Charities Act 2011;

(12) to pay out of the funds of the charity the costs of forming and registering the charity both as a company and as a charity.

Article 5 Analysis

Article 5 provides a summary of the main powers of the company with the associated legislation.

Article 5(1) allows the charity to raise funds with the caveat it does not engage in any taxable permanent trading activity. Provided the charity only trades to help its aims and objectives, its 'primary purpose trading', then no tax liability on profits will be created.[10]

Article 5(2) outlines the company's powers to acquire land, the powers are subject to the articles so may be restrictive in nature or outline a specific

10 Small trading tax exemption is available.

process to acquire land.[11] The company may acquire land to further its charitable purposes or for investment purposes.[12]

Article 5(3) reinforces the requirements of section 117 of the Charities Act 2011 when disposing of land[13] and the required statements concerning the disposition of land.[14]

Article 5(4) allows a general power to borrow money, if the lender requires a charge over the charity's property the company must comply with section 124 of the Charities Act 2011 restrictions on mortgages,[15] section 125 on required statements[16] and section 126 on land registration.[17]

Article 5(10) provides powers to invest money, employ an investment manager and appoint a nominee. The articles may restrict or place specific limitations on the powers of investment and exclude certain types of risky products. The charity may wish to invest only in ethical investments or local social enterprises.[18]

Article 5(11) allows the company to arrange for the purchase of indemnity insurance subject to the requirement of section 189 of the Charities Act 2011.[19]

Article 6 Application of income and property

3.7

6(1) The income and property of the charity shall be applied solely towards the promotion of the Objects.

(2) (a) A director is entitled to be reimbursed from the property of the charity or may pay out of such property reasonable expenses properly incurred by him or her when acting on behalf of the charity.

(b) A director may benefit from trustee indemnity insurance cover purchased at the charity's expense in accordance with, and subject to the conditions in, section 189 of the Charities Act 2011.

(c) A director may receive an indemnity from the charity in the circumstances specified in article 57.

(d) A director may not receive any other benefit or payment unless it is authorised by article 7.

11 If the company is holding property on trust, the powers in the Trusts of Land and Appointment of Trustees Act 1996 and the Trustee Act 2000 are available to the company.
12 Charity Commission Guidance CC33 'Acquiring land'.
13 Charities Act 2011, s 117 (Restrictions on dispositions of land: general).
14 Charities Act 2011, s 122 (Instruments concerning dispositions of land: required statements, etc.).
15 Charities Act 2011, s 124 (Restrictions on mortgages).
16 Charities Act 2011, s 125 (Mortgages: required statements, etc).
17 Charities Act 2011, s 126 (Mortgages of charity land and land registration).
18 Charity Commission Guidance CC14 'Charities and investment matters: a guide for trustees'.
19 Charities Act 2011, s 189 (Indemnity insurance for charity trustees and trustees).

(3) Subject to article 7, none of the income or property of the charity may be paid or transferred directly or indirectly by way of dividend bonus or otherwise by way of profit to any member of the charity. This does not prevent a member who is not also a director receiving:

(a) a benefit from the charity in the capacity of a beneficiary of the charity;

(b) reasonable and proper remuneration for any goods or services supplied to the charity.

Article 6 Analysis

Article 6 defines the established principle that trustees, subject to authorisation by the articles, statute, court or the Charity Commission shall not receive benefits from the charity. Sections 185–188 of the Charities Act 2011[20] provide the statutory rights concerning the remuneration of trustees and the payment of expenses. Section 189[21] provides statutory powers to allow the charity to provide indemnity insurance for trustees.

With the exception of reasonable expenses and indemnity insurance a director may not receive any other benefit from the charity unless authorised by the following (article 7).

Article 7 Benefits and payments to charity directors and connected persons

General provisions

3.8

7(1) No director or connected person may:

(a) buy any goods or services from the charity on terms preferential to those applicable to members of the public;

(b) sell goods, services, or any interest in land to the charity;

(c) be employed by, or receive any remuneration from, the charity;

(d) receive any other financial benefit from the charity; unless the payment is permitted by sub-clause (2) of this article, or authorised by the court or the prior written consent of the Charity Commission has been obtained.

20 Charities Act 2011.
21 Charities Act 2011, s 189 (Indemnity insurance for charity trustees and trustees).

In this article a 'financial benefit' means a benefit, direct or indirect, which is either money or has a monetary value.

> *Article 7(1) Analysis*
>
> The preliminary section above, reiterates that no director or connected person[22] shall benefit financially from the charity unless so authorised by the following provisions.

Scope and powers permitting directors' or connected persons' benefits

(2)(a) A director or connected person may receive a benefit from the charity in the capacity of a beneficiary of the charity provided that a majority of the directors do not benefit in this way.

(b) A director or connected person may enter into a contract for the supply of services, or of goods that are supplied in connection with the provision of services, to the charity where that is permitted in accordance with, and subject to the conditions in, sections 185 and 186 of the Charities Act 2011.

(c) Subject to sub-clause (3) of this article a director or connected person may provide the charity with goods that are not supplied in connection with services provided to the charity by the director or connected person.

(d) A director or connected person may receive interest on money lent to the charity at a reasonable and proper rate which must be not more than the Bank of England bank rate (also known as the base rate).

(e) A director or connected person may receive rent for premises let by the director or connected person to the charity. The amount of the rent and the other terms of the lease must be reasonable and proper. The director concerned must withdraw from any meeting at which such a proposal or the rent or other terms of the lease are under discussion.

(f) A director or connec ted person may take part in the normal trading and fundraising activities of the charity on the same terms as members of the public.

> *Article 7(2) Analysis*
>
> The Charities Act 2011 allows for a director or a connected person to provide goods and services subject to sections 185 and 186.[23] The directors

22 Charities Act 2011, s 188 (Meaning of 'connected person'). See article 61 'Interpretation' for the definition of connected person.

23 Charities Act 2011.

have a fiduciary duty to act with a 'single-minded loyalty' in the interests of the charity.[24] In *Bray v Ford*, Lord Herschell elucidated:

> 'It is an inflexible rule of a Court of Equity that a person in a fiduciary position … is not, unless otherwise expressly provided, entitled to make a profit; he is not allowed to put himself in a position where his interest and duty conflict. It does not appear to me that this rule is, as has been said, founded upon principles of morality. I regard it rather as based on the consideration that, human nature being what it is, there is danger, in such circumstances, of the person holding a fiduciary position being swayed by interest rather than by duty, and thus prejudicing those whom he was bound to protect.'[25]

Fiduciary duty is the grounding principle for charity trustees and the application of the rule is inflexible, for example a defence the trustee acted honestly and in good faith is not accepted by the courts.[26]

A charity may permit a breach of fiduciary duty by an express provision in the articles of association, article 7(2)(c)–(d) provides the authorisation mechanism.

Payment for supply of goods only – controls

(3) The charity and its directors may only rely upon the authority provided by sub-clause (2)(c) of this article if each of the following conditions is satisfied:

(a) The amount or maximum amount of the payment for the goods is set out in an agreement in writing between the charity or its directors (as the case may be) and the director or connected person supplying the goods ('the supplier') under which the supplier is to supply the goods in question to or on behalf of the charity.

(b) The amount or maximum amount of the payment for the goods does not exceed what is reasonable in the circumstances for the supply of the goods in question.

(c) The other directors are satisfied that it is in the best interests of the charity to contract with the supplier rather than with someone who is not a director or connected person. In reaching that decision the directors must balance the advantage of contracting with a director or connected person against the disadvantages of doing so.

(d) The supplier is absent from the part of any meeting at which there is discussion of the proposal to enter into a contract or arrangement with him or her or it with regard to the supply of goods to the charity.

24 *Bristol & West Building Society v Mothew* [1998] Ch 1, 15 by Millett LJ.
25 *Bray v Ford* [1896] AC 44, 51.
26 *Bray v Ford* [1896] AC 44, 48.

(e) The supplier does not vote on any such matter and is not to be counted when calculating whether a quorum of directors is present at the meeting.

(f) The reason for their decision is recorded by the directors in the minute book.

(g) A majority of the directors then in office are not in receipt of remuneration or payments authorised by article 7.

(4) In sub-clauses (2) and (3) of this article:

(a) 'charity' includes any company in which the charity:

  (i) holds more than 50% of the shares; or

  (ii) controls more than 50% of the voting rights attached to the shares; or

  (iii) has the right to appoint one or more directors to the board of the company.

(b) 'connected person' includes any person within the definition in article 61 'Interpretation'.

Article 7(3) Analysis

Article 7(3) reiterates the powers of section 185 of the Charities Act 2011:[27]

185 Remuneration of charity trustees or trustees etc. providing services to charity[28]

(1) The amount of the remuneration is set out in a written agreement between the charity and the provider of the services ("P") and does not exceed what is reasonable in the circumstances.[29]

(2) The charity trustees are satisfied that it would be in the best interests of the charity for the services to be provided by P on the terms of the agreement.[30]

(3) The agreement does not result in a majority of the trustees of the charity being persons who are:

  (a) party to an agreement within (1) above;

  (b) entitled to receive remuneration out of the funds of the charity otherwise than by virtue of such an agreement; or

  (c) connected with a person falling within (a) or (b) above.[31]

27 Charities Act 2011.

28 For a full discussion on remuneration for the supply of goods and the power to award equitable allowances, see Law Commission Consultation Paper No 220 'Technical issues in charity law a Consultation Paper', Ch 10, p 147.

29 Charities Act 2011, s 185(2), Condition A.

30 Charities Act 2011, s 185(2), Condition B. The duty of care in the Trustee Act 2000, s 1(1) applies to a charity trustee when making this decision: Charities Act 2011, s 185(5).

31 Charities Act 2011, s 185(2), Condition C.

(4) The trusts of the charity do not contain any express provision that prohibits P from receiving the remuneration.[32]

Article 7 Key points[33]

- Trustees providing their services unpaid is a fundamental principle of the charity sector.
- Trustees hold a fiduciary duty.
- Trustees are entitled to fair expenses and to have the costs of indemnity insurance met by the charity.
- Charities can pay trustees for the supply of goods and services if authorised by the articles of association. The articles of association may prohibit such activity.
- The charity trustees must have regard to any guidance given by the Commission concerning the making of such agreements.
- Any authorisation is subject to section 185 of the Charities Act 2011.

Article 8 Declaration of directors' interests

3.9

8 A director must declare the nature and extent of any interest, direct or indirect, which he or she has in a proposed transaction or arrangement with the charity or in any transaction or arrangement entered into by the charity which has not previously been declared. A director must absent himself or herself from any discussions of the charity directors in which it is possible that a conflict will arise between his or her duty to act solely in the interests of the charity and any personal interest (including but not limited to any personal financial interest).

Article 8 Analysis

The directors of the company in addition to fiduciary duties, must implement and apply the duties defined in law by the Companies Act 2006. Section 177(1) asserts: 'If a director of a company is in any way, directly or indirectly, interested in a proposed transaction or arrangement with the

32 Charities Act 2011, s 185(2), Condition D. The 'trusts' of a charity are 'the provisions establishing it as a charity and regulating its purposes and administration, whether those provisions take effect by way of trust or not': Charities Act 2011, s 353(1).

33 Charity Commission Guidance CC11 'Trustee expenses and payments'.

company, he must declare the nature and extent of that interest to the other directors'.[34] In addition, transactional conflicts of interest are specified by section 182.[35]

See analysis of article 14 in **2.17**.

Article 9 Conflicts of interests and conflicts of loyalties

3.10

9(1) If a conflict of interests arises for a director because of a duty of loyalty owed to another organisation or person and the conflict is not authorised by virtue of any other provision in the articles, the unconflicted directors may authorise such a conflict of interests where the following conditions apply:

(a) the conflicted director is absent from the part of the meeting at which there is discussion of any arrangement or transaction affecting that other organisation or person;

(b) the conflicted director does not vote on any such matter and is not to be counted when considering whether a quorum of directors is present at the meeting; and

(c) the unconflicted directors consider it is in the interests of the charity to authorise the conflict of interests in the circumstances applying.

(2) In this article a conflict of interests arising because of a duty of loyalty owed to another organisation or person only refers to such a conflict which does not involve a direct or indirect benefit of any nature to a director or to a connected person.

Article 9 Analysis

Article 9 allows the unconflicted directors to authorise a conflicted director, only in the instance of a duty of loyalty owed to another individual or organisation.[36] The Companies Act 2006 allows a private company to authorise any conflicting or transactional matter, if authorised by the articles

34 Companies Act 2006, s 177 (Duty to declare interest in proposed transaction or arrangement).
35 Companies Act 2006, s 182 (Declaration of interest in existing transaction or arrangement).
36 Charity Commission (GD1), 'The Commission considers that such a procedure should be limited to conflicts arising from a duty of loyalty to another organisation or person where there is no direct or indirect benefit of whatever nature to the director or to a connected person. In other circumstances involving a situation leading to a conflict of interests on the part of a director, the Commission is able to authorise the director to act notwithstanding the conflict where it is satisfied that this would be expedient in the interests of the charity (section 105 of the Charities Act 2011).'

or the directors,[37] to counteract the contradictory rules. Section 175[38] is thus modified by section 181.[39]

See analysis of article 14 in **2.17**.

Article 10 Members

3.11

10(1) The subscribers to the memorandum are the first members of the charity.

(2) Membership is open to other individuals or organisations who:

(a) apply to the charity in the form required by the directors; and

(b) are approved by the directors.

(3)(a) The directors may only refuse an application for membership if, acting reasonably and properly, they consider it to be in the best interests of the charity to refuse the application.

(b) The directors must inform the applicant in writing of the reasons for the refusal within twenty-one days of the decision.

(c) The directors must consider any written representations the applicant may make about the decision. The directors' decision following any written representations must be notified to the applicant in writing but shall be final.

(4) Membership is not transferable.

(5) The directors must keep a register of names and addresses of the members.

Article 10 Analysis

Article 10 is drawn from company law,[40] section 112 asserts 'the subscribers of a company's memorandum are deemed to have agreed to become members of the company, and on its registration become members and must be entered as such in its register of members'.

Article 10(5) is a legal requirement of section 113 of the Companies Act 2006, every company must keep a register of its members.

37 Companies Act 2006, s 175(5)(a) (Duty to avoid conflicts of interest).
38 Companies Act 2006.
39 Companies Act 2006, s 181 (Modification of provisions in relation to charitable companies).
40 Companies Act 2006.

Article 11 Classes of membership

3.12

11(1) The directors may establish classes of membership with different rights and obligations and shall record the rights and obligations in the register of members.

(2) The directors may not directly or indirectly alter the rights or obligations attached to a class of membership.

(3) The rights attached to a class of membership may only be varied if:

(a) three-quarters of the members of that class consent in writing to the variation; or

(b) a special resolution is passed at a separate general meeting of the members of that class agreeing to the variation.

(4) The provisions in the articles about general meetings shall apply to any meeting relating to the variation of the rights of any class of members.

> *Article 11 Analysis*
>
> Article 11 refers to section 113 of the Companies Act 2006, 'In the case of a company that does not have a share capital but has more than one class of members, there must be entered in the register, with the names and addresses of the members, a statement of the class to which each member belongs'.[41]

Article 12 Termination of membership

3.13

12 Membership is terminated if:

(1) the member dies or, if it is an organisation, ceases to exist;

(2) the member resigns by written notice to the charity unless, after the resignation, there would be less than two members;

(3) any sum due from the member to the charity is not paid in full within six months of it falling due;

(4) the member is removed from membership by a resolution of the directors that it is in the best interests of the charity that his or her or

41 Companies Act 2006, s 113(6) (Register of members).

its membership is terminated. A resolution to remove a member from membership may only be passed if:

(a) the member has been given at least twenty-one days' notice in writing of the meeting of the directors at which the resolution will be proposed and the reasons why it is to be proposed;

(b) the member or, at the option of the member, the member's representative (who need not be a member of the charity) has been allowed to make representations to the meeting.

> *Article 12 Analysis*
>
> See analysis of article 22 in **2.25**.

Articles 13 and 14 General meetings

3.14

13(1) The charity must hold its first annual general meeting within eighteen months after the date of its incorporation.

[(2) An annual general meeting must be held in each subsequent year and not more than fifteen months may elapse between successive annual general meetings.]

14 The directors may call a general meeting at any time.

> *Article 13 Analysis*
>
> The Companies Act 2006, together with the Charities Act 2011 do not require an annual general meeting, hence if the charity decides to obviate the requirement of an AGM, article 13(2) may be deleted. It should be noted, articles 15(1)(a), 15(3), 32, 33(2) and 37(2) would require adaptation.

Articles 15 and 16 Notice of general meetings

3.15

15(1) The minimum periods of notice required to hold a general meeting of the charity are:

(a) twenty-one clear days for an annual general meeting or a general meeting called for the passing of a special resolution;

(b) fourteen clear days for all other general meetings.

(2) A general meeting may be called by shorter notice if it is so agreed by a majority in number of members having a right to attend and vote at the meeting, being a majority who together hold not less than 90 percent of the total voting rights.

(3) The notice must specify the date time and place of the meeting and the general nature of the business to be transacted. If the meeting is to be an annual general meeting, the notice must say so. The notice must also contain a statement setting out the right of members to appoint a proxy under section 324 of the Companies Act 2006 and article 22.

(4) The notice must be given to all the members and to the directors and auditors.

16 The proceedings at a meeting shall not be invalidated because a person who was entitled to receive notice of the meeting did not receive it because of an accidental omission by the charity.

Article 15 Analysis

Article 15[42] defines the notice required for general meetings, article 15(1)(a)(b)[43] reflects the current company law.[44] The articles may provide for a longer[45] or reduced[46] notice period if agreed by the members. A proxy may attend and vote at general meetings in place of a member of the company. The Companies Act 2006 provides statutory rights to appoint proxies by virtue of the provisions defined in sections 324–331.[47]

Articles 17 and 18 Proceedings at general meetings

3.16

(1) No business shall be transacted at any general meeting unless a quorum is present.

42 Companies Act 2006, s 307 (Notice required of general meeting).
43 Companies Act 2006, s 307(2)(a)(b) (Notice required of general meeting).
44 Companies Act 2006.
45 Companies Act 2006, s 307 (Notice required of general meeting). '(3) The company's articles may require a longer period of notice than that specified in subsection (1) or (2).'
46 Companies Act 2006, s 307 (Notice required of general meeting). '(4) A general meeting may be called by shorter notice than that otherwise required if shorter notice is agreed by the members.'
47 Companies Act 2006.

(2) A quorum is:

(a) [ ] members present in person or by proxy and entitled to vote upon the business to be conducted at the meeting; or

(b) one tenth of the total membership at the time whichever is the greater.

(3) The authorised representative of a member organisation shall be counted in the quorum.

18(1) If:

(a) a quorum is not present within half an hour from the time appointed for the meeting; or

(b) during a meeting a quorum ceases to be present; the meeting shall be adjourned to such time and place as the directors shall determine.

(2) The directors must reconvene the meeting and must give at least seven clear days' notice of the reconvened meeting stating the date, time and place of the meeting.

(3) If no quorum is present at the reconvened meeting within fifteen minutes of the time specified for the start of the meeting the members present in person or by proxy at that time shall constitute the quorum for that meeting.

Articles 17 and 18 Analysis

Articles 17 and 18[48] summarise the requirements for a valid quorum, in the case of a company having only one member, one qualifying person present at a meeting is a quorum.[49] In any other case and subject to the articles, two qualifying people are required to form a quorum. Article 18 allows for automatic adjournment in the event a meeting fails to form a quorum.[50]

A quorum is the minimum number of directors required to vote at a meeting. Case law provides any decisions made at an inquorate board meeting are void (see *Re North Eastern Insurance Co Ltd*).[51]

48 Schedule 2 Regulation 3 Model articles for private companies limited by guarantee, adapted, Article 11 Quorum for directors' meetings.

49 Companies Act 2006, s 318(1) (Quorum at meetings).

50 Companies Act 2006, s 318(2) (Quorum at meetings).

51 [1919] 1 Ch 198.

Article 19 Proceedings at general meetings

3.17

19(1) General meetings shall be chaired by the person who has been appointed to chair meetings of the directors.[52]

(2) If there is no such person or he or she is not present within fifteen minutes of the time appointed for the meeting a director nominated by the directors shall chair the meeting.

(3) If there is only one director present and willing to act, he or she shall chair the meeting.

(4) If no director is present and willing to chair the meeting within fifteen minutes after the time appointed for holding it, the members present in person or by proxy and entitled to vote must choose one of their number to chair the meeting.

> *Article 19 Analysis*
>
> Article 19 is founded on company law, section 319,[53] which allows a member to be elected as chairman in a general meeting by passing a resolution.

Article 20 Proceedings at general meetings

3.18

20(1) The members present in person or by proxy at a meeting may resolve by ordinary resolution that the meeting shall be adjourned.

(2) The person who is chairing the meeting must decide the date, time and place at which the meeting is to be reconvened unless those details are specified in the resolution.

(3) No business shall be conducted at a reconvened meeting unless it could properly have been conducted at the meeting had the adjournment not taken place.

(4) If a meeting is adjourned by a resolution of the members for more than seven days, at least seven clear days' notice shall be given of the reconvened meeting stating the date, time and place of the meeting.

52 Schedule 2 Regulation 3 Model articles for private companies limited by guarantee, adapted, Article 12 Chairing of directors' meetings.

53 Companies Act 2006, s 319 (Chairman of meeting).

> *Article 20 Analysis*
>
> With the exception of section 332,[54] the Companies Act 2006 says very little on the issue of adjournment of meetings, therefore, article 20 is based on common law principles. If considering an adjournment, the chairman ought not to act alone (even with powers conferred by the articles), instead he should gain consent or direction from the members present.
>
> The decision to adjourn ought to be decided on the facts at hand and the urgency of the matter (*Byng v London Life Association Ltd*).[55]

Article 21 Proceedings at general meetings

3.19

21 (1) Any vote at a meeting shall be decided by a show of hands unless before, or on the declaration of the result of, the show of hands a poll is demanded:

(a) by the person chairing the meeting; or

(b) by at least two members present in person or by proxy and having the right to vote at the meeting; or

(c) by a member or members present in person or by proxy representing not less than one-tenth of the total voting rights of all the members having the right to vote at the meeting.

(2) (a) The declaration by the person who is chairing the meeting of the result of a vote shall be conclusive unless a poll is demanded.

(b) The result of the vote must be recorded in the minutes of the charity but the number or proportion of votes cast need not be recorded.

(3) (a) A demand for a poll may be withdrawn, before the poll is taken, but only with the consent of the person who is chairing the meeting.

(b) If the demand for a poll is withdrawn the demand shall not invalidate the result of a show of hands declared before the demand was made.

(4) (a) A poll must be taken as the person who is chairing the meeting directs, who may appoint scrutineers (who need not be members) and who may fix a time and place for declaring the results of the poll.

(b) The result of the poll shall be deemed to be the resolution of the meeting at which the poll is demanded.

54 Companies Act 2006, s 332 (Resolution passed at adjourned meeting). 'Where a resolution is passed at an adjourned meeting of a company, the resolution is for all purposes to be treated as having been passed on the date on which it was in fact passed, and is not to be deemed passed on any earlier date.'
55 [1990] Ch 170.

(5) (a) A poll demanded on the election of a person to chair a meeting or on a question of adjournment must be taken immediately.

(b) A poll demanded on any other question must be taken either immediately or at such time and place as the person who is chairing the meeting directs.

(c) The poll must be taken within thirty days after it has been demanded.

(d) If the poll is not taken immediately at least seven clear days' notice shall be given specifying the time and place at which the poll is to be taken.

(e) If a poll is demanded the meeting may continue to deal with any other business that may be conducted at the meeting.

Article 21 Analysis

The rules on voting are provided by section 284[56] of the Companies Act 2006, which outlines that each member has one vote in the case of a written resolution, show of hands or poll.

The general position outlined in article 21 is that votes at general meetings are decided on a show of hands. If the vote is unclear or possibly disputed, then a poll may be called.

Article 21(1)(b) summarises the rules and describes who has the right to demand a poll. The foundations of the provisions are founded on section 321[57] and therefore members are provided statutory rights to call a poll, regardless of the company's constitution.

Any latitude for adapting the articles is somewhat curtailed by the provisions in the Act, which without ambiguity state that any provisions that exclude rights to demand a poll are void, with the exception of electing a chairman or adjournment of a meeting.[58]

Article 22 Content of proxy notices

3.20

22(1) Proxies may only validly be appointed by a notice in writing (a 'proxy notice') which -

(a) states the name and address of the member appointing the proxy;

(b) identifies the person appointed to be that member's proxy and the general meeting in relation to which that person is appointed;

56 Companies Act 2006, s 284 (Votes: general rules).
57 Companies Act 2006, s 321 (Right to demand a poll).
58 Companies Act 2006, s 321(1).

(c) is signed by or on behalf of the member appointing the proxy, or is authenticated in such manner as the directors may determine; and

(d) is delivered to the charity in accordance with the articles and any instructions contained in the notice of the general meeting to which they relate.

(2) The charity may require proxy notices to be delivered in a particular form, and may specify different forms for different purposes.

(3) Proxy notices may specify how the proxy appointed under them is to vote (or that the proxy is to abstain from voting) on one or more resolutions.

(4) Unless a proxy notice indicates otherwise, it must be treated as –

(a) allowing the person appointed under it as a proxy discretion as to how to vote on any ancillary or procedural resolutions put to the meeting; and

(b) appointing that person as a proxy in relation to any adjournment of the general meeting to which it relates as well as the meeting itself.

Article 22 Analysis

A proxy may attend and vote at general meetings in place of a member of the company. The Companies Act 2006 provides statutory rights to appoint proxies by virtue of the provisions defined in sections 324–331. It should be noted article 22 is a direct reproduction of article 31 of the Model articles for private companies limited by guarantee.

Article 22A Delivery of proxy notices

3.21

22A(1) A person who is entitled to attend, speak or vote (either on a show of hands or on a poll) at a general meeting remains so entitled in respect of that meeting or any adjournment of it, even though a valid proxy notice has been delivered to the charity by or on behalf of that person.

(2) An appointment under a proxy notice may be revoked by delivering to the charity a notice in writing given by or on behalf of the person by whom or on whose behalf the proxy notice was given.

(3) A notice revoking a proxy appointment only takes effect if it is delivered before the start of the meeting or adjourned meeting to which it relates.

(4) If a proxy notice is not executed by the person appointing the proxy, it must be accompanied by written evidence of the authority of the person who executed it to execute it on the appointor's behalf.

Article 22A Analysis

Article 22(A) is somewhat mistitled, as it describes the revocation of proxy notices and the procedures thereof. Article 22A(1) reiterates statutory rights under the Act.[59] Article 22A(2) again mirrors the Companies Act 2006,[60] requiring written submissions to enable revocation. It should be noted in accordance with section 330(6) the articles cannot be modified to reduce the timeframes for delivery of any notice of termination to below the statutory 48 hours for meetings.[61] The articles may be adapted to nominate a specific person that notices ought to be given to,[62] which replaces the relatively vague description of 'company' in the article above.

Article 22(A) is a direct reproduction of Schedule 2 Regulation 3 Model articles for a private companies limited by guarantee, article 32.

Article 23 Written resolutions

3.22

23(1) A resolution in writing agreed by a simple majority (or in the case of a special resolution by a majority of not less than 75%) of the members who would have been entitled to vote upon it had it been proposed at a general meeting shall be effective provided that:

(a) a copy of the proposed resolution has been sent to every eligible member;

(b) a simple majority (or in the case of a special resolution a majority of not less than 75%) of members has signified its agreement to the resolution; and

(c) it is contained in an authenticated document which has been received at the registered office within the period of 28 days beginning with the circulation date.

(2) A resolution in writing may comprise several copies to which one or more members have signified their agreement.

59 Companies Act 2006, s 330(2).

60 Companies Act 2006, s 330 (Notice required of termination of proxy's authority). '(A1) In the case of a traded company the termination of the authority of a person to act as proxy must be notified to the company in writing.'

61 Companies Act 2006, s 330(6) '(6) Any provision of the company's articles is void in so far as it would have the effect of requiring any such appointment or document to be received by the company or another person earlier than the following time—

(a) in the case of a meeting or adjourned meeting, 48 hours before the time for holding the meeting or adjourned meeting;

(b) in the case of a poll taken more than 48 hours after it was demanded, 24 hours before the time appointed for the taking of the poll;'.

62 Companies Act 2006, s 330(4).

(3) In the case of a member that is an organisation, its authorised representative may signify its agreement.

> *Article 23 Analysis*
>
> Article 23 outlines the procedures for written resolutions, the provisions are subject to sections 288–298 of the Companies Act 2006.

Articles 24–26 Votes of members

3.23

24 Subject to article 11, every member, whether an individual or an organisation, shall have one vote.

25 Any objection to the qualification of any voter must be raised at the meeting at which the vote is tendered and the decision of the person who is chairing the meeting shall be final.

26(1) Any organisation that is a member of the charity may nominate any person to act as its representative at any meeting of the charity.

(2) The organisation must give written notice to the charity of the name of its representative. The representative shall not be entitled to represent the organisation at any meeting unless the notice has been received by the charity. The representative may continue to represent the organisation until written notice to the contrary is received by the charity.

(3) Any notice given to the charity will be conclusive evidence that the representative is entitled to represent the organisation or that his or her authority has been revoked. The charity shall not be required to consider whether the representative has been properly appointed by the organisation.

> *Articles 24–26 Analysis*
>
> Article 24 is subject to article 11, which allows for different classes of membership with possibly enhanced voting rights. The default position is: one member – one vote. Article 26 allows an organisation that is a member of a charity to appoint an individual to cast votes on its behalf.

Articles 27–30 Directors

3.24

27(1) A director must be a natural person aged 16 years or older.

(2) No one may be appointed a director if he or she would be disqualified from acting under the provisions of article 39.

28 The minimum number of directors shall be [ ] but (unless otherwise determined by ordinary resolution) shall not be subject to any maximum.

29 The first directors shall be those persons notified to Companies House as the first directors of the charity.

30 A director may not appoint an alternate director or anyone to act on his or her behalf at meetings of the directors.

Articles 27–30 Analysis

Article 27 is founded on company law, a private company must have at least one director,[63] who has attained the age of 16.[64] Additionally, one director must be a natural person[65] (not a corporation). Article 27(2) appointments of directors are subject to article 39 Disqualification and removal of directors.

The minimum number of directors is two, set by the Charity Commission (see article 42(2)).[66] Alternative directors (article 30), where a director may appoint as an alternate any other director, or any other person approved by resolution of the directors, to exercise that director's powers, and carry out that director's responsibilities, in relation to the taking of decisions by the directors in the absence of the alternate's appointor, are prohibited by the articles.

Article 31 Powers of directors

3.25

31(1) The directors shall manage the business of the charity and may exercise all the powers of the charity unless they are subject to any restrictions imposed by the Companies Acts, the articles or any special resolution.

(2) No alteration of the articles or any special resolution shall have retrospective effect to invalidate any prior act of the directors.

(3) Any meeting of directors at which a quorum is present at the time the relevant decision is made may exercise all the powers exercisable by the directors.

63 Companies Act 2006, s 154 (Companies required to have directors).
64 Companies Act 2006, s 157 (Minimum age for appointment as director).
65 Companies Act 2006, s 155 (Companies required to have at least one director who is a natural person).
66 Charity Commission (GD1), 'As good operational practice we recommend a minimum of three directors. This will help with the quality of decision making and the sharing of directors' responsibilities and duties. Note that article 42(2) requires a quorum of at least two directors.'

Article 31 Analysis

Article 31(1) provides that all power lies with the board of directors, or more accurately the managing director powers are an implied delegation by the board.[67] The term 'all powers' requires the directors to act within the confines of the company constitution and they may only be exercised for the purpose they are granted.

The company's articles may also restrict directors' duties, however they must not fetter the statutory obligations of the directors' duties specified in sections 170–177[68] of the Companies Act 2006.

It should be noted article 31 is adapted from article 3 Directors' general authority and article 4 Members' reserve power.[69]

Articles 32 and 33 Retirement of directors

3.26

32 At the first annual general meeting all the directors must retire from office unless by the close of the meeting the members have failed to elect sufficient directors to hold a quorate meeting of the directors. At each subsequent annual general meeting one-third of the directors or, if their number is not three or a multiple of three, the number nearest to one-third, must retire from office. If there is only one director he or she must retire.

33(1) The directors to retire by rotation shall be those who have been longest in office since their last appointment. If any directors became or were appointed directors on the same day those to retire shall (unless they otherwise agree among themselves) be determined by lot.

(2) If a director is required to retire at an annual general meeting by a provision of the articles the retirement shall take effect upon the conclusion of the meeting.

Articles 32 and 33 Analysis

Article 32 provides default rules on the retirement of directors. Unless the length of service is specified by the articles the director's appointment will continue until the trustee dies, resigns or is removed from office.[70] The articles may specify the term of any appointment and powers of re-appointment.

67 *Hely-Hutchinson v Brayhead Ltd* [1968] 1 QB 549.
68 Companies Act 2006, Ch 2 (General duties of directors).
69 Schedule 2 Regulation 3 Model articles for private companies limited by guarantee.
70 Charity Commission Guidance on Charity trustees: resignation and removal.

The Companies Act 2006 provides statutory powers to remove a director[71] and the right of a director to protest their removal.[72]

Articles 34–38 Appointment of directors

3.27

34 The charity may by ordinary resolution:

(1) appoint a person who is willing to act to be a director; and

(2) determine the rotation in which any additional directors are to retire.

35 No person other than a director retiring by rotation may be appointed a director at any general meeting unless:

(1) he or she is recommended for re-election by the directors; or

(2) not less than fourteen nor more than thirty-five clear days before the date of the meeting, the charity is given a notice that:

- (a) is signed by a member entitled to vote at the meeting;
- (b) states the member's intention to propose the appointment of a person as a director;
- (c) contains the details that, if the person were to be appointed, the charity would have to file at Companies House; and
- (d) is signed by the person who is to be proposed to show his or her willingness to be appointed.

Articles 34–38 Analysis

Article 34 provides the process for appointing new directors, it should be noted and proposed a director must meet the requirements of the Companies Act 2006.[73] The courts' view is any director not appointed in accordance with the articles is considered invalid (*Sierra Leone Telecommunications Co Ltd v Barclays Bank Plc*).[74]

Article 36 provides that all members who are entitled to receive notice of a general meeting must be given not less than seven nor more than 28 clear days'

71 Companies Act 2006, s 168 (Resolution to remove director).
72 Companies Act 2006, s 169 (Director's right to protest against removal).
73 Companies Act 2006, Chapter 1 Appointment and removal of directors.
74 [1998] 2 All ER 821.

notice of any resolution to be put to the meeting to appoint a director other than a director who is to retire by rotation.

Article 37(1) provides the directors may appoint a person who is willing to act to be a director. Article 37(2) provides that a director appointed by a resolution of the other directors must retire at the next annual general meeting and must not be taken into account in determining the directors who are to retire by rotation.

Article 38 provides that the appointment of a director, whether by the charity in general meeting or by the other directors, must not cause the number of directors to exceed any number fixed as the maximum number of directors.

Article 39 Disqualification and removal of directors

3.28

39 A director shall cease to hold office if he or she:

(1) ceases to be a director by virtue of any provision in the Companies Acts or is prohibited by law from being a director;

(2) is disqualified from acting as a trustee by virtue of sections 178 and 179 of the Charities Act 2011 (or any statutory re-enactment or modification of those provisions);

(3) ceases to be a member of the charity;

(4) in the written opinion, given to the company, of a registered medical practitioner treating that person, has become physically or mentally incapable of acting as a director and may remain so for more than three months;

(5) resigns as a director by notice to the charity (but only if at least two directors will remain in office when the notice of resignation is to take effect); or

(6) is absent without the permission of the directors from all their meetings held within a period of six consecutive months and the directors resolve that his or her office be vacated.

Article 39 Analysis

Article 39 provides the default provisions for automatic exclusion as a director of the charity. The Charities Act 2011 provides statutory powers of removal and clarifies the main criteria for disqualification.[75]

75 Charities Act 2011, s 178 (Persons disqualified from being charity trustees or trustees of a charity).

Article 40 Remuneration of directors

3.29

40 The directors must not be paid any remuneration unless it is authorised by article 7.

> *Article 40 Analysis*
>
> Article 40 reiterates the charity principle that trustees ought not to receive payment expected for fair expenses and insurance. Subject to article 7 trustees may receive payment for goods and services if authorised by the board.

Articles 41–45 Proceedings of directors

3.30

41(1) The directors may regulate their proceedings as they think fit, subject to the provisions of the articles.

(2) Any director may call a meeting of the directors.

(3) The secretary (if any) must call a meeting of the directors if requested to do so by a director.

(4) Questions arising at a meeting shall be decided by a majority of votes.

[Optional

(5) In the case of an equality of votes, the person who is chairing the meeting shall have a second or casting vote.]

[(6) A meeting may be held by suitable electronic means agreed by the directors in which each participant may communicate with all the other participants.]

42(1) No decision may be made by a meeting of the directors unless a quorum is present at the time the decision is purported to be made. ['Present' includes being present by suitable electronic means agreed by the directors in which a participant or participants may communicate with all the other participants.]

(2) The quorum shall be two or the number nearest to one-third of the total number of directors, whichever is the greater, or such larger number as may be decided from time to time by the directors.

(3) A director shall not be counted in the quorum present when any decision is made about a matter upon which that director is not entitled to vote.

43 If the number of directors is less than the number fixed as the quorum, the continuing directors or director may act only for the purpose of filling vacancies or of calling a general meeting.

44(1) The directors shall appoint a director to chair their meetings and may at any time revoke such appointment.

(2) If no-one has been appointed to chair meetings of the directors or if the person appointed is unwilling to preside or is not present within ten minutes after the time appointed for the meeting, the directors present may appoint one of their number to chair that meeting.

(3) The person appointed to chair meetings of the directors shall have no functions or powers except those conferred by the articles or delegated to him or her by the directors.

45(1) A resolution in writing or in electronic form agreed by all of the directors entitled to receive notice of a meeting of the directors and to vote upon the resolution shall be as valid and effectual as if it had been passed at a meeting of the directors duly convened and held.

(2) The resolution in writing may comprise several documents containing the text of the resolution in like form to each of which one or more directors has signified their agreement.

Articles 41–45 Analysis

The articles may specify if the chairman shall hold a casting vote.

Article 46 Delegation

3.31

46(1) The directors may delegate any of their powers or functions to a committee of two or more directors but the terms of any delegation must be recorded in the minute book.

(2) The directors may impose conditions when delegating, including the conditions that:

(a) the relevant powers are to be exercised exclusively by the committee to whom they delegate;

(b) no expenditure may be incurred on behalf of the charity except in accordance with a budget previously agreed with the directors.

(3) The directors may revoke or alter a delegation.

(4) All acts and proceedings of any committees must be fully and promptly reported to the directors.

Article 46 Analysis

See analysis of article 5 in **2.8**.

Article 47 Validity of directors' decisions

3.32

47(1) Subject to article 47(2), all acts done by a meeting of directors, or of a committee of directors, shall be valid notwithstanding the participation in any vote of a director:

(a) who was disqualified from holding office;

(b) who had previously retired or who had been obliged by the constitution to vacate office;

(c) who was not entitled to vote on the matter, whether by reason of a conflict of interests or otherwise; if without:

(d) the vote of that director; and

(e) that director being counted in the quorum;

the decision has been made by a majority of the directors at a quorate meeting.

(2) Article 47(1) does not permit a director or a connected person to keep any benefit that may be conferred upon him or her by a resolution of the directors or of a committee of directors if, but for article 47(1), the resolution would have been void, or if the director has not complied with article 8.

Article 48 Seal

3.33

48 If the charity has a seal it must only be used by the authority of the directors or of a committee of directors authorised by the directors. The directors may

determine who shall sign any instrument to which the seal is affixed and unless otherwise so determined it shall be signed by a director and by the secretary (if any) or by a second director.

Article 48 Analysis

See analysis of article 35 in **2.38**.

Article 49 Minutes

3.34

49 The directors must keep minutes of all:

(1) appointments of officers made by the directors;

(2) proceedings at meetings of the charity;

(3) meetings of the directors and committees of directors including:

- (a) the names of the directors present at the meeting;
- (b) the decisions made at the meetings; and
- (c) where appropriate the reasons for the decisions.

Article 50 Accounts

3.35

50(1) The directors must prepare for each financial year accounts as required by the Companies Acts. The accounts must be prepared to show a true and fair view and follow accounting standards issued or adopted by the Accounting Standards Board or its successors and adhere to the recommendations of applicable Statements of Recommended Practice.[76]

(2) The directors must keep accounting records as required by the Companies Act.

76 The charities' statement of recommended practice (SORP) gives a framework for accounting and reporting, designed to help charity trustees meet their legal requirement for their accounts, to give a true and fair view encourage consistency in charity accounting standards and give recommendations for charity annual reporting. All charities must use the SORP to prepare their accounts unless the trustees have opted to prepare receipts and payments accounts and their charity is a non-company charity which had an income of £250,000 or less in the reporting period. See Charity Commission Guidance 'The Charities Statement of Recommended Practice (SORP)', available at https://www.gov.uk/government/publications/charities-sorp-2005.

Article 51 Annual Report and Return and Register of Charities

3.36

51(1) The directors must comply with the requirements of the Charities Act 2011 with regard to the:

(a) transmission of a copy of the statements of account to the Commission;

(b) preparation of an Annual Report and the transmission of a copy of it to the Commission;

(c) preparation of an Annual Return and its transmission to the Commission.

(2) The directors must notify the Commission promptly of any changes to the charity's entry on the Central Register of Charities.

> *Articles 50 and 51 Analysis*
>
> Articles 50 and 51 include the Charities Act 2011 requirements on accounting procedures for companies. Section 169[77] is concerned with the preparation of annual accounts, section 163[78] provides statutory obligations for the transmission of annual reports. It should be noted, as per article 50(1) the charity must adhere to the accounting and filing requirements of company house and the statement of recommended practice.[79]

Articles 52–56 Means of communication to be used

3.37

52(1) Subject to the articles, anything sent or supplied by or to the charity under the articles may be sent or supplied in any way in which the Companies Act 2006 provides for documents or information which are authorised or required by any provision of that Act to be sent or supplied by or to the charity.

(2) Subject to the articles, any notice or document to be sent or supplied to a director in connection with the taking of decisions by directors may also be

77 Charities Act 2011, s 169 (Annual returns by registered charities).

78 Charities Act 2011, s 163 (Transmission of annual reports to Commission in certain cases).

79 All charities must use the SORP to prepare their accounts unless the trustees have opted to prepare receipts and payments accounts and their charity is a non-company charity which had an income of £250,000 or less in the reporting period. See Charity Commission Guidance 'The Charities Statement of Recommended Practice (SORP)', available at https://www.gov.uk/government/publications/charities-sorp-2005.

sent or supplied by the means by which that director has asked to be sent or supplied with such notices or documents for the time being.

53 Any notice to be given to or by any person pursuant to the articles:

(1) must be in writing; or

(2) must be given in electronic form.

54(1) The charity may give any notice to a member either:

(a) personally; or

(b) by sending it by post in a prepaid envelope addressed to the member at his or her address; or

(c) by leaving it at the address of the member; or

(d) by giving it in electronic form to the member's address.

(e) by placing the notice on a website and providing the person with a notification in writing or in electronic form of the presence of the notice on the website. The notification must state that it concerns a notice of a company meeting and must specify the place date and time of the meeting.

(2) A member who does not register an address with the charity or who registers only a postal address that is not within the United Kingdom shall not be entitled to receive any notice from the charity.

55 A member present in person at any meeting of the charity shall be deemed to have received notice of the meeting and of the purposes for which it was called.

56(1) Proof that an envelope containing a notice was properly addressed, prepaid and posted shall be conclusive evidence that the notice was given.

(2) Proof that an electronic form of notice was given shall be conclusive where the company can demonstrate that it was properly addressed and sent, in accordance with section 1147 of the Companies Act 2006.

(3) In accordance with section 1147 of the Companies Act 2006 notice shall be deemed to be given:

(a) 48 hours after the envelope containing it was posted; or

(b) in the case of an electronic form of communication, 48 hours after it was sent.

Article 52 Analysis

Article 52 corresponds with article 34 of the model articles.[80] The Companies Act 2006 addresses electronic communications and the manner in which notices of meetings are given.[81] Section 333 pertains to matters when sending documents in electronic form.[82] Sections 1143–1148[83] discuss the statutory obligations for sending or supplying documents or information.

Article 57 Indemnity

Option 1

3.38

57(1) The charity may indemnify a relevant director against any liability incurred in that capacity, to the extent permitted by sections 232 to 234 of the Companies Act 2006.

(2) In this article a 'relevant director' means any director or former director of the charity.

Option 2

57(1) The charity shall indemnify a relevant director against any liability incurred in that capacity, to the extent permitted by sections 232 to 234 of the Companies Act 2006

(2) In this article a 'relevant director' means any director or former director of the charity.

Option 3

57(1) The charity shall indemnify a relevant director against any liability incurred in successfully defending legal proceedings in that capacity, or in connection with any application in which relief is granted by the Court from liability for negligence, default, or breach of duty or breach of trust in relation to the charity.

(2) In this article a 'relevant director' means any director or former director of the charity.

80 Schedule 2 Regulation 3 Model articles for private companies limited by guarantee.
81 Companies Act 2006, s 308 (Manner in which notice to be given).
82 Companies Act 2006, s 333 (Sending documents relating to meetings etc in electronic form).
83 Companies Act 2006, s 1144 (Sending or supplying documents or information).

Optional

57A The charity may indemnify an auditor against any liability incurred by him or her or it

(1) in defending proceedings (whether civil or criminal) in which judgment is given in his or her or its favour or he or she or it is acquitted; or

(2) in connection with an application under section 1157 of the Companies Act 2006 (power of Court to grant relief in case of honest and reasonable conduct) in which relief is granted to him or her or it by the Court.

Article 57 Analysis

Article 57 affords three options to the charity for the provision of indemnity insurance. Options 1 and 2 provide the charity will indemnify relevant directors, the former without any binding contract to do so. Option 3 limits the scope of the liability insurance to defending court proceedings. Article 57A is optional and indemnifies any appointed charity auditors as permitted by section 533.[84]

Article 58 Rules

3.39

58(1) The directors may from time to time make such reasonable and proper rules or bye laws as they may deem necessary or expedient for the proper conduct and management of the charity.

(2) The bye laws may regulate the following matters but are not restricted to them:

(a) the admission of members of the charity (including the admission of organisations to membership) and the rights and privileges of such members, and the entrance fees, subscriptions and other fees or payments to be made by members;

(b) the conduct of members of the charity in relation to one another, and to the charity's employees and volunteers;

(c) the setting aside of the whole or any part or parts of the charity's premises at any particular time or times or for any particular purpose or purposes;

84 Companies Act 2006, s 533 (Indemnity for costs of successfully defending proceedings).

(d) the procedure at general meetings and meetings of the directors in so far as such procedure is not regulated by the Companies Acts or by the articles;

(e) generally, all such matters as are commonly the subject matter of company rules.

(3) The charity in general meeting has the power to alter, add to or repeal the rules or bye laws.

(4) The directors must adopt such means as they think sufficient to bring the rules and bye laws to the notice of members of the charity.

(5) The rules or bye laws shall be binding on all members of the charity. No rule or bye law shall be inconsistent with, or shall affect or repeal anything contained in, the articles.

> *Article 58 Analysis*
>
> Article 58 allows the directors, subject to the articles, to make further rules. It should be noted any rules must not fetter any acts of Parliament relevant to the charity, in particular the Companies Act 2006 and the Charities Act 2011.
>
> Article 58(2)(d) provides that the ability of directors to make further rules in term of decision making appears in the new model articles of private companies limited by guarantee.[85]

Article 59 Disputes

3.40

59 If a dispute arises between members of the charity about the validity or propriety of anything done by the members of the charity under these articles, and the dispute cannot be resolved by agreement, the parties to the dispute must first try in good faith to settle the dispute by mediation before resorting to litigation.[86]

85 Schedule 2 Regulation 3 Model articles for private companies limited by guarantee, see Article 16 Directors' discretion to make further rules. '16.Subject to the articles, the directors may make any rule which they think fit about how they take decisions, and about how such rules are to be recorded or communicated to directors.'

86 Charity Commission (GD1) 'Article 59 – It is good practice to include provisions for dealing with any disputes that arise between members of the charity. Litigation can be expensive, and litigation about the internal affairs of a charity would almost certainly constitute 'charity proceedings', which can be taken only with the Commission's authority. We would usually require the parties to a dispute to have tried mediation first.'

Article 60 Dissolution

3.41

60(1) The members of the charity may at any time before, and in expectation of, its dissolution resolve that any net assets of the charity after all its debts and liabilities have been paid, or provision has been made for them, shall on or before the dissolution of the charity be applied or transferred in any of the following ways:

(a) directly for the Objects; or

(b) by transfer to any charity or charities for purposes similar to the Objects; or

(c) to any charity or charities for use for particular purposes that fall within the Objects.

(2) Subject to any such resolution of the members of the charity, the directors of the charity may at any time before and in expectation of its dissolution resolve that any net assets of the charity after all its debts and liabilities have been paid, or provision made for them, shall on or before dissolution of the charity be applied or transferred:

(a) directly for the Objects; or

(b) by transfer to any charity or charities for purposes similar to the Objects; or

(c) to any charity or charities for use for particular purposes that fall within the Objects.

(3) In no circumstances shall the net assets of the charity be paid to or distributed among the members of the charity (except to a member that is itself a charity) and if no resolution in accordance with article 60(1) is passed by the members or the directors the net assets of the charity shall be applied for charitable purposes as directed by the Court or the Commission.

Article 60 Analysis

Article 60 summarises the procedure for closing a charity. Charities may dissolve for various reasons: mergers, loss of funding, lack of members and transferring from a company to a charitable incorporated organisation.[87] If the charity is a company, it must follow the dissolution process detailed in the articles of association,[88] and comply with the relevant rules to strike

87 Charity Commission Guidance, 'How to close a charity'.
88 Charity Commission Guidance, 'Remove a charity from the charities register'.

off the limited company at Companies House.[89] If the charity does not meet the requirements to strike off, the directors may need to arrange a liquidation.

Article 61 Interpretation

3.42

61. In article 7, sub-clause (2) of article 9 and sub-clause (2) of article 47 'connected person' means:

(1) a child, parent, grandchild, grandparent, brother or sister of the director;

(2) the spouse or civil partner of the director or of any person falling within sub-clause (1) above;

(3) a person carrying on business in partnership with the director or with any person falling within sub-clause (1) or (2) above;

(4) an institution which is controlled –

 (a) by the director or any connected person falling within sub-clause (1), (2), or (3) above; or

 (b) by two or more persons falling within sub-clause 4(a), when taken together

(5) a body corporate in which –

 (a) the director or any connected person falling within subclauses (1) to (3) has a substantial interest; or

 (b) two or more persons falling within sub-clause (5)(a) who, when taken together, have a substantial interest.

 (c) Sections 350–352 of the Charities Act 2011 apply for the purposes of interpreting the terms used in this article.

Article 61 Analysis

The interpretation section of article 61 reproduces section 188 of the Charities Act 2011.[90]

89 You can close down your limited company by getting it 'struck off' the companies register, but only if it: hasn't traded or sold off any stock in the last three months, hasn't changed names in the last three months, isn't threatened with liquidation, or has no agreements with creditors, eg a Company Voluntary Arrangement (CVA).

90 Charities Act 2011, s 188 (Meaning of 'connected person'). Remuneration of charity trustees and trustees.

Chapter 4 Analysis of the Model Articles of Association for a Right to Manage Company

Introduction

4.1

The following chapter provides analysis and commentary of the prescribed articles of association for a right to manage company that incorporates as a company under the Companies Act 2006.

SCHEDULE Regulation 2

ARTICLES OF ASSOCIATION OF A RTM COMPANY

THE COMPANIES ACT 2006

ARTICLES OF ASSOCIATION OF [NAME] RTM COMPANY LIMITED BY GUARANTEE AND NOT HAVING A SHARE CAPITAL

Part 1 Interpretation, names and objects of RTM company and limitation of liability

Article 1 Defined terms

1.—(1) In the articles, unless the context requires otherwise—

"articles" means the company's articles of association;

"bankruptcy" includes individual insolvency proceedings in a jurisdiction other than England and Wales or Northern Ireland which have an effect similar to that of bankruptcy;

"chairman" has the meaning given in article 17;

"chairman of the meeting" has the meaning given in article 30;

"Companies Acts" means the Companies Acts as defined in section 2 of the Companies Act 2006(1), in so far as they apply to the company;

"director" means a director of the company, and includes any person occupying the position of director, by whatever name called;

"document" includes, unless otherwise specified, any document sent or supplied in electronic form;

"electronic form" has the meaning given in section 1168 of the Companies Act 2006 ("the 2006 Act");

"immediate landlord" in relation to a unit in the Premises, means the person who—

(a) if the unit is subject to a lease, is the landlord under the lease; or

(b) if the unit is subject to two or more leases, is the landlord under whichever of the leases is inferior to the others;

"member" has the meaning given in section 112 of the 2006 Act;

"ordinary resolution" has the meaning given in section 282 of the 2006 Act;

"participate", in relation to a directors' meeting, has the meaning given in article 15;

"the Premises" means [*name and address*];

"proxy notice" has the meaning given in article 36;

"residential unit" means a flat or any other separate set of premises which is constructed or adapted for use for the purposes of a dwelling;

"RTM company" (Right to Manage Company) has the meaning given in section 73 of the Commonhold and Leasehold Reform Act 2002

"special resolution" has the meaning given in section 283 of the 2006 Act;

"subsidiary" has the meaning given in section 1159 of the 2006 Act;

"writing" means the representation or reproduction of words, symbols or other information in a visible form by any method or combination of methods, whether sent or supplied in electronic form or otherwise; and

"2002 Act" means the Commonhold and Leasehold Reform Act 2002.

(2) Unless the context otherwise requires, other words or expressions contained in these articles bear the same meaning as in the Companies Act 2006 as in force on the date when the RTM Companies (Model Articles) (England) Regulations 2009 are made.

Name and objects of RTM company

Article 2

4.2

2. The name of the company is [*name*][1]

RTM Company Limited.

1 A non RTM company is restricted from registering using the following in any part of its registered name: 'RTM Company Limited', 'Right to Manage' or 'RTM' in response to the First EC Company Law Directive (First Directive) (68/151/EEC).

Article 3

4.3

3. The registered office of the company will be situated at [*address*]

> *Articles 2 and 3 Analysis*
>
> The company name must end with RTM Company Limited. For companies incorporated prior to 9 November 2009, the name and registered address appeared in the memorandum of association.

Articles 4–6

4.4

4. The objects for which the company is established are to acquire and exercise in accordance with the 2002 Act the right to manage the Premises.

5. These objects shall not be restrictively construed but the widest interpretation shall be given to them. In furtherance of the objects, but not otherwise, the company shall have power to do all such things as may be authorised or required to be done by a RTM company by and under the 2002 Act, and in particular (but without derogation from the generality of the foregoing)—

(a) to prepare, make, pursue or withdraw a claim to acquire the right to manage the Premises;

(b) to exercise management functions under leases of the whole or any part of the Premises in accordance with sections 96 and 97 of the 2002 Act;

(c) to exercise functions in relation to the grant of approvals under long leases of the whole or any part of the Premises in accordance with sections 98 and 99 of the 2002 Act;

(d) in accordance with sections 100 and 101 of the 2002 Act, to monitor, keep under review, report to the landlord, and procure or enforce the performance by any person of the terms of any covenant, undertaking, duty or obligation in any way connected with or affecting the Premises or any of its occupants;

(e) to negotiate for and make applications for the variation of leases pursuant to Part 4 of the Landlord and Tenant Act 1987 (“the 1987 Act”);

(f) to do such other things and to perform such other functions in relation to the Premises or any leases of the whole or any part of the Premises as may be agreed from time to time with the landlord or landlords or any other parties to the leases, as the case may be;

(g) to provide and maintain services and amenities of every description in relation to the Premises;

(h) to maintain, redecorate, repair, renew, repaint and clean the Premises; and to cultivate, maintain, landscape and plant any gardens, grounds or land comprised in the Premises;

(i) to enter into contracts with builders, cleaners, contractors, decorators, gardeners, tenants, or any other person;

(j) to consult and retain any professional advisers;

(k) to employ any staff and managing or other agents;

(l) to pay, remunerate or reward in any way any person supplying goods or services to the company;

(m) to make any appropriate or consequential agreements or arrangements for the right to manage the Premises to cease to be exercisable by the company;

(n) to issue and receive any notice, counter-notice, consent or other communication and to enter into any correspondence concerning or in any way affecting the Premises, the management of the Premises, the occupants of the Premises, the company, any of its activities, or any of its members;

(o) to commence, defend, participate in or pursue any application to, or other proceeding before, any court or tribunal of any description;

(p) to insure the Premises or any other property of the company or in which it has an interest up to and including the full cost of rebuilding and reinstating the Premises, including VAT, architects', engineers', solicitors', surveyors', and all other professional persons' fees, the fees payable on any applications for planning permission or other permits or consents that may be required in relation to rebuilding or reinstating the Premises, the cost of preparation of the site including debris removal, demolition, shoring-up, site clearance and any works that may be required by statute, and incidental expenses, subject to such excesses, exclusions or limitations as are usual in the London insurance market. To insure the company and its directors, officers or auditors against public liability and any other risks which it may consider prudent or desirable to insure against;

(q) to collect in or receive monies from any person on account of administration charges, service charges, or other charges in relation to the Premises and, where required by law to do so, to deal with, hold or invest the monies in accordance with the provisions of the 1987 Act and any orders or regulations made under that Act from time to time;

(r) to establish, undertake and execute any trusts which may lawfully be, or which are required by law to be, established, executed or undertaken by the company;

(s) to establish and maintain capital reserves, management funds and any form of sinking fund in order to pay, or contribute towards, all costs, fees, and other expenses incurred in the implementation of the company's objects;

(t) to invest any money of the company in the United Kingdom by depositing it at interest with any financial institution with which a trust fund of service charge contributions might be held in accordance with the 1987 Act; or to invest it in such other manner (including the purchase of securities and other investments) as the company in general meeting may authorise from time to time; and to hold, sell or otherwise dispose of any such investments;

(u) subject to any conditions or limitations imposed by the company in general meeting from time to time, and subject to the provision of adequate security and the payment of interest, to advance and lend money or give credit to any person; to enter into guarantees, contracts of indemnity and surety; to receive money on deposit or loan; and to secure or guarantee the payment of any sum of money or the performance of any obligation by any person;

(v) subject to any limitations or conditions imposed by the company in general meeting from time to time, to borrow and raise money in any manner and to secure the repayment of any money borrowed, raised or owing by mortgage, charge, standard security, lien or other security upon the whole or part of the company's property or assets (whether present or future);

(w) to operate bank accounts and to draw, make, accept, endorse, discount, negotiate, execute and issue cheques, bills of exchange, debentures, promissory notes, and other negotiable or transferable instruments;

(x) to pay all or any expenses incurred in connection with the promotion, formation and incorporation of the company, or to contract with any person to pay such expenses;

(y) to monitor and determine for the purpose of voting, or for any other purpose, the physical dimensions of the Premises and any part or parts of the Premises and to take or obtain any appropriate measurements;

(z) to enter into any agreements or arrangements with any Minister of the Crown, authority (central, municipal, local, or otherwise) that may seem conducive to the attainment of the company's objects, and to obtain from any such Minister of the Crown or authority any charters, decrees, rights, privileges or concessions which the company may think desirable, and to carry out, exercise, and comply with any such charters, decrees, rights, privileges and concessions;

(aa) to do all things specified for the time being in the articles of association of the company;

(bb) to do or procure or arrange for the doing of all or any of the things or matters mentioned above in any part of the world and either as principals, agents, contractors or otherwise, and by or through agents, brokers, sub-contractors or otherwise and either alone or in conjunction with others; and

(cc) to do all such other lawful things as may be incidental or conducive to the pursuit or attainment of the company's objects.

6. The income of the company, from wherever derived, shall be applied solely in promoting the company's objects, and, save on a winding up of the company, no distribution shall be made to its members in cash or otherwise.

Article 4–6 Analysis

For companies incorporated prior to 9 November 2009, the objects appeared in the memorandum of association. The Companies Act 2006 allowed the company's objects to be unrestricted, unless the articles of association specifically apply a restriction.[2] In the 2009 consultation[3] it was proposed to include the existing prescribed objects for RTM companies in the new articles.

Limitation of liability

Article 7 Liability of members

4.5

7. The liability of each member is limited to £1, being the amount that each member undertakes to contribute to the assets of the company in the event of its being wound up while he is a member or within one year after he ceases to be a member, for—

(a) payment of the company's debts and liabilities contracted before he ceases to be a member,

(b) payment of the costs, charges and expenses of winding up; and

(c) adjustment of the rights of the contributories among themselves.

Article 7 Analysis

See analysis of article 2 in **2.5**.

2 Companies Act 2006, s 31 (Statement of company's objects).

3 Department for Communities and Local Government, 'Consultation on right to manage company articles' (London, June 2009).

Part 2 Directors – Directors' powers and responsibilities

Article 8 Directors' general authority

4.6

8. Subject to the articles, the directors are responsible for the management of the company's business, for which purpose they may exercise all the powers of the company.

> *Article 8 Analysis*
>
> See analysis of article 3 in **2.6**.

Article 9 Members' reserve power

4.7

9.—(1) The members may, by special resolution, direct the directors to take, or refrain from taking, specified action.

(2) No such special resolution invalidates anything which the directors have done before the passing of the resolution.

> *Article 9 Analysis*
>
> See analysis of article 4 in **2.7**.

Article 10 Directors may delegate

4.8

10.—(1) Subject to the articles, the directors may delegate any of the powers which are conferred on them under the articles—

(a) to such person or committee;

(b) by such means (including by power of attorney);

(c) to such an extent;

(d) in relation to such matters; and

(e) on such terms and conditions;

as they think fit.

(2) If the directors so specify, any such delegation may authorise further delegation of the directors' powers by any person to whom they are delegated.

(3) The directors may revoke any delegation in whole or part, or alter its terms and conditions.

> *Article 10 Analysis*
>
> See analysis of article 5 in **2.8**.

Article 11 Committees

4.9

11.—(1) Committees to which the directors delegate any of their powers must follow procedures which are based, so far as they are applicable, on those provisions of the articles which govern the taking of decisions by directors.

> *Article 11 Analysis*
>
> The model articles for private companies limited by guarantee[4] include article 6(2) 'The directors may make rules of procedure for all or any committees, which prevail over rules derived from the articles if they are not consistent with them.' The RTM prescribed articles omit the right of directors to make rules.
>
> See analysis of article 6 in **2.9**.

Decision-making by directors

Article 12 Directors to take decisions collectively

4.10

12.—(1) The general rule about decision-making by directors is that any decision of the directors must be either a majority decision at a meeting or a decision taken in accordance with article 13.

(2) If—

(a) the company only has one director, and

(b) no provision of the articles requires it to have more than one director,

4 Schedule 2 Regulation 3 Model articles for private companies limited by guarantee.

the general rule does not apply, and the director may take decisions without regard to any of the provisions of the articles relating to directors' decision-making.

> *Article 12 Analysis*
>
> See analysis of article 7 in **2.10**.

Article 13 Unanimous decisions

4.11

13.—(1) A decision of the directors is taken in accordance with this article when all eligible directors indicate to each other by any means that they share a common view on a matter.

(2) Such a decision may take the form of a resolution in writing, copies of which have been signed by each eligible director or to which each eligible director has otherwise indicated agreement in writing.

(3) References in this article to eligible directors are to directors who would have been entitled to vote on the matter had it been proposed as a resolution at a directors' meeting.

(4) A decision may not be taken in accordance with this article if the eligible directors would not have formed a quorum at such a meeting.

> *Article 13 Analysis*
>
> See analysis of article 8 in **2.11**.

Article 14 Calling a directors' meeting

4.12

14.—(1) Any director may call a directors' meeting by giving notice of the meeting to the directors or by authorising the company secretary (if any) to give such notice.

(2) Notice of any directors' meeting must indicate—

(a) its proposed date and time;

(b) where it is to take place; and

(c) if it is anticipated that directors participating in the meeting will not be in the same place, how it is proposed that they should communicate with each other during the meeting.

(3) Notice of a directors' meeting must be given to each director, but need not be in writing.

(4) Notice of a directors' meeting need not be given to directors who waive their entitlement to notice of that meeting, by giving notice to that effect to the company not more than 7 days after the date on which the meeting is held. Where such notice is given after the meeting has been held, that does not affect the validity of the meeting, or of any business conducted at it.

Article 14 Analysis

See analysis of article 9 in **2.12**.

Article 15 Participation in directors' meetings

4.13

15.—(1) Subject to the articles, directors participate in a directors' meeting, or part of a directors' meeting, when—

(a) the meeting has been called and takes place in accordance with the articles, and

(b) they can each communicate to the others any information or opinions they have on any particular item of the business of the meeting.

(2) In determining whether directors are participating in a directors' meeting, it is irrelevant where any director is or how they communicate with each other.

(3) If all the directors participating in a meeting are not in the same place, they may decide that the meeting is to be treated as taking place wherever any of them is.

Article 15 Analysis

See analysis of article 10 in **2.13**.

Article 16 Quorum for directors' meetings

4.14

16.—(1) At a directors' meeting, unless a quorum is participating, no proposal is to be voted on, except a proposal to call another meeting.

(2) The quorum for directors' meetings may be fixed from time to time by a decision of the directors, but it must never be less than two, and unless otherwise fixed it is two.

(3) If the total number of directors for the time being is less than the quorum required, the directors must not take any decision other than a decision—

(a) to appoint further directors, or

(b) to call a general meeting so as to enable the members to appoint further directors.

> *Article 16 Analysis*
>
> See analysis of article 11 in **2.14**.

Article 17 Chairing of directors' meetings

4.15

17.—(1) The directors may appoint a director to chair their meetings.

(2) The person so appointed for the time being is known as the chairman.

(3) The directors may terminate the chairman's appointment at any time.

(4) If the chairman is not participating in a directors' meeting within ten minutes of the time at which it was to start, the participating directors must appoint one of themselves to chair it.

> *Article 17 Analysis*
>
> See analysis of article 12 in **2.15**.

Article 18 Casting vote

4.16

18.—(1) If the numbers of votes for and against a proposal are equal, the chairman or other director chairing the meeting has a casting vote.

(2) But this does not apply if, in accordance with the articles, the chairman or other director is not to be counted as participating in the decision-making process for quorum or voting purposes.

> *Article 18 Analysis*
>
> See analysis of article 13 in **2.16**.

Article 19 Conflicts of interest

4.17

19.—(1) If a proposed decision of the directors is concerned with an actual or proposed transaction or arrangement with the company in which a director is interested, that director is not to be counted as participating in the decision-making process for quorum or voting purposes.

(2) But if paragraph (3) applies, a director who is interested in an actual or proposed transaction or arrangement with the company is to be counted as participating in the decision-making process for quorum and voting purposes.

(3) This paragraph applies when—

(a) the company by ordinary resolution disapplies the provision of the articles which would otherwise prevent a director from being counted as participating in the decision-making process;

(b) the director's interest cannot reasonably be regarded as likely to give rise to a conflict of interest; or

(c) the director's conflict of interest arises from a permitted cause.

(4) For the purposes of this article, the following are permitted causes—

(a) a guarantee given, or to be given, by or to a director in respect of an obligation incurred by or on behalf of the company or any of its subsidiaries;

(b) subscription, or an agreement to subscribe, for securities of the company or any of its subsidiaries, or to underwrite, sub-underwrite, or guarantee subscription for any such securities; and

(c) arrangements pursuant to which benefits are made available to employees and directors or former employees and directors of the company or any of its subsidiaries which do not provide special benefits for directors or former directors.

(5) For the purposes of this article, references to proposed decisions and decision-making processes include any directors' meeting or part of a directors' meeting.

(6) Subject to paragraph (7), if a question arises at a meeting of directors or of a committee of directors as to the right of a director to participate in the meeting (or part of the meeting) for voting or quorum purposes, the question may, before the conclusion of the meeting, be referred to the chairman whose ruling in relation to any director other than the chairman is to be final and conclusive.

(7) If any question as to the right to participate in the meeting (or part of the meeting) should arise in respect of the chairman, the question is to be decided by a decision of the directors at that meeting, for which purpose the chairman is not to be counted as participating in the meeting (or that part of the meeting) for voting or quorum purposes.

Article 19 Analysis

See analysis of article 14 in **2.17**.

Article 20 Records of decisions to be kept

4.18

20. The directors must ensure that the company keeps a record, in writing, for at least 10 years from the date of the decision recorded, of every unanimous or majority decision taken by the directors.

Article 20 Analysis

See analysis of article 15 in **2.18**.

Article 21 Directors' discretion to make further rules

4.19

21. Subject to the articles, the directors may make any rule which they think fit about how they take decisions, and about how such rules are to be recorded or communicated to directors.

> *Article 21 Analysis*
>
> See analysis of article 16 in **2.19**.

Appointment of directors

Article 22 Methods of appointing directors

4.20

22.—(1) Any person who is willing to act as a director, and is permitted by law to do so, may be appointed to be a director—

(a) by ordinary resolution, or

(b) by a decision of the directors.

(2) In any case where, as a result of death, the company has no members and no directors, the personal representatives of the last member to have died have the right, by notice in writing, to appoint a person to be a director.

(3) For the purposes of paragraph (2), where 2 or more members die in circumstances rendering it uncertain who was the last to die, a younger member is deemed to have survived an older member.

> *Article 22 Analysis*
>
> See analysis of article 17 in **2.20**.

Article 23 Termination of director's appointment

4.21

23. A person ceases to be a director as soon as—

(a) that person ceases to be a director by virtue of any provision of the Companies Acts 2006 or is prohibited from being a director by law;

(b) a bankruptcy order is made against that person;

(c) a composition is made with that person's creditors generally in satisfaction of that person's debts;

(d) a registered medical practitioner who is treating that person gives a written opinion to the company stating that that person has become physically or mentally incapable of acting as a director and may remain so for more than three months;

(e) by reason of that person's mental health, a court makes an order which wholly or partly prevents that person from personally exercising any powers or rights which that person would otherwise have;

(f) notification is received by the company from the director that the director is resigning from office, and such resignation has taken effect in accordance with its terms.

Article 23 Analysis

The model articles for private companies limited by guarantee[5] omit article 18(e) pursuant to The Mental Health (Discrimination) Act 2013.

See analysis of article 18 in **2.21**.

Article 24 Directors' remuneration

4.22

24. Except with the consent of the company in general meeting, the directors shall not be entitled to any remuneration. Any resolution giving such consent shall specify the amount of remuneration to be paid to the directors, and unless the resolution provides otherwise, the remuneration shall be deemed to accrue from day to day.

Article 24 Analysis

Article 24 is a condensed version of article 19,[6] with the express provision that any agreement for a director to receive remuneration is passed by a resolution in a general meeting.

See analysis of article 19 in **2.22**.

5 Schedule 2 Regulation 3 Model articles for private companies limited by guarantee.
6 Schedule 2 Regulation 3 Model articles for private companies limited by guarantee.

Article 25 Directors' expenses

4.23

25. The company may pay any reasonable expenses which the directors properly incur in connection with their attendance at—

(a) meetings of directors or committees of directors,

(b) general meetings, or

(c) separate meetings of the holders of debentures of the company, or otherwise in connection with the exercise of their powers and the discharge of their responsibilities in relation to the company.

> *Article 25 Analysis*
>
> See analysis of article 20 in **2.23**.

Part 3 Becoming and ceasing to be a member

Article 26 Becoming a member

4.24

26.—(1) Every person who is entitled to be, and who wishes to become, a member of the company shall deliver to the company an application for membership executed by him in the following form (or in a form as near to the following form as circumstances allow or in any other form which is usual or which the directors may approve).

To the Board of [name of company]I, [name]of [address]am a qualifying tenant of [address of flat] and wish to become a member of [name of company] subject to the provisions of the Articles of Association of the company and to any rules made under those Articles. I agree to pay the company an amount of up to £1 if the company is wound up while I am a member or for up to 12 months after I have ceased to become a member. Signed [ ] Dated [ ]

(2) No person shall be admitted to membership of the company unless that person, whether alone or jointly with others, is—

(a) a qualifying tenant of a flat contained in the Premises as specified in section 75 of the 2002 Act; or

(b) from the date upon which the company acquires the right to manage the Premises pursuant to the 2002 Act, a landlord under a lease of the whole or any part of the Premises.

(3) Membership of the company shall not be transferable.

(4) A person who, together with another or others, is to be regarded as jointly being the qualifying tenant of a flat, or as jointly constituting the landlord under a lease of the whole or any part of the Premises, shall, once admitted, be regarded as jointly being a member of the company in respect of that flat or lease (as the case may be).

(5) Applications for membership by persons who are to be regarded as jointly being the qualifying tenant of a flat, or who jointly constitute the landlord under a lease of the whole or any part of the Premises, shall state the names and addresses of all others who are jointly interested with them, and the order in which they wish to appear on the register of members in respect of such flat or lease (as the case may be).

(6) The directors shall, upon being satisfied as to a person's application and entitlement to membership, register such person as a member of the company.

Article 27 Ceasing to be a member

4.25

27.—(1) A member who at any time fails to satisfy the requirements for membership set out in article 26 shall cease to be a member of the company with immediate effect.

(2) If a member (or joint member) dies or becomes bankrupt, his personal representatives or trustee in bankruptcy will be entitled to be registered as a member (or joint member as the case may be) upon notice in writing to the company.

(3) A member may withdraw from the company and thereby cease to be a member by giving at least seven clear days' notice in writing to the company. Any such notice shall not be effective if given in the period beginning with the date on which the company gives notice of its claim to acquire the right to manage the Premises and ending with the date which is either—

(a) the acquisition date in accordance with section 90 of the 2002 Act; or

(b) the date of withdrawal or deemed withdrawal of that notice in accordance with sections 86 or 87 of that Act.

(4) If, for any reason—

(a) a person who is not a member of the company becomes a qualifying tenant or landlord jointly with persons who are members of the company, but fails to apply for membership within 28 days, or

(b) a member who is a qualifying tenant or landlord jointly with such persons dies or becomes bankrupt and his personal representatives or trustee in bankruptcy do not apply for membership within 56 days, or

(c) a member who is a qualifying tenant or landlord jointly with such persons resigns from membership pursuant to article 27(3),

those persons shall, unless they are otherwise entitled to be members of the company by reason of their interest in some other flat or lease, also cease to be members of the company with immediate effect. All such persons shall, however, be entitled to re-apply for membership in accordance with article 26.

Articles 26 and 27 Analysis

Article 26 outlines the legislative requirements for membership of the RTM company. Members must meet the requirement of section 75.[7] Article 27 summarises the company rules concerning the cessation of membership.

See analysis of articles 21 and 22 in **2.24** and **2.25**.

Part 4 Decision-making by members – Organisation of general meetings

Article 28 Attendance and speaking at general meetings

4.26

28.—(1) A person is able to exercise the right to speak at a general meeting when that person is in a position to communicate to all those attending the meeting, during the meeting, any information or opinions which that person has on the business of the meeting.

(2) A person is able to exercise the right to vote at a general meeting when—

(a) that person is able to vote, during the meeting, on resolutions put to the vote at the meeting, and

(b) that person's vote can be taken into account in determining whether or not such resolutions are passed at the same time as the votes of all the other persons attending the meeting.

7 Commonhold and Leasehold Reform Act 2002, s 75 (Qualifying tenants).

(3) The directors may make whatever arrangements they consider appropriate to enable those attending a general meeting to exercise their rights to speak or vote at it.

(4) In determining attendance at a general meeting, it is immaterial whether any two or more members attending it are in the same place as each other.

(5) Two or more persons who are not in the same place as each other attend a general meeting if their circumstances are such that if they have (or were to have) rights to speak and vote at that meeting, they are (or would be) able to exercise them.

Article 28 Analysis

See analysis of article 23 in **2.26**.

Article 29 Quorum for general meetings

4.27

29.—(1) No business other than the appointment of the chairman of the meeting is to be transacted at a general meeting if the persons attending it do not constitute a quorum as set out at 29 paragraph (2).

(2) The quorum for the meeting shall be 20 per cent of the members of the company entitled to vote upon the business to be transacted, or two members of the company so entitled (whichever is the greater) present in person or by proxy.

Article 29 Analysis

The model articles for a private company limited by guarantee[8] include article 24, the RTM articles include paragraph (2) above which provides the requirements for a quorum.

See analysis of article 24 in **2.27**.

Article 30 Chairing general meetings

4.28

30.—(1) If the directors have appointed a chairman, the chairman shall chair general meetings if present and willing to do so.

8 Schedule 2 Regulation 3 Model articles for private companies limited by guarantee.

(2) If the directors have not appointed a chairman, or if the chairman is unwilling to chair the meeting or is not present within ten minutes of the time at which a meeting was due to start—

(a) the directors present, or

(b) (if no directors are present), the meeting,

must appoint a director or member to chair the meeting, and the appointment of the chairman of the meeting must be the first business of the meeting.

(3) The person chairing a meeting in accordance with this article is referred to as "the chairman of the meeting".

> *Article 30 Analysis*
>
> See analysis of article 25 in **2.28**.

Article 31 Attendance and speaking by directors and non-members

4.29

31.—(1) Directors may attend and speak at general meetings, whether or not they are members.

(2) The chairman of the meeting may permit other persons who are not members of the company to attend and speak at a general meeting.

> *Article 31 Analysis*
>
> See analysis of article 26 in **2.29**.

Article 32 Adjournment

4.30

32.—(1) If the persons attending a general meeting within half an hour of the time at which the meeting was due to start do not constitute a quorum, or if during a meeting a quorum ceases to be present, the chairman of the meeting must adjourn it.

(2) The chairman of the meeting may adjourn a general meeting at which a quorum is present if—

(a) the meeting consents to an adjournment, or

(b) it appears to the chairman of the meeting that an adjournment is necessary to protect the safety of any person attending the meeting or ensure that the business of the meeting is conducted in an orderly manner.

(3) The chairman of the meeting must adjourn a general meeting if directed to do so by the meeting.

(4) When adjourning a general meeting, the chairman of the meeting must—

(a) either specify the time and place to which it is adjourned or state that it is to continue at a time and place to be fixed by the directors, and

(b) have regard to any directions as to the time and place of any adjournment which have been given by the meeting.

(5) If the continuation of an adjourned meeting is to take place more than 14 days after it was adjourned, the company must give at least 7 clear days' notice of it (that is, excluding the day of the adjourned meeting and the day on which the notice is given)—

(a) to the same persons to whom notice of the company's general meetings is required to be given, and

(b) containing the same information which such notice is required to contain.

(6) No business may be transacted at an adjourned general meeting which could not properly have been transacted at the meeting if the adjournment had not taken place.

Article 32 Analysis

See analysis of article 27 in **2.30**.

Voting at general meetings

Article 33 Voting: general

4.31

33.—(1) A resolution put to the vote of a general meeting must be decided on a show of hands unless a poll is duly demanded in accordance with the articles.

(2) If there are no landlords under leases of the whole or any part of the Premises who are members of the company, then one vote shall be available to be cast in respect of each flat in the Premises. The vote shall be cast by the member who is the qualifying tenant of the flat.

(3) At any time at which there are any landlords under leases of the whole or any part of the Premises who are members of the company, the votes available to be cast shall be determined as follows—

(a) there shall first be allocated to each residential unit in the Premises the same number of votes as equals the total number of members of the company who are landlords under leases of the whole or any part of the Premises. Landlords under a lease who are regarded as jointly being a member of the company shall be counted as one member for this purpose;

(b) if at any time the Premises includes any non-residential part, a total number of votes shall be allocated to that part as shall equal the total number of votes allocated to the residential units multiplied by a factor of A/B, where A is the total internal floor area of the non-residential parts and B is the total internal area of all the residential parts. Internal floor area shall be determined in accordance with paragraph 1(4) of Schedule 6 to the 2002 Act. Calculations of the internal floor area shall be measured in square metres, fractions of floor area of less than half a square metre shall be ignored and fractions of floor area in excess of half a square metre shall be counted as a whole square metre;

(c) the votes allocated to each residential unit shall be entitled to be cast by the member who is the qualifying tenant of that unit, or if there is no qualifying tenant of the unit, by the member who is the immediate landlord. The immediate landlord will not be entitled to the vote of a residential unit held by a qualifying tenant who is not a member of the RTM company;[9]

(d) the votes allocated to any non-residential part included in the Premises shall be entitled to be cast by the immediate landlord of that part, or where there is no lease of a non-residential part, by the freeholder. Where there is more than one such person, the total number of votes allocated to the non-residential part shall be divided between them in proportion to the internal floor area of their respective parts. Any resulting entitlement to a fraction of a vote shall be ignored;

(e) if a residential unit is not subject to any lease, no votes shall be entitled to be cast in respect of it;

(f) any person who is a landlord under a lease or leases of the whole or any part of the Premises and who is a member of the company but is not otherwise entitled to any votes, shall be entitled to one vote.

(4) In the case of any persons who are to be regarded as jointly being members of the company, any such person may exercise the voting rights to which such

9 Previous provision. (c) the votes allocated to each residential unit shall be entitled to be cast by the member who is the qualifying tenant of that unit, or if there is no member who is a qualifying tenant of the unit, by the member who is the immediate landlord.

members are jointly entitled, but where more than one such person tenders a vote, whether in person or by proxy, the vote of the senior shall be accepted to the exclusion of the votes of the others, and seniority shall be determined by the order in which the names of such persons appear in the register of members in respect of the flat or lease (as the case may be) in which they are interested.

Article 33 Analysis

Article 33 provides the company rules for voting at general meetings, they are more convoluted compared to the model articles.

See analysis of article 28 in **2.31**.

The provisions specify the allocation of votes, where there are landlords under leases who are members of the RTM company. The votes are weighted to take account of the respective interests of members of the property. Landlords under leases who are members of the company are entitled to at least one vote with weighted votes being available to reflect their interest in non-residential parts of the premises.

It should be noted the consultation made changes to 39(c) that provides that the votes of those flats of qualifying tenants who are not members of the RTM company are to be exercised by the immediate landlord of that flat. The consultation agreed that giving the landlord the votes of those flats in such circumstances is not the correct approach.[10]

Article 34 Errors and disputes

4.32

34.—(1) No objection may be raised to the qualification of any person voting at a general meeting except at the meeting or adjourned meeting at which the vote objected to is tendered, and every vote not disallowed at the meeting is valid.

(2) Any such objection must be referred to the chairman of the meeting whose decision is final.

Article 34 Analysis

See analysis of article 29 in **2.32**.

10 Department for Communities and Local Government, 'Consultation on right to manage company articles' (London, June 2009).

Article 35 Poll votes

4.33

35.—(1) A poll on a resolution may be demanded—

(a) in advance of the general meeting where it is to be put to the vote, or

(b) at a general meeting, either before a show of hands on that resolution or immediately after the result of a show of hands on that resolution is declared.

(2) A poll may be demanded by—

(a) the chairman of the meeting;

(b) the directors;

(c) two or more persons having the right to vote on the resolution; or

(d) a person or persons representing not less than one tenth of the total voting rights of all the members having the right to vote on the resolution.

(3) A demand for a poll may be withdrawn if—

(a) the poll has not yet been taken, and

(b) the chairman of the meeting consents to the withdrawal.

(4) Polls must be taken immediately and in such manner as the chairman of the meeting directs.

> *Article 35 Analysis*
>
> See analysis of article 30 in **2.33**.

Article 36 Content of proxy notices

4.34

36.—(1) Proxies may only validly be appointed by a notice in writing (a "proxy notice") which—

(a) states the name and address of the member appointing the proxy;

(b) identifies the person appointed to be that member's proxy and the general meeting in relation to which that person is appointed;

(c) is signed by or on behalf of the member appointing the proxy, or is authenticated in such manner as the directors may determine; and

(d) is delivered to the company in accordance with the articles and any instructions contained in the notice of the general meeting to which they relate.

(2) The company may require proxy notices to be delivered in a particular form, and may specify different forms for different purposes.

(3) Proxy notices may specify how the proxy appointed under them is to vote (or that the proxy is to abstain from voting) on one or more resolutions.

(4) Unless a proxy notice indicates otherwise, it must be treated as—

(a) allowing the person appointed under it as a proxy discretion as to how to vote on any ancillary or procedural resolutions put to the meeting, and

(b) appointing that person as a proxy in relation to any adjournment of the general meeting to which it relates as well as the meeting itself.

Article 36 Analysis

See analysis of article 31 in **2.34**.

Article 37 Delivery of proxy notices

4.35

37.—(1) A person who is entitled to attend, speak or vote (either on a show of hands or on a poll) at a general meeting remains so entitled in respect of that meeting or any adjournment of it, even though a valid proxy notice has been delivered to the company by or on behalf of that person.

(2) An appointment under a proxy notice may be revoked by delivering to the company a notice in writing given by or on behalf of the person by whom or on whose behalf the proxy notice was given.

(3) A notice revoking a proxy appointment only takes effect if it is delivered before the start of the meeting or adjourned meeting to which it relates.

(4) If a proxy notice is not executed by the person appointing the proxy, it must be accompanied by written evidence of the authority of the person who executed it to execute it on the appointor's behalf.

Article 37 Analysis

See analysis of article 32 in **2.35**.

Article 38 Amendments to resolutions

4.36

38.—(1) An ordinary resolution to be proposed at a general meeting may be amended by ordinary resolution if—

(a) notice of the proposed amendment is given to the company in writing by a person entitled to vote at the general meeting at which it is to be proposed not less than 48 hours before the meeting is to take place (or such later time as the chairman of the meeting may determine), and

(b) the proposed amendment does not, in the reasonable opinion of the chairman of the meeting, materially alter the scope of the resolution.

(2) A special resolution to be proposed at a general meeting may be amended by ordinary resolution, if—

(a) the chairman of the meeting proposes the amendment at the general meeting at which the resolution is to be proposed, and

(b) the amendment does not go beyond what is necessary to correct a grammatical or other non-substantive error in the resolution.

(3) If the chairman of the meeting, acting in good faith, wrongly decides that an amendment to a resolution is out of order, the chairman's error does not invalidate the vote on that resolution.

Article 38 Analysis

See analysis of article 33 in **2.36**.

Part 5 Administrative arrangements

Article 39 Means of communication to be used

4.37

39.—(1) Subject to the articles, anything sent or supplied by or to the company under the articles may be sent or supplied in any way in which the Companies

Acts provides for documents or information which are authorised or required by any provision of those Acts to be sent or supplied by or to the company.

(2) Subject to the articles, any notice or document to be sent or supplied to a director in connection with the taking of decisions by directors may also be sent or supplied by the means by which that director has asked to be sent or supplied with such notices or documents for the time being.

(3) A director may agree with the company that notices or documents sent to that director in a particular way are to be deemed to have been received within a specified time of their being sent, and for the specified time to be less than 48 hours.

Article 39 Analysis

See analysis of article 34 in **2.37**.

Article 40 Company seals

4.38

40.—(1) Any common seal may only be used by the authority of the directors.

(2) The directors may decide by what means and in what form any common seal is to be used.

(3) Unless otherwise decided by the directors, if the company has a common seal and it is affixed to a document, the document must also be signed by at least one authorised person in the presence of a witness who attests the signature.

(4) For the purposes of this article, an authorised person is—

(a) any director of the company;

(b) the company secretary (if any); or

(c) any person authorised by the directors for the purpose of signing documents to which the common seal is applied.

Article 40 Analysis

See analysis of article 35 in **2.38**.

Article 41 Inspection and copying of accounts and other records

4.39

41.—(1) In addition to, and without derogation from, any right conferred by statute, any member shall have the right, on reasonable notice, at such time and place as shall be convenient to the company, to inspect, and to be provided with a copy of, any book, minute, document or accounting record of the company, upon payment of any reasonable charge for copying. Such rights shall be subject to any resolution of the company in general meeting.

(2) In the case of any book, minute, document or accounting record which the directors reasonably consider contains confidential material, the disclosure of which would be contrary to the interests of the company, to the exclusion or excision of such confidential material (the fact of such exclusion or excision being disclosed to the member), and to any other reasonable conditions that the directors may impose.

> *Article 41 Analysis*
>
> Article 41(1) provides the right, conferred by the articles, to inspect accounts and other records. The model articles[11] for private companies limited by guarantee provisions provide that members have no entitlement to inspect the company accounts or other records by virtue of being a member.
>
> Article 41(2) allows confidential information to be withheld if not in the best interests of the company. Its should be noted, Companies House provides information freely to members for inspection and covers the majority of requirements under the Act.
>
> See analysis and context of article 36 in **2.39**.

Article 42 Provision for employees on cessation of business

4.40

42. The directors may decide to make provision for the benefit of persons employed or formerly employed by the company or any of its subsidiaries (other than a director or former director or shadow director) in connection with the cessation or transfer to any person of the whole or part of the undertaking of the company or that subsidiary.

11 Schedule 2 Regulation 3 Model articles for private companies limited by guarantee.

Article 42 Analysis

See analysis of article 37 in **2.40**.

Part 6 Directors' indemnity and insurance

Article 43 Indemnity

4.41

43.—(1) Subject to paragraph (2), a relevant director of the company or an associated company may be indemnified out of the company's assets against—

(a) any liability incurred by that director in connection with any negligence, default, breach of duty or breach of trust in relation to the company or an associated company,

(b) any liability incurred by that director in connection with the activities of the company or an associated company in its capacity as a trustee of an occupational pension scheme (as defined in section 235(6) of the Companies Act 2006),

(c) any other liability incurred by that director as an officer of the company or an associated company.

(2) This article does not authorise any indemnity which would be prohibited or rendered void by any provision of the Companies Acts or by any other provision of law.

(3) In this article—

(a) companies are associated if one is a subsidiary of the other or both are subsidiaries of the same body corporate, and

(b) a "relevant director" means any director or former director of the company or an associated company.

Article 44 Insurance

4.42

44.—(1) The directors may decide to purchase and maintain insurance, at the expense of the company, for the benefit of any relevant director in respect of any relevant loss.

(2) In this article—

(a) a "relevant director" means any director or former director of the company or an associated company,

(b) a "relevant loss" means any loss or liability which has been or may be incurred by a relevant director in connection with that director's duties or powers in relation to the company, any associated company or any pension fund or employees' share scheme of the company or associated company, and

(c) companies are associated if one is a subsidiary of the other or both are subsidiaries of the same body corporate.

Articles 43 and 44 Analysis

See analysis of articles 38 and 39 in **2.41** and **2.42**.

Chapter 5 Analysis of the Model Articles of Association for a Community Interest Company

CIC Limited by Guarantee, Schedule 1, Large Membership

INTERPRETATION

Article 1 Defined terms

5.1

1. In the Articles, unless the context requires otherwise, the following terms shall have the following meanings:

Term	Meaning
"Address"	includes a number or address used for the purposes of sending or receiving Documents by Electronic Means;
"Articles"	the Company's articles of association;
"Authorised Representative"	means any individual nominated by a Member Organisation to act as its representative at any meeting of the Company in accordance with Article 39;
"asset-locked body"	means (i) a community interest company, a charity[i] or a Permitted Industrial and Provident Society; or (ii) a body established outside the United Kingdom that is equivalent to any of those;
"bankruptcy"	includes individual insolvency proceedings in a jurisdiction other than England and Wales or Northern Ireland which have an effect similar to that of bankruptcy;
"Chair"	has the meaning given in Article 10;
"chairman of the meeting"	has the meaning given in Article 35;
"Circulation Date"	in relation to a written resolution, has the meaning given to it in the Companies Acts;

Term	Meaning
"Clear Days"	in relation to the period of a notice, that period excluding the day when the notice is given or deemed to be given and the day for which it is given or on which it is to take effect;
"community"	is to be construed in accordance with accordance with Section 35(5) of the Company's (Audit, Investigations and Community Enterprise) Act 2004;
"Companies Acts"	means the Companies Acts (as defined in Section 2 of the Companies Act 2006), in so far as they apply to the Company;
"Company"	[ ] [Community Interest Company/C.I.C.];
"Conflict of Interest"	any direct or indirect interest of a Director (whether personal, by virtue of a duty of loyalty to another organisation or otherwise) that conflicts, or might conflict with the interests of the Company;
"Director"	a director of the Company, and includes any person occupying the position of director, by whatever name called;
"Document"	includes, unless otherwise indicated, any Document sent or supplied in Electronic Form;
"Electronic Form" and "Electronic Means"	have the meanings respectively given to them in Section 1168 of the Companies Act 2006;
"Hard Copy Form"	has the meaning given to it in the Companies Act 2006;
"Memorandum"	the Company's memorandum of association;
"paid"	means paid or credited as paid;
"participate"	in relation to a Directors' meeting, has the meaning given in Article 15;
"Permitted Industrial and Provident Society"	an industrial and provident society which has a restriction on the use of its assets in accordance with Regulation 4 of the Community Benefit Societies (Restriction on Use of Assets) Regulations 2006 or Regulation 4 of the Community Benefit Societies (Restriction on Use of Assets) Regulations (Northern Ireland) 2006;
"Proxy Notice"	has the meaning given in Article 42;
"the Regulator"	means the Regulator of Community Interest Companies;
"Secretary"	the secretary of the Company (if any);

Term	Meaning
"specified"	means specified in the memorandum and articles of association of the Company for the purposes of this paragraph;
"subsidiary"	has the meaning given in section 1159 of the Companies Act 2006;
"transfer"	includes every description of disposition, payment, release or distribution, and the creation or extinction of an estate or interest in, or right over, any property; and
"Writing"	the representation or reproduction of words, symbols or other information in a visible form by any method or combination of methods, whether sent or supplied in Electronic Form or otherwise.

1.1 Subject to clause 3 of this Schedule, any reference in the Articles to an enactment includes a reference to that enactment as re-enacted or amended from time to time and to any subordinate legislation made under it.

1.2 Unless the context otherwise requires, other words or expressions contained in these Articles bear the same meaning as in the Companies Act 2006 as in force on the date when the Articles become binding on the Company.

Exclusion of model articles

The relevant model articles for a company limited by guarantee are hereby expressly excluded.

Article 1 Analysis

In the model articles[1] article 1, the defined terms appear at the end of the document, for comparison to the new model articles, this section has been transferred to the front of the articles.

Provision 3.1 which excludes the model articles for a private company limited by guarantee[2] appears in article 52 of the model articles,[3] in order to explicitly state the exclusion it is good practice to provide the provision at the beginning of the document and specifically refer to the model articles regulations. It should be noted for companies incorporated under previous Companies Acts, the relevant articles should be expressed and excluded.

1 CIC Limited by Guarantee, Schedule 1, Large Membership.
2 Schedule 2 Regulation 3 Model articles for private companies limited by guarantee.
3 CIC Limited by Guarantee, Schedule 1, Large Membership.

> *Alternative precedent*
>
> The model articles for private companies limited by guarantee contained or incorporated in Schedule 1 to the Companies (Model Articles) Regulations 2008, SI 2008/3229 as amended prior to the date of adoption of these articles (the 'Model Articles') shall not apply to the Company, save insofar as they are varied or excluded by, or are inconsistent with, the following articles.

COMMUNITY AND INTEREST COMPANY AND ASSET LOCK

Article 2 Community Interest Company

5.2

The Company is to be a community interest company.

> *Article 2 Analysis*
>
> A company limited by shares or a company limited by guarantee and not having a share capital may be formed as or become a community interest company, and a company limited by guarantee and having a share capital may become a community interest company.[4]
>
> In terms of conversion: the company is required to alter its articles to state that it is to be a CIC. Adaptation may be required to ensure they conform to the requirements of CIC legislation and the name of the company will require alteration to include one of the CIC designations.[5]

Article 3 Asset Lock

5.3

3.1 The Company shall not transfer any of its assets other than for full consideration.

3.2 Provided the conditions in Article 3.3 are satisfied, Article 3.1 shall not apply to:

(a) the transfer of assets to any specified asset-locked body, or (with the consent of the Regulator) to any other asset-locked body; and

4 Companies (Audit, Investigations and Community Enterprise) Act 2004, s 26 (Community interest companies).

5 Office of the Regulator of Community Interest Companies: Information and guidance notes, Chapter 4: Creating a Community Interest Company (CIC), May 2016 (4.2. Converting an existing company to a CIC).

(b) the transfer of assets made for the benefit of the community other than by way of a transfer of assets into an asset-locked body.

3.3 The conditions are that the transfer of assets must comply with any restrictions on the transfer of assets for less than full consideration which may be set out elsewhere in the Memorandum and Articles of the Company.

3.4 If the Company is wound up under the Insolvency Act 1986; and all its liabilities have been satisfied any residual assets shall be given or transferred to the asset-locked body specified in Article 3.5 below.

3.5 For the purposes of this Article 3, the following asset-locked body is specified as a potential recipient of the Company's assets under Articles 3.2 and 3.4:

Asset Locked Body Name

Charity Registration Number (if applicable): [ ]

Company Registration Number (if applicable): [ ]

Registered Office: [ ]

Article 3 Analysis

The asset lock is the fundamental feature of the CIC, it is designed to ensure the company assets are specifically used for the benefit of the company.

Chapter 6[6] of the regulator's guidance provides further guidance. It should be noted the provisions cannot be edited or amended.[7]

Article 4 Not for profit

5.4

The Company is not established or conducted for private gain: any surplus or assets are used principally for the benefit of the community.

6 Office of the Regulator of Community Interest Companies: Information and guidance notes, Chapter 6: The Asset Lock, May 2016.

7 CICs are also able to adopt asset lock rules that impose more stringent requirements, provided they also include these basic provisions.

Article 4 Analysis

Article 4 provides the 'not for profit' guarantee. This article does not appear in the model articles and together with article 3 provides the CIC operates on a genuine not for profit basis. The traditional private company limited by guarantee holds the ability and obligation to pay the directors.

OBJECTS, POWERS AND LIMITATION OF LIABILITY

Article 5 Objects

5.5

The objects of the Company are to carry on activities which benefit the community and in particular (without limitation) to: [insert here].

Article 5 Analysis

Article 5 requires the objects of the company to be restricted. For example, 'to provide day care and transport facilities for the elderly and physically disadvantaged in North Essex'. If the objects are not restricted by the articles it would follow the company would not meet the community interest test.[8]

Article 6 Powers

5.6

To further its objects the Company may do all such lawful things as may further the Company's objects and, in particular, but, without limitation, may borrow or raise and secure the payment of money for any purpose including for the purposes of investment or of raising funds.

Article 6 Analysis

The company will have statutory powers and obligations conferred by the Companies Act 2006 and the Community Interest Company Regulations 2005, SI 2005/1788.

Article 6 prescribes that the main powers must be used to further the company's objects and all actions must be lawful. It is possible to limit the powers of the company. It should be noted, any adaptation of the provisions in the articles must not fetter the statutory powers bestowed by legislation.

8 Office of the Regulator of Community Interest Companies: Information and guidance notes, Chapter 5: Constitutional Documents, May 2016.

Article 7 Liability of members

5.7

The liability of each member is limited to £1, being the amount that each member undertakes to contribute to the assets of the Company in the event of its being wound up while he or she is a member or within one year after he or she ceases to be a member, for:

7.1 payment of the Company's debts and liabilities contracted before he or she ceases to be a member;

7.2 payment of the costs, charges and expenses of winding up; and

7.3 adjustment of the rights of the contributories among themselves.

Article 7 Analysis

Typically, the guarantors limit any liability to £1. The members may underwrite its activities by guaranteeing a larger sum. Article 7 provides the members are not liable for the company's debts, on the assumption no fraud or illegal actions have transpired that may fetter the limited liability.

DIRECTORS

DIRECTORS' POWERS AND RESPONSIBILITIES

Article 8 Directors' general authority

5.8

Subject to the Articles, the Directors are responsible for the management of the Company's business, for which purpose they may exercise all the powers of the Company.

Article 8 Analysis

See analysis of article 3 in **2.6**.

Article 9 Members' reserve power

5.9

9.1 The members may, by special resolution, direct the Directors to take, or refrain from taking, specific action.

9.2 No such special resolution invalidates anything which the Directors have done before the passing of the resolution.

> *Article 9 Analysis*
>
> See analysis of article 4 in **2.7**.

Article 10 Chair

5.10

The Directors may appoint one of their number to be the chair of the Directors for such term of office as they determine and may at any time remove him or her from office.

> *Article 10 Analysis*
>
> See analysis of article 12 in **2.15**.

Article 11 Directors may delegate

5.11

11.1 Subject to the Articles, the Directors may delegate any of the powers which are conferred on them under the Articles:

(a) to such person or committee;

(b) by such means (including by power of attorney);

(c) to such an extent;

(d) in relation to such matters or territories; and

(e) on such terms and conditions;

(f) as they think fit.

11.2 If the Directors so specify, any such delegation may authorise further delegation of the Directors' powers by any person to whom they are delegated.

11.3 The Directors may revoke any delegation in whole or part, or alter its terms and conditions.

> *Article 11 Analysis*
>
> See analysis of article 5 in **2.8**.

Article 12 Committees

5.12

12.1 Committees to which the Directors delegate any of their powers must follow procedures which are based as far as they are applicable on those provisions of the Articles which govern the taking of decisions by Directors.

12.2 The Directors may make rules of procedure for all or any committees, which prevail over rules derived from the Articles if they are not consistent with them.

> *Article 12 Analysis*
>
> See analysis of article 6 in **2.9**.

DECISION-MAKING BY DIRECTORS

Article 13 Directors to take decisions collectively

5.13

Any decision of the Directors must be either a majority decision at a meeting or a decision taken in accordance with Article 19.

> *Article 13 Analysis*
>
> See analysis of article 7 in **2.10**.

Article 14 Calling a Directors' meeting

5.14

14.1 Two Directors may (and the Secretary, if any, must at the request of two Directors) call a Directors' meeting.

14.2 A Directors' meeting must be called by at least seven Clear Days' notice unless either, all the Directors agree; or urgent circumstances require shorter notice.

14.3 Notice of Directors' meetings must be given to each Director.

14.4 Every notice calling a Directors' meeting must specify: the place, day and time of the meeting; and if it is anticipated that Directors participating in the meeting will not be in the same place, how it is proposed that they should communicate with each other during the meeting.

14.5 Notice of Directors' meetings need not be in Writing.

14.6 Notice of Directors' meetings may be sent by Electronic Means to an Address provided by the Director for the purpose.

> *Article 14 Analysis*
>
> Article 14.1 requires two directors to call a meeting as opposed to 'any' director in the model articles.[9]
>
> See analysis of article 9 in **2.12**.

Article 15 Participation in Directors' meetings

5.15

15.1 Subject to the Articles, Directors participate in a Directors' meeting, or part of a Directors' meeting, when:

(a) the meeting has been called and takes place in accordance with the Articles; and

(b) they can each communicate to the others any information or opinions they have on any particular item of the business of the meeting.

15.2 In determining whether Directors are participating in a Directors' meeting, it is irrelevant where any Director is or how they communicate with each other.ii

15.3. If all the Directors participating in a meeting are not in the same place, they may decide that the meeting is to be treated as taking place wherever any of them is.

> *Article 15 Analysis*
>
> See analysis of article 10 in **2.13**.

Article 16 Quorum for Directors' meetings

5.16

16.1 At a Directors' meeting, unless a quorum is participating, no proposal is to be voted on, except a proposal to call another meeting.

9 Schedule 2 Regulation 3 Model articles for private companies limited by guarantee.

16.2 The quorum for Directors' meetings may be fixed from time to time by a decision of the Directors, but it must never be less than two, and unless otherwise fixed it is [two].

16.3 If the total number of Directors for the time being is less than the quorum required, the Directors must not take any decision other than a decision:

(a) to appoint further Directors; or

(b) to call a general meeting so as to enable the members to appoint further Directors.

> *Article 16 Analysis*
>
> See analysis of article 11 in **2.14**.

Article 17 Chairing of Directors' meetings

5.17

The chair, if any, or in his or her absence another Director nominated by the Directors present shall preside as chair of each Directors' meeting.

> *Article 17 Analysis*
>
> See analysis of article 12 in **2.15**.

Article 18 Decision making at a meeting

5.18

Questions arising at a Directors' meeting shall be decided by a majority of votes. In all proceedings of Directors each Director must not have more than one vote. In case of an equality of votes, the chair shall have a second or casting vote.

> *Article 18 Analysis*
>
> See analysis of article 12 in **2.15**.

Article 19 Decisions without a meeting

5.19

19.1 The Directors may take a unanimous decision without a Directors' meeting by indicating to each other by any means, including without limitation by Electronic Means, that they share a common view on a matter. Such a decision may, but need not, take the form of a resolution in Writing, copies of which have been signed by each Director or to which each Director has otherwise indicated agreement in Writing.

19.2 A decision which is made in accordance with Article 19.1 shall be as valid and effectual as if it had been passed at a meeting duly convened and held, provided the following conditions are complied with:

(a) approval from each Director must be received by one person being either such person as all the Directors have nominated in advance for that purpose or such other person as volunteers if necessary ("the Recipient"), which person may, for the avoidance of doubt, be one of the Directors;

(b) following receipt of responses from all of the Directors, the Recipient must communicate to all of the Directors by any means whether the resolution has been formally approved by the Directors in accordance with this Article 19.2;

(c) the date of the decision shall be the date of the communication from the Recipient confirming formal approval;

(d) the Recipient must prepare a minute of the decision in accordance with Article 48.

> *Article 19 Analysis*
>
> See analysis of article 8 in **2.11**.

Article 20 Conflicts of interest

5.20

20.1 Whenever a Director finds himself or herself in a situation that is reasonably likely to give rise to a Conflict of Interest, he or she must declare his or her interest to the Directors unless, or except to the extent that, the other Directors are or ought reasonably to be aware of it already.

20.2 If any question arises as to whether a Director has a Conflict of Interest, the question shall be decided by a majority decision of the other Directors.

20.3 Whenever a matter is to be discussed at a meeting or decided in accordance with Article 19 and a Director has a Conflict of Interest in respect of that matter then, subject to Article 21, he or she must:

(a) remain only for such part of the meeting as in the view of the other Directors is necessary to inform the debate;

(b) not be counted in the quorum for that part of the meeting; and

(c) withdraw during the vote and have no vote on the matter.

20.4 When a Director has a Conflict of Interest which he or she has declared to the Directors, he or she shall not be in breach of his or her duties to the Company by withholding confidential information from the Company if to disclose it would result in a breach of any other duty or obligation of confidence owed by him or her.

Article 21 Directors' power to authorise a conflict of interest

5.21

21.1 The Directors have power to authorise a Director to be in a position of Conflict of Interest provided:

(a) in relation to the decision to authorise a Conflict of Interest, the conflicted Director must comply with Article 20.3;

(b) in authorising a Conflict of Interest, the Directors can decide the manner in which the Conflict of Interest may be dealt with and, for the avoidance of doubt, they can decide that the Director with a Conflict of Interest can participate in a vote on the matter and can be counted in the quorum;

(c) he decision to authorise a Conflict of Interest can impose such terms as the Directors think fit and is subject always to their right to vary or terminate the authorisation; and

21.2 If a matter, or office, employment or position, has been authorised by the Directors in accordance with Article 21.1 then, even if he or she has been authorised to remain at the meeting by the other Directors, the Director may absent himself or herself from meetings of the Directors at which anything relating to that matter, or that office, employment or position, will or may be discussed.

21.3. A Director shall not be accountable to the Company for any benefit which he or she derives from any matter, or from any office, employment or position, which has been authorised by the Directors in accordance with Article 21.1 (subject to any limits or conditions to which such approval was subject).

Article 22 Register of Directors' interests

5.22

The Directors shall cause a register of Directors' interests to be kept. A Director must declare the nature and extent of any interest, direct or indirect, which he or she has in a proposed transaction or arrangement with the Company or in any transaction or arrangement entered into by the Company which has not previously been declared.

Articles 20–22 Analysis

See analysis of article 14 in **2.17**.

APPOINTMENT AND RETIREMENT OF DIRECTORS

Article 23 Methods of appointing directors

5.23

23.1 Those persons notified to the Registrar of Companies as the first Directors of the Company shall be the first Directors.

23.2 Any person who is willing to act as a Director, and is permitted by law to do so, may be appointed to be a Director:

(a) by ordinary resolution; or

(b) by a decision of the Directors.

23.3 In any case where, as a result of death, the Company has no members and no Directors, the personal representatives of the last member to have died have the right, by notice in writing, to appoint a person to be a member.

23.4 For the purposes of Article 23.3, where two or more members die in circumstances rendering it uncertain who was the last to die, a younger member is deemed to have survived an older member.

Article 23 Analysis

See analysis of article 17 in **2.20**.

Article 24 Termination of Director's appointment

5.24

A person ceases to be a Director as soon as:

(a) that person ceases to be a Director by virtue of any provision of the Companies Acts, or is prohibited from being a Director by law;

(b) a bankruptcy order is made against that person, or an order is made against that person in individual insolvency proceedings in a jurisdiction other than England and Wales or Northern Ireland which have an effect similar to that of bankruptcy;

(c) a composition is made with that person's creditors generally in satisfaction of that person's debts;

(d) notification is received by the Company from the Director that the Director is resigning from office, and such resignation has taken effect in accordance with its terms (but only if at least two Directors will remain in office when such resignation has taken effect);

(e) the Director fails to attend three consecutive meetings of the Directors and the Directors resolve that the Director be removed for this reason; or

(f) at a general meeting of the Company, a resolution is passed that the Director be removed from office, provided the meeting has invited the views of the Director concerned and considered the matter in the light of such views.

> *Article 24 Analysis*
>
> See analysis of article 18 in **2.21**.

Article 25 Directors' remuneration

5.25

25.1 Directors may undertake any services for the Company that the Directors decide.

25.2 Directors are entitled to such remuneration as the Directors determine:

(a) for their services to the Company as Directors; and

(b) for any other service which they undertake for the Company.

25.3 Subject to the Articles, a Director's remuneration may:

(a) take any form; and

(b) include any arrangements in connection with the payment of a pension, allowance or gratuity, or any death, sickness or disability benefits, to or in respect of that director.

25.4 Unless the Directors decide otherwise, Directors' remuneration accrues from day to day.

25.5 Unless the Directors decide otherwise, Directors are not accountable to the Company for any remuneration which they receive as Directors or other officers or employees of the Company's subsidiaries or of any other body corporate in which the Company is interested.

Article 25 Analysis

As per the provisions of article 25, a CIC may provide remuneration to its directors. The central disparity, in terms of private company limited by guarantee, incorporated under the Companies Act 2006 and using the model articles[10] is the directors have no restrictions or rules to abide by.

The CIC regulator[11] provides the following principles in relation to directors' remuneration:[12]

- Directors may be paid for their services.
- Directors' remuneration should never be more than is reasonable.[13]
- Directors' remuneration arrangements should always be transparent.[14]
- The Regulator – or the members of a CIC – may take action if a CIC director's remuneration appears to be too high.[15]

For further analysis and comparison see article 19 in **2.22**.

Article 26 Directors' expenses

5.26

The Company may pay any reasonable expenses which the Directors properly incur in connection with their attendance at:

(a) meetings of Directors or committees of Directors;

(b) general meetings; or

(c) separate meetings of any class of members or of the holders of any debentures of the Company,

or otherwise in connection with the exercise of their powers and the discharge of their responsibilities in relation to the Company.

Article 26 Analysis

See analysis of article 20 in **2.23**.

10 Schedule 2 Regulation 3 Model articles for private companies limited by guarantee.
11 Office of the Regulator of Community Interest Companies.
12 Office of the Regulator of Community Interest Companies: Information and guidance notes, Chapter 9: Corporate governance, May 2016 (9.3. Directors' remuneration).
13 Reasonable – having regard to the contribution which they make to the success of the company and the benefits it provides for the community (9.3.6. What is 'reasonable' remuneration).
14 All companies are required to keep copies of directors' service contracts, or memoranda of their terms, available at an appropriate place for inspection by their members (9.3.7. Transparency).
15 If the Regulator becomes aware of potentially excessive director remuneration, the Regulator is likely to wish to discuss the matter further with the CIC concerned (9.3.8. Action by the Regulator).

MEMBERS

BECOMING AND CEASING TO BE A MEMBER

Article 27 Becoming a member

5.27

27.1 The subscribers to the Memorandum are the first members of the Company.

27.2 Such other persons as are admitted to membership in accordance with the Articles shall be members of the Company.

27.3 No person shall be admitted a member of the Company unless he or she is approved by the Directors.

27.4 Every person who wishes to become a member shall deliver to the Company an application for membership in such form (and containing such information) as the Directors require and executed by him or her.

> *Article 27 Analysis*
>
> See analysis of article 21 in **2.24**.

Article 28 Termination of membership

5.28

28.1 Membership is not transferable to anyone else.

28.2 Membership is terminated if:

(a) the member dies or ceases to exist;

(b) otherwise in accordance with the Articles; or

(c) at a meeting of the Directors at which at least half of the Directors are present, a resolution is passed resolving that the member be expelled on the ground that his or her continued membership is harmful to or is likely to become harmful to the interests of the Company. Such a resolution may not be passed unless the member has been given at least 14 Clear Days' notice that the resolution is to be proposed, specifying the circumstances alleged to justify expulsion, and has been afforded a reasonable opportunity of being heard by or of making written representations to the Directors. A member expelled by such a resolution will nevertheless remain liable to pay to the Company any subscription or other sum owed by him or her.

Article 28 Analysis

Article 28 expands the basic provisions of article 22 of the model articles. It should be noted section (c) could lead to misunderstanding and lacks clarity around the provisions. In particular: how is the board to define the term harmful? In what manner is the 14 days' notice to be issued? Does the 14 days begin on receipt or the board resolution?

The option of being heard presents the board with the challenge of offering the member the support of a friend or family and in certain instances legal representation. Although not stated, the assumption is the member has no right to appeal.

For further analysis see article 22 in **2.25**.

ORGANISATION OF GENERAL MEETINGS

Article 29 General meetings

5.29

29.1 The Directors may call a general meeting at any time.

29.2 The Directors must call a general meeting if required to do so by the members under the Companies Acts.

Article 30 Length of notice

5.30

All general meetings must be called by either:

30.1 at least 14 Clear Days' notice; or

30.2 shorter notice if it is so agreed by [a majority of the members having a right to attend and vote at that meeting. Any such majority must together represent at least [90%] of the total voting rights at that meeting of all the members].

Article 31 Contents of notice

5.31

31.1 Every notice calling a general meeting must specify the place, day and time of the meeting, whether it is a general or an annual general meeting, and the general nature of the business to be transacted.

31.2 If a special resolution is to be proposed, the notice must include the proposed resolution and specify that it is proposed as a special resolution.

31.3 In every notice calling a meeting of the Company there must appear with reasonable prominence a statement informing the member of his or her rights to appoint another person as his or her proxy at a general meeting.

Article 32 Service of notice

5.32

Notice of general meetings must be given to every member, to the Directors and to the auditors of the Company.

Articles 29–32 Analysis

Articles 29–32 do not appear in the Model Articles for Private Companies Limited by Guarantee. Provision 29.1 refers to sections 302[16] and 303[17] which allow the directors to call a general meeting and allow the members to require the directors to call a general meeting.

The company is required by section 307(2)(a) to provide 14 days' notice, the Act[18] allows a shorter period if by majority of 90% or higher (not exceeding 95%) agrees, the articles may in addition specify the requisite percentage required.[19]

Article 31 reiterates the provisions of the Companies Act 2006 section 311,[20] article 32.1 simplifies section 310[21] of the Companies Act 2006. It should be noted the condition to provide notice to the company's auditors is not required by statute.

Article 33 Attendance and speaking at general meetings

5.33

33.1 A person is able to exercise the right to speak at a general meeting when that person is in a position to communicate to all those attending the meeting, during the meeting, any information or opinions which that person has on the business of the meeting.

16 Companies Act 2006, s 302 (Directors' power to call general meetings).
17 Companies Act 2006, s 303 (Members' power to require directors to call general meeting).
18 Companies Act 2006.
19 Companies Act 2006, s 307(6)(a) (Notice required of general meeting).
20 Companies Act 2006, s 311 (Contents of notice of meetings).
21 Companies Act 2006, s 310 (Persons entitled to receive notice of meetings).

33.2 A person is able to exercise the right to vote at a general meeting when:

(a) that person is able to vote, during the meeting, on resolutions put to the vote at the meeting; and

(b) that person's vote can be taken into account in determining whether or not such resolutions are passed at the same time as the votes of all the other persons attending the meeting.

33.3 The Directors may make whatever arrangements they consider appropriate to enable those attending a general meeting to exercise their rights to speak or vote at it.

33.4 In determining attendance at a general meeting, it is immaterial whether any two or more members attending it are in the same place as each other.

33.5 Two or more persons who are not in the same place as each other attend a general meeting if their circumstances are such that if they have (or were to have) rights to speak and vote at that meeting, they are (or would be) able to exercise them.

Article 33 Analysis

See analysis of article 23 in **2.26**.

Article 34 Quorum for general meetings

5.34

34.1 No business (other than the appointment of the chair of the meeting) may be transacted at any general meeting unless a quorum is present.

34.2 Two persons entitled to vote on the business to be transacted (each being a member, a proxy for a member or a duly Authorised Representative of a member); or 10% of the total membership (represented in person or by proxy), whichever is greater, shall be a quorum.

34.3 If a quorum is not present within half an hour from the time appointed for the meeting, the meeting shall stand adjourned to the same day in the next week at the same time and place, or to such time and place as the Directors may determine, and if at the adjourned meeting a quorum is not present within half an hour from the time appointed for the meeting those present and entitled to vote shall be a quorum.

Article 34 Analysis

See analysis of article 24 in **2.27**.

Article 35 Chairing general meetings

5.35

35.1 The chair (if any) or in his or her absence some other Director nominated by the Directors will preside as chair of every general meeting.

35.2 If neither the chair nor such other Director nominated in accordance with Article 35.1 (if any) is present within fifteen minutes after the time appointed for holding the meeting and willing to act, the Directors present shall elect one of their number to chair the meeting and, if there is only one Director present and willing to act, he or she shall be chair of the meeting.

35.3 If no Director is willing to act as chair of the meeting, or if no Director is present within fifteen minutes after the time appointed for holding the meeting, the members present in person or by proxy and entitled to vote must choose one of their number to be chair of the meeting, save that a proxy holder who is not a member entitled to vote shall not be entitled to be appointed chair of the meeting.

Article 35 Analysis

See analysis of article 25 in **2.28**.

Article 36 Attendance and speaking by Directors and non-members

5.36

36.1 A Director may, even if not a member, attend and speak at any general meeting.

36.2 The chair of the meeting may permit other persons who are not members of the Company to attend and speak at a general meeting.

Article 36 Analysis

See analysis of article 26 in **2.29**.

Article 37 Adjournment

5.37

37.1 The chair of the meeting may adjourn a general meeting at which a quorum is present if:

(a) the meeting consents to an adjournment; or

(b) it appears to the chair of the meeting that an adjournment is necessary to protect the safety of any person attending the meeting or ensure that the business of the meeting is conducted in an orderly manner.

37.2 The chair of the meeting must adjourn a general meeting if directed to do so by the meeting.

37.3 When adjourning a general meeting, the chair of the meeting must:

(a) either specify the time and place to which it is adjourned or state that it is to continue at a time and place to be fixed by the Directors; and

(b) have regard to any directions as to the time and place of any adjournment which have been given by the meeting.

37.4 If the continuation of an adjourned meeting is to take place more than 14 days after it was adjourned, the Company must give at least seven Clear Days' notice of it:

(a) to the same persons to whom notice of the Company's general meetings is required to be given; and

(b) containing the same information which such notice is required to contain.

37.5 No business may be transacted at an adjourned general meeting which could not properly have been transacted at the meeting if the adjournment had not taken place.

> *Article 37 Analysis*
>
> See analysis of article 27 in **2.30**.

VOTING AT GENERAL MEETINGS

Article 38 Voting: general

5.38

38.1 A resolution put to the vote of a general meeting must be decided on a show of hands unless a poll is duly demanded in accordance with the Articles.

38.2 A person who is not a member of the Company shall not have any right to vote at a general meeting of the Company; but this is without prejudice to any right to vote on a resolution affecting the rights attached to a class of the Company's debentures.

38.3 Article 38.2 shall not prevent a person who is a proxy for a member or a duly Authorised Representative from voting at a general meeting of the Company.

Article 38 Analysis

See analysis of article 28 in **2.31**.

Article 39 Votes

5.39

39.1 On a vote on a resolution on a show of hands at a meeting every person present in person (whether a member, proxy or Authorised Representative of a member) and entitled to vote shall have a maximum of one vote.

39.2 On a vote on a resolution on a poll at a meeting every member present in person or by proxy or Authorised Representative shall have one vote.

39.3 In the case of an equality of votes, whether on a show of hands or on a poll, the chair of the meeting shall not be entitled to a casting vote in addition to any other vote he or she may have.

39.4 No member shall be entitled to vote at any general meeting unless all monies presently payable by him, her or it to the Company have been paid.

39.5 The following provisions apply to any organisation that is a member ("a Member Organisation"):

(a) a Member Organisation may nominate any individual to act as its representative ("an Authorised Representative") at any meeting of the Company;

(b) the Member Organisation must give notice in Writing to the Company of the name of its Authorised Representative. The Authorised Representative will not be entitled to represent the Member Organisation at any meeting of the Company unless such notice has been received by the Company. The Authorised Representative may continue to represent the Member Organisation until notice in Writing is received by the Company to the contrary;

(c) a Member Organisation may appoint an Authorised Representative to represent it at a particular meeting of the Company or at all meetings of the Company until notice in Writing to the contrary is received by the Company;

(d) any notice in Writing received by the Company shall be conclusive evidence of the Authorised Representative's authority to represent the Member Organisation or that his or her authority has been revoked. The Company shall not be required to consider whether the Authorised Representative has been properly appointed by the Member Organisation;

(e) an individual appointed by a Member Organisation to act as its Authorised Representative is entitled to exercise (on behalf of the Member Organisation) the same powers as the Member Organisation could exercise if it were an individual member;

(f) on a vote on a resolution at a meeting of the Company, the Authorised Representative has the same voting rights as the Member Organisation would be entitled to if it was an individual member present in person at the meeting; and

(g) the power to appoint an Authorised Representative under this Article 39.5 is without prejudice to any rights which the Member Organisation has under the Companies Acts and the Articles to appoint a proxy or a corporate representative.

Article 39 Analysis

See analysis of article 28 in **2.31**.

Article 40 Poll votes

5.40

40.1 A poll on a resolution may be demanded:

(a) in advance of the general meeting where it is to be put to the vote; or

(b) at a general meeting, either before a show of hands on that resolution or immediately after the result of a show of hands on that resolution is declared.

40.2 A poll may be demanded by:

(a) the chair of the meeting;

(b) the Directors;

(c) two or more persons having the right to vote on the resolution;

(d) any person, who, by virtue of being appointed proxy for one or more members having the right to vote at the meeting, holds two or more votes; or

(e) a person or persons representing not less than one tenth of the total voting rights of all the members having the right to vote on the resolution.

40.3 A demand for a poll may be withdrawn if:

(a) the poll has not yet been taken; and

(b) the chair of the meeting consents to the withdrawal.

40.4 Polls must be taken immediately and in such manner as the chair of the meeting directs.

Article 40 Analysis

See analysis of article 30 in **2.33**.

Article 41 Errors and disputes

5.41

41.1 No objection may be raised to the qualification of any person voting at a general meeting except at the meeting or adjourned meeting at which the vote objected to is tendered, and every vote not disallowed at the meeting is valid.

41.2 Any such objection must be referred to the chair of the meeting whose decision is final.

Article 41 Analysis

See analysis of article 29 in **2.32**.

Article 42 Content of proxy notices

5.42

42.1 Proxies may only validly be appointed by a notice in writing (a "Proxy Notice") which:

(a) states the name and address of the member appointing the proxy;

(b) identifies the person appointed to be that member's proxy and the general meeting in relation to which that person is appointed;

(c) is signed by or on behalf of the member appointing the proxy, or is authenticated in such manner as the directors may determine; and

(d) is delivered to the Company in accordance with the Articles and any instructions contained in the notice of the general meeting to which they relate.

42.2 The Company may require Proxy Notices to be delivered in a particular form, and may specify different forms for different purposes.

42.3 Proxy Notices may specify how the proxy appointed under them is to vote (or that the proxy is to abstain from voting) on one or more resolutions.

42.4 Unless a Proxy Notice indicates otherwise, it must be treated as:

(a) allowing the person appointed under it as a proxy discretion as to how to vote on any ancillary or procedural resolutions put to the meeting; and

(b) appointing that person as a proxy in relation to any adjournment of the general meeting to which it relates as well as the meeting itself.

Article 42 Analysis

See analysis of article 31 in **2.34**.

Article 43 Delivery of proxy notices

5.43

43.1 A person who is entitled to attend, speak or vote (either on a show of hands or on a poll) at a general meeting remains so entitled in respect of that meeting or any adjournment of it, even though a valid Proxy Notice has been delivered to the Company by or on behalf of that person.

43.2 An appointment under a Proxy Notice may be revoked by delivering to the Company a notice in Writing given by or on behalf of the person by whom or on whose behalf the Proxy Notice was given.

43.3 A notice revoking the appointment of a proxy only takes effect if it is delivered before the start of the meeting or adjourned meeting to which it relates.

Article 43 Analysis

See analysis of article 32 in **2.35**.

Article 44 Amendments to resolutions

5.44

44.1 An ordinary resolution to be proposed at a general meeting may be amended by ordinary resolution if:

(a) notice of the proposed amendment is given to the Company in Writing by a person entitled to vote at the general meeting at which it is to be proposed not less than 48 hours before the meeting is to take place (or such later time as the chair of the meeting may determine); and

(b) the proposed amendment does not, in the reasonable opinion of the chair of the meeting, materially alter the scope of the resolution.

44.2 A special resolution to be proposed at a general meeting may be amended by ordinary resolution, if:

(a) the chair of the meeting proposes the amendment at the general meeting at which the resolution is to be proposed; and

(b) the amendment does not go beyond what is necessary to correct a grammatical or other non-substantive error in the resolution.

44.3 If the chair of the meeting, acting in good faith, wrongly decides that an amendment to a resolution is out of order, the chair's error does not invalidate the vote on that resolution.

Article 44 Analysis

See analysis of article 33 in **2.36**.

WRITTEN RESOLUTIONS

Article 45 Written resolutions

5.45

45.1 Subject to Article 44.3, a written resolution of the Company passed in accordance with this Article 44 shall have effect as if passed by the Company in general meeting:

(a) A written resolution is passed as an ordinary resolution if it is passed by a simple majority of the total voting rights of eligible members.

(b) A written resolution is passed as a special resolution if it is passed by members representing not less than 75% of the total voting rights of eligible members. A written resolution is not a special resolution unless it states that it was proposed as a special resolution.

45.2 In relation to a resolution proposed as a written resolution of the Company the eligible members are the members who would have been entitled to vote on the resolution on the circulation date of the resolution.

45.3 A members' resolution under the Companies Acts removing a Director or an auditor before the expiration of his or her term of office may not be passed as a written resolution.

45.4 A copy of the written resolution must be sent to every member together with a statement informing the member how to signify their agreement to the resolution and the date by which the resolution must be passed if it is not to lapse. Communications in relation to written notices shall be sent to the Company's auditors in accordance with the Companies Acts.

45.5 A member signifies their agreement to a proposed written resolution when the Company receives from him or her an authenticated Document identifying the resolution to which it relates and indicating his or her agreement to the resolution.

(a) If the Document is sent to the Company in Hard Copy Form, it is authenticated if it bears the member's signature.

(b) If the Document is sent to the Company by Electronic Means, it is authenticated [if it bears the member's signature] or [if the identity of the member is confirmed in a manner agreed by the Directors] or [if it is accompanied by a statement of the identity of the member and the Company has no reason to doubt the truth of that statement] or [if it is from an email Address notified by the member to the Company for the purposes of receiving Documents or information by Electronic Means].

45.6 A written resolution is passed when the required majority of eligible members have signified their agreement to it.

45.7 A proposed written resolution lapses if it is not passed within 28 days beginning with the circulation date.

Article 45 Analysis

Article 45 does not appear in any versions of the new model articles, under the Companies Act 2006.

The provisions outline the requirements of section 288[22] as detailed in article 45.1 to pass a written resolution.

A written resolution, which may take the form of an ordinary or special resolution, is proposed and passed in writing, as opposed to a more traditional general meeting where each member votes.

All decisions in a private limited company can be dealt with by written resolution, with the exception of the removal of a director as stipulated by

22 Companies Act 2006, s 288 (Written resolutions of private companies).

article 45.3 which provides that a written resolution may not be passed to remove a director before his expiration of period of office.[23] Article 45.7 reiterates section 297,[24] if it is not passed within 28 days beginning with the circulation date, it shall lapse.

ADMINISTRATIVE ARRANGEMENTS AND MISCELLANEOUS

Article 46 Means of communication to be used

5.46

46.1 Subject to the Articles, anything sent or supplied by or to the Company under the Articles may be sent or supplied in any way in which the Companies Act 2006 provides for Documents or information which are authorised or required by any provision of that Act to be sent or supplied by or to the Company.

46.2 Subject to the Articles, any notice or Document to be sent or supplied to a Director in connection with the taking of decisions by Directors may also be sent or supplied by the means by which that Director has asked to be sent or supplied with such notices or Documents for the time being.

46.3 A Director may agree with the Company that notices or Documents sent to that Director in a particular way are to be deemed to have been received within an agreed time of their being sent, and for the agreed time to be less than 48 hours.

Article 46 Analysis

See analysis of article 34 in **2.37**.

Article 47 Irregularities

5.47

The proceedings at any meeting or on the taking of any poll or the passing of a written resolution or the making of any decision shall not be invalidated by reason of any accidental informality or irregularity (including any accidental omission to give or any non-receipt of notice) or any want of qualification in any of the persons present or voting or by reason of any business being considered which is not referred to in the notice unless a provision of the Companies Acts specifies that such informality, irregularity or want of qualification shall invalidate it.

23 Companies Act 2006, s 288(2)(a) (Written resolutions of private companies).
24 Companies Act 2006, s 297 (Period for agreeing to written resolution).

> *Article 47 Analysis*
>
> This article does not appear in any versions of the new model articles.

Article 48 Minutes

5.48

48.1 The Directors must cause minutes to be made in books kept for the purpose:

(a) of all appointments of officers made by the Directors;

(b) of all resolutions of the Company and of the Directors; and

(c) of all proceedings at meetings of the Company and of the Directors, and of committees of Directors, including the names of the Directors present at each such meeting;

and any such minute, if purported to be signed (or in the case of minutes of Directors' meetings signed or authenticated) by the chair of the meeting at which the proceedings were had, or by the chair of the next succeeding meeting, shall, as against any member or Director of the Company, be sufficient evidence of the proceedings.

48.2 The minutes must be kept for at least ten years from the date of the meeting, resolution or decision.

> *Article 48 Analysis*
>
> Article 48 restates section 248[25] detailing the company's requirements to cause minutes to be recorded and kept for a period of no less than 10 years. It should be noted, failure to record minutes is a criminal offence.
>
> This article does not appear in any versions of the new model articles.

Article 49 Records and accounts

5.49

The Directors shall comply with the requirements of the Companies Acts as to maintaining a members' register, keeping financial records, the audit or

25 Companies Act 2006, s 248 (Minutes of directors' meetings).

examination of accounts and the preparation and transmission to the Registrar of Companies and the Regulator of:

49.1 annual reports;

49.2 annual returns; and

49.3 annual statements of account.

> *Article 49 Analysis*
>
> Article 49 provides an overview of section 386[26] which states any company must keep adequate accounting records.
>
> This article does not appear in any versions of the new model articles.

Article 50 Indemnity

5.50

50.1 Subject to Article 49.2 a relevant Director of the Company or an associated company may be indemnified out of the Company's assets against:

(a) any liability incurred by that Director in connection with any negligence, default, breach of duty or breach of trust in relation to the Company or an associated company;

(b) any liability incurred by that Director in connection with the activities of the Company or an associated company in its capacity as a trustee of an occupational pension scheme (as defined in section 235(6) of the Companies Act 2006); and

(c) any other liability incurred by that Director as an officer of the Company or an associated company.

50.2 This Article does not authorise any indemnity which would be prohibited or rendered void by any provision of the Companies Acts or by any other provision of law.

50.3 In this Article:

(a) companies are associated if one is a subsidiary of the other or both are subsidiaries of the same body corporate; and

(b) a "relevant Director" means any Director or former Director of the Company or an associated company.

26 Companies Act 2006, s 386 (Duty to keep accounting records).

Article 51 Insurance

5.51

51.1 The Directors may decide to purchase and maintain insurance, at the expense of the Company, for the benefit of any relevant Director in respect of any relevant loss.

51.2 In this Article:

(a) a "relevant Director" means any Director or former Director of the Company or an associated company;

(b) a "relevant loss" means any loss or liability which has been or may be incurred by a relevant Director in connection with that Director's duties or powers in relation to the Company, any associated company or any pension fund or employees' share scheme of the company or associated company; and

(c) companies are associated if one is a subsidiary of the other or both are subsidiaries of the same body corporate.

> *Articles 50 and 51 Analysis*
>
> See analysis of articles 38 and 39 in **2.42**.

CIC Limited by Shares, Schedule 2, Large Membership

INTERPRETATION

Article 1 Defined terms

5.52

1. In the Articles, unless the context requires otherwise, the following terms shall have the following meanings:

Term	**Meaning**
"Address"	includes a number or address used for the purposes of sending or receiving Documents by Electronic Means;
"Articles"	means the Company's articles of association;

Term	Meaning
"asset-locked body"	means (i) a community interest Company or a charity or a Permitted Society; or (ii) a body established outside the United Kingdom that is equivalent to any of those;
"Authorised Representative"	means any individual nominated by a Shareholder Organisation to act as its representative at any meeting of the Company in accordance with Article 53;
"bankruptcy"	includes individual insolvency proceedings in a jurisdiction other than England and Wales or Northern Ireland which have an effect similar to that of bankruptcy;
"Chair"	has the meaning given in Article 10;
"chairman of the meeting"	has the meaning given in Article 50;
"Circulation Date"	in relation to a written resolution, has the meaning given to it in the Companies Acts;
"Clear Days"	in relation to the period of a notice, that period excluding the day when the notice is given or deemed to be given and the day for which it is given or on which it is to take effect;
"community"	is to be construed in accordance with the section 35(5) of the Companies (Audit, Investigations and Community Enterprise) Act 2004;
"Companies Acts"	means the Companies Acts (as defined in section 2 of the Companies Act 2006), in so far as they apply to the Company;
"Company"	[Community Interest Company/C.I.C.];
"Conflict of Interest"	any direct or indirect interest of a Director (whether personal, by virtue of a duty of loyalty to another organisation or otherwise) that conflicts or might conflict with the interests of the Company;
"Director"	means a director of the Company, and includes any person occupying the position of director, by whatever name called;
"distribution recipient"	has the meaning given in Article 38;
"Document"	includes, unless otherwise indicated, any document sent or supplied in Electronic Form;

Term	Meaning
"Electronic Form and Electronic Means"	have the meanings respectively given to them in section 1168 of the Companies Act 2006;
"fully paid"	in relation to a share, means that the nominal value and any premium to be paid to the Company in respect of that share have been paid to the Company;
"Hard Copy Form"	has the meaning given in section 1168 of the Companies Act 2006;
"holder"	in relation to shares means the person whose name is entered in the register of shareholders as the holder of the shares;
"instrument"	means a Document in Hard Copy Form;
"Memorandum"	the Company's memorandum of association;
"paid"	means paid or credited as paid;
"participate"	in relation to a Directors' meeting, has the meaning given in Article 15;
"Permitted Registered Society"	Means: A registered society within the meaning given by section 1(1) of the Co-operative and Community Benefit Societies Act 2014; or A society registered or deemed to be registered under the Industrial and Provident Societies Act (Northern Ireland) 1969;
"Proxy Notice"	has the meaning given in Article 56;
"the Regulator"	means the Regulator of Community Interest Companies;
"the Regulations"	means the Community Interest Company Regulations 2005 (as amended);
"Secretary"	the secretary of the Company (if any);
"shareholder"	means a person who is the holder of a share;
"shares"	means shares in the Company;
"specified"	means specified in the articles of association of the Company for the purposes of this paragraph;
"subsidiary"	has the meaning given in section 1159 of the Companies Act 2006;
"transfer"	includes every description of disposition, payment, release or distribution, and the creation or extinction of an estate or interest in, or right over, any property;

Term	Meaning
"transmittee"	means a person entitled to a share by reason of the death or bankruptcy of a shareholder or otherwise by operation of law; and
"Writing"	means the representation or reproduction of words, symbols or other information in a visible form by any method or combination of methods, whether sent or supplied in Electronic Form or otherwise.

2. Subject to clause 3 of this Schedule, any reference in the Articles to an enactment includes a reference to that enactment as re-enacted or amended from time to time and to any subordinate legislation made under it.

3. Unless the context otherwise requires, other words or expressions contained in these Articles bear the same meaning as in the Companies Act 2006 as in force on the date when the Articles become binding on the Company.

Exclusion of model articles

The relevant model articles for a company limited by guarantee are hereby expressly excluded.

Article 1 Analysis

In the model articles[27] article 1, the defined terms appear at the end of the document, for comparison to the new model articles, this section has been transferred to the front of the articles.

Provision 3.1 which excludes the model articles for a private company limited by guarantee[28] appears in article 52 of the model articles,[29] in order to explicitly state the exclusion, it is good practice to provide the provision at the beginning of the document and specifically refer to the model articles regulations. It should be noted for companies incorporated under previous Companies Acts, the relevant articles should be expressed and excluded.

Alternative precedent

The model articles for private companies limited by guarantee contained or incorporated in Schedule 1 to the Companies (Model Articles) Regulations 2008, SI 2008/3229 as amended prior to the date of adoption of these articles (the 'Model Articles') shall not apply to the Company, save insofar as they are varied or excluded by, or are inconsistent with, the following articles.

27 CIC Limited by Guarantee, Schedule 1, Large Membership.
28 Schedule 2 Regulation 3 Model articles for private companies limited by guarantee.
29 CIC Limited by Guarantee, Schedule 1, Large Membership.

COMMUNITY INTEREST COMPANY AND ASSET LOCK

Article 2 Community Interest Company

5.53

The Company shall be a community interest company.

Article 2 Analysis
See analysis of article 2 in **5.2**.

Article 3 Asset Lock[30]

5.54

3.1 The Company shall not transfer any of its assets other than for full consideration.

3.2 Provided the conditions in Article 3.3 are satisfied, Article 3.1 shall not apply to:

(a) the transfer of assets to any specified asset-locked body, or (with the consent of the Regulator) to any other asset-locked body; and

(b) the transfer of assets made for the benefit of the community other than by way of a transfer of assets into an asset-locked body.

3.3 The conditions are that the transfer of assets must comply with any restrictions on the transfer of assets for less than full consideration which may be set out elsewhere in the Memorandum or Articles of the Company.

3.4 If the Company is wound up under the Insolvency Act 1986; and all its liabilities have been satisfied any residual assets shall be given or transferred to the asset-locked body specified in Article 3.5 below.

3.5 For the purposes of this Article 3, the following asset-locked body is specified as a potential recipient of the Company's assets under Articles 3.2 and 3.4:

Asset Locked Body Name

Charity Registration Number (if applicable): [ ]

30 Mandatory provision. The Community Interest Company Regulations 2005, SI 2005/1788, Schedule 2, Provisions prescribed for the memorandum or articles of a community interest company limited by shares, or limited by guarantee with a share capital.

Company Registration Number (if applicable): [ ]

Registered Office: [ ]

> *Article 3 Analysis*
>
> See analysis of article 3 in **5.3**.

Article 4 Not for profit

5.55

The Company is not established or conducted for private gain: any surplus or assets are used principally for the benefit of the community.

> *Article 4 Analysis*
>
> See analysis of article 4 in **5.4**.

OBJECTS, POWERS AND LIMITATION OF LIABILITY

Article 5 Objects

5.56

The objects of the Company are to carry on activities which benefit the community and in particular (without limitation) to: [insert here].

> *Article 5 Analysis*
>
> See analysis of article 5 in **5.5**.

Article 6 Powers

5.57

To further its objects the Company may do all such lawful things as may further the Company's objects and, in particular, but, without limitation, may borrow or raise and secure the payment of money for any purpose including for the purposes of investment or of raising funds.

> *Article 6 Analysis*
>
> See analysis of article 6 in **5.6**.

Article 7 Liability of shareholders

5.58

The liability of the shareholders is limited to the amount, if any, unpaid on the shares held by them.

> *Article 7 Analysis*
>
> Article 7 previously appeared in the old style memorandum of association and defines the liability for the members. The provision must not be altered or omitted, its inclusion means once all shares are fully paid up, the shareholders have no further liability.
>
> Article 7 corresponds with the new model articles for private companies limited by shares.[31]

DIRECTORS

DIRECTORS' POWERS AND RESPONSIBILITIES

Article 8 Directors' general authority

5.59

Subject to the Articles, the Directors are responsible for the management of the Company's business, for which purpose they may exercise all the powers of the Company.

> *Article 8 Analysis*
>
> See analysis of article 3 in **2.6**.

Article 9 Shareholders[32] *reserve power*

5.60

9.1 The shareholders may, by special resolution, direct the Directors to take, or refrain from taking, specific action.

31 Schedule 1 Regulation 2 Model articles for private companies limited by shares.

32 'Shareholders' replaces 'members'.

9.2 No such special resolution invalidates anything which the Directors have done before the passing of the resolution.

> *Article 9 Analysis*
>
> See analysis of article 4 in **2.7**.

Article 10 Chair

5.61

The Directors may appoint one of their number to be the chair of the Directors for such term of office as they may determine and may at any time remove him or her from office.

> *Article 10 Analysis*
>
> See analysis of article 12 in **2.15**.

Article 11 Directors may delegate

5.62

11.1 Subject to the Articles, the Directors may delegate any of the powers which are conferred on them under the Articles:

(a) to such person or committee;

(b) by such means (including by power of attorney);

(c) to such an extent;

(d) in relation to such matters or territories; and

(e) on such terms and conditions;

as they think fit.

11.2 If the Directors so specify, any such delegation may authorise further delegation of the Directors' powers by any person to whom they are delegated.

11.3 The Directors may revoke any delegation in whole or part, or alter its terms and conditions.

> *Article 11 Analysis*
>
> See analysis of article 5 in **2.8**.

Article 12 Committees

5.63

12.1 Committees to which the Directors delegate any of their powers must follow procedures which are based as far as they are applicable on those provisions of the Articles which govern the taking of decisions by Directors.

12.2 The Directors may make rules of procedure for all or any committees, which prevail over rules derived from the Articles if they are not consistent with them.

> *Article 12 Analysis*
>
> See analysis of article 6 in **2.9**.

DECISION-MAKING BY DIRECTORS

Article 13 Directors to take decisions collectively

5.64

Any decision of the Directors must be either a majority decision at a meeting or a decision taken in accordance with Article 19.

> *Article 13 Analysis*
>
> See analysis of article 7 in **2.10**.

Article 14 Calling a Directors' meeting

5.65

14.1 Two Directors may (and the Secretary, if any, must at the request of two Directors) call a Directors' meeting.

14.2 A Directors' meeting must be called by at least seven Clear Days' notice unless either all the Directors agree; or urgent circumstances require shorter notice.

14.3 Notice of Directors' meetings must be given to each Director.

14.4 Every notice calling a Directors' meeting must specify: the place, day and time of the meeting; and if it is anticipated that Directors participating in the meeting will not be in the same place, how it is proposed that they should communicate with each other during the meeting.

14.5 Notice of Directors' meetings need not be in Writing.

14.6 Notice of Directors' meetings may be sent by Electronic Means to an Address provided by the Director for the purpose.

Article 14 Analysis

Article 14.1 requires two directors to call a meeting as opposed to 'any' director in the model articles.[33]

See analysis of article 9 in **2.12**.

Article 15 Participation in Directors' meetings

5.66

15.1 Subject to the Articles, Directors participate in a Directors' meeting, or part of a Directors' meeting, when:

(a) the meeting has been called and takes place in accordance with the Articles; and

(b) they can each communicate to the others any information or opinions they have on any particular item of the business of the meeting.

15.2 In determining whether Directors are participating in a Directors' meeting, it is irrelevant where any Director is or how they communicate with each other.

15.3 If all the Directors participating in a meeting are not in the same place, they may decide that the meeting is to be treated as taking place wherever any of them is.

Article 15 Analysis

See analysis of article 10 in **2.13**.

Article 16 Quorum for Directors' meetings

5.67

16.1 At a Directors' meeting, unless a quorum is participating, no proposal is to be voted on, except a proposal to call another meeting.

33 Schedule 2 Regulation 3 Model articles for private companies limited by guarantee.

16.2 The quorum for Directors' meetings may be fixed from time to time by a decision of the Directors, but it must never be less than two, and unless otherwise fixed it is [two].

16.3 If the total number of Directors for the time being is less than the quorum required, the Directors must not take any decision other than a decision:

(a) to appoint further Directors; or

(b) to call a general meeting so as to enable the shareholders to appoint further Directors.

> *Article 16 Analysis*
>
> See analysis of article 11 in **2.14**.

Article 17 Chairing of Directors' meetings

5.68

The chair, if any, or in his or her absence another Director nominated by the Directors present shall preside as chair of each Directors' meeting.

> *Article 17 Analysis*
>
> See analysis of article 12 in **2.15**.

Article 18 Voting

5.69

18.1 Questions arising at a Directors' meeting shall be decided by a majority of votes.

18.2 In all proceedings of Directors each director must not have more than one vote.[34]

18.3 In case of an equality of votes, the chair shall have a second or casting vote.

> *Article 18 Analysis*
>
> Article 18 reflects paragraph 4 of Schedule 2 to the Regulations, which is mandatory to include in the articles of all community interest companies.

34 Mandatory provision. The Community Interest Company Regulations 2005, SI 2005/1788, Schedule 2, Provisions prescribed for the memorandum or articles of a community interest company limited by shares, or limited by guarantee with a share capital.

Article 18.3 is optional, which allows the chair a casting vote. the ability of the chair to cast a further vote may prevent the deadlocking of the board. Depending on the extent of the board, the casting vote ought not to provide continual bias or the balance of power being abused.

Article 19 Decisions without a meeting

5.70

19.1 The Directors may take a unanimous decision without a Directors' meeting by indicating to each other by any means, including without limitation by Electronic Means, that they share a common view on a matter. Such a decision may, but need not, take the form of a resolution in Writing, copies of which have been signed by each Director or to which each Director has otherwise indicated agreement in Writing.

19.2 A decision which is made in accordance with Article 19.1 shall be as valid and effectual as if it had been passed at a meeting duly convened and held, provided the following conditions are complied with:

(a) approval from each Director must be received by one person being either such person as all the Directors have nominated in advance for that purpose or such other person as volunteers if necessary ("the Recipient"), which person may, for the avoidance of doubt, be one of the Directors;

(b) following receipt of responses from all of the Directors, the Recipient must communicate to all of the Directors by any means whether the resolution has been formally approved by the Directors in accordance with this Article 19.2;

(c) the date of the decision shall be the date of the communication from the Recipient confirming formal approval;

(d) the Recipient must prepare a minute of the decision in accordance with Article 62.

Article 19 Analysis

See analysis of article 8 in **2.11**.

Article 20 Conflicts of interest

5.71

20.1 Whenever a Director finds himself or herself in a situation that is reasonably likely to give rise to a Conflict of Interest, he or she must declare his or her interest to the Directors unless, or except to the extent that, the other Directors are or ought reasonably to be aware of it already.

20.2 Whenever a matter is to be discussed at a meeting or decided in accordance with Article 19 and a Director has a Conflict of Interest in respect of that matter then, subject to Article 21, he or she must:

(a) remain only for such part of the meeting as in the view of the other Directors is necessary to inform the debate;

(b) not be counted in the quorum for that part of the meeting; and

(c) withdraw during the vote and have no vote on the matter.

20.3 If any question arises as to whether a Director has a Conflict of Interest, the question shall be decided by a majority decision of the other Directors.

20.4 When a Director has a Conflict of Interest which he or she has declared to the Directors, he or she shall not be in breach of his or her duties to the Company by withholding confidential information from the Company if to disclose it would result in a breach of any other duty or obligation of confidence owed by him or her.

Article 21 Directors' power to authorise a conflict of interest

5.72

21.1 The Directors have power to authorise a Director to be in a position of Conflict of Interest provided:

(a) in relation to the decision to authorise a Conflict of Interest, the conflicted Director must comply with Article 20.3;

(b) in authorising a Conflict of Interest, the Directors can decide the manner in which the Conflict of Interest may be dealt with and, for the avoidance of doubt, they can decide that the Director with a Conflict of Interest can participate in a vote on the matter and can be counted in the quorum;

(c) the decision to authorise a Conflict of Interest can impose such terms as the Trustees think fit and is subject always to their right to vary or terminate the authorisation; and

21.2 If a matter, or office, employment or position, has been authorised by the Directors in accordance with Article 21.1 then, even if he or she has been authorised to remain at the meeting by the other Directors, the Director may absent himself or herself from meetings of the Directors at which anything relating to that matter, or that office, employment or position, will or may be discussed.

21.3 A Director shall not be accountable to the Company for any benefit which he or she derives from any matter, or from any office, employment or position, which has been authorised by the Directors in accordance with Article 21.1 (subject to any limits or conditions to which such approval was subject).

Article 22 Register of Directors' interests

5.73

The Directors shall cause a register of Directors' interests to be kept. A Director must declare the nature and extent of any interest, direct or indirect, which he or she has in a proposed transaction or arrangement with the Company or in any transaction or arrangement entered into by the Company which has not previously been declared.

> *Articles 20–22 Analysis*
>
> See analysis of article 14 in **2.17**.

APPOINTMENT AND RETIREMENT OF DIRECTORS

Article 23 Methods of appointing Directors

5.74

23.1 Those persons notified to the Registrar of Companies as the first Directors of the Company shall be the first Directors.

23.2 Any person who is willing to act as a Director, and is permitted by law to do so, may be appointed to be a Director:

(a) by ordinary resolution; or

(b) by a decision of the Directors.

23.3 In any case where, as a result of death, the Company has no shareholders and no Directors, the personal representatives of the last shareholder to have died have the right, by notice in Writing, to appoint a person to be a Director.

23.4 For the purposes of Article 23.3, where 2 or more shareholders die in circumstances rendering it uncertain who was the last to die, a younger shareholder is deemed to have survived an older shareholder.

> *Article 23 Analysis*
>
> See analysis of article 17 in **2.20**.

Article 24 Termination of director's appointment

5.75

A person ceases to be a Director as soon as:

(a) that person ceases to be a Director by virtue of any provision of the Companies Act 2006, or is prohibited from being a Director by law;

(b) a bankruptcy order is made against that person, or an order is made against that person in individual insolvency proceedings in a jurisdiction other than England and Wales or Northern Ireland which have an effect similar to that of bankruptcy;

(c) a composition is made with that person's creditors generally in satisfaction of that person's debts;

(d) notification is received by the Company from the Director that the Director is resigning from office, and such resignation has taken effect in accordance with its terms (but only if at least two Directors will remain in office when such resignation has taken effect); or

(e) the Director fails to attend three consecutive meetings of the Directors and the Directors resolve that the Director be removed for this reason.

> *Article 24 Analysis*
>
> See analysis of article 18 in **2.21**.

Article 25 Directors' remuneration

5.76

25.1 Directors may undertake any services for the Company that the Directors decide.

25.2 Subject to the Articles and in particular Article 3 Directors are entitled to such remuneration as the Directors determine:

(a) for their services to the Company as Directors; and

(b) for any other service which they undertake for the Company.

25.3 Subject to the Articles and in particular Article 3, a director's remuneration may:

(a) take any form; and

(b) include any arrangements in connection with the payment of a pension, allowance or gratuity, or any death, sickness or disability benefits, to or in respect of that director.

25.4 Unless the Directors decide otherwise, Directors' remuneration accrues from day to day.

25.5 Unless the Directors decide otherwise, Directors are not accountable to the Company for any remuneration which they receive as Directors or other officers or employees of the Company's subsidiaries or of any other body corporate in which the Company is interested.

Article 25 Analysis

As per the provisions of article 25, a CIC may provide remuneration to its directors. The central disparity in terms of private companies limited by guarantee, incorporated under the Companies Act 2006 and using the model articles,[35] is the directors have no restrictions or rules to abide by.

The CIC regulator[36] provides the following principles in relation to directors' remuneration:[37]

- Directors may be paid for their services.
- Directors' remuneration should never be more than is reasonable.[38]
- Directors' remuneration arrangements should always be transparent.[39]
- The Regulator – or the members of a CIC – may take action if a CIC director's remuneration appears to be too high.[40]

For further analysis and comparison see article 19 in **2.22**.

Article 26 Directors' expenses

5.77

The Company may pay any reasonable expenses which the Directors properly incur in connection with their attendance at:

(a) meetings of Directors or committees of Directors;

(b) general meetings; or

35 Schedule 2 Regulation 3 Model articles for private companies limited by guarantee.
36 Office of the Regulator of Community Interest Companies.
37 Office of the Regulator of Community Interest Companies: Information and guidance notes, Chapter 9: Corporate governance, May 2016 (9.3. Directors' remuneration).
38 Reasonable – having regard to the contribution which they make to the success of the company and the benefits it provides for the community (9.3.6. What is 'reasonable' remuneration).
39 All companies are required to keep copies of directors' service contracts, or memoranda of their terms, available at an appropriate place for inspection by their members (9.3.7. Transparency).
40 If the Regulator becomes aware of potentially excessive director remuneration, the Regulator is likely to wish to discuss the matter further with the CIC concerned (9.3.8. Action by the Regulator).

(c) separate meetings of the holders of any class of shares or of debentures of the Company,

or otherwise in connection with the exercise of their powers and the discharge of their responsibilities in relation to the Company.

> *Article 26 Analysis*
>
> See analysis of article 20 in **2.23**.

SHARES AND DISTRIBUTIONS

SHARES

Article 27 All shares to be fully paid up

5.78

27.1 No share is to be issued for less than the aggregate of its nominal value and any premium to be paid to the Company in consideration for its issue.

27.2 This does not apply to shares taken on the formation of the Company by the subscribers to the Company's Memorandum.

> *Article 27 Analysis*
>
> The majority of CICs are predominately SMEs and therefore are unlikely to use share classes that are part or nil paid. Stating and implementing a strategy to only use fully paid up share classes removes the need for lengthy provisions on liens and forfeiture.
>
> It ought to be noted that should a company wish to issue part or nil paid shares the articles of association would require amendment to reflect the new share classes issued by the company, with additional new provisions for liens and forfeiture.

Article 28 Powers to issue different classes of share

5.79

28.1 Subject to the Articles, but without prejudice to the rights attached to any existing share, the Company may issue shares with such rights or restrictions as may be determined by ordinary resolution.

28.2 The Company may issue shares which are to be redeemed, or are liable to be redeemed at the option of the Company or the holder, and the Directors may determine the terms, conditions and manner of redemption of any such shares.

Article 28 Analysis

Shares carry rights. On the basis the article permits, the company is free to define the rights attached to the share classes issued. The most common rights relate to: dividends, capital on winding up and voting. Redeemable shares are issued with rights to repurchase the shares back at a specified date in the future, or by agreement with the directors; they are primally used for outside investors and employee share schemes. Financing redemption, payment and cancellation of the shares is restricted by the Companies Act 2006,[41] therefore care should be taken if adapting the article.

This article aligns with section 685[42] which permits the directors of a limited company to determine the terms, conditions and manner of redemption of shares if they are authorised by either the company's articles or by a resolution of the company. The articles may restrict or exclude the issue of redeemable shares[43] for private limited companies. It should be noted a company may not issue redeemable share classes without initially issuing non-redeemable shares.[44]

A public limited company may only issue redeemable shares if it is authorised to do so by its articles.[45]

Article 29 Company not bound by less than absolute interests

5.80

Except as required by law, no person is to be recognised by the Company as holding any share upon any trust, and except as otherwise required by law or the Articles, the Company is not in any way to be bound by or recognise any interest in a share other than the holder's absolute ownership of it and all the rights attaching to it.

Article 29 Analysis

It is common for shares to be held in trust funds (usually discretionary trusts), senior family members may wish to pass on shares to their issue and still retain a modicum of control over the shareholdings.

Shares held on trust presents the issue of who holds the rights to the shares. Article 29 enforces section 126[46] which provides that any trust fund is not

41 Companies Act 2006, Pt 18, Ch 3 (Redeemable shares).

42 Companies Act 2006, s 685 (Terms and manner of redemption).

43 Companies Act 2006, s 684(2) 'The articles of a private limited company may exclude or restrict the issue of redeemable shares'.

44 Companies Act 2006, s 684(4).

45 Companies Act 2006, s 684(3).

46 Companies Act 2006, s 126 (Trusts not to be entered on register). 'No notice of any trust, expressed, implied or constructive, shall be entered on the register of members of a company registered in England and Wales or Northern Ireland, or be receivable by the registrar.'

recognised by virtue that it cannot register as members of a company in England, Wales or Northern Ireland.

Thought needs to be given when settling shares into trusts as to whom will be the registered holders: if the trustees are registered, the beneficiaries will be excluded by the company and will only be required to deal with the trustees.

It should be noted the company may take actions requested by the trustees (assuming they are the registered entity) that may breach the trust rules. The company cannot be held accountable for such infringements of trust law or rules, the prescribed particulars of the shares are not interchangeable between trustee and beneficiary, the rights attaching from the company perspective are provided to the registered entity.

The beneficiaries cannot insist the company accepts their vote over the trustees if they are not registered, section 145[47] allows a member to nominate another person to 'enjoy or exercise all or any specified rights of the member in relation to the company'. If the company is aware that shareholdings are held in trust or by intermediaries the articles ought to be redrafted to specifically allow section 145 to be enforced; without the adapted article section 145 will not apply.

Article 30 Share certificates

5.81

30.1 The Company must issue each shareholder, free of charge, with one or more certificates in respect of the shares which that shareholder holds.

30.2 Every certificate must specify:

(a) in respect of how many shares, of what class, it is issued;

(b) the nominal value of those shares;

(c) that the shares are fully paid; and

(d) any distinguishing numbers assigned to them.

30.3 No certificate may be issued in respect of shares of more than one class.

30.4 If more than one person holds a share, only one certificate may be issued in respect of it.

47 Companies Act 2006, s 145 (Effect of provisions of articles as to enjoyment or exercise of members' rights).

30.5 Certificates must:

(a) have affixed to them the Company's common seal; or

(b) be otherwise executed in accordance with the Companies Acts.

> *Article 30 Analysis*
>
> Article 30 outlines the company's procedure when issuing share certificates by allotment or transfer, share certificates by virtue of section 768[48] are still prima facie evidence of title to the shares.
>
> Article 30(5) asserts certificates must have affixed the company's common seal, by virtue of section 44.[49] If the company will execute all share certificates by signature,[50] then the provision may be removed or adapted.
>
> Careful drafting may be required if article 27 is considered for amendment, (all shares to be fully paid up) to include part paid shares as article 30(2)(c) indicates, shares are fully paid up, article 27 and article 30(2)(c) would require deletion or amendment should anything other than fully paid up shares be issued by the company.
>
> Section 769 certificates on allotment and section 776 certificates on transfer both specify a time limit of two months, article 30(1) can be amended to include the time frame required by the Companies Act 2006.
>
> If the company does not have a common seal, share certificates can be executed by two directors, by one director and the secretary (if there is one), or by one director in the presence of an independent witness.

Article 31 Replacement share certificates

5.82

31.1 If a certificate issued in respect of a shareholder's shares is:

(a) damaged or defaced; or

(b) said to be lost, stolen or destroyed,

that shareholder is entitled to be issued with a replacement certificate in respect of the same shares.

31.2 A shareholder exercising the right to be issued with such a replacement certificate:

48 Companies Act 2006, s 768 (Share certificate to be evidence of title).

49 Companies Act 2006, s 44 (Execution of documents).

50 Companies Act 2006, s 44(2) 'A document is validly executed by a company if it is signed on behalf of the company – (a) by two authorised signatories, or (b) by a director of the company in the presence of a witness who attests the signature.'

(a) may at the same time exercise the right to be issued with a single certificate or separate certificates;

(b) must return the certificate which is to be replaced to the Company if it is damaged or defaced; and

(c) must comply with such conditions as to evidence, indemnity and the payment of a reasonable fee as the Directors decide.

Article 31 Analysis

Article 31 describes the company rules on issuing replacement share certificates. The typical procedure if a company is required to provide replacement certificates is for the member to return the damaged or defaced certificates and provided the company an indemnity, for example:

> 'The original share certificate in respect of 100 Class A Ordinary shares in ABC Limited has been lost or destroyed.'

Article 32 Share transfers

5.83

32.1 Shares may be transferred by means of an instrument of transfer in any usual form or any other form approved by the Directors, which is executed by or on behalf of the transferor.

32.2 No fee may be charged for registering any instrument of transfer or other Document relating to or affecting the title to any share.

32.3 The Company may retain any instrument of transfer which is registered.

32.4 The transferor remains the holder of a share until the transferee's name is entered in the register of shareholders as holder of it.

Mandatory[51]

32.5 The Directors may refuse to register the transfer of a share to a person of whom they do not approve.[52]

32.6 They may also refuse to register the transfer unless it is lodged at the registered office of the Company or at such other place as the Directors may

51 Articles 32.5 to 32.8 are mandatory, reflecting paragraph 2 of Schedule 2 to the Regulations. However, the model constitution does not contain any other restrictions on the transfer of shares. Note specifically that the directors may refuse to register a transfer to persons of whom they do not approve.

52 The Community Interest Company Regulations 2005, SI 2005/1788, Schedule 2, Provisions prescribed for the memorandum or articles of a community interest company limited by shares, or limited by guarantee with a share capital.

appoint and is accompanied by such evidence as the Directors may reasonably require to show the right of the transferor to make the transfer, and by such other information, as they may reasonably require.

32.7 If the Directors refuse to register such a transfer, they shall, within two months after the date on which the transfer was lodged with the Company send to the transferee notice of the refusal.

32.8 The provisions of this Article apply in addition to any restrictions on the transfer of a share which maybe set out elsewhere in the Memorandum or Articles of the Company.

> *Article 32 Analysis*
>
> A company will require control over its shares and to whom they can be transferred. Article 32 outlines the procedure to transfer the company shares, article 32.5 allows for refusal of any share transfer. It should be noted, in addition, the Companies Act 2006 requires the directors to provide further information specifying the reasons for any refusal.[53]

Article 33 Purchase of own shares

5.84

Subject to the Articles, the Company may purchase its own shares (including any redeemable shares) and may make a payment in respect of the redemption or purchase of its own shares otherwise than out of the distributable profits of the Company or the proceeds of a fresh issue of shares. Any share so purchased shall be purchased at its nominal value.

> *Article 33 Analysis*
>
> The legislation concerning a limited company acquiring its own shares is complex and must only be completed with adherence to Part 18[54] of the Companies Act 2006.

It should be noted, the articles here are only concerned with CICs incorporated under Schedule 2,[55] ie a company which only intends to pay dividends to asset-locked bodies.

53 Companies Act 2006, s 771(1)(b) (Procedure on transfer being lodged).
54 Companies Act 2006, Part 18 (Acquisition by limited company of its own shares).
55 The Community Interest Company Regulations 2005, SI 2005/1788, Schedule 2, Provisions prescribed for the memorandum or articles of a community interest company limited by shares, or limited by guarantee with a share capital.

The company is restricted when instigating a purchase of its own shares to those shares which are held by another asset-locked body. The company may not distribute assets by repurchasing shares from members unless the amount paid is not in excess of the paid up value of the share.[56] Any share purchase must adhere to the asset lock provisions: the transfer of assets to any specified asset-locked body, or (with the consent of the Regulator) to any other asset-locked body.[57]

The Companies Act legislation is complicated,[58] adding the supplementary community interest regulations[59] means legal advice should always be sought before instigating a share buy back.

Article 34 Transmission of shares[60]

5.85

34.1 If title to a share passes to a transmittee, the Company may only recognise the transmittee as having any title to that share.

34.2 A transmittee who produces such evidence of entitlement to shares as the Directors may properly require:

(a) may, subject to the Articles, choose either to become the holder of those shares or to have them transferred to another person; and

(b) subject to the Articles, and pending any transfer of the shares to another person, has the same rights as the holder had.

34.3 But transmittees do not have the right to attend or vote at a general meeting, or agree to a proposed written resolution, in respect of shares to which they are entitled, by reason of the holder's death or bankruptcy or otherwise, unless they become the holders of those shares.

Article 34 Analysis

The transmission of shares is concerned with the procedure when a person becomes entitled to a shareholding by the operation of law. In the majority

56 The Community Interest Company Regulations 2005, SI 2005/1788, reg 24 (Redemption and purchase of shares). A relevant company may not distribute assets to its members by way of the redemption or purchase of the company's own shares, unless the amount to be paid by the company in respect of any such a share does not exceed the paid up value of the share.

57 The Community Interest Company Regulations 2005, SI 2005/1788, Schedule 2, Provisions prescribed for the memorandum or articles of a community interest company limited by shares, or limited by guarantee with a share capital.

58 Companies Act 2006.

59 The Community Interest Company Regulations 2005, SI 2005/1788.

60 In the event of the death of a shareholder, the share will pass according to the will of the deceased shareholder, or the intestacy rules.

of cases transmission will occur on the death of the registered shareholder or if they become bankrupt.

Transmission is the automatic transfer of a share for a particular legal reason. This will occur for example when a shareholder dies and leaves a will, their shares will be automatically transferred to the executor of the will.

When a shareholder dies without leaving a will, their shares will be automatically transferred to their administrator when the court grants the letters of administration appointing the administrator as their personal representative. If a shareholder is declared bankrupt, their shares will be transferred to their personal representative.

All transfers, or request for transfers, are subject to the articles of association, and without express permission of the directors they may be refused.

Article 35 Exercise of transmittees' rights

5.86

35.1 Transmittees who wish to become the holders of shares to which they have become entitled must notify the Company in Writing of that wish.

35.2 If the transmittee wishes to have a share transferred to another person, the transmittee must execute an instrument of transfer in respect of it.

35.3 Any transfer made or executed under this Article is to be treated as if it were made or executed by the person from whom the transmittee has derived rights in respect of the share, and as if the event which gave rise to the transmission had not occurred.

Article 35 Analysis

This article allows the individual who becomes entitled to the shareholdings either by death or an act of law to elect to become a member himself or another entity by executing an instrument of transfer.

Article 36 Transmittees bound by prior notices

5.87

If a notice is given to a shareholder in respect of shares and a transmittee is entitled to those shares, the transmittee is bound by the notice if it was given to the shareholder before the transmittee's name has been entered in the register of shareholders.

Article 36 Analysis

This is a new article, the purpose of which is to ensure the transfer provisions detailed in the articles of association are adhered to.

DIVIDENDS AND OTHER DISTRIBUTIONS

Article 37 Procedure for declaring dividends[61]

5.88

37.1 Subject to the Companies Acts, the Regulations and the Articles, the Company may by ordinary resolution declare dividends, and the Directors may, provided that such decision is authorised by an ordinary resolution of the shareholders, decide to pay interim dividends.

37.2 For the avoidance of doubt the payment of dividends shall be considered to be a transfer of assets other than for full consideration and shall not be permitted other than in the circumstances prescribed in Article 3.

37.3 A dividend must not be declared unless the Directors have made a recommendation as to its amount. Such a dividend must not exceed the amount recommended by the Directors.

37.4 No dividend may be declared or paid unless it is in accordance with shareholders' respective rights.

37.5 Unless the shareholders' resolution to declare or Directors' decision to pay a dividend, or the terms on which shares are issued, specify otherwise, it must be paid by reference to each shareholder's holding of shares on the date of the resolution or decision to declare or pay it.

37.6 If the Company's share capital is divided into different classes, no interim dividend may be paid on shares carrying deferred or non-preferred rights if, at the time of payment, any preferential dividend is in arrear.

37.7 The Directors may pay at intervals any dividend payable at a fixed rate if it appears to them that the profits available for distribution justify the payment.

61 A company which does not intend to pay dividends or make other distributions to private investors (ie a company which adopts the provisions of Schedule 2 to the Regulations rather than those of Schedule 3) must not make use of this provision to pay dividends on any share held by a private investor, as the payment of any such dividends will amount to a breach of the asset lock provisions set out in paragraph 1 of Schedule 2 and article 3. In article 37.2 these words reflect the prohibition on paying dividends to private investors when the provisions set out in Schedule 2 to the Regulations are adopted as part of a CIC's articles.

37.8 If the Directors act in good faith, they do not incur any liability to the holders of shares conferring preferred rights for any loss they may suffer by the lawful payment of an interim dividend on shares with deferred or non-preferred rights.

Article 37 Analysis

Part 23 of the Companies Act 2006 provides statutory obligations the company must adhere to when declaring dividends, in particular section 830[62] which specifies dividends can only be paid from profits. Article 37(1) provides precise terminology for the declaration and payment of dividends.

Final dividends are declared by the company's board of directors based on the full year's financial statements and cannot be revoked by shareholders, an interim dividend can be paid out of surplus profits from any previous financial year, if recommended by the board.

The final dividend is debt of the company when declared, an interim dividend is a mere resolution to pay and does not create any obligation or debt, this allows the directors to revoke the interim dividends should they so wish (*Potel v IRC*).[63]

Article 38 Payment of dividends and other distributions

5.89

38.1 Where a dividend or other sum which is a distribution is payable in respect of a share, it must be paid by one or more of the following means:

(a) transfer to a bank or building society account indicated by the distribution recipient either in Writing or as the Directors may otherwise decide;

(b) sending a cheque made payable to the distribution recipient by post to the distribution recipient at the distribution recipient's registered Address (if the distribution recipient is a holder of the share), or (in any other case) to an Address indicated by the distribution recipient either in Writing or as the Directors may otherwise decide;

(c) sending a cheque made payable to such person by post to such person at such Address as the distribution recipient has indicated either in Writing or as the Directors may otherwise decide; or

(d) any other means of payment as the Directors agree with the distribution recipient either in Writing or by such other means as the Directors decide.

62 Companies Act 2006, s 830 (Distributions to be made only out of profits available for the purpose).
63 [1971] 2 All ER 504.

38.2 In the Articles, "the distribution recipient" means, in respect of a share in respect of which a dividend or other sum is payable:

(a) the holder of the share; or

(b) if the share has two or more joint holders, whichever of them is named first in the register of members; or

(c) if the holder is no longer entitled to the share by reason of death or bankruptcy, or otherwise by operation of law, the transmittee.

Article 38 Analysis

The article outlines the company procedure for the physical payment of dividends. Article 38(a) allows for electronic transfer of dividend payments, regulation 106 of Table A prescribed payment by cheque sent to the registered address of the person entitled to receive the payment.

Article 38(b) allows cheque payments to be sent to any address specified in writing, it is unlikely today a small company would issue dividend payments by cheque, it was somewhat fortuitous when the articles were drafted in 2005 that article 38(d) allows any means of payments agreed between the directors and the recipient.

The articles provide (without amendment) for payment using online money transfers or e-commerce payment systems such as PayPal or Google Wallet.

Article 38(2)(c) relates to the previous articles 34 and 35 and affirms dividends will be paid to the personal representative in the case of a bankrupt or executor in the case of death, prior to any potential transfer.

Article 39 No interest on distributions

5.90

The Company may not pay interest on any dividend or other sum payable in respect of a share unless otherwise provided by:

(a) the terms on which the share was issued; or

(b) the provisions of another agreement between the holder of that share and the Company.

Article 39 Analysis

This article states the common practice that interest is not payable on distributions. The Companies Act 2006 does not prevent interest being paid and the article could be amended accordingly to reflect any interest payments agreed between the company and the shareholder.

Article 40 Unclaimed distributions

5.91

40.1 All dividends or other sums which are:

(a) payable in respect of shares; and

(b) unclaimed after having been declared or become payable,

may be invested or otherwise made use of by the Directors for the benefit of the Company until claimed.

40.2 The payment of any such dividend or other sum into a separate account does not make the Company a trustee in respect of it.

40.3 If:

(a) twelve years have passed from the date on which a dividend or other sum became due for payment; and

(b) the distribution recipient has not claimed it,

the distribution recipient is no longer entitled to that dividend or other sum and it ceases to remain owing by the Company.

Article 40 Analysis

This article provides clarity between the company and the shareholder. If dividend payments are unclaimed, as discussed in article 40, final dividends are a debt to the company and unclaimed dividends would be reflected on the company's balance sheet. Article 40(3)(a) allows the company after a period of 12 years to write off the debt.

The Limitation Act 1980 provides that the time limit is generally six years, the sample model articles of association under the Companies Act 2006 state a 12-year period and most companies allow for 12 years. It is possible to reduce the period for unclaimed dividends (but not shares) down to six years by amending the company's articles of association.

Unpaid dividends by (UK) companies in 2018 amount to a staggering £100 billion.[64] Public companies are keen to move the debt from its balance sheet; Rentokil Initial plc whose unpaid dividends amount to £1 million has instigated a novel strategy by adapting its articles of association and used unclaimed shares and unclaimed dividends to support good causes.[65]

64 www.linkassetservices.com/.

65 www.rentokil-initial.com/media/news-releases/news-2019/new-approach-puts-unclaimed-dividends-and-shares-to-good-use.aspx.

Article 41 Non-cash distributions

5.92

41.1 Subject to the terms of issue of the share in question, the Company may, by ordinary resolution on the recommendation of the Directors, decide to pay all or part of a dividend or other distribution payable in respect of a share by transferring non-cash assets of equivalent value (including, without limitation, shares or other securities in any company).

41.2 For the purposes of paying a non-cash distribution, the Directors may make whatever arrangements they think fit, including, where any difficulty arises regarding the distribution:

(a) fixing the value of any assets;

(b) paying cash to any distribution recipient on the basis of that value in order to adjust the rights of recipients; and

(c) vesting any assets in trustees.

> *Article 41 Analysis*
>
> The article allows a distribution *in specie*, although a dividend ought to be paid in cash (*Wood v Odessa Waterworks Co*).[66] Where a dividend is declared in cash, but satisfied by a transfer of assets, it is called 'dividend *in specie*'.
>
> A distribution *in specie* occurs where a company makes a distribution of an identified non-cash asset, such as without first declaring an amount in cash. Distributions *in specie* are detailed under section 845 of the Companies Act 2006.[67]
>
> Both dividend *in specie* and distribution *in specie* must be made in accordance with Part 23 of the Companies Act 2006.[68]

Article 42 Waiver of distributions

5.93

Distribution recipients may waive their entitlement to a dividend or other distribution payable in respect of a share by giving the Company notice in Writing to that effect, but if:

(a) the share has more than one holder; or

66 (1889) 42 Ch D 636.
67 Companies Act 2006, s 845 (Distributions in kind: determination of amount).
68 Part 23 Distributions.

(b) more than one person is entitled to the share, whether by reason of the death or bankruptcy of one or more joint holders, or otherwise,

the notice is not effective unless it is expressed to be given, and signed, by all the holders or persons otherwise entitled to the share.

Article 42 Analysis

Article 42 is a new addition, with no previous regulation in Table A. Care ought to be taken in regards of waiver if the company has two or three directors and is a family concern.

A strategy to avoid tax by allowing all the dividends to be paid to a spouse was explored in (*Buck v Revenue and Customs Comrs*),[69] there must be a commercial reason for waiving rights to dividends by a member. The 'arm's length' test stipulates, would the member have waived his rights to dividends if they had been operating at arm's length?

Article 42(b) relates to previous articles on transmission, that if entitlement to dividends could be claimed by multiple individuals, then permission and signature must be sought from all those with a valid claim.

It should be noted, tax advice should be sought before consideration of the waiver of distributions.

CAPITALISATION OF PROFITS

Article 43 Authority to capitalise and appropriation of capitalised sums

5.94

43.1 Subject to the Articles, the Directors may, if they are so authorised by an ordinary resolution:

(a) decide to capitalise any profits of the Company (whether or not they are available for distribution) which are not required for paying a preferential dividend, or any sum standing to the credit of the Company's share premium account or capital redemption reserve; and

(b) appropriate any sum which they so decide to capitalise (a "capitalised sum") to the persons who would have been entitled to it if it were distributed by way of dividend (the "persons entitled") and in the same proportions.

43.2 Capitalised sums must be applied:

(a) on behalf of the persons entitled and

(b) in the same proportions as a dividend would have been distributed to them.

69 [2009] STC (SCD) 6.

43.3 Any capitalised sum may be applied in paying up new shares of a nominal amount equal to the capitalised sum which are then allotted credited as fully paid to the persons entitled or as they may direct.

43.4 A capitalised sum which was appropriated from profits available for distribution may be applied in paying up new debentures of the Company which are then allotted credited as fully paid to the persons entitled or as they may direct.

43.5 Subject to the Articles the Directors may:

(a) apply capitalised sums in accordance with Articles 43.3 and 43.4 partly in one way and partly in another;

(b) make such arrangements as they think fit to deal with shares or debentures becoming distributable in fractions under this Article (including the issuing of fractional certificates or the making of cash payments); and

(c) authorise any person to enter into an agreement with the Company on behalf of all the persons entitled which is binding on them in respect of the allotment of shares and debentures to them under this Article.

Article 43 Analysis

The article and its provisions allow the company by ordinary resolution to capitalise on profits by converting the company's retained earnings into capital stock. The capitalisation of profits process usually involves issuing bonus shares to existing shareholders. This allocation is achieved by issuing shares in proportion to the existing members' shareholdings.

DECISION-MAKING BY SHAREHOLDERS

ORGANISATION OF GENERAL MEETINGS

Article 44 General meetings

5.95

44.1 The Directors may call a general meeting at any time.

44.2 The Directors must call a general meeting if required to do so by the shareholders under the Companies Acts.

Article 45 Length of notice

5.96

All general meetings must be called by either:

45.1 at least 14 Clear Days' notice; or

45.2 shorter notice if it is so agreed by [a majority of the shareholders having a right to attend and vote at that meeting. Any such majority must together represent at least [90%] of the total voting rights at that meeting of all the shareholders].

Article 46 Contents of notice

5.97

46.1 Every notice calling a general meeting must specify the place, day and time of the meeting, whether it is a general or an annual general meeting, and the general nature of the business to be transacted.

46.2 If a special resolution is to be proposed, the notice must include the proposed resolution and specify that it is proposed as a special resolution.

46.3 In every notice calling a meeting of the Company there must appear with reasonable prominence a statement informing the shareholder of his or her rights to appoint another person as his or her proxy at a general meeting.

Article 47 Service of notice

5.98

Notice of general meetings must be given to every shareholder, to the Directors and to the auditors of the Company.

> *Articles 44–47 Analysis*
>
> See analysis of articles 29–32 in **5.32**.

Article 48 Attendance and speaking at general meetings

5.99

48.1 A person is able to exercise the right to speak at a general meeting when that person is in a position to communicate to all those attending the meeting, during the meeting, any information or opinions which that person has on the business of the meeting.

48.2 A person is able to exercise the right to vote at a general meeting when:

(a) that person is able to vote, during the meeting, on resolutions put to the vote at the meeting; and

(b) that person's vote can be taken into account in determining whether or not such resolutions are passed at the same time as the votes of all the other persons attending the meeting.

48.3 The Directors may make whatever arrangements they consider appropriate to enable those attending a general meeting to exercise their rights to speak or vote at it.

48.4 In determining attendance at a general meeting, it is immaterial whether any two or more shareholders attending it are in the same place as each other.

48.5 Two or more persons who are not in the same place as each other attend a general meeting if their circumstances are such that if they have (or were to have) rights to speak and vote at that meeting, they are (or would be) able to exercise them.

> *Article 48 Analysis*
>
> See analysis of article 23 in **2.26**.

Article 49 Quorum for general meetings

5.100

49.1 No business other than the appointment of the chairman of the meeting is to be transacted at a general meeting if the persons attending it do not constitute a quorum.

49.2 The quorum for a general meeting shall be two persons entitled to vote on the business to be transacted (each being a shareholder, a proxy for a shareholder or a duly authorised representative of a shareholder) or 10% of the total shareholding (represented in person or by proxy) whichever is greater.

> *Article 49 Analysis*
>
> See analysis of article 24 in **2.27**.

Article 50 Chairing general meetings

5.101

50.1 If the Directors have appointed a chairman, the chairman shall chair general meetings if present and willing to do so.

50.2 If the Directors have not appointed a chairman, or if the chairman is unwilling to chair the meeting or is not present within ten minutes of the time at which a meeting was due to start:

(a) the Directors present; or

(b) (if no Directors are present), the meeting, must appoint a Director or shareholder to chair the meeting, and the appointment of the chairman of the meeting must be the first business of the meeting.

50.3 The person chairing a meeting in accordance with this Article is referred to as "the chairman of the meeting".

> *Article 50 Analysis*
>
> See analysis of article 25 in **2.28**.

Article 51 Attendance and speaking by Directors and non-shareholders

5.102

51.1 Directors may attend and speak at general meetings, whether or not they are shareholders.

51.2 The chairman of the meeting may permit other persons who are not:

(a) shareholders of the Company; or

(b) otherwise entitled to exercise the rights of shareholders in relation to general meetings, to attend and speak at a general meeting.

> *Article 51 Analysis*
>
> See analysis of article 26 in **2.29**.

Article 52 Adjournment

5.103

52.1 If the persons attending a general meeting within half an hour of the time at which the meeting was due to start do not constitute a quorum, or if during a meeting a quorum ceases to be present, the chairman of the meeting must adjourn it.

52.2 The chairman of the meeting may adjourn a general meeting at which a quorum is present if:

(a) the meeting consents to an adjournment; or

(b) it appears to the chairman of the meeting that an adjournment is necessary to protect the safety of any person attending the meeting or ensure that the business of the meeting is conducted in an orderly manner.

52.3 The chairman of the meeting must adjourn a general meeting if directed to do so by the meeting.

52.4 When adjourning a general meeting, the chairman of the meeting must:

(a) either specify the time and place to which it is adjourned or state that it is to continue at a time and place to be fixed by the Directors; and

(b) have regard to any directions as to the time and place of any adjournment which have been given by the meeting.

52.5 If the continuation of an adjourned meeting is to take place more than 14 days after it was adjourned, the Company must give at least 7 Clear Days' notice of it (that is, excluding the day of the adjourned meeting and the day on which the notice is given):

(a) to the same persons to whom notice of the Company's general meetings is required to be given; and

(b) containing the same information which such notice is required to contain.

52.6 No business may be transacted at an adjourned general meeting which could not properly have been transacted at the meeting if the adjournment had not taken place.

Article 52 Analysis

See analysis of article 27 in **2.30**.

VOTING AT GENERAL MEETINGS

Article 53 Voting: general

5.104

53.1 A resolution put to the vote of a general meeting must be decided on a show of hands unless a poll is duly demanded in accordance with the Articles.

53.2 A person who is not a shareholder of the Company shall not have any right to vote at a general meeting of the Company; but this is without prejudice to any right to vote on a resolution affecting the rights attached to a class of the Company's debentures.[70]

53.3 Article 53.2 shall not prevent a person who is a proxy for a shareholder or an Authorised Representative from voting at a general meeting of the Company.

53.4 On a vote on a resolution on a show of hands at a meeting every person present in person (whether a shareholder, proxy or Authorised Representative of a shareholder) and entitled to vote shall have a maximum of one vote.

53.5 On a vote on a resolution on a poll at a meeting every shareholder present in person or by proxy or Authorised Representative shall have one vote.

53.6 In the case of an equality of votes, whether on a show of hands or on a poll, the chair of the meeting shall not be entitled to a casting vote in addition to any other vote he or she may have.

53.7 No shareholder shall be entitled to vote at any general meeting unless all monies presently payable by him, her or it to the Company have been paid.

53.8 The following provisions apply to any organisation that is a shareholder ("a Shareholder Organisation"):

(a) a Shareholder Organisation may nominate any individual to act as its representative ("an Authorised Representative") at any meeting of the Company;

(b) the Shareholder Organisation must give notice in Writing to the Company of the name of its Authorised Representative. The Authorised Representative will not be entitled to represent the Shareholder Organisation at any meeting of the Company unless such notice has been

70 Mandatory provision. The Community Interest Company Regulations 2005, SI 2005/1788, Schedule 2, Provisions prescribed for the memorandum or articles of a community interest company limited by shares, or limited by guarantee with a share capital.

received by the Company. The Authorised Representative may continue to represent the Shareholder Organisation until notice in Writing is received by the Company to the contrary;

(c) a Shareholder Organisation may appoint an Authorised Representative to represent it at a particular meeting of the Company or at all meetings of the Company until notice in Writing to the contrary is received by the Company;

(d) any notice in Writing received by the Company shall be conclusive evidence of the Authorised Representative's authority to represent the Shareholder Organisation or that his or her authority has been revoked. The Company shall not be required to consider whether the Authorised Representative has been properly appointed by the Shareholder Organisation;

(e) an individual appointed by a Shareholder Organisation to act as its Authorised Representative is entitled to exercise (on behalf of the Shareholder Organisation) the same powers as the Shareholder Organisation could exercise if it were an individual shareholder;

(f) on a vote on a resolution at a meeting of the Company, the Authorised Representative has the same voting rights as the Shareholder Organisation would be entitled to if it was an individual shareholder present in person at the meeting; and

(g) the power to appoint an Authorised Representative under this Article 53.8 is without prejudice to any rights which the Shareholder Organisation has under the Companies Acts and the Articles to appoint a proxy or a corporate representative.

Article 53 Analysis

See analysis of article 28 in **2.31**.

Article 54 Poll votes

5.105

54.1 A poll on a resolution may be demanded:

(a) in advance of the general meeting where it is to be put to the vote; or

(b) at a general meeting, either before a show of hands on that resolution or immediately after the result of a show of hands on that resolution is declared.

54.2 A poll may be demanded by:

(a) the chairman of the meeting;

(b) the Directors;

(c) two or more persons having the right to vote on the resolution;

(d) any person, who, by virtue of being appointed proxy for one or more members having the right to vote at the meeting, holds two or more votes; or

(e) a person or persons representing not less than one tenth of the total voting rights of all the shareholders having the right to vote on the resolution.

54.3 A demand for a poll may be withdrawn if:

(a) the poll has not yet been taken; and

(b) the chairman of the meeting consents to the withdrawal.

54.4 Polls must be taken immediately and in such manner as the chairman of the meeting directs.

Article 54 Analysis

See analysis of article 30 in **2.33**.

Article 55 Errors and disputes

5.106

55.1 No objection may be raised to the qualification of any person voting at a general meeting except at the meeting or adjourned meeting at which the vote objected to is tendered, and every vote not disallowed at the meeting is valid.

55.2 Any such objection must be referred to the chairman of the meeting, whose decision is final.

Article 55 Analysis

See analysis of article 29 in **2.32**.

Article 56 Content of Proxy Notices

5.107

56.1 Proxies may only validly be appointed by a notice in Writing (a "Proxy Notice") which:

(a) states the name and Address of the shareholder appointing the proxy;

(b) identifies the person appointed to be that shareholder's proxy and the general meeting in relation to which that person is appointed;

(c) is signed by or on behalf of the shareholder appointing the proxy, or is authenticated in such manner as the Directors may determine; and

(d) is delivered to the Company in accordance with the Articles and any instructions contained in the notice of the general meeting to which they relate.

56.2 The Company may require Proxy Notices to be delivered in a particular form, and may specify different forms for different purposes.

56.3 Proxy notices may specify how the proxy appointed under them is to vote (or that the proxy is to abstain from voting) on one or more resolutions.

56.4 Unless a Proxy Notice indicates otherwise, it must be treated as:

(a) allowing the person appointed under it as a proxy discretion as to how to vote on any ancillary or procedural resolutions put to the meeting; and

(b) appointing that person as a proxy in relation to any adjournment of the general meeting to which it relates as well as the meeting itself.

Article 56 Analysis

See analysis of article 31 in **2.34**.

Article 57 Delivery of Proxy Notices

5.108

57.1 A person who is entitled to attend, speak or vote (either on a show of hands or on a poll) at a general meeting remains so entitled in respect of that meeting or any adjournment of it, even though a valid Proxy Notice has been delivered to the Company by or on behalf of that person.

57.2 An appointment under a Proxy Notice may be revoked by delivering to the Company a notice in Writing given by or on behalf of the person by whom or on whose behalf the Proxy Notice was given.

57.3 A notice revoking a proxy appointment only takes effect if it is delivered before the start of the meeting or adjourned meeting to which it relates.

57.4 If a Proxy Notice is not executed by the person appointing the proxy, it must be accompanied by written evidence of the authority of the person who executed it to execute it on the appointor's behalf.

> *Article 57 Analysis*
>
> See analysis of article 32 in **2.35**.

Article 58 Amendments to resolutions

5.109

58.1 An ordinary resolution to be proposed at a general meeting may be amended by ordinary resolution if:

(a) notice of the proposed amendment is given to the Company in Writing by a person entitled to vote at the general meeting at which it is to be proposed not less than 48 hours before the meeting is to take place (or such later time as the chairman of the meeting may determine); and

(b) the proposed amendment does not, in the reasonable opinion of the chairman of the meeting, materially alter the scope of the resolution.

58.2 A special resolution to be proposed at a general meeting may be amended by ordinary resolution, if:

(a) the chairman of the meeting proposes the amendment at the general meeting at which the resolution is to be proposed; and

(b) the amendment does not go beyond what is necessary to correct a grammatical or other non-substantive error in the resolution.

58.3 If the chairman of the meeting, acting in good faith, wrongly decides that an amendment to a resolution is out of order, the chairman's error does not invalidate the vote on that resolution.

> *Article 58 Analysis*
>
> See analysis of article 33 in **2.36**.

WRITTEN RESOLUTIONS

Article 59 Written resolutions

5.110

59.1 Subject to Article 59.3, a written resolution of the Company passed in accordance with this Article 59 shall have effect as if passed by the Company in general meeting:

(a) A written resolution is passed as an ordinary resolution if it is passed by a simple majority of the total voting rights of eligible shareholders.

(b) A written resolution is passed as a special resolution if it is passed by shareholders representing not less than 75% of the total voting rights of eligible shareholders. A written resolution is not a special resolution unless it states that it was proposed as a special resolution.

59.2 In relation to a resolution proposed as a written resolution of the Com pany the eligible shareholders are the shareholders who would have been entitled to vote on the resolution on the Circulation Date of the resolution.

59.3 A shareholders' resolution under the Companies Acts removing a Director or an auditor before the expiration of his or her term of office may not be passed as a written resolution.

59.4 A copy of the written resolution must be sent to every shareholder together with a statement informing the shareholder how to signify their agreement to the resolution and the date by which the resolution must be passed if it is not to lapse. Communications in relation to written notices shall be sent to the Company's auditors in accordance with the Companies Acts.

59.5 A shareholder signifies their agreement to a proposed written resolution when the Company receives from him or her an authenticated Document identifying the resolution to which it relates and indicating his or her agreement to the resolution.

(a) If the Document is sent to the Company in Hard Copy Form, it is authenticated if it bears the shareholder's signature.

(b) If the Document is sent to the Company by Electronic Means, it is authenticated [if it bears the shareholder's signature] or [if the identity of the shareholder is confirmed in a manner agreed by the Directors] or [if it is accompanied by a statement of the identity of the shareholder and the Company has no reason to doubt the truth of that statement] or [if it is from an email Address notified by the shareholder to the Company for the purposes of receiving Documents or information by Electronic Means].

59.6 A written resolution is passed when the required majority of eligible shareholders have signified their agreement to it.

59.7 A proposed written resolution lapses if it is not passed within 28 days beginning with the Circulation Date.

> *Article 59 Analysis*
>
> See analysis of article 45 in **5.45**.

ADMINISTRATIVE ARRANGEMENTS AND MISCELLANEOUS

Article 60 Means of communication to be used

5.111

60.1 Subject to the Articles, anything sent or supplied by or to the Company under the Articles may be sent or supplied in any way in which the Companies Act 2006 provides for Documents or information which are authorised or required by any provision of that Act to be sent or supplied by or to the Company.

60.2 Subject to the Articles, any notice or Document to be sent or supplied to a Director in connection with the taking of decisions by Directors may also be sent or supplied by the means by which that Director has asked to be sent or supplied with such notices or Documents for the time being.

60.3 A Director may agree with the Company that notices or Documents sent to that Director in a particular way are to be deemed to have been received within an agreed time of their being sent, and for the agreed time to be less than 48 hours.

> *Article 60 Analysis*
>
> See analysis of article 34 in **2.37**.

Article 61 Irregularities

5.112

The proceedings at any meeting or on the taking of any poll or the passing of a written resolution or the making of any decision shall not be invalidated by reason of any accidental informality or irregularity (including any accidental omission to give or any non-receipt of notice) or any want of qualification in any of the persons present or voting or by reason of any business being considered which is not referred to in the notice unless a provision of the Companies Acts specifies that such informality, irregularity or want of qualification shall invalidate it.

> *Article 61 Analysis*
>
> See analysis of article 47 in **5.47**.

Article 62 Minutes

5.113

62.1 The Directors must cause minutes to be made in books kept for the purpose:

(a) of all appointments of officers made by the Directors;

(b) of all resolutions of the Company and of the Directors (including, without limitation, decisions of the Directors made without a meeting); and

(c) of all proceedings at meetings of the Company and of the Directors, and of committees of Directors, including the names of the Directors present at each such meeting;

and any such minute, if purported to be signed (or in the case of minutes of Directors' meetings signed or authenticated) by the chair of the meeting at which the proceedings were had, or by the chair of the next succeeding meeting, shall, as against any shareholder or Director of the Company, be sufficient evidence of the proceedings.

62.2 The minutes must be kept for at least ten years from the date of the meeting, resolution or decision.

> *Article 62 Analysis*
>
> See analysis of article 48 in **5.48**.

Article 63 Records and accounts

5.114

The Directors shall comply with the requirements of the Companies Acts as to maintaining a shareholders' register, keeping financial records, the audit or examination of accounts and the preparation and transmission to the Registrar of Companies and the Regulator of:

63.1 annual reports;

63.2 annual returns; and

63.3 annual statements of account.

63.4 Except as provided by law or authorised by the Directors or an ordinary resolution of the Company, no person is entitled to inspect any of the Company's accounting or other records or Documents merely by virtue of being a shareholder.

Article 63 Analysis
See analysis of article 49 in **5.49**.

Article 64 Indemnity

5.115

64.1 Subject to Article 64.2, a relevant Director of the Company or an associated company may be indemnified out of the Company's assets against:

(a) any liability incurred by that Director in connection with any negligence, default, breach of duty or breach of trust in relation to the Company or an associated company;

(b) any liability incurred by that Director in connection with the activities of the Company or an associated company in its capacity as a trustee of an occupational pension scheme (as defined in section 235(6) of the Companies Act 2006);

(c) any other liability incurred by that Director as an officer of the Company or an associated company.

64.2 This Article does not authorise any indemnity which would be prohibited or rendered void by any provision of the Companies Acts or by any other provision of law.

64.3 In this Article:

(a) companies are associated if one is a subsidiary of the other or both are subsidiaries of the same body corporate; and

(b) a "relevant Director" means any Director or former Director of the Company or an associated company.

Article 65 Insurance

5.116

65.1 The Directors may decide to purchase and maintain insurance, at the expense of the Company, for the benefit of any relevant director in respect of any relevant loss.

65.2 In this Article:

(a) a "relevant Director" means any Director or former Director of the Company or an associated company;

(b) a "relevant loss" means any loss or liability which has been or may be incurred by a relevant Director in connection with that Director's duties or powers in relation to the Company, any associated company or any pension fund or employees' share scheme of the Company or associated company; and

(c) companies are associated if one is a subsidiary of the other or both are subsidiaries of the same body corporate.

Articles 64 and 65 Analysis

See analysis of articles 38 and 39 in **2.42**.

Chapter 6 Analysis of the Model Articles for a Company and Trust with Employee Ownership

Part E Model articles of a trustee company and a company with employee ownership

Assumptions

6.1

- The model documentation assumes the use of a Corporate Trustee as this protects against the risks of potential unlimited personal liability.[1]
- The model documentation provides for the Corporate Trustee to be a company limited by guarantee (as recommended in the Nuttall Review).
- If a Corporate Trustee is used, the directors of the Trustee Company will, in effect, be the Trustees and have the same fiduciary duties owed to the beneficiaries of the Trust as if they were themselves the Trustees.
- The model documentation suggests that the Articles of Association of the Trustee Company provide for there to be between three and five Trustee Directors all of whom are resident in the UK for UK tax purposes. Of these, at least one shall be an Independent Trustee Director and the rest either current or former employees.
- The model documentation further provides for this Trustee Company to be a directly wholly-owned subsidiary of the Company.

6.2

The model articles for a trust company contain bespoke provisions concerning the appointment and dismissal of company and external trustees. Broadly, with the exceptions detailed in the following analysis, the articles follow the provisions of the model articles prescribed by the Companies Act 2006.[2]

1 The model documentation could easily be adapted to use Individual Trustees.
2 Schedule 2 Regulation 3 Model articles for private companies limited by guarantee.

The following articles are omitted

6.3

Article 4 Members' reserve power

Article 5 Trustee directors may delegate

Article 6 Committees

Article 15 Records of decisions to be kept

Article 17 Methods of appointing trustee directors

Article 18 Termination of director's appointment

Model articles will apply

6.4

It should be noted the articles here do not include a provision excluding or modifying the model articles[3] as required by section 20 of the Companies Act 2006.[4] If the articles are registered without modification, the model articles will still apply.[5]

This position could encompass provisions from Table A if the company was originally incorporated under the Companies Act 1985, or indeed any previous act. Articles 17 and 18 would conflict with the bespoke provisions that appear in section 3.

Therefore the following article(s), subject to the requirements of the company ought to be added.

Model articles shall not apply

Precedent 1

6.5

Neither the model articles for private companies limited by shares prescribed pursuant to the 2006 Act, nor any other articles of association (whether

3 Schedule 2 Regulation 3 Model articles for private companies limited by guarantee.

4 Companies Act 2006, s 20 (Default application of model articles).

5 Companies Act 2006, s 20 (Default application of model articles). '(1) On the formation of a limited company: (a) if articles are not registered, or (b)if articles are registered, in so far as they do not exclude or modify the relevant model articles, the relevant model articles (so far as applicable) form part of the company's articles in the same manner and to the same extent as if articles in the form of those articles had been duly registered.'

prescribed pursuant to the 2006 Act or set out in any other statute, statutory instrument or other subordinate legislation concerning companies) shall apply to the company.

In these articles any reference to any statutory provision shall be deemed to include a reference to each and every statutory amendment, modification, re-enactment and extension thereof for the time being in force.

If applicable:

Precedent 2

6.6

Table A in the Schedule to the Companies (Tables A to F) Regulations 1985 (as amended) ("Table A") shall not apply to the Company.[6]

In these Articles and the Model Articles any reference to any statutory provision shall be deemed to include a reference to each and every statutory amendment, modification, re-enactment and extension thereof for the time being in force.

6 The article is only needed if the Company was incorporated before 1 October 2009.

Model Articles of Association of a Company Limited by Guarantee with Employee Ownership

THE COMPANIES ACT 2006

PRIVATE COMPANY LIMITED BY GUARANTEE

ARTICLES OF ASSOCIATION

of

[INSERT NAME] EMPLOYEES' TRUSTEES LIMITED

("the Company")

(Adopted by written special resolution on [date])

Article 1 Defined terms

6.7

1. In the articles, unless the context requires otherwise—

"articles" means the company's articles of association;

"bankruptcy" includes individual insolvency proceedings in a jurisdiction other than England and Wales or Northern Ireland which have an effect similar to that of bankruptcy;

"chairman" has the meaning given in article 12;

"chairman of the meeting" has the meaning given in article 25;

"Companies Acts" means the Companies Acts (as defined in section 2 of the Companies Act 2006), in so far as they apply to the company;

"director" means a director of the company, and includes any person occupying the position of director, by whatever name called;

"document" includes, unless otherwise specified, any document sent or supplied in electronic form;

"electronic form" has the meaning given in section 1168 of the Companies Act 2006;

"member" has the meaning given in section 112 of the Companies Act 2006;

"ordinary resolution" has the meaning given in section 282 of the Companies Act 2006;

"participate", in relation to a trustee directors' meeting, has the meaning given in article 10;

"proxy notice" has the meaning given in article 31;

"special resolution" has the meaning given in section 283 of the Companies Act 2006;

"subsidiary" has the meaning given in section 1159 of the Companies Act 2006; and

"writing" means the representation or reproduction of words, symbols or other information in a visible form by any method or combination of methods, whether sent or supplied in electronic form or otherwise.

2. Unless the context otherwise requires, other words or expressions contained in these articles bear the same meaning as in the Companies Act 2006 as in force on the date when these articles become binding on the company.

Article 2 Liability of members

6.8

2. The liability of each member is limited to £1, being the amount that each member undertakes to contribute to the assets of the company in the event of its being wound up while he is a member or within one year after he ceases to be a member, for:

(a) payment of the company's debts and liabilities contracted before he ceases to be a member,

(b) payment of the costs, charges and expenses of winding up, and

(c) adjustment of the rights of the contributories among themselves.

Article 2 Analysis

See analysis of article 2 in **2.5**.

Part 2 Directors

Article 3 Appointment and removal of trustee directors

6.9

3.(1) Subject to the following provisions of these articles, each Trustee Director shall be appointed, and may be removed from office as a Trustee Director, by ordinary resolution.

(2) For so long as the Company is a trustee of the [INSERT NAME] Employees' Share Trust, there shall at all times be:

(a) at least [three] and not more than [five] Trustee directors, all of whom are resident in the UK for UK tax purposes;

(b) at least one Trustee Director who is an Independent Trustee Director and not less than [one-half] of the other Trustee directors shall be Employee Trustee directors; and

(c) every Trustee Director who is not an Independent Trustee Director shall be an individual who is, or has been, an employee or director of a member or former member of the Group SAVE THAT the number of Independent Trustee directors shall not exceed one-third in number of the Trustee directors.

(3) In the event of any change of Control of the Company with Employee Ownership, the power of the members of the Company to remove and appoint a Trustee Director shall be suspended for the period of [30] days beginning with the date of such change of Control.

Article 4 Independent Trustee Director

6.10

4.(1) An Independent Trustee Director may be appointed a Trustee Director upon such terms as to remuneration and otherwise as may be agreed at the time of his appointment by the Company (on the one hand) and the Independent Trustee Director (on the other hand) PROVIDED ALWAYS that such an appointment shall be valid only if the terms provide that such Independent Trustee Director may be removed at any time in accordance with these articles.

(2) An Independent Trustee Director shall automatically cease to hold office as a Trustee Director if he or she becomes a director or employee of any other member of the Group or if all of the other Trustee directors together determine that his or her independence has been compromised for any reason and give notice in writing to that effect to such Independent Trustee Director.

(3) If, in consequence of a reduction in the number of Trustee directors, the number of Independent Trustee directors would otherwise exceed the limit on the number of Independent Trustee directors in article 3.2, one or more of the Independent Trustee directors shall immediately resign from office as a Trustee Director so as to ensure that such limit is not exceeded, and in the event

of disagreement as to which Independent Trustee Director(s) should resign, an Independent Trustee Director who was most recently appointed or last re-appointed a Trustee Director shall resign in preference to an Independent Trustee Director who was earlier appointed or last re-appointed.]

Article 5 Employee Trust Trustee directors

6.11

5.(1) No person shall be appointed to hold office as an Employee Trustee Director unless:

(a) [he or she has been selected and nominated to hold office as a Trustee Director in accordance with a procedure determined by the Employees' Council and which is not inconsistent with the terms of the Constitution; and]

(b) he or she has confirmed in writing his or her willingness to hold such office.

Article 6 Retirement of employee trust trustee directors

6.12

6.(1) An Employee Trustee Director shall automatically cease to hold office as a Trustee Director if he or she [gives or receives notice of termination of employment with any member of the Group or ceases for any reason to be an employee of any member of the Group or retires by rotation].

(2) On the [third] anniversary of the first acquisition by the Trustee of shares in the Company with Employee Ownership and, for so long as the Trustee holds shares or other securities in the Company with Employee Ownership, at the end of every subsequent anniversary of that date, one Employee Trustee Director shall retire by rotation.

(3) The Employee Trustee Director to retire by rotation shall be the [one] who has [have] been longest in office since his or her last appointment or reappointment, but as between persons who became or were last reappointed Employee Trustee directors on the same day the one to retire shall (unless they otherwise agree among themselves) be determined by lot.

(4) An Employee Trustee Director retiring by rotation shall be eligible to be nominated as a candidate to fill the vacancy.

Article 7 Retirement of trustee directors

6.13

7.(1) A Trustee Director shall retire and his office as a director of the Company shall automatically be vacated if:

(a) that person ceases for any reason to be resident in the UK for UK tax purposes; or

(b) that person ceases to be a director by virtue of any provision of the Companies Act 2006 or is prohibited from being a director by law;

(c) a bankruptcy order is made against that person;

(d) a composition is made with that person's creditors generally in satisfaction of that person's debts;

(e) a registered medical practitioner who is treating that person gives a written opinion to the Trustee Company stating that that person has become physically or mentally incapable of acting as a director and may remain so for more than three months; and

(f) notification is received by the Trustee Company from that person that that person is resigning from office as a Trustee Director, and such resignation has taken effect in accordance with its terms.

Article 8 Initial Trustee directors

6.14

8.(1) The initial Trustee directors shall be the individuals whose names appear in Column A of the table below, each of whom has been selected to hold such office in the capacity referred to opposite his or her name in Column B of that table and in accordance with the rules of this Schedule applicable to such Independent Trustee Director, Employee Trustee Director or other Trustee Director.

(2) Table of Initial Trustee directors of the Original Trustee

Column A	Column B
Name of Director	Status of Trustee Director
[name of director(s)]	Independent Trustee Director(s)
[name of director(s)]	Employee Trustee Director(s)
[name of director(s)]	other Trustee Director(s)

Trustee directors' powers and responsibilities

Article 9 Trustee directors' general authority

6.15

9.(1) Subject to the articles, the "trustee" directors are responsible for the management of the company's business, for which purpose they may exercise all the powers of the company.

> *Article 9 Analysis*
>
> See analysis of article 3 in **2.6**.

Decision-making by trustee directors

Article 10 Trustee directors to take decisions collectively

6.16

10.(1) The general rule about decision-making by trustee directors is that any decision of the "trustee" trustee directors must be either a majority decision at a meeting or a decision taken in accordance with article 11.

> *Article 10 Analysis*
>
> See analysis of article 7 in **2.10**.

Article 11 Unanimous decisions

6.17

11.(1) A decision of the trustee directors is taken in accordance with this article when all eligible trustee directors indicate to each other by any means that they share a common view on a matter.

(2) Such a decision may take the form of a resolution in writing, copies of which have been signed by each eligible director or to which each eligible director has otherwise indicated agreement in writing.

(3) References in this article to eligible trustee directors are to trustee directors who would have been entitled to vote on the matter had it been proposed as a resolution at a trustee directors' meeting.

(4) A decision may not be taken in accordance with this article if the eligible trustee directors would not have formed a quorum at such a meeting.

> *Article 11 Analysis*
>
> See analysis of article 8 in **2.11**.

Article 12 Calling a trustee directors' meeting

6.18

12.(1) Any director may call a trustee directors' meeting by giving notice of the meeting to the trustee directors or by authorising the company secretary (if any) to give such notice.

(2) Notice of any trustee directors' meeting must indicate:

(a) its proposed date and time;

(b) where it is to take place; and

(c) if it is anticipated that trustee directors participating in the meeting will not be in the same place, how it is proposed that they should communicate with each other during the meeting.

(3) Notice of a trustee directors' meeting must be given to each director, but need not be in writing.

(4) Notice of a trustee directors' meeting need not be given to trustee directors who waive their entitlement to notice of that meeting, by giving notice to that effect to the company not more than 7 days after the date on which the meeting is held. Where such notice is given after the meeting has been held, that does not affect the validity of the meeting, or of any business conducted at it.

> *Article 12 Analysis*
>
> See analysis of article 9 in **2.12**.

Article 13 Participation in trustee directors' meetings

6.19

13.(1) Subject to the articles, trustee directors participate in a trustee directors' meeting, or part of a trustee directors' meeting, when:

(a) the meeting has been called and takes place in accordance with the articles, and

(b) they can each communicate to the others any information or opinions they have on any particular item of the business of the meeting.

(2) In determining whether trustee directors are participating in a trustee directors' meeting, it is irrelevant where any director is or how they communicate with each other.

(3) If all the trustee directors participating in a meeting are not in the same place, they may decide that the meeting is to be treated as taking place wherever any of them is.

Article 13 Analysis

See analysis of article 10 in **2.13**.

Article 14 Quorum for trustee directors' meetings

6.20

14.(1) At a meeting of the Trustee Directors, unless a quorum is participating, no proposal is to be voted on, except a proposal to call another meeting.

(2) The quorum for the conduct of business of the Trustee Directors shall:

(a) if there are [5] Trustee Directors, be [3] Trustee Directors, of whom at least one is an Independent Trustee Director and at least one is an Employee Trustee Director; or

(b) if there are fewer than [5] Trustee Directors, be [2] Trustee Directors, of whom one is an Independent Trustee Director and at least one is an Employee Trustee Director.

(3) If the total number of Trustee Directors for the time being is less than the quorum required, the Trustee Directors must not take any decision other than a decision to call another meeting of the Trustee Directors or a general meeting

so as to enable the members to appoint, or if there is only one member, to call upon that member to select and appoint one or more additional Trustee Directors in accordance with the articles.

> *Article 14 Analysis*
>
> Article 14 reflects the main elements of the new model articles. The provisions specify the quorum should include an independent director and an employee director, the two latter individuals would not be applicable to a standard private limited company limited by guarantee. The article may be amended to reflect the actual number of trustees.
>
> See analysis of article 11 in **2.14**.

Article 15 Chairing of trustee directors' meetings

6.21

15.(1) The trustee directors may appoint a director to chair their meetings.

(2) The person so appointed for the time being is known as the chairman.

(3) The trustee directors may terminate the chairman's appointment at any time.

(4) If the chairman is not participating in a trustee directors' meeting within ten minutes of the time at which it was to start, the participating trustee directors must appoint one of themselves to chair it.

> *Article 15 Analysis*
>
> See analysis of article 12 in **2.15**.

Article 16 Casting vote

6.22

16.(1) If the numbers of votes for and against a proposal are equal, the chairman or other director chairing the meeting has a casting vote.

(2) But this does not apply if, in accordance with the articles, the chairman or other director is not to be counted as participating in the decision-making process for quorum or voting purposes.

> *Article 16 Analysis*
>
> See analysis of article 13 in **2.16**.

Article 17 Conflicts of interest

6.23

17.(1) Subject to articles 17.2 and 17.6, if a proposed decision of the Trustee Directors is concerned with an actual or proposed transaction or arrangement with the Company in which a Trustee Director is interested, that Trustee Director is not to be counted as participating in the decision-making process for quorum or voting purposes.

(2) If article 17.3 applies, a Trustee Director who is interested in an actual or proposed transaction or arrangement with the Company is to be counted as participating in the decision-making process for quorum and voting purposes.

(3) This paragraph applies when:

(a) the conflict arises by reason only of the fact that the Trustee Director is:

- (i) an employee or director of the Company with Employee Ownership or of any other member of the Group; or
- (ii) is an employee or director of another member of the Group;

(b) the Trustee Director's conflict of interest arises from:

- (i) a guarantee given, or to be given, by or to a Trustee Director in respect of an obligation incurred by or on behalf of the Company;
- (ii) arrangements pursuant to which benefits are made available to employees or former employees of the Company with Employee Ownership or any other member of the Group which do not provide special benefits for Trustee Directors or former Trustee Directors.

(4) Subject to paragraph 17.6, if a question arises at a meeting of Trustee Directors or of a committee of Trustee Directors as to the right of a Trustee Director to participate in the meeting (or part of the meeting) for voting or quorum purposes, the question may, before the conclusion of the meeting, be referred to the chairman whose ruling in relation to any Trustee Director other than the chairman is to be final and conclusive.

(5) If any question as to the right to participate in the meeting (or part of the meeting) should arise in respect of the chairman, the question is to be decided

by a decision of the Trustee Directors at that meeting, for which purpose the chairman is not to be counted as participating in the meeting (or that part of the meeting) for voting or quorum purposes.

(6) The Trustee Directors may authorise, to the fullest extent permitted by law, any matter proposed to them which would otherwise result in a Trustee Director infringing his duty under section 175 of the Companies Act 2006 to avoid a situation in which such Trustee Director has, or can have, a direct or indirect interest that conflicts, or possibly may conflict, with the interests of the Company and which may reasonably be regarded as likely to give rise to a conflict of interest.

(7) Authorisation of a matter under article 17.6 is effective only if:

(a) the matter has been proposed to the Trustee Directors by its being submitted in writing for consideration at a meeting of the Trustee Directors or for the authorisation of the Trustee Directors by resolution in writing and in accordance with the Trustee Directors' normal procedures or in such other manner as the Trustee Directors may approve;

(b) any requirement as to quorum at the meeting of the Trustee Directors at which the matter is considered is met without counting the Trustee Director in question and any other interested Trustee Director; and

(c) the matter has been agreed to without the Trustee Director in question and any other interested Trustee Director voting or would have been agreed to if their votes had not been counted.

(8) Any authorisation of a matter under article 17.6 shall extend to any actual or potential conflict of interest which may reasonably be expected to arise out of the matter so authorised.

(9) The Trustee Directors may authorise a matter on such terms and for such duration, or impose such limits or conditions on it, as the Trustee Directors may decide and may vary the terms of duration of such an authorisation (including any limits or conditions imposed on such authorisation) or revoke such authorisation. A Trustee Director shall comply with any obligations imposed on him by the Trustee Directors pursuant to any such authorisation.

(10) Any terms imposed by the Trustee Directors under article 17.9 may include (without limitation):

(a) whether the Trustee Director may vote (or be counted in the quorum) at a meeting of the Trustee Directors or any committee or sub-committee of the Trustee Directors in relation to any resolution relating to the relevant matter;

(b) whether the Trustee Director is to be given any documents or other information in relation to the relevant matter; and

(c) whether the Trustee Director is to be excluded from discussions in relation to the relevant matter at a meeting of the Trustee Directors or any committee or subcommittee of the Trustee Directors or otherwise.

(11) The Trustee Director shall not be required to disclose any confidential information obtained in relation to the relevant matter (other than through his position as a Trustee Director of the Company) to the Company or to use to apply it in performing his duties as a Trustee Director if to do so would result in a breach of a duty or obligation of confidence owed to him in relation to or in connection with that matter.

(12) A Trustee Director does not infringe any duty he owes to the Company by virtue of sections 171 to 177 of the Act if he acts in accordance with such terms, limits and conditions (if any) as the Trustee Directors may impose in respect of its authorisation of the Trustee Director's conflict of interest or possible conflict of interest under article 17.6.

(13) A Trustee Director shall not, save as otherwise agreed by him, be accountable to the Company for any benefit which he (or a person connected with him) derives from any matter authorised by the Trustee Directors under article 17.6 and any contract, transaction or arrangement relating thereto shall not be liable to be avoided on the grounds of any such benefit.

(14) A reference in these articles to a conflict of interest includes a conflict of interest and duty and a conflict of duties.

Article 17 Analysis

Article 17 reflects article 14 in the new model articles.[7] Typically, if a director is conflicted, they are restricted from participating in the quorum, therefore they are excluded in the decision-making process concerning the conflicted matter.

The directors may pass an ordinary resolution and disapply the restriction. In addition, the conflicted director may be included in the quorum, if their interest is a permitted cause.[8] Article 17.2 acknowledges that employees, employee trustees and directors of the company will be conflicted on the basis of their relationship with the main company. The provisions do not require an ordinary resolution to authorise the conflict. The provisions allow the company to disapply the requirements of section 175[9] and apply conditions as they see fit.

For further analysis and comparison see article 14 in **2.17**.

7 Schedule 2 Regulation 3 Model articles for private companies limited by guarantee
8 Schedule 2 Regulation 3 Model articles for private companies limited by guarantee, article 14(4).
9 Companies Act 2006, s 175 (Duty to avoid conflicts of interest).

Article 18 Trustee directors' discretion to make further rules

6.24

18.(1) Subject to the articles, the trustee directors may make any rule which they think fit about how they take decisions, and about how such rules are to be recorded or communicated to trustee directors.

> *Article 18 Analysis*
>
> See analysis of article 16 in **2.19**.

Article 19 Directors' remuneration

6.25

19.(1) Except as mentioned in article 4.1,[10] Trustee Directors are not entitled to remuneration for their services to the Company as Trustee Directors.

(2) An Independent Trustee Director is not accountable to the Company for any remuneration which he or she receives as a Trustee Director in accordance with article 4.1.

> *Article 19 Analysis*
>
> Article 19 explicitly states the trustee directors shall not be remunerated. The appointed independent trustee director may receive payment for his or her services agreed between the company and the independent trustee. In contrast the model articles[11] allow all directors in the company to be remunerated.[12]
>
> For further analysis and comparison see article 19 in **2.22**.

10 See article 4(1) above: 'An Independent Trustee Director may be appointed a Trustee Director upon such terms as to remuneration and otherwise as may be agreed at the time of his appointment by the Company (on the one hand) and the Independent Trustee Director (on the other hand) PROVIDED ALWAYS that such an appointment shall be valid only if the terms provide that such Independent Trustee Director may be removed at any time in accordance with these articles.'

11 Schedule 2 Regulation 3 Model articles for private companies limited by guarantee.

12 Schedule 2 Regulation 3 Model articles for private companies limited by guarantee, article 19(2) 'Directors are entitled to such remuneration as the directors determine.'

Article 20 Trustee directors' expenses

6.26

20.(1) The company may pay any reasonable expenses which the trustee directors properly incur in connection with their attendance at:

(a) meetings of trustee directors or committees of trustee directors,

(b) general meetings, or

(c) or otherwise in connection with the exercise of their powers and the discharge of their responsibilities in relation to the company.

> *Article 20 Analysis*
>
> See analysis of article 20 in **2.23**.

Part 3 Members – Becoming and ceasing to be a member

Article 21 Applications for membership

6.27

21.(1) No person shall become a member of the company unless:

(a) that person has completed an application for membership in a form approved by the trustee directors, and

(b) the existing member or members has or have, by ordinary resolution, approved the application or, if the new member or members are to be appointed upon or in consequence of the withdrawal from membership of a sole member of the Company, the Trustee Directors have approved the application.[13]

> *Article 21 Analysis*
>
> Paragraph 21(b) differs from the model articles, allowing for a sole member leaving i.e. if there are no members (employees) to approve the application, the trustee directors may approve the membership. The articles, in addition, require membership to be approved by ordinary resolution.
>
> See analysis of article 21 in **2.24**.

13 Schedule 2 Regulation 3 Model articles for private companies limited by guarantee, article 21(b) 'the trustee directors have approved the application' is replaced with 21(b) above.

Article 22 Termination of membership

6.28

22.(1) A member may withdraw from membership of the company by giving 7 days' notice to the company in writing (provided always that a sole member of the Company may not withdraw from membership of the Company before the appointment of one or more other members of the Company).

(2) Membership is not transferable.

(3) A person's membership terminates when that person dies or ceases to exist (or when such person withdraws from membership in accordance with article 22.1).

> *Article 22 Analysis*
>
> Article 22 reflects the new model articles. In addition, article 22.1 requires the company must always have one member. The last member (sole member) cannot withdraw without appointing a new member.

Organisation of general meetings

Article 23 Attendance and speaking at general meetings[14]

6.29

23.(1) A person is able to exercise the right to speak at a general meeting when that person is in a position to communicate to all those attending the meeting, during the meeting, any information or opinions which that person has on the business of the meeting.

(2) A person is able to exercise the right to vote at a general meeting when:

(a) that person is able to vote, during the meeting, on resolutions put to the vote at the meeting, and

(b) that person's vote can be taken into account in determining whether or not such resolutions are passed at the same time as the votes of all the other persons attending the meeting.

14 This article replicates article 23 in the Schedule 2 Regulation 3 Model articles for private companies limited by guarantee.

(3) The trustee directors may make whatever arrangements they consider appropriate to enable those attending a general meeting to exercise their rights to speak or vote at it.

(4) In determining attendance at a general meeting, it is immaterial whether any two or more members attending it are in the same place as each other.

(5) Two or more persons who are not in the same place as each other attend a general meeting if their circumstances are such that if they have (or were to have) rights to speak and vote at that meeting, they are (or would be) able to exercise them.

> *Article 23 Analysis*
>
> See analysis of article 23 in **2.26**.

Article 24 Quorum for general meetings

6.30

24.(1) If the Company has only one member, every resolution of the member shall be passed as a written resolution[15] in accordance with Chapter 2 of Part 13 of the Companies Act 2006.[16]

(2) (If the Company has more than one member), No business other than the appointment of the chairman of the meeting is to be transacted at a general meeting if the persons attending it do not constitute a quorum.

> *Article 24 Analysis*
>
> Article 24 reflects the new model articles.[17] Article 24(1) requires the sole member to pass a written resolution, this prevents the sole member removing a director or an auditor.[18]

15 Companies Act 2006, s 288 (Written resolutions of private companies).

16 Companies Act 2006, Part 13, Chapter 2 (Written resolutions. General provisions about written resolutions).

17 Schedule 2 Regulation 3 Model articles for private companies limited by guarantee.

18 Companies Act 2006, s 288(2) 'The following may not be passed as a written resolution: (a) a resolution under section 168 removing a director before the expiration of his period of office; (b) a resolution under section 510 removing an auditor before the expiration of his term of office.'

Article 25 Chairing general meetings

6.31

25.(1) If the trustee directors have appointed a chairman, the chairman shall chair general meetings if present and willing to do so.

(2) If the trustee directors have not appointed a chairman, or if the chairman is unwilling to chair the meeting or is not present within ten minutes of the time at which a meeting was due to start—

(a) the trustee directors present, or

(b) (if no trustee directors are present), the meeting,

must appoint a director or member to chair the meeting, and the appointment of the chairman of the meeting must be the first business of the meeting.

(3) The person chairing a meeting in accordance with this article is referred to as "the chairman of the meeting".

> *Article 25 Analysis*
>
> See analysis of article 25 in **2.28**.

Article 26 Attendance and speaking by trustee directors and non-members

6.32

26.(1) Trustee directors may attend and speak at general meetings, whether or not they are members.

(2) The chairman of the meeting may permit other persons who are not members of the company to attend and speak at a general meeting.

> *Article 26 Analysis*
>
> See analysis of article 26 in **2.29**.

Article 27 Adjournment

6.33

27.(1) If the persons attending a general meeting within half an hour of the time at which the meeting was due to start do not constitute a quorum, or if during a meeting a quorum ceases to be present, the chairman of the meeting must adjourn it.

(2) The chairman of the meeting may adjourn a general meeting at which a quorum is present if—

(a) the meeting consents to an adjournment, or

(b) it appears to the chairman of the meeting that an adjournment is necessary to protect the safety of any person attending the meeting or ensure that the business of the meeting is conducted in an orderly manner.

(3) The chairman of the meeting must adjourn a general meeting if directed to do so by the meeting.

(4) When adjourning a general meeting, the chairman of the meeting must—

(a) either specify the time and place to which it is adjourned or state that it is to continue at a time and place to be fixed by the trustee directors, and

(b) have regard to any directions as to the time and place of any adjournment which have been given by the meeting.

(5) If the continuation of an adjourned meeting is to take place more than 14 days after it was adjourned, the company must give at least 7 clear days' notice of it (that is, excluding the day of the adjourned meeting and the day on which the notice is given)—

(a) to the same persons to whom notice of the company's general meetings is required to be given, and

(b) containing the same information which such notice is required to contain.

(6) No business may be transacted at an adjourned general meeting which could not properly have been transacted at the meeting if the adjournment had not taken place.

Article 27 Analysis

See analysis of article 27 in **2.30**.

Voting at general meetings

Article 28 Voting: general

6.34

28. A resolution put to the vote of a general meeting must be decided on a show of hands unless a poll is duly demanded in accordance with the articles.

> *Article 28 Analysis*
>
> See analysis of article 28 in **2.31**.

Article 29 Errors and disputes

6.35

29.(1) No objection may be raised to the qualification of any person voting at a general meeting except at the meeting or adjourned meeting at which the vote objected to is tendered, and every vote not disallowed at the meeting is valid.

(2) Any such objection must be referred to the chairman of the meeting whose decision is final.

> *Article 29 Analysis*
>
> See analysis of article 29 in **2.32**.

Article 30 Poll votes

6.36

30.(1) A poll on a resolution may be demanded—

(a) in advance of the general meeting where it is to be put to the vote, or

(b) at a general meeting, either before a show of hands on that resolution or immediately after the result of a show of hands on that resolution is declared.

(2) A poll may be demanded by—

(a) the chairman of the meeting;

(b) the trustee directors;

(c) two or more persons having the right to vote on the resolution; or

(d) a person or persons representing not less than one tenth of the total voting rights of all the members having the right to vote on the resolution.

(3) A demand for a poll may be withdrawn if—

(a) the poll has not yet been taken, and

(b) the chairman of the meeting consents to the withdrawal.

(4) Polls must be taken immediately and in such manner as the chairman of the meeting directs.

> *Article 30 Analysis*
>
> See analysis of article 30 in **2.33**.

Article 31 Content of proxy notices

6.37

31.(1) Proxies may only validly be appointed by a notice in writing (a "proxy notice") which—

(a) states the name and address of the member appointing the proxy;

(b) identifies the person appointed to be that member's proxy and the general meeting in relation to which that person is appointed;

(c) is signed by or on behalf of the member appointing the proxy, or is authenticated in such manner as the trustee directors may determine; and

(d) is delivered to the company in accordance with the articles and any instructions contained in the notice of the general meeting to which they relate.

(2) The company may require proxy notices to be delivered in a particular form, and may specify different forms for different purposes.

(3) Proxy notices may specify how the proxy appointed under them is to vote (or that the proxy is to abstain from voting) on one or more resolutions.

(4) Unless a proxy notice indicates otherwise, it must be treated as—

(a) allowing the person appointed under it as a proxy discretion as to how to vote on any ancillary or procedural resolutions put to the meeting, and

(b) appointing that person as a proxy in relation to any adjournment of the general meeting to which it relates as well as the meeting itself.

Article 31 Analysis

See analysis of article 31 in **2.34**.

Article 32 Delivery of proxy notices

6.38

32.(1) A person who is entitled to attend, speak or vote (either on a show of hands or on a poll) at a general meeting remains so entitled in respect of that meeting or any adjournment of it, even though a valid proxy notice has been delivered to the company by or on behalf of that person.

(2) An appointment under a proxy notice may be revoked by delivering to the company a notice in writing given by or on behalf of the person by whom or on whose behalf the proxy notice was given.

(3) A notice revoking a proxy appointment only takes effect if it is delivered before the start of the meeting or adjourned meeting to which it relates.

(4) If a proxy notice is not executed by the person appointing the proxy, it must be accompanied by written evidence of the authority of the person who executed it to execute it on the appointor's behalf.

Article 32 Analysis

See analysis of article 32 in **2.35**.

Article 33 Amendments to resolutions

6.39

33.(1) An ordinary resolution to be proposed at a general meeting may be amended by ordinary resolution if—

(a) notice of the proposed amendment is given to the company in writing by a person entitled to vote at the general meeting at which it is to be proposed not less than 48 hours before the meeting is to take place (or such later time as the chairman of the meeting may determine), and

(b) the proposed amendment does not, in the reasonable opinion of the chairman of the meeting, materially alter the scope of the resolution.

(2) A special resolution to be proposed at a general meeting may be amended by ordinary resolution, if—

(a) the chairman of the meeting proposes the amendment at the general meeting at which the resolution is to be proposed, and

(b) the amendment does not go beyond what is necessary to correct a grammatical or other non-substantive error in the resolution.

(3) If the chairman of the meeting, acting in good faith, wrongly decides that an amendment to a resolution is out of order, the chairman's error does not invalidate the vote on that resolution.

Article 33 Analysis

See analysis of article 33 in **2.36**.

Part 4 Administrative arrangements

Article 34 Means of communication to be used

6.40

34.(1) Subject to the articles, anything sent or supplied by or to the company under the articles may be sent or supplied in any way in which the Companies Act 2006 provides for documents or information which are authorised or required by any provision of that Act to be sent or supplied by or to the company.

(2) Subject to the articles, any notice or document to be sent or supplied to a director in connection with the taking of decisions by trustee directors may also be sent or supplied by the means by which that director has asked to be sent or supplied with such notices or documents for the time being.

(3) A director may agree with the company that notices or documents sent to that director in a particular way are to be deemed to have been received within a specified time of their being sent, and for the specified time to be less than 48 hours.

Article 34 Analysis

See analysis of article 34 in **2.37**.

Article 35 Company seals

6.41

35.(1) Any common seal may only be used by the authority of the trustee directors.

(2) The trustee directors may decide by what means and in what form any common seal is to be used.

(3) Unless otherwise decided by the trustee directors, if the company has a common seal and it is affixed to a document, the document must also be signed by at least one authorised person in the presence of a witness who attests the signature.

(4) For the purposes of this article, an authorised person is—

(a) any director of the company;

(b) the company secretary (if any); or

(c) any person authorised by the trustee directors for the purpose of signing documents to which the common seal is applied.

Article 35 Analysis
See analysis of article 35 in **2.38**.

Article 36 No right to inspect accounts and other records

6.42

36(1) A sole member of the Company shall have the right to inspect any of the Company's accounting or other records or documents on giving reasonable notice to the Trustee directors.

(2) Subject to article 36.1, except as provided by law or authorised by the Trustee directors or an ordinary resolution of the Company, no person is entitled to inspect any of the Company's accounting or other records or documents merely by virtue of being a member.

Article 36 Analysis
See analysis of article 36 in **2.39**.

Article 37 Provision for employees on cessation of business

6.43

37. The "trustee" trustee directors may decide to make provision for the benefit of persons employed or formerly employed by the company or any of its subsidiaries (other than a director or former director or shadow director) in connection with the cessation or transfer to any person of the whole or part of the undertaking of the company or that subsidiary.

> *Article 37 Analysis*
>
> See analysis of article 37 in **2.40**.

Trustee directors' indemnity and insurance

Article 38 Indemnity

6.44

38.(1) Subject to paragraph (2), a relevant director of the company or an associated company may be indemnified out of the company's assets against—

(a) any liability incurred by that director in connection with any negligence, default, breach of duty or breach of trust in relation to the company or an associated company,

(b) any liability incurred by that director in connection with the activities of the company or an associated company in its capacity as a trustee of an occupational pension scheme (as defined in section 235(6) of the Companies Act 2006),

(c) any other liability incurred by that director as an officer of the company or an associated company.

(2) This article does not authorise any indemnity which would be prohibited or rendered void by any provision of the Companies Acts or by any other provision of law.

(3) In this article—

(a) companies are associated if one is a subsidiary of the other or both are subsidiaries of the same body corporate, and

(b) a "relevant director" means any director or former director of the company or an associated company.

Article 39 Insurance

6.45

39.(1) The trustee directors may decide to purchase and maintain insurance, at the expense of the company, for the benefit of any relevant director in respect of any relevant loss.

(2) In this article—

(a) a "relevant director" means any director or former director of the company or an associated company,

(b) a "relevant loss" means any loss or liability which has been or may be incurred by a relevant director in connection with that director's duties or powers in relation to the company, any associated company or any pension fund or employees' share scheme of the company or associated company, and

(c) companies are associated if one is a subsidiary of the other or both are subsidiaries of the same body corporate

Articles 38 and 39 Analysis

See analysis of articles 38 and 39 in **2.42**.

Analysis of the model articles of association of a company with employee ownership

Assumptions

6.46

- The model documentation provides for the establishment of an Employees' Council.
- The model documentation presents an example of rules that could be used to govern a postal ballot of employees.

Model Articles of Association of a Company Limited by Shares with Employee Ownership

THE COMPANIES ACT 2006

PRIVATE COMPANY LMITED BY SHARES

ARTICLES OF ASSOCIATION

of

[INSERT NAME] LIMITED

("the Company")

(Adopted by written special resolution on [date])

Article 1 Defined terms

6.47

1 In these Articles, unless the context requires otherwise:

"the Act" means the Companies Act 2006 (as amended)

"the Companies Acts" has the meaning given by section 2 of the Companies Act 2006 which may, by virtue of that or any other such enactment, be cited together with the Act as the "Companies Acts" (with or without the addition of an indication of the date of any such enactment)

"Compulsory Transfer Notice" means a transfer notice deemed to be given pursuant to Articles 7.14, 7.15 or 7.22(b)

"Control" has the meaning given in section 995 of the Income Tax Act 2007

"Director" means a director of the Company

"the Directors" means the board of directors of the Company

"Employee" means a bona fide employee of a member of the Group

"Employees' Council" means the body mentioned in Article 9

"Employee Director" means a Director whose appointment and removal as a Director is as mentioned in Article 11

"Employees' Share Scheme" has the meaning given in section 1166 of the Act "the Group" means the Company and any other company which is for the time being both a subsidiary of the Company and under the Control of the Company

"HMRC" means Her Majesty's Revenue and Customs

"ITEPA" means the Income Tax (Earnings and Pensions) Act 2003

"Leaves" means ceases to hold employment within the Group

"Leaving Date" means, in relation to an Employee or former Employee, the date on which he or she Leaves

"the Model Articles" means, the model articles for private companies limited by shares contained in Schedule 1 of the Companies (Model Articles) Regulations 2008 (SI 2008/3229) as amended prior to the date of adoption of these Articles

"the Principles" means the principles set out in Part 2 of the document entitled 'Guide to the Constitution of [name of the Company]' as that document is amended from time to time

"securities" has the meaning given in section 420 of ITEPA

"Share Incentive Plan" means a share incentive plan approved by HMRC pursuant to section 488 and Schedule 2 of ITEPA

"Shares" means shares in the capital of the Company

"Statutory Market Value" means, in relation to any Shares, the market value of such Shares determined in accordance with Part 8 of the Taxation of Chargeable Gains Act 1992 (as amended or reenacted)

"Transferee" means a person who agrees to acquire Shares in accordance with these Articles.

"Transfer Notice" means, in respect of any Shares, a notice given or deemed to be given to the Company that the holder of such Shares wishes, or is obliged, to offer such Shares for sale and transfer in accordance with the provisions of these Articles.

"Transfer Price" means the price per Share at which Transfer Shares may be sold and transferred as determined in accordance with these Articles.

"Transfer Shares" means Shares which are the subject of a Transfer Notice

"Transferor" means a person wishing, or obliged, to offer Shares for sale and transfer pursuant to these Articles

"the Trust" means The [INSERT NAME] Employees' Share Trust established by the Trust Deed

"the Trust Deed" means the trust deed dated [……….] between the Company and [INSERT NAME] Employees' Trustees Limited, a company limited by guarantee registered in England & Wales with registered no. [ ] (being the original trustee of that trust), which established the Trust (as amended from time to time)

"the Trustee" means the trustee or trustees for the time being of the Trust (and references to the Trustee shall be construed as referring only to such person or persons acting in their capacity as trustee of that trust)

"Voluntary Transfer Notice" means a Transfer Notice voluntarily given pursuant to Article 7.5

2 For the purposes of these Articles:

(a) a person shall not be treated as ceasing to hold office or employment within the Group unless and until he or she is no longer an employee or director of any member of the Group;

(b) references to any statute order or regulation includes a reference to such statute as amended, modified, re-enacted or replaced from time to time;

(c) words and phrases which are defined or referred to in or for the purposes of the Companies Acts have the same meanings in these Articles unless they are already defined within the Articles or the context otherwise requires;

(d) headings are for ease of reference and shall not affect the interpretation of these Articles.

Article 2 Application of the Model Articles

6.48

2.(1) The Model Articles shall apply to the Company save as expressly excluded or modified by these Articles or as are inconsistent with the provisions of these Articles.

(2) Model Articles 14(1)–14(4), 26, 27(2) shall not apply.

Article 2 Analysis

Alternative Precedent – Model articles shall apply by reference[19]

Precedent 1

The model articles for private companies limited by shares contained or incorporated in Schedule 1 to the Companies (Model Articles) Regulations 2008, SI 2008/3229 as amended prior to the date of adoption of these

19 See 'Model articles shall not apply' in **6.5** above.

articles (the 'Model Articles') shall apply to the company, save insofar as they are varied or excluded by, or are inconsistent with, the following articles:

Model articles 14(1)–14(4), 26, 27(2) shall not apply.

In these articles and the Model Articles any reference to any statutory provision shall be deemed to include a reference to each and every statutory amendment, modification, re-enactment and extension thereof for the time being in force.

If applicable:

Precedent 2

Table A in the Schedule to the Companies (Tables A to F) Regulations 1985 (as amended) ('Table A') shall not apply to the Company.[20]

In these Articles and the Model Articles any reference to any statutory provision shall be deemed to include a reference to each and every statutory amendment, modification, re-enactment and extension thereof for the time being in force.

Article 3 Private limited company

6.49

3.(1) The Company is a private company and no shares or debentures of the Company may be offered for sale to the public.

Article 3 Analysis

Article 3 reflects section 755,[21] a private company must not offer shares to the general public. It should be noted, subject to the articles, the company can however offer shares to existing shareholders, or to professional investors and companies.

Article 4 Share capital

6.50

4.(1) The share capital of the Company at the date of the adoption of these Articles is £[...........] divided into [............] Shares.

20 The article is only needed if the company was incorporated before 1 October 2009.

21 Companies Act 2006, s 755 (Prohibition of public offers by private company). '(1) A private company limited by shares or limited by guarantee and having a share capital must not: (a) offer to the public any securities of the company.'

> *Article 4 Analysis*
>
> The article describes the share capital structure of the company, the article does not appear in the model articles.[22]

Article 5 Special consent

6.51

5.(1) The following matters shall each require either the prior consent in writing of members together holding Shares representing at least 75 per cent of the issued equity share capital of the Company or the passing of a special resolution of the members of the Company at a general meeting of the company:

(a) [the grant of any right to subscribe for shares in the capital of the Company or any other member of the Group otherwise than pursuant to an Employees' Share Scheme;

(b) an issue of any shares in the capital of the Company otherwise than pursuant to the exercise of a right granted as mentioned in sub-clause (a) above and authorised pursuant to this Article 5.1 or a right granted as mentioned in sub-clause 5.2(a) below and authorised pursuant to Article 5.2;

(c) the transfer of any shares in the capital of the Company (not being a transfer permitted by Article 7.4) to any person other than an existing member of the Company;

(d) a winding-up of the Company or of any other member of the Group (other than a company which is dormant);

(e) the disposal of the whole or a substantial part of the undertaking or assets of the Company;

(f) any change of status of the Company to a public limited company or application for any shares in the Company or in any parent undertaking of the Company to be dealt in on a public market;

(g) the removal of [INSERT NAME] Employees' Trustees Limited as trustee of the Trust;

(h) the appointment of any person, other than [INSERT NAME] Employees' Trustees Limited, as trustee of the Trust.]

(2) The following matters shall each require either the prior consent in writing of members together holding Shares representing at least 50 per cent of the issued equity share capital of the Company or the passing of an ordinary

22 Schedule 1 Regulation 2 Model articles for private companies limited by shares.

resolution of the members of the Company at a general meeting of the company:

(a) [the grant of any right to subscribe for shares in the capital of the Company pursuant to an Employees' Share Scheme;

(b) the acquisition by the Company or by any other member of the Group (other than by the Trustee) of an interest in the equity share capital of the Company;

(c) the payment of dividends;

(d) the payment to an Employee or Employees of a bonus out of the profits of the Company which would otherwise be available for distribution (as mentioned in section 830 of the Act);

(e) the payment or award to any Employee of a bonus (in cash or kind) of an amount which represents more than [25] per cent of the annual rate of basic salary payable to such Employee, being a bonus paid otherwise than in accordance with a binding obligation to make such payment or award under the terms of such Employee's contract of employment;

(f) the disposal or the entering into of a binding agreement to dispose, to a person who is not a member of the Group, of:

   (i) shares or securities in any member of the Group;

   (ii) any business or assets with a value in excess of £[ ] or, if less, 10 per cent of the net asset value of the Group;

(g) the making of a loan to any person in excess of £[ ] or, if less, 10 per cent of the net asset value of the Group;

(h) any alteration of or addition to the Trust Deed.]

Article 5 Analysis

The article describes the situations where special consent is required to take certain actions. The provisions here are often detailed in the shareholder agreement, it should be noted the articles of association are public documents. The directors may decide not to publish sensitive rules on Companies House.The actions in article 5(1) require a special resolution, in article 5(2) the voting consent requires a simple majority.

Alternative provisions

- 'Investor Director Consent' means the prior written consent of all the Investor Directors.
- 'Investor Director Consent' means the prior written consent of at least 50% of the Investor Directors.

- 'Investor Majority' means 75% of Series A Shares from time to time.
- 'Investor Majority Consent' means the prior written consent of the Investor Majority.

The provisions requiring consent are not limited to those detailed in article 5, the company ought to review any possible situation or occurrence where the company would require a special resolution to be passed. Depending on the share and voting structure, care should be taken to not fetter the right of minority shareholders or indeed, in reverse, allow a small shareholder minority to sway the power of the company.

The special consent may require a percentage over and above that of a special resolution, for example 80 per cent. Care should be taken not to entrench provisions, resulting in certain articles becoming almost impossible to amend,[23] as this may impede the directors' power to run the company effectively.

Companies House – notification procedures for entrenched articles

If the company includes entrenched provisions, or makes alterations to any entrenched provisions in the company's articles, a notification is required to be sent to Companies House.

The article does not appear in the model articles.[24]

Article 6 Lien on shares

6.52

6.(1) The Company shall have a first and paramount lien on all Shares (whether or not such shares are fully-paid) registered in the name of a person indebted or under liability to the Company (whether such person is the sole holder of the shares or one of two or more joint holders) for all moneys (whether presently payable or not) payable at a fixed time or called, and to all distributions and other moneys and property attributable to such shares.

(2) The Directors may at any time declare any Share to be wholly or in part exempt from the provisions of this Article 6.

23 Absolute entrenchment is no longer available for companies incorporated after 1 October 2006. To interpret the legislation, a company's articles may contain provision for entrenchment, only in terms that specified provisions may be amended or repealed only if they are more restrictive than passing a special resolution. Therefore an article requiring 80% of the eligible votes to pass would be described as entrenched, or alternatively 'all members' must agree. It was the intention of the Act to allow for 'absolute entrenchment' due to Companies Act 2006, ss 22(3)(a),23 being added at committee stage (and being at odds with absolute entrenchment). The original clause, that specified articles could not be amended or repealed, was removed.

24 Schedule 1 Regulation 2 Model articles for private companies limited by shares.

(3) The Company's lien on a Share shall extend to any amounts presently payable to the Company by the registered holder of such share or if such registered holder has died, his or her estate.

> *Article 6 Analysis*
>
> Article 6 is omitted from the private limited company articles.
>
> If the company requires the ability to issue partly paid shares, this article may be inserted into the company articles. Partly paid shares typically are issued to employees as an incentive, and included here on the basis the company will issue partly paid shares to employees. The articles provide the ability to transact partly paid shares and the relevant rules.
>
> The article appears in the model articles for public companies.[25]

Article 7 Share transfers

6.53

7.(1) No Share or any interest in a Share may be transferred otherwise than in accordance with the provisions of this Article and Model Article 26 shall have effect subject to the following provisions of these Articles.

(2) For the purpose of ensuring that a transfer of Shares is duly authorised or required under these Articles, the Directors may require any member or legal representatives of any deceased member or any person named as transferee in any transfer lodged for registration or such other person as the Directors may reasonably believe to have information relevant to such purpose, to furnish to the Company such information and evidence as the Directors may think fit regarding any matter which they deem relevant to such purpose including (but not limited to) the names, addresses and interests of all persons respectively having interests in the Shares from time to time registered in that member's name. Failing such information and evidence being furnished to the satisfaction of the Directors within a period of 28 days after such request, the Directors may refuse to register the transfer in question.

(3) Subject to Article 7.2, the Directors shall be bound to register a transfer of any Share made in accordance with the following provisions of this Article 7 but may otherwise refuse to register the transfer of a share and, if they do so, the instrument of transfer must be returned to the transferee with the notice of refusal unless they suspect that the proposed transfer may be fraudulent.

25 Schedule 3 Regulation 4 Model articles for public companies, article 52.

Article 7(1)–7(3) Analysis

A company will require control over its shares and to whom they can be transferred. A conventional procedure used regularly by companies is to offer shares on a pre-emptive basis. The member wishing to dispose of their shareholding offers first refusal to other members, this may include the company purchasing the shares, if the articles allow it.

It is unlikely that any potential external purchaser would consider acquiring a minority shareholding, typically a sale of a company would involve all members and the purchaser buying the company outright on terms favourable to majority and minority shareholders.

On the basis a minority shareholder prompted the company or its members to buy out the holding and employed the pre-emptive provisions (assuming they are drafted in the company's constitution), funds may not be available to complete the transaction.

A common occurrence where share buybacks and pre-emption rights cause difficulties for a company is on the death of a shareholder who has by will or intestacy allowed the shareholding to pass to his beneficiaries or executors.

It should be noted shareholders ought to agree on a rolling three-year basis the value of the members' shares on the assumption any of them shall die in that period. Once a fixed price is agreed a cross-option agreement can be put in place with the option of a life insurance policy on each member's life to cover the share purchase from the beneficiary. There are a number of common circumstances that company directors ought to plan for and draft suitable precedents in the articles of association to prevent expensive litigation. Broadly the following issues should be addressed on a regular basis and a suitable strategy implemented:

- The death of a member and cross options agreements.
- Deadlocked company.
- Permitted transfers to family members.
- Voluntary transfers.
- Mandatory transfer for good and bad leavers.
- Drag and tag along.

Permitted transfers

(4) Any Share may at any time be transferred without restriction as to price or otherwise:

(a) to the Trustee;

(b) by the Trustee to any individual who is within the class of beneficiaries of the Trust;

(c) by the Trustee to the trustee or trustee of any other trust for the benefit of persons who are employees of members of the Group and which is an Employees' Share Scheme;

(d) to the trustee or trustees of a Share Incentive Plan;

(e) by the trustee or trustees of a Share Incentive Plan to any individual pursuant to and in accordance with the rules of such Share Incentive Plan;

(f) to any person appointed as the Trustee upon a change of trustee, or upon the appointment of a new trustee, of the Trust;

(g) to any person appointed as trustee upon a change of trustee, or the appointment of a new trustee, of a Share Incentive Plan;

(h) to any person appointed as trustee of any such other trust as mentioned in subparagraph (c) above upon a change of trustee, or the appointment of a new trustee, of such trust; or

(i) subject to the Companies Act, to the Company for cancellation or to be held in treasury.

Article 7(4) Analysis

The article prescribes that no share restriction shall apply on the transfer of shares to the trustee company or share incentive plan.

Simplified Precedent

Permitted transfers by investors

1. Subject to any other provision of these articles the following transfers of shares may be made by the investor directors without restriction or any authorisation:
2. [transfer to a holding company];
3. [company investment trust];
4. [trustee or trust];
5. [company investment investor];
6. [company investment house];
7. [company fund manager].

Voluntary transfers

(5) Subject to Article 7.18, any person wishing to transfer a Share or any interest in a Share otherwise than as mentioned in Article 7.4 must give to the Company a Transfer Notice in writing in respect of such Share. A Voluntary

Transfer Notice, once given, may not be withdrawn without the agreement of the Directors. A Voluntary Transfer Notice may be given subject to a condition that it shall be revoked if either:

(a) the Transferor and the Directors cannot reach agreement as to the Transfer Price (as mentioned in Article 7.19(a)); or

(b) offers are not received by the Directors for all of the Transfer Shares.

> *Article 7(5) Analysis*
>
> Article 7.5 reflects the Companies Act 2006, that a company may not register a share transfer unless a proper instrument of transfer has been delivered to the company.[26] It should be noted, the article is typically expanded to provide a simple process of delivery and contents of the transfer notice, if clarity is required.

Effect of a transfer notice

(6) A Transfer Notice shall constitute the Company as agent of the Transferor for the sale and transfer of the Shares in respect of which such Transfer Notice is given or is deemed to be given at a price per Share determined in accordance with the following provisions of these Articles.

(7) The Directors shall, within 14 days beginning with the date on which the Transfer Notice is given or is deemed to be given, first offer the Transfer Shares to the Trustee, and if and insofar as the Trustee does not, within the period of [21] days following receipt of such offer, accept such offer in respect of any of the Transfer Shares:

(a) offer the Transfer Shares for sale at the Transfer Price to any one or more of the following persons (and, if more than one, in such proportions as the Directors may determine):

  (i) the trustee or trustees of any Share Incentive Plan established by the Company;

  (ii) any one or more Employees;

  (iii) the trustee or trustees of any such other trust as is mentioned in sub-paragraph (c) of Article 7.4; (iv) the Company; or

(b) offer the Transfer Shares, or the balance remaining of the Transfer Shares, to all of the holders of Shares (other than the Transferor) by making an offer of such Shares to each of such holders in proportion to or as nearly

26 Companies Act 2006, s 770 (Registration of transfer).

as may be in proportion to their respective holdings of Shares ("a General Offer"); or

(c) offer a proportion of the Transfer Shares as mentioned in (a) above and make a General Offer in respect of the balance of the Transfer Shares.

(8) If a General Offer is made, the Directors shall also invite each holder of Shares to state in his reply to the General Offer the number of additional Shares (if any) in excess of his proportion which such holder desires to purchase. If any holder of Shares does not accept the General Offer in respect of his respective proportion in full, the Shares not so accepted shall be used to satisfy requests for additional Shares as nearly as may be in proportion to the number of Shares already held by those holders who have made such requests respectively, provided that no holder shall be obliged to purchase more Shares than he shall have applied for. If any Shares shall not be capable of being so offered without fractions of those Shares being offered to the holders of Shares in proportion to their existing holdings, such Shares shall be offered to the holders of Shares, or some of them, in such proportions or in such manner as the Directors shall determine.

(9) If or to the extent that any offer or offers made as mentioned in Article 7.7(a) is or are not accepted in respect of all of the Transfer Shares within 28 days of such offer or offers having been made, the Directors shall make a General Offer in respect of the balance of such Shares.

(10) A General Offer shall be open for acceptance for 60 days or such shorter period as the Directors may determine from the date on which it is made and insofar as it is not then accepted, it shall lapse.

(11) If after the expiry of any such General Offer any Shares remain unsold or if any Transferee fails to complete his purchase of Shares within 28 days of the time from his date of acceptance of any such offer, the Directors may offer such Shares for sale at the Transfer Price to any such other person or persons as the Directors may determine PROVIDED ALWAYS that, if any such person is not already a member of the Company, the admission of such person or persons as a member of the Company is, in the opinion of the Directors, in the best interests of the Company.

(12) If any such offer to purchase Transfer Shares is accepted in respect of any number of Transfer Shares, the Transferor shall (save, in the case of a Voluntary Transfer Notice, if a condition imposed as mentioned in Article 7.5 is not satisfied) be bound to accept such offer and to transfer such Shares in accordance with, and subject to, the provisions of this Article 7.

(13) If in any case the Transferor, after having become bound to sell any Transfer Shares, defaults in transferring them, the Directors may receive the purchase money on his behalf, and the Transferor shall be deemed to have appointed

as his attorney any Director for the purpose of authorising such Director to execute a transfer of such Shares on behalf of the Transferor in favour of the Transferee. The receipt of the Company for the purchase money shall be a good discharge to the Transferee and such purchase monies shall be paid by the Company into a separate bank account in the name of the Transferor.

Article 7(6)–7(13) Analysis

Article 7(6) explains the pre-emption process if shares become available for purchase in accordance with a voluntary transfer. It is common to appoint the company the agent for the sale, who then offers on the shares on behalf of the vendor to those specified in article 7(7).

The general offer allows all the shareholders to buy the shares in direct proportion to their existing shareholding, at the transfer price, the general offer is open for 60 days, subject to the articles. If shares remain unallocated, the company may, in accordance with article 7(11), offer the shares to whomever they deem suitable, on the basis the sale is in the best interests of the company. Typically, the clause is amended to allow the company to buy the shareholding from distributable profits, referred to as treasury shares,[27] this more preferable option negates the possibility of the shares being sold to external individuals or corporate bodies. It should be noted, treasury shares is a complicated area of company law and legal advice should be sought if including provisions for the company to buy back its own shares.

Compulsory Transfer Notice

(14) If any holder of Shares, being an Employee, Leaves, he or she ("the Relevant Person") shall thereupon be deemed to have given a Transfer Notice (as mentioned in Article 7.5) in respect of all of the Shares which he then holds on [the first anniversary of] the Leaving Date of the Relevant Person.

(15) If any person not being an Employee ("the Newly-Acquiring Shareholder") acquires Shares in pursuance of rights or interests obtained by that, or any other, person at a time when that, or such other, person ("the Relevant Person") was an Employee, the Newly-Acquiring Shareholder shall, upon acquiring such Shares, be deemed to have given a Transfer Notice in respect of all such Shares [on the first anniversary of the Leaving Date of the Relevant Person].

(16) The provisions of Articles 7.5 to 7.13 (inclusive) shall apply in relation to any transfer of Shares made pursuant to the application of Articles 7.14, 7.15 and 7.22(b).

27 Companies Act 2006, s 724 (Treasury shares).

(17) If no willing purchaser can be found from amongst the persons to whom the Transfer Shares have been offered by the Directors for any of the Transfer Shares in respect of which a Compulsory Transfer Notice is given or deemed to be given, the balance remaining of the Transfer Shares shall, subject to Article 9, remain registered in the name of the Transferor but the Company shall have the right, exercisable at any time, to require the Transferor to sell and transfer such Shares to a willing purchaser at the Transfer Price.

(18) If on any occasion a Compulsory Transfer Notice is deemed to be given in respect of any Shares, any Voluntary Transfer Notice previously given or deemed to be given in respect of such Shares shall cease to be of any effect so that the provisions of this Article 7 shall apply in relation to such Compulsory Transfer Notice and shall cease to apply in relation to such

Article 7(14)–7(18) Analysis

Compulsory transfer notices, or deemed transfer notices, mean the shares are automatically transferred without the need for A share transfer notice, or any other instrument of transfer. The article prescribes that in relation to any employee leaving the company, on the assumption that employee has transferred shares to a family member (for example a spouse or child), all shares connected to the leaver will be deemed to have been transferred in accordance with the provisions of 7(14) and 7(15). The date of transfer is specified as the leaving date or an anniversary period. The later part of the article reaffirms the pre-emption process the company must follow to allocate the leaver's shareholding.

Voluntary Transfer Notice – Transfer Price

(19) The Transfer Price shall:

(a) if the Transfer Notice is a Voluntary Transfer Notice, be such price as the Transferor and Transferee and the Directors may agree or, in the absence of such agreement, the market value of the Transfer Shares at the time of transfer of the Transfer Shares, determined as mentioned in Articles 7.20 or 7.21; or

(b) if the Transfer Notice is a Compulsory Transfer Notice, be (subject to Article 7.21), the market value of the Transfer Shares at the Leaving Date or, if the Shares are transferred pursuant to the Company exercising its right under Article 7.17, at the time of transfer of the Transfer Shares, determined (in either case) as mentioned in Article 7.20.

Article 7(19) Analysis

The provisions summarise the price for voluntary and compulsory share transfers, in the case of a voluntary share transfer, the value is based on agreement between the parties or an independent valuation in accordance with article 7(20). If a compulsory transfer (leaver), the shares are purchased at the market value on the date of leaving, the market value may be ascertained by way of independent valuation.

The model articles for an employee ownership company do not provide for a 'bad leaver' and assume the leaver is in accordance with article 7(14), has not caused the company any detriment, or committed any fraudulent or illegal acts.

It would be abhorrent to the remaining shareholders if a leaver left after embezzling company funds or causing damage to its reputation, then received full market value for their shareholding. Therefore, it is common to include a 'bad leaver' provision, if the leaver is deemed a bad leaver, they shall receive only the nominal value of their shareholding. The following precedent may be adapted to the requirements of the existing articles.

Precedent

Bad leavers

Any person who ceases to be an employee for reasons other than:

1. on his death;
2. bankruptcy;
3. wrongful dismissal;
4. permanent disability or incapacity through ill health; or
5. retirement at normal retirement age,

(shall be deemed a 'bad leaver').

A 'bad leaver' of the company shall be deemed to have immediately served a transfer notice (a 'mandatory transfer notice') and his shareholding 'leaver's shares' shall be dealt with (unless the directors resolve otherwise) in accordance with the following provisions.

The sale price for the leaver's shares shall be:

1. the lower of the issue price and the fair price.

[If the parties agree the sale price shall be the issue price then paragraphs 39.5–39.8 shall not apply to these articles.] [The bad leaver and the company shall agree the issue price and fair price.]

If the parties fail to agree a 'fair price' within 7 business days of the company receiving the mandatory transfer notice the company will immediately appoint the 'expert' to determine the fair price for the 'leaver's shares'.

The expert will be a firm of chartered accountants nominated by the 'leaver' and the company.

> The 'expert' shall certify the 'fair price' as soon as possible and will without evidence of inaccuracy or fault be final and binding on the 'leaver' and the company.
>
> The cost of obtaining the 'fair price' will be divided equally by the 'seller' and the company unless the directors decide otherwise.

Valuation of a share

(20) Subject to Article 7.21, the market value of any Shares at a given time shall be the amount which is certified in writing to the Directors to be, in the expert opinion of an independent adviser (not being the auditors of any member of the Group) nominated by the Directors and who, in their opinion, is appropriately qualified to value shares in unquoted companies, the Statutory Market Value of the Shares at that time. Upon receipt of such certificate, the Directors shall as soon as practicable inform all members of the market value so determined. It shall be the responsibility of the Directors to obtain such an opinion as soon as reasonably practicable after a Transfer Notice has been given or has been deemed to be given. The costs of obtaining any such certificate shall be borne by the company [unless the Transfer Notice is a Voluntary Transfer Notice, in which case the Transferor shall bear such costs].

(21) If for any purpose the company has reached agreement with HMRC as to what is the Statutory Market Value of a Share as at the relevant time, the Directors may determine that such Statutory Market Value shall be taken to be the market value of Shares for the purposes of Article 7.19 and, in this event, the provisions of Article 7.20 shall not apply in relation to the relevant transfer of such Shares.

> *Article 7(20) Analysis*
>
> The article summarises the valuation process, including the ability to appoint an independent valuer.

Transmission of shares

(22) In the application of Articles 27 to 29 of the Model Articles to the Company:

(a) any person becoming entitled to a Share in consequence of the death or bankruptcy of a holder of a Share shall give a Transfer Notice in respect of such Share before he elects in respect of that Share to be registered himself or to execute a transfer;

(b) if a person so becoming entitled shall not have given a Transfer Notice in respect of any Share within three months of the death or bankruptcy, the Directors may at any time thereafter give notice requiring such a person within 14 working days to give a Transfer Notice in respect of all of the Shares to which he has so become entitled and for which he has not previously given a Transfer Notice and if it does not do so he shall at the end of such 14 day period be deemed to have given a Transfer Notice in respect of those Shares in relation to which he has still not given a Transfer Notice.

Article 7(22) Analysis

The article here reflects the legal position on the death of a shareholder. The individual who is entitled to the shares of the deceased is termed the transmittee, typically the executor of the will. Section (b) allows for a deemed transfer notice if the shares are not transferred in a timely manner.

Article 8 [suspension of voting rights after member leaves

6.54

8.(1) Shares held by an Employee who acquired such Shares pursuant to a right or opportunity made available by reason of the [office or] employment of such person with any member of the Group shall, if such person Leaves, immediately cease to carry any right to vote on a resolution of members or to attend or be counted in the quorum at a general meeting of members of the Company.

(2) The suspension of voting rights, and of the right to attend and be counted in the quorum at a general meeting of members of the Company, attaching to Shares held by a former Employee shall cease to have effect when such Shares are transferred to any other person or persons pursuant to the provisions of Article 7.]

Article 8 Analysis

The optional article that suspends voting rights and attendance of meetings by a leaver, or indeed a bad leaver. A leaver of the company may, for various reasons, hold a negative view of the company and therefore seek to disrupt and impede the normal running of company meetings.

Article 9 Employees' Council

6.55

9.(1) The Directors shall procure the establishment of a body of Employees and [at least one] Director to be known as the Employees' Council of which:

(a) the selection and appointment and removal of its members; and

(b) the governance and regulation of its affairs are conducted in accordance with a written set of rules initially approved by [ordinary resolution of the members of the Company] and which may from time to time be amended or added to by resolution in writing of the Employees' Council in accordance with those rules.

Article 10 Directors

6.56

10.(1) The minimum number of Directors shall be [3].

(2) The maximum number of Directors shall be [5].

(3) The Directors from time to time may choose any one of their number to act as Chairman of the Company.

Article 11 [Employee Director(s)

6.57

11.(1) At least [ ] of the Directors shall be an Employee who has, or Employees each of whom have, been selected and nominated for appointment, and who shall resign, or be removed, from office as a Director in accordance with such procedure as may from time to time be determined by the Employees' Council.

(2) An Employee Director shall be appointed for an initial fixed term of [3] years beginning with the date of his or her appointment as a Director and shall automatically cease to hold office as a Director at the end of that period and if there will then be no Employee Director, the remaining Directors shall, as soon as practicable, call upon the Employees' Council to select and nominate an eligible Employee to hold office as a Director.

(3) As soon as practicable after the Company receives notice in writing of the name and address of an Employee who has been selected and nominated for appointment as an Employee Director, the remaining Directors or the members shall procure that such individual is appointed to hold office as an

Employee Director [SAVE THAT neither the remaining Directors nor the members shall be obliged to appoint such individual as a Director if, in their unanimous opinion, such appointment would not be in the best interests of the Company and in this event the Secretary of the Company shall invite the Employees' Council to select and nominate another eligible Employee for appointment as an Employee Director].

(4) The Employees' Council may at any time, by giving notice in writing to the Company, request that an Employee Director be removed from office as a Director and, if such Employee Director does not resign as a Director, the Directors shall requisition a written resolution of members of the Company pursuant to section 168 of the Act.]

Article 12 [Decision-making by Directors

6.58

12.(1) In making any decision, the Directors shall have regard to the Principles and to the views of the Employees' Council and Model Article 7 shall be construed accordingly.]

Articles 9–12 Analysis

Article 9 describes the process of establishing the Employee Council, questionably, these provisions are best suited in a shareholder agreement (or similar document).

Article 9(1)(b) refers to the establishment of rules for the Employee Council. It would seem appropriate to remove the provisions for an Employee Council from the articles of association and include the relevant procedures in the external rule book or similar document, the advantage being they can be changed and edited as the company grows without the requirement of passing a special resolution and resubmission to Companies House. Also, the Employee Council agreement is not subject to public scrutiny.

Article 11, the appointment of an Employee Director, may impede the overall operation of the company (and certainly cause conflicts of interest) and ought to avoided.

Article 13 Conflicts of interest

6.59

13.(1) The Directors may authorise, to the fullest extent permitted by law, any matter proposed to them which would otherwise result in a Director infringing his duty under section 175 of the Act to avoid a situation in which such Director has, or can have, a direct or indirect interest that conflicts, or possibly may conflict, with the interests of the Company and which may reasonably be regarded as likely to give rise to a conflict of interest.

(2) Authorisation of a matter under Article 13.1 is effective only if:

(a) the matter has been proposed to the Directors by its being submitted in writing for consideration at a meeting of the Directors or for the authorisation of the Directors by resolution in writing and in accordance with the Directors' normal procedures or in such other manner as the Directors may approve;

(b) any requirement as to quorum at the meeting of the Directors at which the matter is considered is met without counting the Director in question and any other interested Director; and

(c) the matter has been agreed to without the Director in question and any other interested Director voting or would have been agreed to if their votes had not been counted.

(3) Any authorisation of a matter under Article 13.1 shall extend to any actual or potential conflict of interest which may reasonably be expected to arise out of the matter so authorised.

(4) The Directors may authorise a matter on such terms and for such duration, or impose such limits or conditions on it, as the Directors may decide and may vary the terms of duration of such an authorisation (including any limits or conditions imposed on such authorisation) or revoke such authorisation. A Director shall comply with any obligations imposed on him by the Directors pursuant to any such authorisation.

(5) Any terms imposed by the Directors under Article 13.4 may include (without limitation):

(a) whether the Director may vote (or be counted in the quorum) at a meeting of the Directors or any committee or sub-committee of the Directors in relation to any resolution relating to the relevant matter;

(b) whether the Director is to be given any documents or other information in relation to the relevant matter; and

(c) whether the Director is to be excluded from discussions in relation to the relevant matter at a meeting of the Directors or any committee or sub-committee of the Directors or otherwise.

(6) The Director shall not be required to disclose any confidential information obtained in relation to the relevant matter (other than through his position as a Director of the Company) to the Company or to use to apply it in performing

his duties as a Director if to do so would result in a breach of a duty or obligation of confidence owed to him in relation to or in connection with that matter.

(7) A Director does not infringe any duty he owes to the Company by virtue of sections 171 to 177 of the Act if he acts in accordance with such terms, limits and conditions (if any) as the Directors may impose in respect of its authorisation of the Director's conflict of interest or possible conflict of interest under Article 13.1.

(8) A Director shall not, save as otherwise agreed by him, be accountable to the Company for any benefit which he (or a person connected with him) derives from any matter authorised by the Directors under Article 13.1 and any contract, transaction or arrangement relating thereto shall not be liable to be avoided on the grounds of any such benefit.

(9) A reference in these Articles to a conflict of interest includes a conflict of interest and duty and a conflict of duties.

Article 13 Analysis

See analysis in **6.23** above.

Article 14 Annual general meeting

6.60

14.(1) The Company must hold a general meeting as its annual general meeting not less than once in each calendar year beginning 1 January and not more than [fifteen] months after the last preceding annual general meeting.

(2) A notice calling an annual general meeting of the Company must state that the meeting is an annual general meeting.

(3) The members of the Company may require the Company to give, to members of the Company entitled to receive notice of the next annual general meeting, notice of a resolution which may properly be moved and is intended to be moved at that meeting.

(4) A resolution may properly be moved at an annual general meeting unless:

(a) it would, if passed, be ineffective (whether by reason of inconsistency with any enactment or the constitution of the Company or otherwise);

(b) it is defamatory of any person; or

(c) it is frivolous or vexatious.

(5) The Company shall give notice of a resolution once it has received requests that it do so from [the Employees' Council or] members representing at least [5] per cent of the total voting rights of all the members who have a right to vote on the resolution at the annual general meeting to which the requests relate (excluding any voting rights attached to any shares in the Company held as treasury shares).

(6) A request mentioned in Article 14.5:

(a) may be in hard copy form or in electronic form;

(b) must identify the resolution of which notice is to be given;

(c) must be authenticated by the person or persons making it; and

(d) must be received by the secretary of the Company not later than:

  (i) 6 weeks before the annual general meeting to which the requests relate; or

  (ii) if later, the time at which notice is given of that meeting.

(7) If the Company is required to give notice of a resolution, it must send a copy of such resolution to each member of the Company entitled to receive notice of the annual general meeting in the same manner as notice of the meeting and at the same time as, or as soon as reasonably practicable after, it gives notice of the meeting.

(8) The expenses of the Company in complying with the requirements of this Article 14 shall be borne by the Company and not by the members who requested the circulation of the resolution.

Precedents

Precedent 1: Not for Profit Company Articles of Association

General comments

The following not for profit company precedent is based upon the Schedule 2 Regulation 3 model articles for private companies limited by guarantee.

Key changes

- A numbering structure providing increased clarity. Additions, deletions and variations have been made to improve the reading and understanding of the provisions.
- Provisions for electing a chair and other officers.
- The membership articles are extended to provide improved provisions for joining and leaving.
- Membership, rights to appeal.

Drafting assumptions

- The company is a private limited company limited by guarantee and incorporated in England and Wales under the Companies Act 2006.
- The company is not a registered charity.
- The company's objects are restricted, companies incorporated prior to 1 October 2009 specified their objects in the memorandum of association, a separate document to the articles that restricted the activities the company could undertake. The Companies Act 2006 allowed a company by default unrestricted objects.[1] It is arguably good practice for a not for profit to restrict its objects in the articles of association.
- The company may not appoint alternative directors.
- The model articles will not apply.

1 Companies Act 2006, s 31 (Statement of company's objects). '(1) Unless a company's articles specifically restrict the objects of the company, its objects are unrestricted.'

- The terms 'directors',[2] 'trustees' and 'board' or any other term to describe the governing body of the company are company directors and therefore must comply with the Companies Act 2006. It should be noted if the company is a charity the directors are deemed by law to be trustees.

Boiler plate clauses

The following are generic provisions, commonly referred to as 'boiler plate'. The provisions provide certain statements, specific actions or limitations to the articles of association. The clauses are typically simple to understand, do not act with other clauses and can be inserted and amended without controversy.

Powers to represent the membership

The company [charity] represents the [membership] to other third parties or the general public on issues that positively or negatively impact the company [charity].

The company [charity] may, individually or with other organisations, approved by the directors, seek to influence public opinion, make representations to local and central governmental bodies and institutions regarding the reform, development and implementation of appropriate policies, legislation and regulations, on matters that impact on the objects of the company [charity].

Provided that and subject to the Companies Act 2006, all such activities shall be confined to those which an English and Welsh company [charity] may properly undertake and in line with any guidance published by the Charity Commission.

Not for profit

The company is not established or conducted for private gain: any surplus or assets are used principally for the benefit of the community.

Powers

To further its objects the company may do all such lawful things as may further the company's objects and, in particular, but, without limitation, may borrow

2 The Companies Act 2006 defines a company director as 'any person occupying the position of director, by whatever name called'.

or raise and secure the payment of money for any purpose including for the purposes of investment or of raising funds.

Irregularities

The proceedings at any meeting or on the taking of any poll or the passing of a written resolution or the making of any decision shall not be invalidated by reason of any accidental informality or irregularity.

This shall include any accidental omission to give or any non-receipt of notice or any want of qualification in any of the persons present or voting or by reason of any business being considered which is not referred to in the notice unless a provision of the Companies Acts specifies that such informality, irregularity or want of qualification shall invalidate it.

Winding up

If any property remains after the company [charity] has been wound up or dissolved **'residue property'** and the debts and liabilities have been satisfied it may not be paid to or distributed among the members of the company [charity].

Residue property must be given to some other organisation with similar objects to the [company][charity]. The organisation or organisations to benefit may be selected by special resolution of the [directors][trustees] at or before the time of winding up or dissolution.

The prior approval of the [Council][Associated body][Directors by special resolution] shall be required to voluntarily wind up the company.

Dissolution (alternative)

The members may at any time before, and in expectation of, its dissolution resolve that any net assets of the [company][charity] after all its debts and liabilities have been paid, or provision has been made for them, shall on or before the dissolution of the Trust be applied or transferred to;

Charity Registration Number (if applicable):

Company Registration Number (if applicable):

Registered Office:

Reviewing and amending the memorandum and articles

The [company][charity] shall be required to review the provisions of the articles of association on a bi-yearly basis. Any amendment to the articles of association shall require the following:

(a) the prior approval of [membership council][associated body][specific committee];

(b) the prior approval of the [local authority]regulatory body];

(c) a special resolution of the [directors]trustees]; and

(d) such other approvals, consents and filings as may from time to time be required by the Companies Act 2006.

Conflicts of interest – deceleration

The [directors][trustees] shall affect a register of trustees' interests. Subject to the articles and the Companies Act 2006, a [directors][trustees] must declare the nature and extent of any interest, direct or indirect, which he or she has in a proposed transaction or arrangement with the [company][charity] or in any transaction or arrangement entered into by the [company][charity] which has not previously been declared.

The trustees shall also adopt (and may review and amend from time to time) a policy in relation to conflicts of interest.

Code of conduct

The [directors][trustees] shall establish rules that all members shall be required to observe a 'code of conduct', including, but not limited to, when members are participating in activities or at events that are administered or organised by the [club][association[charity][company].

The code of conduct shall include rules and regulations, as the [directors][trustees] see fit, from time to time, including the suspension or removal of any or all of the rights and privileges of membership, including the holding of office, in relation to the contravention of the code of conduct by a member. [For the avoidance of doubt, members shall not have a right of appeal.]

Articles of Association

Company Number: [NUMBER]

THE COMPANIES ACT 2006

PRIVATE COMPANY LIMITED BY GUARANTEE

ARTICLES OF ASSOCIATION OF [Name] Limited

[(Adopted by Special Resolution passed on [DATE])]

Article 1 Interpretation

1. In the articles, unless the context requires otherwise—

'articles' means the company's articles of association;

'bankruptcy' includes individual insolvency proceedings in a jurisdiction other than England and Wales or Northern Ireland which have an effect similar to that of bankruptcy;

'chairman' has the meaning given in article 12;

'chairman of the meeting' has the meaning given in article 28;

'Companies Acts' means the Companies Acts (as defined in section 2 of the Companies Act 2006), in so far as they apply to the company;

'company' shall include any corporation or other body corporate incorporated under the Companies Act 2006;

'director' means a director of the company, and includes any person occupying the position of director, by whatever name called;

'document' includes, unless otherwise specified, any document sent or supplied in electronic form;

'electronic form' has the meaning given in section 1168 of the Companies Act 2006;

'member' has the meaning given in section 112 of the Companies Act 2006;

'ordinary resolution' has the meaning given in section 282 of the Companies Act 2006;

'participate', in relation to a directors' meeting, has the meaning given in article 10;

'person' includes a: natural person, corporate or unincorporated body, legal representative and trustee;

'proxy notice' has the meaning given in article 34;

'special resolution' has the meaning given in section 283 of the Companies Act 2006;

'subsidiary' has the meaning given in section 1159 of the Companies Act 2006; and

'writing' means the representation or reproduction of words, symbols or other information in a visible form by any method or combination of methods, whether sent or supplied in electronic form or otherwise.

Unless the context otherwise requires, other words or expressions contained in these articles bear the same meaning as in the Companies Act 2006 as in force on the date when these articles become binding on the company.

Words denoting the singular shall include the plural and vice versa; words denoting a gender shall include all genders unless the context otherwise requires; and references to these articles or any other document shall be construed as references to these articles, that provision or that document as in force and as amended from time to time.

The terms 'including', 'include', 'in particular' or any similar expression, shall not limit the sense or application of any words preceding those terms.

No right to inspect accounts and other records. Except as provided by law or authorised by the Board by ordinary resolution, no member of the club is entitled to request or inspect any:

- accounting records;
- board documents;
- membership information.

[The directors may decide to make provision for the benefit of persons employed or formerly employed by the club or any of its subsidiaries (other than a director or former director or shadow director) in connection with the cessation or transfer to any person of the whole or part of the undertaking of the company or that subsidiary.]

Model articles shall not apply

The model articles for private companies limited by guarantee as prescribed by the Companies Act 2006 shall not apply to the company.

Article 2 Liability of members

2.1. The liability of each member is limited to £1, being the amount that each member undertakes to contribute to the assets of the company in the event of its being wound up while he is a member or within one year after he ceases to be a member, for:

(a) payment of the company's debts and liabilities contracted before he ceases to be a member;

(b) payment of the costs, charges and expenses of winding up; and

(c) adjustment of the rights of the contributories among themselves.

Article 3 Directors' general authority

3.1. Subject to these articles, the directors are responsible for the management of the company's business, for which purpose they may exercise all the powers of the company.

Article 4 Members' reserve power

4.1. The members may, by special resolution, direct the directors to take, or refrain from taking, specified action.

4.2. No such special resolution invalidates anything which the directors have done before the passing of the resolution.

Article 5 Directors may delegate

5.1. Subject to the articles, the directors may delegate any of the powers which are conferred on them under these articles:

(a) to such person or committee;

(b) by such means (including by power of attorney);

(c) to such an extent;

(d) in relation to such matters or territories; and

(e) on such terms and conditions; as they think fit.

5.2. If the directors so specify, any such delegation may authorise further delegation of the directors' powers by any person to whom they are delegated.

5.3. The directors may revoke any delegation as they see fit at any time in whole or part, or alter its terms and conditions.

Article 6 Committees

6.1. Committees to which the directors delegate any of their powers must follow procedures which are based as far as they are applicable on those provisions of the articles which govern the taking of decisions by directors.

6.2. The directors may make rules of procedure for all or any committees, which prevail over rules derived from the articles if they are not consistent with them.

Article 7 Directors to take decisions collectively

7.1. The general rule about decision-making by directors is that any decision of the directors must be either a majority decision at a meeting or a unanimous decision taken in accordance with article 8.

Article 8 Unanimous decisions

8.1. A decision of the directors is taken in accordance with this article when all eligible directors indicate to each other by any means that they share a common view on a matter.

8.2. Such a decision may take the form of a resolution in writing, copies of which have been signed by each eligible director or to which each eligible director has otherwise indicated agreement in writing.

8.3. References in this article to eligible directors are to directors who would have been entitled to vote on the matter had it been proposed as a resolution at a directors' meeting.

8.4. A decision may not be taken in accordance with this article if the eligible directors would not have formed a quorum at such a meeting.

Article 9 Calling a directors' meeting

9.1. Any director may call a directors' meeting by giving notice of the meeting to the directors.

9.2. Notice of any directors' meeting must indicate:

(a) its proposed date and time;

(b) where it is to take place;

(c) if it is anticipated that directors participating in the meeting will not be in the same place, how it is proposed that they should communicate with each other during the meeting.

9.3. Notice of a directors' meeting must be given to each director, but need not be in writing.

9.4. Notice of a directors' meeting need not be given to directors who waive their entitlement to notice of that meeting, by giving notice to that effect to the company not more than 7 days after the date on which the meeting is held. Where such notice is given after the meeting has been held, that does not affect the validity of the meeting, or of any business conducted at it.

Article 10 Participation in directors' meetings

10.1. Subject to the articles, directors participate in a directors' meeting, or part of a directors' meeting, when:

(a) the meeting has been called and takes place in accordance with the articles; and

(b) they can each communicate to the others any information or opinions they have on any particular item of the business of the meeting.

10.2. In determining whether directors are participating in a directors' meeting, it is irrelevant where any director is or how they communicate with each other.

10.3. If all the directors participating in a meeting are not in the same place, they may decide that the meeting is to be treated as taking place wherever any of them is.

Article 11 Quorum for directors' meetings

11.1. At a directors' meeting, unless a quorum is participating, no proposal is to be voted on, except a proposal to call another meeting.

11.2. The quorum for directors' meetings may be fixed from time to time by a decision of the directors, but it must never be less than two, and unless otherwise fixed it is two.

11.3. If the total number of directors for the time being is less than the quorum required, the directors must not take any decision other than a decision to appoint further directors or to call a general meeting so as to enable the members to appoint further directors.

Article 12 Chairing of directors' meetings

12.1. Subject to article 22, the directors may appoint a director to chair their meetings.

12.2. The person so appointed for the time being is known as the chairman. The directors may terminate the chairman's appointment at any time.

12.3. If the chairman is not participating in a directors' meeting within ten minutes of the time at which it was to start, the participating directors must appoint one of themselves to chair it.

Article 13 Casting vote

13.1. If the numbers of votes for and against a proposal are equal, the chairman or other director chairing the meeting has a casting vote.

13.2. But this does not apply if, in accordance with the articles, the chairman or other director is not to be counted as participating in the decision-making process for quorum or voting purposes.

Article 14 Situational conflicts of interest

14.1. A director of the company must avoid a situation in which he can have a direct or indirect interest that conflicts or possibly may conflict with the interests of the company.

14.2. Any director in breach of paragraph 14.1 is deemed a 'conflicted director'.

Authorisation of conflicts of interest

14.3. Subject to the provisions of section 175 of the Companies Act 2006 and the provisions of this article the directors may authorise a 'conflicted director'.

14.4. **An 'authorisation' is effective only if:**

(a) any requirement as to the quorum at the meeting at which the matter is considered is met without counting the director in question or any other interested director; and

(b) the matter was agreed to without their voting or would have been agreed to if their votes had not been counted.

14.5. In accordance with section 175(5)(a) of the Companies Act 2006 in respect of a 'conflicted director' who has proposed that the board of directors authorise his conflicted interest ('board authorisation') may for the avoidance of doubt:

(a) apply such terms and conditions as they see fit to any authorisation;

(b) vary or terminate any authorisation at any time by the directors or committee as they see fit.

Article 15 Transactional conflicts of interest

15.1. If a 'conflicted director' of the company is directly or indirectly interested in a proposed transaction ('transaction') or arrangement with the company he must declare the nature and extent of that interest to the other directors.

15.2. Subject to the provisions of section 177 and section 182 of the Companies Act 2006:

(a) If a proposed decision of the directors is concerned with an actual or proposed transaction or arrangement with the company in which a director is interested, that director is not to be counted as participating in the decision-making process for quorum or voting purposes.

(b) *[If a proposed decision of the directors is concerned with an actual or proposed transaction or arrangement with the company in which a director is interested, that director is not to be counted as participating in the decision-making process for quorum or voting purposes.]*

15.3. The 'conflicted director' shall not be required to disclose to the company any benefit he or any of his connected persons derive as a result of any 'authorised conflict'.

Article 16 Records of decisions to be kept

16.1. The directors must ensure that the company keeps a record, in writing, for at least 10 years from the date of the decision recorded, of every unanimous or majority decision taken by the directors.

Article 17 Directors' discretion to make further rules

17.1. Subject to the articles, the directors may make any rule which they think fit about how they take decisions, and about how such rules are to be recorded or communicated to directors.

Appointments of directors

Article 18 Methods of appointing directors

18.1. Any person who is willing to act as a director, and is permitted by law to do so, may be appointed to be a director:

(a) by ordinary resolution; or

(b) by a decision of the directors.

18.2. In any case where, as a result of death, the company has no members and no directors, the personal representatives of the last member to have died have the right, by notice in writing, to appoint a person to be a director.

18.3. For the purposes of paragraph 18.2, where two or more members die in circumstances rendering it uncertain who was the last to die, a younger member is deemed to have survived an older member.

Article 19 Termination of director's appointment

19.1. A person ceases to be a director as soon as:

(a) that person ceases to be a director by virtue of any provision of the Companies Act 2006 or is prohibited from being a director by law;

(b) a bankruptcy order is made against that person;

(c) a composition is made with that person's creditors generally in satisfaction of that person's debts;

(d) a registered medical practitioner who is treating that person gives a written opinion to the company stating that that person has become physically or mentally incapable of acting as a director and may remain so for more than three months;

(e) notification is received by the company from the director that the director is resigning from office, and such resignation has taken effect in accordance with its terms.

Article 20 Directors' remuneration

20.1. Directors may undertake any services for the company that the directors decide.

20.2. Directors are entitled to such remuneration as the directors determine:

(a) for their services to the company as directors;

(b) for any other service which they undertake for the company.

20.3. Subject to the articles, a director's remuneration may:

(a) Take any form, and include any arrangements in connection with the payment of a pension, allowance or gratuity, or any death, sickness or disability benefits, to or in respect of that director.

(b) Unless the directors decide otherwise, directors' remuneration accrues from day to day.

(c) Unless the directors decide otherwise, directors are not accountable to the company for any remuneration which they receive as directors or other officers or employees of the company's subsidiaries or of any other body corporate in which the company is interested.

Article 21 Directors' expenses

21.1. The company may pay any reasonable expenses which the directors properly incur in connection with their attendance at:

(a) meetings of directors;

(b) committees of directors;

(c) general meetings; or

(d) otherwise in connection with the exercise of their powers and the discharge of their responsibilities in relation to the company.

Appointments and elections

Article 22 Election of the chairman

22.1. At the annual general meeting each year a chairman will be elected in accordance with article 23.

22.2. The term of chairman shall be for [2] years 'board term'. The chairman will have full voting rights subject to these articles.

22.3. A chairman shall not be eligible for reelection after the 'board term' for a period of [5] years.

22.4. The board on the appointment of a chairman in accordance with article 23 shall, 14 days after the date of the AGM, appoint or revoke any 'board position' by ordinary resolution from time to time as they see fit. For the avoidance of doubt 'board position' means:

(a) vice-chairman;

(b) secretary;

(c) treasurer;

together 'board position'.

Article 23 Board elections

23.1. A voting member of the club may nominate another member 'nominee' for any board position.

23.2. Nominations shall be made by the 'nominee form' authorised by the board from time to time.

23.3. The board shall provide nominee forms to voting members at least [14] days prior to the agreed date of the annual general meeting.

23.4. Nominee forms shall be returned to the board [5] days prior to the 'AGM'.

23.5. A nominee shall be a voting member of the club in good standing with a least [2] years continuous membership of the club.

23.6. If the board shall receive only one nomination then he shall be appointed without election or the matter shall be put to board for election at the 'AGM' on terms the directors agree.

Becoming and ceasing to be a member

Article 24 Membership

24.1. No person shall become a member of the company unless:

(a) that person has completed an application for membership in a form approved by the directors; and

(b) the board have approved the application.

24.2. The board may from time to time fix the levels of entrance fees and annual subscriptions to be paid by the different categories of members.

24.3. All members shall be subject to these articles and any other club rules authorised by the board.

24.4. Any member whose [annual fee – subscription] is [2] months in arrears shall be deemed to have resigned from the club.

24.5. Any person ceasing to be a member forfeits all rights in relation to and claims upon the club, its property and its funds and has no right to the return of any part of his subscription.

Article 25 Termination of membership

25.1. A member may withdraw from membership of the company by giving 7 days' notice to the company in writing:

(a) Membership is not transferable.

(b) A person's membership terminates when that person dies or ceases to exist.

25.2. The board shall at their discretion request a member 'leaver' withdraw from membership immediately in writing 'leaving notice':

(a) The leaver shall within 14 days of receiving the leaving notice inform the board in writing that he requests a board or any committee to consider his position 'leaver committee'.

25.3. The leaver may:

(a) attend the club premises or any other venue the board sees fit on the date and time of the leaver committee;

(b) not use any club facilities (or than disabled facilities) on the day of his attendance at the leaver committee without the express permission of a member of the leaver committee;

(c) present his case in person or by written submission;

(d) at the discretion of the board the leaver may be allowed to attend the meeting with a third party for the purpose of support only;

(e) no third party present at the meeting may give verbal or written submission.

25.4. Any non-attendance at the leaver's meeting without good reason will result in the leaver being deemed to have resigned from the club.

25.5. On the closing of the written or verbal submission the leaver committee shall vote on the matter:

(a) if the vote is carried the leaver shall be deemed to have resigned from the club.

25.6. The leaver may within 14 days of the date of the leaver's committee request in writing that an appeal be instigated and a full vote be put to a general meeting of the board:

(a) For the avoidance of doubt the leaver shall have no rights to attend the general meeting or present any further written submissions.

(b) The chairman or vice-chairman may prior to the general meeting request any further information he deems fit from the leaver or the leaving committee.

Organisation of general meetings

Article 26 Attendance and speaking at general meetings

26.1. A person is able to exercise the right to speak at a general meeting when that person is in a position to communicate to all those attending the meeting, during the meeting, any information or opinions which that person has on the business of the meeting.

26.2. A person is able to exercise the right to vote at a general meeting when:

(a) that person is able to vote, during the meeting, on resolutions put to the vote at the meeting; and

(b) that person's vote can be taken into account in determining whether or not such resolutions are passed at the same time as the votes of all the other persons attending the meeting.

26.3. The directors may make whatever arrangements they consider appropriate to enable those attending a general meeting to exercise their rights to speak or vote at it.

26.4. In determining attendance at a general meeting, it is immaterial whether any two or more members attending it are in the same place as each other.

26.5. Two or more persons who are not in the same place as each other attend a general meeting if their circumstances are such that if they have (or were to have) rights to speak and vote at that meeting, they are (or would be) able to exercise them.

Article 27 Quorum for general meetings

27.1. No business other than the appointment of the chairman of the meeting is to be transacted at a general meeting if the persons attending it do not constitute a quorum.

Article 28 Chairing general meetings

28.1. The chairman shall chair general meetings if present and willing to do so.

28.2. If the directors have not appointed a chairman, or if the chairman is unwilling to chair the meeting or is not present within ten minutes of the time at which a meeting was due to start:

(a) the directors present; or

(b) (if no directors are present), at the meeting, they must appoint a director or member to chair the meeting, and the appointment of the chairman of the meeting must be the first business of the meeting.

28.3. The person chairing a meeting in accordance with this article is referred to as 'the chairman of the meeting'.

Article 29 Attendance and speaking by directors and non-members

29.1. Directors may attend and speak at general meetings, whether or not they are members.

29.2. The chairman of the meeting may permit other persons who are not members of the company to attend and speak at a general meeting.

Article 30 Adjournment

30.1. If the persons attending a general meeting within half an hour of the time at which the meeting was due to start do not constitute a quorum, or if during a meeting a quorum ceases to be present, the chairman of the meeting must adjourn it.

30.2. The chairman of the meeting may adjourn a general meeting at which a quorum is present if:

(a) the meeting consents to an adjournment; or

(b) it appears to the chairman of the meeting that an adjournment is necessary to protect the safety of any person attending the meeting or ensure that the business of the meeting is conducted in an orderly manner.

30.3. The chairman of the meeting must adjourn a general meeting if directed to do so by the meeting.

30.4. When adjourning a general meeting, the chairman of the meeting must:

(a) either specify the time and place to which it is adjourned or state that it is to continue at a time and place to be fixed by the directors;

(b) and have regard to any directions as to the time and place of any adjournment which have been given by the meeting.

30.5. If the continuation of an adjourned meeting is to take place more than 14 days after it was adjourned, the company must give at least 7 clear days' notice of it (that is, excluding the day of the adjourned meeting and the day on which the notice is given):

(a) to the same persons to whom notice of the company's general meetings is required to be given and containing the same information which such notice is required to contain; and

(b) no business may be transacted at an adjourned general meeting which could not properly have been transacted at the meeting if the adjournment had not taken place.

Voting and general meetings

Article 31 Voting: general

31.1. A resolution put to the vote of a general meeting must be decided on a show of hands unless a poll is duly demanded in accordance with the articles.

Article 32 Errors and disputes

32.1. No objection may be raised to the qualification of any person voting at a general meeting except at the meeting or adjourned meeting at which the vote objected to is tendered, and every vote not disallowed at the meeting is valid.

32.2. Any such objection must be referred to the chairman of the meeting whose decision is final.

Article 33 Poll votes

33.1. A poll on a resolution may be demanded:

(a) in advance of the general meeting where it is to be put to the vote; or

(b) at a general meeting, either before a show of hands on that resolution or immediately after the result of a show of hands on that resolution is declared.

33.2. A poll may be demanded by:

(a) the chairman of the meeting;

(b) the directors;

(c) two or more persons having the right to vote on the resolution; or

(d) a person or persons representing not less than one tenth of the total voting rights of all the members having the right to vote on the resolution.

33.3. A demand for a poll may be withdrawn if:

(a) the poll has not yet been taken; and

(b) the chairman of the meeting consents to the withdrawal.

33.4. Polls must be taken immediately and in such manner as the chairman of the meeting directs.

Article 34 Content of proxy notices

34.1. Proxies may only validly be appointed by a notice in writing (a 'proxy notice'). The proxy notice shall:

(a) state the name and address of the member appointing the proxy;

(b) identify the person appointed to be that member's proxy;

(c) state the general meeting in relation to which that person is appointed;

(d) be signed by or on behalf of the member appointing the proxy, or is authenticated in such manner as the directors may determine;

(e) be delivered to the company in accordance with the articles and any instructions contained in the notice of the general meeting to which they relate.

34.2. The company may require proxy notices to be delivered in a particular form, and may specify different forms for different purposes.

34.3. Proxy notices may specify how the proxy appointed under them is to vote (or that the proxy is to abstain from voting) on one or more resolutions.

34.4. Unless a proxy notice indicates otherwise it shall be treated as:

(a) allowing the person appointed under it as a proxy discretion as to how to vote on any ancillary or procedural resolutions put to the meeting; and

(b) appointing that person as a proxy in relation to any adjournment of the general meeting to which it relates as well as the meeting itself.

Article 35 Delivery of proxy notices

35.1. A person who is entitled to attend, speak or vote (either on a show of hands or on a poll) at a general meeting remains so entitled in respect of that meeting or any adjournment of it, even though a valid proxy notice has been delivered to the company by or on behalf of that person.

35.2. An appointment under a proxy notice may be revoked by delivering to the company a notice in writing given by or on behalf of the person by whom or on whose behalf the proxy notice was given.

35.3. A notice revoking a proxy appointment only takes effect if it is delivered before the start of the meeting or adjourned meeting to which it relates.

35.4. If a proxy notice is not executed by the person appointing the proxy, it must be accompanied by written evidence of the authority of the person who executed it to execute it on the appointor's behalf.

Article 36 Amendments to resolutions

36.1. An ordinary resolution to be proposed at a general meeting may be amended by ordinary resolution if:

(a) notice of the proposed amendment is given to the company in writing by a person entitled to vote at the general meeting at which it is to be proposed not less than 48 hours before the meeting is to take place (or such later time as the chairman of the meeting may determine);

(b) the proposed amendment does not, in the reasonable opinion of the chairman of the meeting, materially alter the scope of the resolution.

36.2. A special resolution to be proposed at a general meeting may be amended by ordinary resolution if:

(a) the chairman of the meeting proposes the amendment at the general meeting at which the resolution is to be proposed; and

(b) the amendment does not go beyond what is necessary to correct a grammatical or other non-substantive error in the resolution.

36.3. If the chairman of the meeting, acting in good faith, wrongly decides that an amendment to a resolution is out of order, the chairman's error does not invalidate the vote on that resolution.

Administrative arrangements

Article 37 Means of communication to be used

37.1. Subject to the articles, anything sent or supplied by or to the company under the articles may be sent or supplied in any way in which the Companies Act 2006 provides for documents or information which are authorised or required by any provision of that Act to be sent or supplied by or to the company.

37.2. Subject to the articles, any notice or document to be sent or supplied to a director in connection with the taking of decisions by directors may also be sent or supplied by the means by which that director has asked to be sent or supplied with such notices or documents for the time being.

37.3. A director may agree with the company that notices or documents sent to that director in a particular way are to be deemed to have been received within a specified time of their being sent, and for the specified time to be less than 48 hours.

Article 38 Company seals

38.1. Any common seal may only be used by the authority of the directors. The directors may decide by what means and in what form any common seal is to be used.

38.2. Unless otherwise decided by the directors, if the company has a common seal and it is affixed to a document, the document must also be signed by at least one authorised person in the presence of a witness who attests the signature.

38.3. For the purposes of this article an authorised person is:

(a) any director of the company;

(b) any person authorised by the directors for the purpose of signing documents to which the common seal is applied.

Indemnity and insurance

Article 39 Indemnity

39.1. Subject to paragraph 39.2 only in relation to the club any relevant director may be indemnified out of the club's resources against any liability incurred by that director in connection with any:

(a) negligence;

(b) default;

(c) breach of duty;

(d) breach of trust;

(e) [liability incurred by that director in connection with the activities of the club in its capacity as a trustee of an occupational pension scheme (as defined in section 235(6) of the Companies Act 2006)];

(f) liability incurred by that director as an officer of the club.

39.2. This article does not authorise any indemnity which would be prohibited or rendered void by any provision of the Companies Acts or by any other provision of law.

39.3. The directors may decide to purchase and maintain insurance, at the expense of the company, for the benefit of any relevant director in respect of any relevant loss.

39.4. In this article 'relevant director' means any director or former director of the club. A 'relevant loss' means any loss or liability which has been or may be incurred by a relevant director in connection with that director's duties or powers in relation to the club or any pension fund or employees' share scheme.

Precedent 2: Membership Organisation Articles of Association

The following membership organisation precedent is based upon the Schedule 2 Regulation 3 model articles for a private company limited by guarantee.[1] The precedent is designed for an association that requires the facility for a wide membership.

An example is a tennis association that organises a local league with 20 club members. The articles empower the board to make most of the decisions, with provisions for the 20 members to elect a chair and two other officers. The number of officers could be extended by adapting the specific clauses. The board has a number of powers to terminate or suspend members, together with powers concerning membership subscriptions.

The precedent endeavours to widen the membership provisions adding:

- multiple membership classes;
- subscriptions;
- termination;
- suspension; and
- appeals.

Together with:

- Duties of members.
- A winding up clause that prevents assets passing to the members.
- The precedent appoints a chairman together with three board members.
- The conflicts of interest articles are updated and in addition include rules on transitional conflicts of interest.

1 Schedule 2 Regulation 3 Model articles for private companies limited by guarantee.

Drafting assumptions

- The company is a private limited company limited by guarantee and incorporated in England and Wales under the Companies Act 2006.
- The company is not a registered charity.
- The company's objects are restricted, companies incorporated prior to 1 October 2009 specified their objects in the memorandum of association, a separate document to the articles that restricted the activities the company could undertake. The Companies Act 2006 allowed a company by default unrestricted objects.[2] It is arguably good practice for a not for profit to restrict its objects in the articles of association.
- The model articles will not apply.
- The terms 'directors',[3] 'trustees' and 'board' or any other term to describe the governing body of the company are company directors and therefore must comply with the Companies Act 2006. It should be noted if the company is a charity the directors are deemed by law to be trustees.

2 Companies Act 2006, s 31 (Statement of company's objects). '(1) Unless a company's articles specifically restrict the objects of the company, its objects are unrestricted.'

3 The Companies Act 2006 defines a company director as 'any person occupying the position of director, by whatever name called'.

Articles of Association

Company Number: [NUMBER]

THE COMPANIES ACT 2006

PRIVATE COMPANY LIMITED BY GUARANTEE

ARTICLES OF ASSOCIATION OF [Name] Limited

[(Adopted by Special Resolution passed on [DATE])]

Article 1 Interpretation

1. In the articles, unless the context requires otherwise—

   'articles' means the company's articles of association;

   'bankruptcy' includes individual insolvency proceedings in a jurisdiction other than England and Wales or Northern Ireland which have an effect similar to that of bankruptcy;

   'chairman' has the meaning given in article 18;

   'chairman of the meeting' has the meaning given in article 32;

   'Companies Acts' means the Companies Acts (as defined in section 2 of the Companies Act 2006), in so far as they apply to the company;

   'company' shall include any corporation or other body corporate incorporated under the Companies Act 2006;

   'director' means a director of the company, and includes any person occupying the position of director, by whatever name called;

   'document' includes, unless otherwise specified, any document sent or supplied in electronic form;

   'electronic form' has the meaning given in section 1168 of the Companies Act 2006;

   'member' has the meaning given in section 112 of the Companies Act 2006;

   'ordinary resolution' has the meaning given in section 282 of the Companies Act 2006;

   'participate', in relation to a directors' meeting, has the meaning given in article 16;

   'person' includes a: natural person, corporate or unincorporated body, legal representative and trustee;

   'proxy notice' has the meaning given in article 38;

'special resolution' has the meaning given in section 283 of the Companies Act 2006;

'subsidiary' has the meaning given in section 1159 of the Companies Act 2006; and

'writing' means the representation or reproduction of words, symbols or other information in a visible form by any method or combination of methods, whether sent or supplied in electronic form or otherwise.

Unless the context otherwise requires, other words or expressions contained in these articles bear the same meaning as in the Companies Act 2006 as in force on the date when these articles become binding on the company.

Words denoting the singular shall include the plural and vice versa; words denoting a gender shall include all genders unless the context otherwise requires; and references to these articles or any other document shall be construed as references to these articles, that provision or that document as in force and as amended from time to time.

The terms **'including'**, **'include'**, **'in particular'** or any similar expression, shall not limit the sense or application of any words preceding those terms.

No right to inspect accounts and other records. Except as provided by law or authorised by the Board by ordinary resolution, no member of the club is entitled to request or inspect any:

- accounting records;
- board documents;
- membership information

[The directors may decide to make provision for the benefit of persons employed or formerly employed by the club or any of its subsidiaries (other than a director or former director or shadow director) in connection with the **cessation** or transfer to any person of the whole or part of the undertaking of the company or that subsidiary.]

Article 2 Model articles shall not apply

2.1. The model articles for private companies limited by guarantee as prescribed by the Companies Act 2006 shall not apply to the company.

2.2. Subject to the Companies Act 2006, any amendment of these articles shall require the prior approval of [individual][body corporate][another affiliated association].

Article 3 Duties of members

3.1. The members shall be subject to the articles of association.

3.2. Subject to the law, members shall undertake to comply with the articles [the association rules] and any lawful direction of the board.

Article 4 Association

4.1. The association is a member of [name] and its members shall abide by its rules.

4.2. The association will seek at all times:

(a) to pursue its objectives without bias toward any political party or religious group; and

(b) that no member is subject to any discrimination or harassment.

Article 5 Objects

5.1. The association objects shall be specifically limited to [insert].

5.2. The objects of the association are the advancement of [insert].

Article 6 Liability of members

6.1. The liability of each member is limited to £1, being the amount that each member undertakes to contribute to the assets of the company in the event of its being wound up while he is a member or within one year after he ceases to be a member, for:

(a) payment of the company's debts and liabilities contracted before he ceases to be a member;

(b) payment of the costs, charges and expenses of winding up; and

(c) adjustment of the rights of the contributories among themselves.

Article 7 Winding up

7.1. If the company is wound up under the Insolvency Act 1986 and all its liabilities have been satisfied, any residual assets shall be given or transferred to the [body corporate] specified in article 7.2.

7.2. The following [body corporate] is specified as a potential recipient of the company's assets.

Charity Registration Number (if applicable):

Company Registration Number (if applicable):

Registered Office

Membership

Article 8 Becoming and ceasing to be a member

8.1. Members of the charity:

(a) Full members.

(b) Associate members.

(c) [Honorary members].

(d) [League members].

8.2. Application for membership:

(a) All members shall apply annually to the board in accordance with the association rules.

(b) The board shall consider all new membership applications submitted and membership shall be decided by the board; the board's decision shall be final and binding.

(c) For the avoidance of doubt the member applications and the board's decision shall not be subject to an appeals process.

8.3. Membership application procedure.

8.4. Each member shall send to the [chief executive] no later than [date]:

(a) [Association application form].

(b) Full name and legal status.

(c) The name and address of its secretary and officers.

(d) The address of the member's principle **'registered ground'** [cricket ground][football ground][sports arena].

(e) For youth [members], its Child Welfare Officer.

(f) The member rules book [or other format applicable].

(g) Articles of association [if applicable].

8.5. **Membership subscriptions**

8.6. Each member shall pay an annual membership fee; the 'membership subscription'. The membership subscription shall be subject to the membership category in accordance with article 8.1.

8.7. The annual rates of the membership subscription shall be proposed and approved by the board in the annual general meeting.

8.8. All member subscriptions shall be paid by [date]; the 'renewal date', any member whose membership subscription remains not fully paid within 60 days of the renewal date shall, if the board so decide, cease to be a member of the charity and be in default 'default member'.

8.9. A default member shall not hold any privileges of membership and cease to have any claim on the property of the charity. [Any liability as provided for in the articles of association of the charity shall nevertheless continue.]

8.10. Members shall have no right to a representative at a general meeting of the charity whose subscription is not paid on or before the due date preceding such general meeting.

8.11. A member, without the written permission of the board may not be associated with or formally apply for membership of another [charity] [association][league] or a body corporate whose objects are for the promotion of [the equivalent objects of these articles].

8.12. Subject to the articles, all members shall remain liable for and shall pay to the charity all monies which may be due by it to the charity. The charity shall not be liable for any debts or obligations of any member.

8.13. **Termination of membership**

8.14. Members may withdraw membership from the charity by:

(a) giving notice in writing to the [Chief Executive][board]chair] 60 days or at least one month before the application date, in accordance with article 8.13

8.15. Subject to any decision by the board, membership will terminate, provided that:

(a) All membership fees have been fully paid in accordance with article 8.5 and no outstanding monies are due to the charity.

(b) The member is not in breach of any of its obligations to the charity.

(c) The member is not subject to any ongoing disciplinary hearing or complaint.

8.16. For the avoidance of doubt membership is not transferable to any individual, charity, trust or body corporate.

8.17. **Suspension of membership**

8.18. For the avoidance of doubt; the board shall have the power to suspend or terminate any member on such grounds as it may consider appropriate, by a majority vote at any general meeting.

8.19. Membership may be suspended or terminated by the board in the following situations by giving 14 clear days' notice in writing to the member: the 'suspension notice':

(a) A member fails to have its registered ground accepted by the board.

(b) Where a member fails for [number] playing seasons to [play] [compete in] the [specified event][competitions] for which it is eligible to take part.

(c) Any member who is subject to article 8.17.

(d) On winding up or insolvency of the members [charity][club] [association].

8.20. **Appeals**

8.21. An appeal against any decision by the board in accordance with article 8.17 shall be directed to the general meeting of the charity in accordance with the rules of the suspension notice.

8.22. The member must appeal in writing 'appeal' to the board, providing any evidence or mitigating circumstances in defence of the board's decision to suspend membership.

8.23. Upon receipt of an 'appeal' the [Chair][CEO] shall take all necessary steps to convene a general meeting of the charity to address the appeal.

Powers and responsibilities

Article 9 Directors' general authority

9.1. Subject to these articles, the directors are responsible for the management of the company's business, for which purpose they may exercise all the powers of the company.

Article 10 Members' reserve power

10.1. The members may, by special resolution, direct the directors to take, or refrain from taking, specified action.

10.2. No such special resolution invalidates anything which the directors have done before the passing of the resolution.

Article 11 Directors may delegate

11.1. Subject to the articles, the directors may delegate any of the powers which are conferred on them under these articles:

(a) to such person or committee;

(b) by such means (including by power of attorney);

(c) to such an extent;

(d) in relation to such matters or territories; and

(e) on such terms and conditions; as they think fit.

11.2. If the directors so specify, any such delegation may authorise further delegation of the directors' powers by any person to whom they are delegated.

11.3. The directors may revoke any delegation as they see fit at any time in whole or part, or alter its terms and conditions.

Article 12 Committees

12.1. Committees to which the directors delegate any of their powers must follow procedures which are based as far as they are applicable on those provisions of the articles which govern the taking of decisions by directors.

12.2. The directors may make rules of procedure for all or any committees, which prevail over rules derived from the articles if they are not consistent with them.

Decision making

Article 13 Directors to take decisions collectively

13.1. The general rule about decision-making by directors is that any decision of the directors must be either a majority decision at a meeting or a unanimous decision taken in accordance with article 14.

Article 14 Unanimous decisions

14.1. A decision of the directors is taken in accordance with this article when all eligible directors indicate to each other by any means that they share a common view on a matter.

14.2. Such a decision may take the form of a resolution in writing, copies of which have been signed by each eligible director or to which each eligible director has otherwise indicated agreement in writing.

14.3. References in this article to eligible directors are to directors who would have been entitled to vote on the matter had it been proposed as a resolution at a directors' meeting.

14.4. A decision may not be taken in accordance with this article if the eligible directors would not have formed a quorum at such a meeting.

Article 15 Calling a directors' meeting

15.1. Any director may call a directors' meeting by giving notice of the meeting to the directors.

15.2. Notice of any directors' meeting must indicate:

(a) its proposed date and time;

(b) where it is to take place;

(c) if it is anticipated that directors participating in the meeting will not be in the same place, how it is proposed that they should communicate with each other during the meeting.

15.3. Notice of a directors' meeting must be given to each director, but need not be in writing.

15.4. Notice of a directors' meeting need not be given to directors who waive their entitlement to notice of that meeting, by giving notice to that effect to the company not more than 7 days after the date on which the meeting is held. Where such notice is given after the meeting has been held, that does not affect the validity of the meeting, or of any business conducted at it.

Article 16 Participation in directors' meetings

16.1. Subject to the articles, directors participate in a directors' meeting, or part of a directors' meeting, when:

(a) the meeting has been called and takes place in accordance with the articles; and

(b) they can each communicate to the others any information or opinions they have on any particular item of the business of the meeting.

16.2. In determining whether directors are participating in a directors' meeting, it is irrelevant where any director is or how they communicate with each other.

16.3. If all the directors participating in a meeting are not in the same place, they may decide that the meeting is to be treated as taking place wherever any of them is.

Article 17 Quorum for directors' meetings

17.1. At a directors' meeting, unless a quorum is participating, no proposal is to be voted on, except a proposal to call another meeting.

17.2. The quorum for directors' meetings may be fixed from time to time by a decision of the directors, but it must never be less than two, and unless otherwise fixed it is two.

17.3. If the total number of directors for the time being is less than the quorum required, the directors must not take any decision other than a decision to appoint further directors or to call a general meeting so as to enable the members to appoint further directors.

Article 18 Chairing of directors' meetings

18.1. The directors may appoint a director to chair their meetings.

18.2. The person so appointed for the time being is known as the chairman. The directors may terminate the chairman's appointment at any time.

18.3. If the chairman is not participating in a directors' meeting within ten minutes of the time at which it was to start, the participating directors must appoint one of themselves to chair it.

Article 19 Casting vote

19.1. If the numbers of votes for and against a proposal are equal, the chairman or other director chairing the meeting has a casting vote.

19.2. But this does not apply if, in accordance with the articles, the chairman or other director is not to be counted as participating in the decision-making process for quorum or voting purposes.

Article 20 Situational conflicts of interest

20.1. A director of the company must avoid a situation in which he can have a direct or indirect interest that conflicts or possibly may conflict with the interests of the company.

20.2. Any director in breach of paragraph 20.1 is deemed a 'conflicted director'.

Authorisation of conflicts of interest

20.3. Subject to the provisions of section 175 of the Companies Act 2006 and the provisions of this article the directors may authorise a 'conflicted director'.

20.4. **An 'authorisation' is effective only if:**

(a) any requirement as to the quorum at the meeting at which the matter is considered is met without counting the director in question or any other interested director; and

(b) the matter was agreed to without their voting or would have been agreed to if their votes had not been counted.

20.5. In accordance with section 175(5)(a) of the Companies Act 2006 in respect of a 'conflicted director' who has proposed that the board of directors authorise his conflicted interest ('board authorisation') may for the avoidance of doubt:

(a) apply such terms and conditions as they see fit to any authorisation;

(b) vary or terminate any authorisation at any time by the directors or committee as they see fit.

Article 21 Transactional conflicts of interest

21.1. If a 'conflicted director' of the company is directly or indirectly interested in a proposed transaction 'transaction' or arrangement with the company he must declare the nature and extent of that interest to the other directors.

21.2. Subject to the provisions of section 177 and section 182 of the Companies Act 2006:

(a) If a proposed decision of the directors is concerned with an actual or proposed transaction or arrangement with the company in which a director is interested, that director is not to be counted as participating in the decision-making process for quorum or voting purposes.

(b) *[If a proposed decision of the directors is concerned with an actual or proposed transaction or arrangement with the company in which a director is interested, that director is not to be counted as participating in the decision-making process for quorum or voting purposes.]*

21.3. The 'conflicted director' shall not be required to disclose to the company any benefit he or any of his connected persons derive as a result of any 'authorised conflict'.

Article 22 Records of decisions to be kept

22.1. The directors must ensure that the company keeps a record, in writing, for at least 10 years from the date of the decision recorded, of every unanimous or majority decision taken by the directors.

Article 23 Directors' discretion to make further rules

23.1. Subject to the articles, the directors may make any rule which they think fit about how they take decisions, and about how such rules are to be recorded or communicated to directors.

Appointments of directors

Article 24 Methods of appointing directors

24.1. Any person who is willing to act as a director, and is permitted by law to do so, may be appointed to be a director:

(a) by ordinary resolution; or

(b) by a decision of the directors.

24.2. In any case where, as a result of death, the company has no members and no directors, the personal representatives of the last member to have died have the right, by notice in writing, to appoint a person to be a director.

24.3. For the purposes of paragraph 24.2, where two or more members die in circumstances rendering it uncertain who was the last to die, a younger member is deemed to have survived an older member.

Article 25 Termination of director's appointment

25.1. A person ceases to be a director as soon as:

(a) that person ceases to be a director by virtue of any provision of the Companies Act 2006 or is prohibited from being a director by law;

(b) a bankruptcy order is made against that person;

(c) a composition is made with that person's creditors generally in satisfaction of that person's debts;

(d) a registered medical practitioner who is treating that person gives a written opinion to the company stating that that person has become physically or mentally incapable of acting as a director and may remain so for more than three months;

(e) notification is received by the company from the director that the director is resigning from office, and such resignation has taken effect in accordance with its terms.

Article 26 Directors' remuneration

26.1. Directors may undertake any services for the company that the directors decide.

26.2. Directors are entitled to such remuneration as the directors determine:

(a) for their services to the company as directors;

(b) for any other service which they undertake for the company.

26.3. Subject to the articles, a director's remuneration may:

(a) Take any form, and include any arrangements in connection with the payment of a pension, allowance or gratuity, or any death, sickness or disability benefits, to or in respect of that director.

(b) Unless the directors decide otherwise, directors' remuneration accrues from day to day.

(c) Unless the directors decide otherwise, directors are not accountable to the company for any remuneration which they receive as directors or other officers or employees of the company's subsidiaries or of any other body corporate in which the company is interested.

Article 27 Directors' expenses

27.1. The company may pay any reasonable expenses which the directors properly incur in connection with their attendance at:

(a) meetings of directors;

(b) committees of directors;

(c) general meetings; or

(d) otherwise in connection with the exercise of their powers and the discharge of their responsibilities in relation to the company.

Appointments and elections

Article 28 Election of the chairman

28.1. At the annual general meeting each year a chairman will be elected in accordance with article 29.

28.2. The term of chairman shall be for [2] years 'board term'. The chairman will have full voting rights subject to these articles.

28.3. A chairman shall not be eligible for reelection after the 'board term' for a period of [5] years.

28.4. The board on the appointment of a chairman in accordance with article 29 shall, 14 days after the date of the AGM, appoint or revoke any 'board position' by ordinary resolution from time to time as they see fit. For the avoidance of doubt 'board position' means:

(a) vice-chairman;

(b) secretary;

(c) treasurer;

together 'board position'.

Article 29 Board elections

29.1. A voting member of the club may nominate another member 'nominee' for any board position.

29.2. Nominations shall be made by the 'nominee form' authorised by the board from time to time.

29.3. The board shall provide nominee forms to voting members at least [14] days prior to the agreed date of the annual general meeting.

29.4. Nominee forms shall be returned to the board [5] days prior to the 'AGM'.

29.5. A nominee shall be a voting member of the club in good standing with a least [2] years continuous membership of the club.

29.6. If the board shall receive only one nomination then he shall be appointed without election or the matter shall be put to board for election at the 'AGM' on terms the directors agree.

Organisation of general meetings

Article 30 Attendance and speaking at general meetings

30.1. A person is able to exercise the right to speak at a general meeting when that person is in a position to communicate to all those attending the meeting, during the meeting, any information or opinions which that person has on the business of the meeting.

30.2. A person is able to exercise the right to vote at a general meeting when:

(a) that person is able to vote, during the meeting, on resolutions put to the vote at the meeting; and

(b) that person's vote can be taken into account in determining whether or not such resolutions are passed at the same time as the votes of all the other persons attending the meeting.

30.3. The directors may make whatever arrangements they consider appropriate to enable those attending a general meeting to exercise their rights to speak or vote at it.

30.4. In determining attendance at a general meeting, it is immaterial whether any two or more members attending it are in the same place as each other.

30.5. Two or more persons who are not in the same place as each other attend a general meeting if their circumstances are such that if they have (or were to have) rights to speak and vote at that meeting, they are (or would be) able to exercise them.

Article 31 Quorum for general meetings

31.1. No business other than the appointment of the chairman of the meeting is to be transacted at a general meeting if the persons attending it do not constitute a quorum.

Article 32 Chairing general meetings

32.1. The chairman shall chair general meetings if present and willing to do so.

32.2. If the directors have not appointed a chairman, or if the chairman is unwilling to chair the meeting or is not present within ten minutes of the time at which a meeting was due to start:

(a) the directors present; or

(b) (if no directors are present), at the meeting, they must appoint a director or member to chair the meeting, and the appointment of the chairman of the meeting must be the first business of the meeting.

32.3. The person chairing a meeting in accordance with this article is referred to as 'the chairman of the meeting'.

Article 33 Attendance and speaking by directors and non-members

33.1. Directors may attend and speak at general meetings, whether or not they are members.

33.2. The chairman of the meeting may permit other persons who are not members of the company to attend and speak at a general meeting.

Article 34 Adjournment

34.1. If the persons attending a general meeting within half an hour of the time at which the meeting was due to start do not constitute a quorum, or if during a meeting a quorum ceases to be present, the chairman of the meeting must adjourn it.

34.2. The chairman of the meeting may adjourn a general meeting at which a quorum is present if:

(a) the meeting consents to an adjournment; or

(b) it appears to the chairman of the meeting that an adjournment is necessary to protect the safety of any person attending the meeting or ensure that the business of the meeting is conducted in an orderly manner.

34.3. The chairman of the meeting must adjourn a general meeting if directed to do so by the meeting.

34.4. When adjourning a general meeting, the chairman of the meeting must:

(a) either specify the time and place to which it is adjourned or state that it is to continue at a time and place to be fixed by the directors;

(b) and have regard to any directions as to the time and place of any adjournment which have been given by the meeting.

34.5. If the continuation of an adjourned meeting is to take place more than 14 days after it was adjourned, the company must give at least 7 clear days' notice of it (that is, excluding the day of the adjourned meeting and the day on which the notice is given):

(a) to the same persons to whom notice of the company's general meetings is required to be given and containing the same information which such notice is required to contain; and

(b) no business may be transacted at an adjourned general meeting which could not properly have been transacted at the meeting if the adjournment had not taken place.

Voting at general meetings

Article 35 Voting: general

35.1. A resolution put to the vote of a general meeting must be decided on a show of hands unless a poll is duly demanded in accordance with the articles.

Article 36 Errors and disputes

36.1. No objection may be raised to the qualification of any person voting at a general meeting except at the meeting or adjourned meeting at which the vote objected to is tendered, and every vote not disallowed at the meeting is valid.

36.2. Any such objection must be referred to the chairman of the meeting whose decision is final.

Article 37 Poll votes

37.1. A poll on a resolution may be demanded:

(a) in advance of the general meeting where it is to be put to the vote; or

(b) at a general meeting, either before a show of hands on that resolution or immediately after the result of a show of hands on that resolution is declared.

37.2. A poll may be demanded by:

(a) the chairman of the meeting;

(b) the directors;

(c) two or more persons having the right to vote on the resolution; or

(d) a person or persons representing not less than one tenth of the total voting rights of all the members having the right to vote on the resolution.

37.3. A demand for a poll may be withdrawn if:

(a) the poll has not yet been taken; and

(b) the chairman of the meeting consents to the withdrawal.

37.4. Polls must be taken immediately and in such manner as the chairman of the meeting directs.

Article 38 Content of proxy notices

38.1. Proxies may only validly be appointed by a notice in writing (a 'proxy notice'). The proxy notice shall:

(a) state the name and address of the member appointing the proxy;

(b) identify the person appointed to be that member's proxy;

(c) state the general meeting in relation to which that person is appointed;

(d) be signed by or on behalf of the member appointing the proxy, or is authenticated in such manner as the directors may determine;

(e) be delivered to the company in accordance with the articles and any instructions contained in the notice of the general meeting to which they relate.

38.2. The company may require proxy notices to be delivered in a particular form, and may specify different forms for different purposes.

38.3. Proxy notices may specify how the proxy appointed under them is to vote (or that the proxy is to abstain from voting) on one or more resolutions.

38.4. Unless a proxy notice indicates otherwise it shall be treated as:

(a) allowing the person appointed under it as a proxy discretion as to how to vote on any ancillary or procedural resolutions put to the meeting; and

(b) and appointing that person as a proxy in relation to any adjournment of the general meeting to which it relates as well as the meeting itself.

Article 39 Delivery of proxy notices

39.1. A person who is entitled to attend, speak or vote (either on a show of hands or on a poll) at a general meeting remains so entitled in respect of that meeting or any adjournment of it, even though a valid proxy notice has been delivered to the company by or on behalf of that person.

39.2. An appointment under a proxy notice may be revoked by delivering to the company a notice in writing given by or on behalf of the person by whom or on whose behalf the proxy notice was given.

39.3. A notice revoking a proxy appointment only takes effect if it is delivered before the start of the meeting or adjourned meeting to which it relates.

39.4. If a proxy notice is not executed by the person appointing the proxy, it must be accompanied by written evidence of the authority of the person who executed it to execute it on the appointor's behalf.

Article 40 Amendments to resolutions

40.1. An ordinary resolution to be proposed at a general meeting may be amended by ordinary resolution if:

(a) notice of the proposed amendment is given to the company in writing by a person entitled to vote at the general meeting at which it is to be proposed not less than 48 hours before the meeting is to take place (or such later time as the chairman of the meeting may determine);

(b) the proposed amendment does not, in the reasonable opinion of the chairman of the meeting, materially alter the scope of the resolution.

40.2. A special resolution to be proposed at a general meeting may be amended by ordinary resolution if:

(a) the chairman of the meeting proposes the amendment at the general meeting at which the resolution is to be proposed; and

(b) the amendment does not go beyond what is necessary to correct a grammatical or other non-substantive error in the resolution.

40.3. If the chairman of the meeting, acting in good faith, wrongly decides that an amendment to a resolution is out of order, the chairman's error does not invalidate the vote on that resolution.

Administrative arrangements

Article 41 Means of communication to be used

41.1. Subject to the articles, anything sent or supplied by or to the company under the articles may be sent or supplied in any way in which the Companies Act 2006 provides for documents or information which are authorised or required by any provision of that Act to be sent or supplied by or to the company.

41.2. Subject to the articles, any notice or document to be sent or supplied to a director in connection with the taking of decisions by directors may also be sent or supplied by the means by which that director has asked to be sent or supplied with such notices or documents for the time being.

41.3. A director may agree with the company that notices or documents sent to that director in a particular way are to be deemed to have been received within a specified time of their being sent, and for the specified time to be less than 48 hours.

Article 42 Company seals

42.1. Any common seal may only be used by the authority of the directors. The directors may decide by what means and in what form any common seal is to be used.

42.2. Unless otherwise decided by the directors, if the company has a common seal and it is affixed to a document, the document must also be signed by at least one authorised person in the presence of a witness who attests the signature.

42.3. For the purposes of this article an authorised person is:

(a) any director of the company;

(b) any person authorised by the directors for the purpose of signing documents to which the common seal is applied.

Indemnity and insurance

Article 43 Indemnity

43.1. Subject to paragraph 43.2 only in relation to the club any relevant director may be indemnified out of the club's resources against any liability incurred by that director in connection with any:

(a) negligence;

(b) default;

(c) breach of duty;

(d) breach of trust;

(e) [liability incurred by that director in connection with the activities of the club in its capacity as a trustee of an occupational pension scheme (as defined in section 235(6) of the Companies Act 2006)];

(f) liability incurred by that director as an officer of the club.

43.2. This article does not authorise any indemnity which would be prohibited or rendered void by any provision of the Companies Acts or by any other provision of law.

43.3. The directors may decide to purchase and maintain insurance, at the expense of the company, for the benefit of any relevant director in respect of any relevant loss.

43.4. In this article 'relevant director' means any director or former director of the club. A 'relevant loss' means any loss or liability which has been or may be incurred by a relevant director in connection with that director's duties or powers in relation to the club or any pension fund or employees' share scheme.

Precedent 3: Charitable Company Articles of Association

The Companies Act 1985 to 2006

Company Limited by Guarantee and not Having a Share Capital

Articles of Association for a Charitable Company

Articles of Association of

Article 1 Company name

1. The company's name is [insert company name].

Article 2 Interpretation

2.1. In the articles:

'address' means a postal address or, for the purposes of electronic communication, a fax number, an e-mail or postal address or a telephone number for receiving text messages in each case registered with the charity;

'connected person' means:

(a) a child, parent, grandchild, grandparent, brother or sister of the director;

(b) the spouse or civil partner of the director or of any person falling within sub-clause (a) above;

(c) a person carrying on business in partnership with the director or with any person falling within sub-clause (a) or (b) above;

(d) an institution which is controlled by the director or any connected person falling within sub-clause (a), (b), or (c) above;

(e) or by two or more persons falling within sub-clause 2.5(d), when taken together;

(f) a body corporate in which:

(a) the director or any connected person falling within subclauses (a) to (c) has a substantial interest;

or

(b) two or more persons falling within sub-clause (f)(a) who, when taken together, have a substantial interest.

(g) Sections 350–352 of the Charities Act 2011 apply for the purposes of interpreting the terms used in this article.

'the articles' means the charity's articles of association;

'the charity' means the company intended to be regulated by the articles;

'clear days' in relation to the period of a notice means a period excluding:

- the day when the notice is given or deemed to be given; and
- the day for which it is given or on which it is to take effect;

'the Commission' means the Charity Commission for England and Wales;

'Companies Acts' means the Companies Acts (as defined in section 2 of the Companies Act 2006) insofar as they apply to the charity;

'the directors' means the directors of the charity. The directors are charity trustees as defined by section 177 of the Charities Act 2011;

'document' includes, unless otherwise specified, any document sent or supplied in electronic form;

'electronic form' has the meaning given in section 1168 of the Companies Act 2006;

'the memorandum' means the charity's memorandum of association;

'officers' includes the directors and the secretary (if any);

'the seal' means the common seal of the charity if it has one;

'secretary' means any person appointed to perform the duties of the secretary of the charity;

'the United Kingdom' means Great Britain and Northern Ireland; and words importing one gender shall include all genders, and the singular includes the plural and vice versa.

2.2. Unless the context otherwise requires, words or expressions contained in the articles have the same meaning as in the Companies Acts but excluding any statutory modification not in force when this constitution becomes binding on the charity.

2.3. Apart from the exception mentioned in the previous paragraph a reference to an Act of Parliament includes any statutory modification or re-enactment of it for the time being in force.

Article 3 Liability of members

3.1. The liability of the members is limited to a sum not exceeding £10, being the amount that each member undertakes to contribute to the assets of the charity in the event of its being wound up while he, she or it is a member or within one year after he, she or it ceases to be a member, for:

(a) payment of the charity's debts and liabilities incurred before he, she or it ceases to be a member;

(b) payment of the costs, charges and expenses of winding up; and

(c) adjustment of the rights of the contributories among themselves.

Article 4 Objects

4.1. The charity's objects ('objects') are specifically restricted to the following:

4.2. [Nothing in the articles shall authorise an application of the property of the charity for purposes which are not charitable in accordance with section 7 of the Charities and Trustee Investment (Scotland) Act 2005 and/or section 2 of the Charities Act (Northern Ireland) 2008.]

Article 5 Powers

5.1. The charity has power to do anything which is calculated to further its object(s) or is conducive or incidental to doing so. In particular, the charity has power:

(a) to raise funds. In doing so, the charity must not undertake any taxable permanent trading activity and must comply with any relevant statutory regulations;

(b) to buy, take on lease or in exchange, hire or otherwise acquire any property and to maintain and equip it for use;

(c) to sell, lease or otherwise dispose of all or any part of the property belonging to the charity. In exercising this power, the charity must comply as appropriate with sections 117 and 122 of the Charities Act 2011;

(d) to borrow money and to charge the whole or any part of the property belonging to the charity as security for repayment of the money borrowed or as security for a grant or the discharge of an obligation. The charity must comply as appropriate with sections 124–126 of the Charities Act 2011 if it wishes to mortgage land;

(e) to cooperate with other charities, voluntary bodies and statutory authorities and to exchange information and advice with them;

(f) to establish or support any charitable trusts, associations or institutions formed for any of the charitable purposes included in the objects;

(g) to acquire, merge with or to enter into any partnership or joint venture arrangement with any other charity;

(h) to set aside income as a reserve against future expenditure but only in accordance with a written policy about reserves;

(i) to employ and remunerate such staff as are necessary for carrying out the work of the charity. The charity may employ or remunerate a director only to the extent it is permitted to do so by article 7 and provided it complies with the conditions in that article;

(j) to deposit or invest funds, employ a professional fund-manager; and arrange for the investments or other property of the charity to be held in the name of a nominee; in the same manner and subject to the same conditions as the trustees of a trust are permitted to do by the Trustee Act 2000;

(k) to provide indemnity insurance for the directors in accordance with, and subject to the conditions in, section 189 of the Charities Act 2011;

(l) to pay out of the funds of the charity the costs of forming and registering the charity both as a company and as a charity.

Article 6 Application of income and property

6.1. The income and property of the charity shall be applied solely towards the promotion of the objects:

(a) A director is entitled to be reimbursed from the property of the charity or may pay out of such property reasonable expenses properly incurred by him or her when acting on behalf of the charity.

(b) A director may benefit from trustee indemnity insurance cover purchased at the charity's expense in accordance with, and subject to the conditions in, section 189 of the Charities Act 2011.

(c) A director may receive an indemnity from the charity in the circumstances specified in article 7.

(d) A director may not receive any other benefit or payment unless it is authorised by article 7.

Transfer of income and property

6.2. Subject to article 7, none of the income or property of the charity may be paid or transferred directly or indirectly by way of dividend bonus or otherwise by way of profit to any member of the charity. This does not prevent a member who is not also a director receiving:

(a) a benefit from the charity in the capacity of a beneficiary of the charity;

(b) reasonable and proper remuneration for any goods or services supplied to the charity.

Article 7 Benefits and payments to charity directors and connected persons

7.1. In this article a 'financial benefit' means a benefit, direct or indirect, which is either money or has a monetary value.

7.2. No director or connected person may:

(a) buy any goods or services from the charity on terms preferential to those applicable to members of the public;

(b) sell goods, services, or any interest in land to the charity;

(c) be employed by, or receive any remuneration from, the charity;

(d) receive any other financial benefit from the charity; unless the payment is permitted by sub-clause 7.3 of this article, or authorised by the court or the prior written consent of the Charity Commission has been obtained.

7.3. **Scope and powers permitting directors' or connected persons' benefits**

For the benefit of doubt, in these articles 7.3 and 7.4, 'charity' includes any company in which the charity: holds more than 50 per cent of the shares; or controls more than 50 per cent of the voting rights attached to the shares; or has the right to appoint one or more directors to the board of the company. A 'connected person' includes any person within the definition in article 2.1.

(a) A director or connected person may receive a benefit from the charity in the capacity of a beneficiary of the charity provided that a majority of the directors do not benefit in this way.

(b) A director or connected person may enter into a contract for the supply of services, or of goods that are supplied in connection with the provision of services, to the charity where that is permitted in accordance with, and subject to the conditions in, sections 185 and 186 of the Charities Act 2011.

(c) Subject to article 7.4 a director or connected person may provide the charity with goods that are not supplied in connection with services provided to the charity by the director or connected person.

(d) A director or connected person may receive interest on money lent to the charity at a reasonable and proper rate which must be not more than the Bank of England bank rate (also known as the base rate).

(e) A director or connected person may receive rent for premises let by the director or connected person to the charity. The amount of the rent and the other terms of the lease must be reasonable and proper. The director concerned must withdraw from any meeting at which such a proposal or the rent or other terms of the lease are under discussion.

(f) A director or connected person may take part in the normal trading and fundraising activities of the charity on the same terms as members of the public.

7.4. **Payment for supply of goods only – controls**

The charity and its directors may only rely upon the authority provided by sub-clause 7.3(c) of this article if each of the following conditions is satisfied:

(a) The amount or maximum amount of the payment for the goods is set out in an agreement in writing between the charity or its directors (as the case may be) and the director or connected person supplying the goods ('the supplier') under which the supplier is to supply the goods in question to or on behalf of the charity.

(b) The amount or maximum amount of the payment for the goods does not exceed what is reasonable in the circumstances for the supply of the goods in question.

(c) The other directors are satisfied that it is in the best interests of the charity to contract with the supplier rather than with someone who is not a director or connected person. In reaching that decision the directors must balance the advantage of contracting with a director or connected person against the disadvantages of doing so.

(d) The supplier is absent from the part of any meeting at which there is discussion of the proposal to enter into a contract or arrangement with him or her or it with regard to the supply of goods to the charity.

(e) The supplier does not vote on any such matter and is not to be counted when calculating whether a quorum of directors is present at the meeting.

(f) The reason for their decision is recorded by the directors in the minute book.

(g) A majority of the directors then in office are not in receipt of remuneration or payments authorised by article 7.

Article 8 Declaration of directors' interests

8.1. A director must declare the nature and extent of any interest, direct or indirect, which he or she has in a proposed transaction or arrangement with the charity or in any transaction or arrangement entered into by the charity which has not previously been declared. A director must absent himself or herself from any discussions of the charity directors in which it is possible that a conflict will arise between his or her duty to act solely in the interests of the charity and any personal interest (including but not limited to any personal financial interest).

Article 9 Conflicts of interests and conflicts of loyalties

9.1. If a conflict of interests arises for a director because of a duty of loyalty owed to another organisation or person and the conflict is not authorised by virtue of any other provision in the articles, the unconflicted directors may authorise such a conflict of interests where the following conditions apply:

(a) the conflicted director is absent from the part of the meeting at which there is discussion of any arrangement or transaction affecting that other organisation or person;

(b) the conflicted director does not vote on any such matter and is not to be counted when considering whether a quorum of directors is present at the meeting; and

(c) the unconflicted directors consider it is in the interests of the charity to authorise the conflict of interests in the circumstances applying.

9.2. In this article a conflict of interests arising because of a duty of loyalty owed to another organisation or person only refers to such a conflict which does not involve a direct or indirect benefit of any nature to a director or to a connected person.

Article 10 Members

10.1. The subscribers to the memorandum are the first members of the charity.

10.2. Membership is open to other individuals or organisations who:

(a) apply to the charity in the form required by the directors; and

(b) are approved by the directors.

10.3. The directors may only refuse an application for membership if, acting reasonably and properly, they consider it to be in the best interests of the charity to refuse the application.

10.4. The directors must inform the applicant in writing of the reasons for the refusal within 21 days of the decision.

10.5. The directors must consider any written representations the applicant may make about the decision. The directors' decision following any written representations must be notified to the applicant in writing but shall be final.

10.6. Membership is not transferable.

10.7. The directors must keep a register of names and addresses of the members.

Article 11 Classes of membership

11.1. The directors may establish classes of membership with different rights and obligations and shall record the rights and obligations in the register of members.

11.2. The directors may not directly or indirectly alter the rights or obligations attached to a class of membership.

11.3. The rights attached to a class of membership may only be varied if:

(a) three-quarters of the members of that class consent in writing to the variation; or

(b) a special resolution is passed at a separate general meeting of the members of that class agreeing to the variation.

11.4. The provisions in the articles about general meetings shall apply to any meeting relating to the variation of the rights of any class of members.

Article 12 Termination of membership

12.1. Membership is terminated if:

(a) the member dies or, if it is an organisation, ceases to exist;

(b) the member resigns by written notice to the charity unless, after the resignation, there would be less than two members;

(c) any sum due from the member to the charity is not paid in full within six months of it falling due;

(d) the member is removed by a resolution of the directors.

12.2. A resolution to remove a member from membership may only be passed if the member has been given at least 21 days' notice in writing of the meeting of the directors at which the resolution will be proposed and the reasons why it is to be proposed:

(a) the member or nominated representative (who need not be a member of the charity) has been allowed to make representations to the meeting.

Article 13 General meetings

13.1. The charity must hold its first annual general meeting within 18 months after the date of its incorporation. An annual general meeting must be held in each subsequent year and not more than 15 months may elapse between successive annual general meetings.

Article 14 Calling a directors meeting

14.1. The directors may call a general meeting at any time.

Article 15 Notice of general meetings

15.1. The minimum periods of notice required to hold a general meeting of the charity are:

(a) 21 clear days for an annual general meeting or a general meeting called for the passing of a special resolution;

(b) 14 clear days for all other general meetings.

15.2. A general meeting may be called by shorter notice if it is so agreed by a majority in number of members having a right to attend and vote at the meeting, being a majority who together hold not less than 90 per cent of the total voting rights.

15.3. The notice must specify the date time and place of the meeting and the general nature of the business to be transacted. If the meeting is to be an annual general meeting, the notice must say so. The notice must also contain a statement setting out the right of members to appoint a proxy under section 324 of the Companies Act 2006 and article 22.

15.4. The notice must be given to all the members and to the directors and auditors.

Article 16 Omissions

16.1. The proceedings at a meeting shall not be invalidated because a person who was entitled to receive notice of the meeting did not receive it because of an accidental omission by the charity.

Article 17 Proceedings at general meetings

17.1. No business shall be transacted at any general meeting unless a quorum is present.

17.2. A quorum is:

(a) four members present in person or by proxy and entitled to vote upon the business to be conducted at the meeting; or

(b) one tenth of the total membership at the time whichever is the greater.

17.3. The authorised representative of a member organisation shall be counted in the quorum.

Article 18 Adjournment

18.1. If a quorum is not present within half an hour from the time appointed for the meeting; or during a meeting a quorum ceases to be present; the meeting shall be adjourned to such time and place as the directors shall determine.

18.2. The directors must reconvene the meeting and must give at least seven clear days' notice of the reconvened meeting stating the date, time and place of the meeting.

18.3. If no quorum is present at the reconvened meeting within 15 minutes of the time specified for the start of the meeting the members present in person or by proxy at that time shall constitute the quorum for that meeting.

Article 19 Chairing general meetings

19.1. General meetings shall be chaired by the person who has been appointed to chair meetings of the directors.

19.2. If there is no such person or he or she is not present within 15 minutes of the time appointed for the meeting a director nominated by the directors shall chair the meeting.

19.3. If there is only one director present and willing to act, he or she shall chair the meeting.

19.4. If no director is present and willing to chair the meeting within 15 minutes after the time appointed for holding it, the members present in person or by proxy and entitled to vote must choose one of their number to chair the meeting.

Article 20 Reconvening the meeting

20.1. The members present in person or by proxy at a meeting may resolve by ordinary resolution that the meeting shall be adjourned.

20.2. The person who is chairing the meeting must decide the date, time and place at which the meeting is to be reconvened unless those details are specified in the resolution.

20.3. No business shall be conducted at a reconvened meeting unless it could properly have been conducted at the meeting had the adjournment not taken place.

20.4. If a meeting is adjourned by a resolution of the members for more than seven days, at least seven clear days' notice shall be given of the reconvened meeting stating the date, time and place of the meeting.

Article 21 Voting

21.1. Any vote at a meeting shall be decided by a show of hands unless before, or on the declaration of the result of, the show of hands a poll is demanded:

(a) by the person chairing the meeting; or

(b) by at least two members present in person or by proxy and having the right to vote at the meeting; or

(c) by a member or members present in person or by proxy representing not less than one-tenth of the total voting rights of all the members having the right to vote at the meeting.

21.2. The declaration by the person who is chairing the meeting of the result of a vote shall be conclusive unless a poll is demanded.

21.3. The result of the vote must be recorded in the minutes of the charity but the number or proportion of votes cast need not be recorded.

Polls

21.4. A demand for a poll may be withdrawn, before the poll is taken, but only with the consent of the person who is chairing the meeting.

(a) If the demand for a poll is withdrawn the demand shall not invalidate the result of a show of hands declared before the demand was made.

(b) A poll must be taken as the person who is chairing the meeting directs, who may appoint scrutineers (who need not be members) and who may fix a time and place for declaring the results of the poll.

21.5. The result of the poll shall be deemed to be the resolution of the meeting at which the poll is demanded.

(a) A poll demanded on the election of a person to chair a meeting or on a question of adjournment must be taken immediately.

(b) A poll demanded on any other question must be taken either immediately or at such time and place as the person who is chairing the meeting directs.

(c) The poll must be taken within 30 days after it has been demanded.

(d) If the poll is not taken immediately at least seven clear days' notice shall be given specifying the time and place at which the poll is to be taken.

(e) If a poll is demanded the meeting may continue to deal with any other business that may be conducted at the meeting.

Article 22 Content of proxy notices

22.1. Proxies may only validly be appointed by a notice in writing (a 'proxy notice') which:

(a) states the name and address of the member appointing the proxy;

(b) identifies the person appointed to be that member's proxy and the general meeting in relation to which that person is appointed;

(c) is signed by or on behalf of the member appointing the proxy, or is authenticated in such manner as the directors may determine; and

(d) is delivered to the charity in accordance with the articles and any instructions contained in the notice of the general meeting to which they relate.

22.2. The charity may require proxy notices to be delivered in a particular form, and may specify different forms for different purposes.

22.3. Proxy notices may specify how the proxy appointed under them is to vote (or that the proxy is to abstain from voting) on one or more resolutions.

22.4. Unless a proxy notice indicates otherwise, it must be treated as:

(a) allowing the person appointed under it as a proxy discretion as to how to vote on any ancillary or procedural resolutions put to the meeting; and

(b) appointing that person as a proxy in relation to any adjournment of the general meeting to which it relates as well as the meeting itself.

Delivery of proxy notices

22.5. A person who is entitled to attend, speak or vote (either on a show of hands or on a poll) at a general meeting remains so entitled in respect of that meeting or any adjournment of it, even though a valid proxy notice has been delivered to the charity by or on behalf of that person.

22.6. An appointment under a proxy notice may be revoked by delivering to the charity a notice in writing given by or on behalf of the person by whom or on whose behalf the proxy notice was given.

22.7. A notice revoking a proxy appointment only takes effect if it is delivered before the start of the meeting or adjourned meeting to which it relates.

22.8. If a proxy notice is not executed by the person appointing the proxy, it must be accompanied by written evidence of the authority of the person who executed it to execute it on the appointor's behalf.

Article 23 Written resolutions

23.1. A resolution in writing agreed by a simple majority (or in the case of a special resolution by a majority of not less than 75 per cent) of the members who would have been entitled to vote upon it had it been proposed at a general meeting shall be effective provided that:

(a) a copy of the proposed resolution has been sent to every eligible member;

(b) a simple majority (or in the case of a special resolution a majority of not less than 75 per cent) of members has signified its agreement to the resolution; and

(c) it is contained in an authenticated document which has been received at the registered office within the period of 28 days beginning with the circulation date.

23.2. A resolution in writing may comprise several copies to which one or more members have signified their agreement.

23.3. In the case of a member that is an organisation, its authorised representative may signify its agreement.

Article 24 Votes of members

24.1. Subject to article 11, every member, whether an individual or an organisation, shall have one vote.

Article 25 Objections

25.1. Any objection to the qualification of any voter must be raised at the meeting at which the vote is tendered and the decision of the person who is chairing the meeting shall be final.

Article 26 Nominations of representatives

26.1. Any organisation that is a member of the charity may nominate any person to act as its representative at any meeting of the charity.

(a) The organisation must give written notice to the charity of the name of its representative. The representative shall not be entitled to represent the organisation at any meeting unless the notice has been received by the charity. The representative may continue to represent the organisation until written notice to the contrary is received by the charity.

(b) Any notice given to the charity will be conclusive evidence that the representative is entitled to represent the organisation or that his or her authority has been revoked. The charity shall not be required to consider whether the representative has been properly appointed by the organisation.

Article 27 Directors

27.1. Any appointment as director is subject to the Companies Act 2006. A director must be a natural person aged 16 years or older.

(a) No one may be appointed a director if he or she would be disqualified from acting under the provisions of article 39.

Article 28 Number of directors

28.1. The minimum number of directors shall be two but (unless otherwise determined by ordinary resolution) shall not be subject to any maximum.

Article 29 First directors appointed

29.1. The first directors shall be those persons notified to Companies House as the first directors of the charity.

Article 30 Restrictions on alternative directors

30.1. A director may not appoint an alternate director or anyone to act on his or her behalf at meetings of the directors.

Article 31 Powers of directors

31.1. The directors shall manage the business of the charity and may exercise all the powers of the charity unless they are subject to any restrictions imposed by the Companies Acts, the articles or any special resolution.

31.2. No alteration of the articles or any special resolution shall have retrospective effect to invalidate any prior act of the directors.

31.3. Any meeting of directors at which a quorum is present at the time the relevant decision is made may exercise all the powers exercisable by the directors.

Article 32 Retirement of directors

32.1. At the first annual general meeting all the directors must retire from office unless by the close of the meeting the members have failed to elect sufficient directors to hold a quorate meeting of the directors. At each subsequent annual general meeting one-third of the directors or, if their number is not three or a multiple of three, the number nearest to one-third, must retire from office. If there is only one director he or she must retire.

Article 33 Retirement by rotation

33.1. The directors to retire by rotation shall be those who have been longest in office since their last appointment. If any directors became or were appointed directors on the same day those to retire shall (unless they otherwise agree among themselves) be determined by lot.

33.2. If a director is required to retire at an annual general meeting by a provision of the articles the retirement shall take effect upon the conclusion of the meeting.

Article 34 Appointment of directors

34.1. The charity may by ordinary resolution:

(a) appoint a person who is willing to act to be a director; and

(b) determine the rotation in which any additional directors are to retire.

Article 35 Reappointment

35.1. No person other than a director retiring by rotation may be appointed a director at any general meeting unless he or she is recommended for re-election by the directors; or not less than 14 nor more than 35 clear days before the date of the meeting, the charity is given a notice that:

(a) is signed by a member entitled to vote at the meeting;

(b) states the member's intention to propose the appointment of a person as a director;

(c) contains the details that, if the person were to be appointed, the charity would have to file at Companies House; and

(d) is signed by the person who is to be proposed to show his or her willingness to be appointed.

Article 36 Notices

36.1. All members who are entitled to receive notice of a general meeting must be given not less than seven nor more than 28 clear days' notice of any resolution to be put to the meeting to appoint a director other than a director who is to retire by rotation.

Article 37 Appointment by directors

37.1. The directors may appoint a person who is willing to act to be a director.

37.2. A director appointed by a resolution of the other directors must retire at the next annual general meeting and must not be taken into account in determining the directors who are to retire by rotation.

Article 38 Maximum number of directors

38.1. The appointment of a director, whether by the charity in general meeting or by the other directors, must not cause the number of directors to exceed any number fixed as the maximum number of directors.

Article 39 Disqualification and removal of directors

39.1. A director shall cease to hold office if he or she:

(a) ceases to be a director by virtue of any provision in the Companies Acts or is prohibited by law from being a director;

(b) is disqualified from acting as a trustee by virtue of sections 178 and 179 of the Charities Act 2011 (or any statutory re-enactment or modification of those provisions);

(c) ceases to be a member of the charity;

(d) in the written opinion, given to the company, of a registered medical practitioner treating that person, has become physically or mentally incapable of acting as a director and may remain so for more than three months;

(e) resigns as a director by notice to the charity (but only if at least two directors will remain in office when the notice of resignation is to take effect); or

(f) is absent without the permission of the directors from all their meetings held within a period of six consecutive months and the directors resolve that his or her office be vacated.

Article 40 Remuneration of directors

40.1. The directors must not be paid any remuneration unless it is authorised by article 7.

Article 41 Proceedings of directors

41.1. The directors may regulate their proceedings as they think fit, subject to the provisions of the articles.

41.2. Any director may call a meeting of the directors.

41.3. The secretary (if any) must call a meeting of the directors if requested to do so by a director.

41.4. Questions arising at a meeting shall be decided by a majority of votes.

Chair casting vote

41.5. In the case of an equality of votes, the person who is chairing the meeting shall have a second or casting vote.

Communication

41.6. A meeting may be held by suitable electronic means agreed by the directors in which each participant may communicate with all the other participants.

Article 42 Quorum for meetings

42.1. No decision may be made by a meeting of the directors unless a quorum is present at the time the decision is purported to be made.

(a) 'Present' includes being present by suitable electronic means agreed by the directors in which a participant or participants may communicate with all the other participants.

42.2. The quorum shall be two or the number nearest to one-third of the total number of directors, whichever is the greater, or such larger number as may be decided from time to time by the directors.

42.3. A director shall not be counted in the quorum present when any decision is made about a matter upon which that director is not entitled to vote.

Article 43 Election of Chair

43.1. If the number of directors is less than the number fixed as the quorum, the continuing directors or director may act only for the purpose of filling vacancies or of calling a general meeting.

Article 44 Appointment

44.1. The directors shall appoint a director to chair their meetings and may at any time revoke such appointment.

44.2. If no-one has been appointed to chair meetings of the directors or if the person appointed is unwilling to preside or is not present within ten minutes after the time appointed for the meeting, the directors present may appoint one of their number to chair that meeting.

44.3. The person appointed to chair meetings of the directors shall have no functions or powers except those conferred by the articles or delegated to him or her by the directors.

Article 45 Resolutions in writing

45.1. A resolution in writing or in electronic form agreed by all of the directors entitled to receive notice of a meeting of the directors and to vote upon the resolution shall be as valid and effectual as if it had been passed at a meeting of the directors duly convened and held.

45.2. The resolution in writing may comprise several documents containing the text of the resolution in like form to each of which one or more directors has signified their agreement.

Article 46 Delegation

46.1. The directors may delegate any of their powers or functions to a committee of two or more directors but the terms of any delegation must be recorded in the minute book.

46.2. The directors may impose conditions when delegating, including the conditions that:

(a) the relevant powers are to be exercised exclusively by the committee to whom they delegate;

(b) no expenditure may be incurred on behalf of the charity except in accordance with a budget previously agreed with the directors.

46.3. The directors may revoke or alter a delegation.

46.4. All acts and proceedings of any committees must be fully and promptly reported to the directors.

Article 47 Validity of directors' decisions

47.1. Subject to article 47(2), all acts done by a meeting of directors, or of a committee of directors, shall be valid notwithstanding the participation in any vote of a director:

(a) who was disqualified from holding office;

(b) who had previously retired or who had been obliged by the constitution to vacate office;

(c) who was not entitled to vote on the matter, whether by reason of a conflict of interests or otherwise;

if without:

(d) the vote of that director; and

(e) that director being counted in the quorum; the decision has been made by a majority of the directors at a quorate meeting.

47.2. Article 47(1) does not permit a director or a connected person to keep any benefit that may be conferred upon him or her by a resolution of the directors or of a committee of directors if, but for article 47(1), the resolution would have been void, or if the director has not complied with article 8.

Article 48 Seal

48.1. If the charity has a seal it must only be used by the authority of the directors or of a committee of directors authorised by the directors. The directors may determine who shall sign any instrument to which the seal is affixed and unless otherwise so determined it shall be signed by a director and by the secretary (if any) or by a second director.

Article 49 Minutes

49.1. The directors must keep minutes of all: appointments of officers made by the directors, proceedings at meetings of the charity, meetings of the directors and committees of directors including:

(a) the names of the directors present at the meeting;

(b) the decisions made at the meetings; and

(c) where appropriate the reasons for the decisions.

Article 50 Accounts

50.1. The directors must prepare for each financial year accounts as required by the Companies Acts. The accounts must be prepared to show a true and fair view and follow accounting standards issued or adopted by the Accounting Standards Board or its successors and adhere to the recommendations of applicable Statements of Recommended Practice.

50.2. The directors must keep accounting records as required by the Companies Act.

Article 51 Annual Report and Return and Register of Charities

51.1. The directors must comply with the requirements of the Charities Act 2011 with regard to the:

(a) transmission of a copy of the statements of account to the Commission;

(b) preparation of an Annual Report and the transmission of a copy of it to the Commission;

(c) preparation of an Annual Return and its transmission to the Commission.

51.2. The directors must notify the Commission promptly of any changes to the charity's entry on the Central Register of Charities.

Article 52 Means of communication to be used

52.1. Subject to the articles, anything sent or supplied by or to the charity under the articles may be sent or supplied in any way in which the Companies Act 2006 provides for documents or information which are authorised or required by any provision of that Act to be sent or supplied by or to the charity.

52.2. Subject to the articles, any notice or document to be sent or supplied to a director in connection with the taking of decisions by directors may also be sent or supplied by the means by which that director has asked to be sent or supplied with such notices or documents for the time being.

Article 53 Notices afforded

53.1. Any notice to be given to or by any person pursuant to the articles:

(a) must be in writing; or

(b) must be given in electronic form.

Article 54 Notices methods of communication

54.1. The charity may give any notice to a member either:

(a) personally; or

(b) by sending it by post in a prepaid envelope addressed to the member at his or her address; or

(c) by leaving it at the address of the member; or

(d) by giving it in electronic form to the member's address.

(e) by placing the notice on a website and providing the person with a notification in writing or in electronic form of the presence of the notice on the website. The notification must state that it concerns a notice of a company meeting and must specify the place date and time of the meeting.

54.2. A member who does not register an address with the charity or who registers only a postal address that is not within the United Kingdom shall not be entitled to receive any notice from the charity.

Article 55 Notices in person

55.1. A member present in person at any meeting of the charity shall be deemed to have received notice of the meeting and of the purposes for which it was called.

Article 56 Notices proof of delivery

56.1. Proof that an envelope containing a notice was properly addressed, prepaid and posted shall be conclusive evidence that the notice was given.

56.2. Proof that an electronic form of notice was given shall be conclusive where the company can demonstrate that it was properly addressed and sent, in accordance with section 1147 of the Companies Act 2006.

56.3. In accordance with section 1147 of the Companies Act 2006 notice shall be deemed to be given:

(a) 48 hours after the envelope containing it was posted; or

(b) in the case of an electronic form of communication, 48 hours after it was sent.

Article 57 Indemnity

57.1. The charity shall indemnify a relevant director against any liability incurred in that capacity, to the extent permitted by sections 232 to 234 of the Companies Act 2006

57.2. In this article a 'relevant director' means any director or former director of the charity.

57.3. The charity may indemnify an auditor against any liability incurred by him or her or it:

(a) in defending proceedings (whether civil or criminal) in which judgment is given in his or her or its favour or he or she or it is acquitted; or

(b) in connection with an application under section 1157 of the Companies Act 2006 (power of Court to grant relief in case of honest and reasonable conduct) in which relief is granted to him or her or it by the Court.]

Article 58 Rules

58.1. The directors may from time to time make such reasonable and proper rules or bye laws as they may deem necessary or expedient for the proper conduct and management of the charity.

58.2. The bye laws may regulate the following matters but are not restricted to them:

(a) the admission of members of the charity (including the admission of organisations to membership) and the rights and privileges of such members, and the entrance fees, subscriptions and other fees or payments to be made by members;

(b) the conduct of members of the charity in relation to one another, and to the charity's employees and volunteers;

(c) the setting aside of the whole or any part or parts of the charity's premises at any particular time or times or for any particular purpose or purposes;

(d) the procedure at general meetings and meetings of the directors in so far as such procedure is not regulated by the Companies Acts or by the articles;

(e) generally, all such matters as are commonly the subject matter of company rules.

58.3. The charity in general meeting has the power to alter, add to or repeal the rules or bye laws.

58.4. The directors must adopt such means as they think sufficient to bring the rules and bye laws to the notice of members of the charity.

58.5. The rules or bye laws shall be binding on all members of the charity. No rule or bye law shall be inconsistent with, or shall affect or repeal anything contained in, the articles.

Article 59 Disputes

59.1. If a dispute arises between members of the charity about the validity or propriety of anything done by the members of the charity under these articles, and the dispute cannot be resolved by agreement, the parties to the dispute must first try in good faith to settle the dispute by mediation before resorting to litigation.

Article 60 Dissolution

60.1. The members of the charity may at any time before, and in expectation of, its dissolution resolve that any net assets of the charity after all its debts and liabilities have been paid, or provision has been made for them, shall on or before the dissolution of the charity be applied or transferred in any of the following ways:

(a) directly for the objects; or

(b) by transfer to any charity or charities for purposes similar to the objects; or

(c) to any charity or charities for use for particular purposes that fall within the objects.

60.2. Subject to any such resolution of the members of the charity, the directors of the charity may at any time before and in expectation of its dissolution resolve that any net assets of the charity after all its debts and liabilities have been paid, or provision made for them, shall on or before dissolution of the charity be applied or transferred:

(a) directly for the objects; or

(b) by transfer to any charity or charities for purposes similar to the objects; or

(c) to any charity or charities for use for particular purposes that fall within the objects.

60.3. In no circumstances shall the net assets of the charity be paid to or distributed among the members of the charity (except to a member that is itself a charity) and if no resolution in accordance with article 60.1 is passed by the members or the directors the net assets of the charity shall be applied for charitable purposes as directed by the Court or the Commission.

Precedent 4: Museum Articles of Association

The following museum precedent is based upon the Schedule 2 Regulation 3 model articles for a private company limited by guarantee.[1]

Drafting assumptions

- The company is a private limited company limited by guarantee and incorporated in England and Wales under the Companies Act 2006.
- The company is not a registered charity.
- The company's objects are restricted, companies incorporated prior to 1 October 2009 specified their objects in the memorandum of association, a separate document to the articles that restricted the activities the company could undertake. The Companies Act 2006 allowed a company by default unrestricted objects.[2] It is arguably good practice for a not for profit to restrict its objects in the articles of association.
- The model articles will not apply.
- The terms 'directors',[3] 'trustees' and 'board' or any other term to describe the governing body of the company are company directors and therefore must comply with the Companies Act 2006. It should be noted if the company is a charity the directors are deemed by law to be trustees.

1 Schedule 2 Regulation 3 Model articles for private companies limited by guarantee.

2 Companies Act 2006, s 31 (Statement of company's objects). '(1) Unless a company's articles specifically restrict the objects of the company, its objects are unrestricted.'

3 The Companies Act 2006 defines a company director as 'any person occupying the position of director, by whatever name called'.

The Companies Act 1985 to 2006

Company Limited by Guarantee and not Having a Share Capital

Articles of Association for a Charitable Company

Articles of Association of

Article 1 Company name

1. The company's name is [insert company name].

Article 2 Interpretation

2.1. In the articles:

'address' means a postal address or, for the purposes of electronic communication, a fax number, an e-mail or postal address or a telephone number for receiving text messages in each case registered with the charity;

'connected person' means:

(a) a child, parent, grandchild, grandparent, brother or sister of the director;

(b) the spouse or civil partner of the director or of any person falling within sub-clause (a) above;

(c) a person carrying on business in partnership with the director or with any person falling within sub-clause (a) or (b) above;

(d) an institution which is controlled by the director or any connected person falling within sub-clause (a), (b), or (c) above;

(e) or by two or more persons falling within sub-clause 2.5(d), when taken together

(f) a body corporate in which:

(a) the director or any connected person falling within subclauses (a) to (c) has a substantial interest;

or

(b) two or more persons falling within sub-clause (f)(a) who, when taken together, have a substantial interest.

(g) Sections 350–352 of the Charities Act 2011 apply for the purposes of interpreting the terms used in this article.

'the articles' means the charity's articles of association;

'the charity' means the company intended to be regulated by the articles;

'clear days' in relation to the period of a notice means a period excluding:

- the day when the notice is given or deemed to be given; and
- the day for which it is given or on which it is to take effect;

'the Commission' means the Charity Commission for England and Wales;

'Companies Acts' means the Companies Acts (as defined in section 2 of the Companies Act 2006) insofar as they apply to the charity;

'the directors' means the directors of the charity. The directors are charity trustees as defined by section 177 of the Charities Act 2011;

'document' includes, unless otherwise specified, any document sent or supplied in electronic form;

'electronic form' has the meaning given in section 1168 of the Companies Act 2006;

'the memorandum' means the charity's memorandum of association;

'officers' includes the directors and the secretary (if any);

'the seal' means the common seal of the charity if it has one;

'secretary' means any person appointed to perform the duties of the secretary of the charity;

'the United Kingdom' means Great Britain and Northern Ireland; and words importing one gender shall include all genders, and the singular includes the plural and vice versa.

2.2. Unless the context otherwise requires words or expressions contained in the articles have the same meaning as in the Companies Acts but excluding any statutory modification not in force when this constitution becomes binding on the charity.

2.3. Apart from the exception mentioned in the previous paragraph a reference to an Act of Parliament includes any statutory modification or re-enactment of it for the time being in force.

Article 3 Liability of members

3.1. The liability of the members is limited to a sum not exceeding £10, being the amount that each member undertakes to contribute to the assets of the charity in the event of its being wound up while he, she or it is a member or within one year after he, she or it ceases to be a member, for:

(a) payment of the charity's debts and liabilities incurred before he, she or it ceases to be a member;

(b) payment of the costs, charges and expenses of winding up; and

(c) adjustment of the rights of the contributories among themselves.

Article 4 Objects

4.1. The charity's objects ('objects') are specifically restricted to the following:

4.2. [Nothing in the articles shall authorise an application of the property of the charity for purposes which are not charitable in accordance with section 7 of the Charities and Trustee Investment (Scotland) Act 2005 and/or section 2 of the Charities Act (Northern Ireland) 2008.]

Article 5 Powers

5.1. The charity has power to do anything which is calculated to further its object(s) or is conducive or incidental to doing so. In particular, the charity has power:

(a) to raise funds. In doing so, the charity must not undertake any taxable permanent trading activity and must comply with any relevant statutory regulations;

(b) to buy, take on lease or in exchange, hire or otherwise acquire any property and to maintain and equip it for use;

(c) to sell, lease or otherwise dispose of all or any part of the property belonging to the charity. In exercising this power, the charity must comply as appropriate with sections 117 and 122 of the Charities Act 2011.

(d) to borrow money and to charge the whole or any part of the property belonging to the charity as security for repayment of the money borrowed or as security for a grant or the discharge of an obligation. The charity must comply as appropriate with sections 124–126 of the Charities Act 2011 if it wishes to mortgage land;

(e) to co-operate with other charities, voluntary bodies and statutory authorities and to exchange information and advice with them;

(f) to establish or support any charitable trusts, associations or institutions formed for any of the charitable purposes included in the objects;

(g) to acquire, merge with or to enter into any partnership or joint venture arrangement with any other charity;

(h) to set aside income as a reserve against future expenditure but only in accordance with a written policy about reserves;

(i) to employ and remunerate such staff as are necessary for carrying out the work of the charity. The charity may employ or remunerate a director only to the extent it is permitted to do so by article 7 and provided it complies with the conditions in that article;

(j) to deposit or invest funds, employ a professional fund-manager; and arrange for the investments or other property of the charity to be held in the name of a nominee; in the same manner and subject to the same conditions as the trustees of a trust are permitted to do by the Trustee Act 2000;

(k) to provide indemnity insurance for the directors in accordance with, and subject to the conditions in, section 189 of the Charities Act 2011;

(l) to pay out of the funds of the charity the costs of forming and registering the charity both as a company and as a charity.

Article 6 Application of income and property

6.1. The income and property of the charity shall be applied solely towards the promotion of the objects.

(a) A director is entitled to be reimbursed from the property of the charity or may pay out of such property reasonable expenses properly incurred by him or her when acting on behalf of the charity.

(b) A director may benefit from trustee indemnity insurance cover purchased at the charity's expense in accordance with, and subject to the conditions in, section 189 of the Charities Act 2011.

(c) A director may receive an indemnity from the charity in the circumstances specified in article 57.

(d) A director may not receive any other benefit or payment unless it is authorised by article 7.

Transfer of income and property

6.2. Subject to article 7, none of the income or property of the charity may be paid or transferred directly or indirectly by way of dividend bonus or otherwise by way of profit to any member of the charity. This does not prevent a member who is not also a director receiving:

(a) a benefit from the charity in the capacity of a beneficiary of the charity;

(b) reasonable and proper remuneration for any goods or services supplied to the charity.

Article 7 Benefits and payments to charity directors and connected persons

7.1. In this article a 'financial benefit' means a benefit, direct or indirect, which is either money or has a monetary value.

7.2. No director or connected person may:

(a) buy any goods or services from the charity on terms preferential to those applicable to members of the public;

(b) sell goods, services, or any interest in land to the charity;

(c) be employed by, or receive any remuneration from, the charity;

(d) receive any other financial benefit from the charity; unless the payment is permitted by sub-clause 7.3 of this article, or authorised by the court or the prior written consent of the Charity Commission has been obtained.

7.3. **Scope and powers permitting directors' or connected persons' benefits**

For the benefit of doubt, in these articles 7.3 and 7.4, 'charity' includes any company in which the charity: holds more than 50 per cent of the shares; or controls more than 50 per cent of the voting rights attached to the shares; or has the right to appoint one or more directors to the board of the company. A 'connected person' includes any person within the definition in article 2.1.

(a) A director or connected person may receive a benefit from the charity in the capacity of a beneficiary of the charity provided that a majority of the directors do not benefit in this way.

(b) A director or connected person may enter into a contract for the supply of services, or of goods that are supplied in connection with the provision of services, to the charity where that is permitted in accordance with, and subject to the conditions in, sections 185 and 186 of the Charities Act 2011.

(c) Subject to article 7.4 a director or connected person may provide the charity with goods that are not supplied in connection with services provided to the charity by the director or connected person.

(d) A director or connected person may receive interest on money lent to the charity at a reasonable and proper rate which must be not more than the Bank of England bank rate (also known as the base rate).

(e) A director or connected person may receive rent for premises let by the director or connected person to the charity. The amount of the rent and the other terms of the lease must be reasonable and proper. The director concerned must withdraw from any meeting at which such a proposal or the rent or other terms of the lease are under discussion.

(f) A director or connected person may take part in the normal trading and fundraising activities of the charity on the same terms as members of the public.

7.4. **Payment for supply of goods only – controls**

The charity and its directors may only rely upon the authority provided by sub-clause 7.3(c) of this article if each of the following conditions is satisfied:

(a) The amount or maximum amount of the payment for the goods is set out in an agreement in writing between the charity or its directors (as the case may be) and the director or connected person supplying the goods ('the supplier') under which the supplier is to supply the goods in question to or on behalf of the charity.

(b) The amount or maximum amount of the payment for the goods does not exceed what is reasonable in the circumstances for the supply of the goods in question.

(c) The other directors are satisfied that it is in the best interests of the charity to contract with the supplier rather than with someone who is not a director or connected person. In reaching that decision the directors must balance the advantage of contracting with a director or connected person against the disadvantages of doing so.

(d) The supplier is absent from the part of any meeting at which there is discussion of the proposal to enter into a contract or arrangement with him or her or it with regard to the supply of goods to the charity.

(e) The supplier does not vote on any such matter and is not to be counted when calculating whether a quorum of directors is present at the meeting.

(f) The reason for their decision is recorded by the directors in the minute book.

(g) A majority of the directors then in office are not in receipt of remuneration or payments authorised by article 7.

Article 8 Declaration of directors' interests

8.1. A director must declare the nature and extent of any interest, direct or indirect, which he or she has in a proposed transaction or arrangement with the charity or in any transaction or arrangement entered into by the charity which has not previously been declared. A director must absent himself or herself from any discussions of the charity directors in which it is possible that a conflict will arise between his or her duty to act solely in the interests of the charity and any personal interest (including but not limited to any personal financial interest).

Article 9 Conflicts of interests and conflicts of loyalties

9.1. If a conflict of interests arises for a director because of a duty of loyalty owed to another organisation or person and the conflict is not authorised by virtue of any other provision in the articles, the unconflicted directors may authorise such a conflict of interests where the following conditions apply:

(a) the conflicted director is absent from the part of the meeting at which there is discussion of any arrangement or transaction affecting that other organisation or person;

(b) the conflicted director does not vote on any such matter and is not to be counted when considering whether a quorum of directors is present at the meeting; and

(c) the unconflicted directors consider it is in the interests of the charity to authorise the conflict of interests in the circumstances applying.

9.2. In this article a conflict of interests arising because of a duty of loyalty owed to another organisation or person only refers to such a conflict which does not involve a direct or indirect benefit of any nature to a director or to a connected person.

Becoming and ceasing to be a member

Article 10 Membership

10.1. The subscribers to the memorandum are the first members of the charity. All persons who at the date of incorporation of [The Museum] shall be full members of the unincorporated association known as [The Museum].

10.2. Membership is not transferable.

10.3. The directors must keep a register of names and addresses of the members.

10.4. Membership is open to any person who is willing to abide by the articles of association and any rules instigated by the board of trustees from time to time, and is authorised by the board.

10.5. Subject to any decision by the board of trustees, membership numbers shall be unrestricted.

10.6. The levels of entrance fees and annual subscriptions to be paid by the different categories of members shall be proposed at the annual general meeting and agreed by a majority vote of the board of trustees, for the avoidance of doubt in the event of a deadlock the chair shall having a casting vote, the casting vote shall not be subject to any appeal.

10.7. No person shall become a member of the museum unless:

(a) that person has completed an application for membership in a form approved by the directors; and

(b) the board have approved the application.

10.8. All members shall be subject to these articles and any other rules authorised by the board of trustees.

10.9. Any member whose [annual fee – subscription] is [2] months in arrears shall be deemed to have resigned from the museum.

10.10. Any person ceasing to be a member forfeits all rights in relation to and claims upon the museum, its property and its funds and has no right to the return of any part of his subscription.

Article 11 Refusal of application

11.1. The directors may only refuse an application for membership if, acting reasonably and properly, they consider it to be in the best interests of the museum to refuse the application.

11.2. The directors must inform the applicant in writing of the reasons for the refusal within 21 days of the decision.

11.3. The directors must consider any written representations the applicant may make about the decision. The directors' decision following any written representations must be notified to the applicant in writing but shall be final.

Article 12 Classes of membership

12.1. The directors may establish classes of membership with different rights and obligations and shall record the rights and obligations in the register of members.

12.2. The directors may not directly or indirectly alter the rights or obligations attached to a class of membership.

12.3. The rights attached to a class of membership may only be varied if:

(a) three-quarters of the members of that class consent in writing to the variation; or

(b) a special resolution is passed at a separate general meeting of the members of that class agreeing to the variation.

12.4. The provisions in the articles about general meetings shall apply to any meeting relating to the variation of the rights of any class of members.

Article 13 Subscriptions

13.1. Subscriptions shall be payable in advance.

13.2. They shall become due annually on the anniversary of the joining date and paid not later than [three] months from this date.

13.3. Subscriptions [by agreement with trustees] shall be paid by instalments, the full subscription by the following anniversary date.

13.4. If the subscription is not paid within one month of the joining anniversary date, or payments fall into arrears, membership shall automatically cease.

13.5. Members cannot seek election, propose, or second nominations to the Board of Management, unless they have completed one year's full membership of the museum.

Article 14 Termination of membership

14.1. A member may withdraw from membership of the museum by giving seven days' notice to the company in writing.

(a) Membership is not transferable.

(b) A person's membership terminates when that person dies or ceases to exist.

14.2. Membership is terminated if:

(a) the member dies or, if it is an organisation, ceases to exist;

(b) the member resigns by written notice to the charity unless, after the resignation, there would be less than two members;

(c) any sum due from the member to the charity is not paid in full within six months of it falling due;

(d) the member is removed by a resolution of the directors.

14.3. The board shall at their discretion request a member withdraw from membership 'leaver' immediately in writing 'leaving notice'.

(a) The leaver shall within 14 days of the receiving of the leaving notice inform the board in writing he requests a board or any committee to consider his position 'leaver committee'.

(b) A resolution to remove a member from membership may only be passed if the member has been given at least 21 days' notice in writing of the meeting of the directors at which the resolution will be proposed and the reasons why it is to be proposed.

14.4. The leaver may:

(a) attend the museum premises or any other venue the board sees fit on the date and time of the leaver committee;

(b) not use any museum facilities (or than disabled facilities) on the day of his or her attendance at the leaver committee without the express permission of a member of the leaver committee;

(c) present his case in person or by written submission;

(d) at the discretion of the board the leaver can be allowed to attend the meeting with a third party for the purpose of support only;

(e) no third party present at the meeting may give verbal or written submission.

14.5. If there is any non-attendance at the leavers meeting without good reason the leaver shall be deemed to have resigned from the museum.

14.6. On the closing of the written or verbal submission the leaver committee shall vote on the matter:

(a) if the vote is carried the leaver shall be deemed to have resigned from the museum.

14.7. The leaver may within 14 days of the date of the leavers committee request in writing that an appeal be instigated and a full vote be put to a general meeting of the board.

(a) For the avoidance of doubt the leaver shall have no rights to attend the general meeting or present any further written submissions.

(b) The chairman or vice-chairman may prior to the general meeting request any further information he deems fit from the leaver or the leaving committee.

Article 15 Trustees

15.1. Unless and until resolved to the contrary by the members, the theatre shall have a board of trustees.

15.2. Number of trustees:

(a) There shall be no fewer than six; and not more than 11 trustees.

Article 16 The composition of the board of management

16.1. The chairman and the secretary; and:

(a) The arts manager.

(b) The members manager.

(c) The treasurer.

(d) The marketing manager.

(e) Head of production.

Article 17 Appointment of trustees

17.1. Those persons notified to the Registrar of Companies as the first directors of the Union shall be the first trustees until and including the effective date. Thereafter, the trustees shall be made up of the following persons:

17.2. Six member trustees (charity officers), elected in accordance with article 18;

17.3. Four external trustees, elected in accordance with article 19; and

17.4. One nominated trustee appointed in accordance with article 20.

17.5. Together, the 'trustee board'.

Article 18 Member trustees and officers

18.1. The member trustees and charity officers shall be elected by [secret] [open] ballot by the 'membership' at an election to be held in accordance with the museum's rules.

18.2. Subject to the museum's rules, charity officers shall be elected in accordance with article 18.1 to such posts, and in such number, as may be required by the museum from time to time.

18.3. A maximum of six charity officers, once elected in accordance with article 18.1, shall also hold office as member trustees.

18.4. Subject to the museum's rules, the member officers shall remain in office for a term of one year from the date of election [year end][start of year] and serve no more than two terms. For the avoidance of doubt, these terms may be either consecutive or non-consecutive.

18.5. A member officer shall become a member trustee of the museum on commencement of his or her term of office as a member officer.

Article 19 External trustee

19.1. Subject to article 21, a maximum of four external trustees shall be appointed by:

(a) A majority vote of the trustee board.

(b) [Charity Rules].

19.2. Subject to article 21, external trustees shall remain in office for a term of two years, from the date of appointment.

19.3. An external trustee may serve a maximum of three terms. For the avoidance of doubt, these terms may be either consecutive or non-consecutive.

Article 20 Nominated trustees

20.1. The trustee board may appoint a suitable and competent person (who is not a member) to fill the vacancy of nominated trustee.

20.2. The trustee board shall consider, subject to any charity rules, at their discretion, any skill gaps required to enhance the trustee board.

(a) Any member of the trustee board, from time to time, by notifying the chair in writing may nominate an individual for the position of nominated trustee, based on the skill gaps identified.

(b) The trustee board shall nominate a minimum of two candidates for the position of nominated trustee taking into account the experience and skills required.

20.3. The trustee board shall select one of the candidates put forward by a majority vote to serve as nominated trustee and that individual shall be appointed by the trustees as the nominated trustee.

20.4. If the numbers of votes for and against are equal, the chair or other trustee chairing the meeting has a casting vote.

20.5. Subject to article 21, the nominated trustee shall remain in office for a term of up to three years calculated from the date of appointment. For the avoidance of doubt, these terms may be either consecutive or non-consecutive, and the re-appointment of a serving nominated trustee shall be by the same process in place for the appointment of a nominated trustee.

20.6. For the avoidance of doubt, the 'nominated trustee' is not a trustee or member and may not vote at trustees' meetings.

20.7. A nominated trustee may appoint a representative:

(a) by giving seven clear days' notice, in writing to the chair 'notice approval', before the date of any trustees' meeting at which the nominated trustee's representative 'nominated trustee representative' is to attend.

(b) On the approval of any 'notice approval' provided the 'nominated trustee representative' may attend any subsequent trustees' board meetings, without prior notification

(c) The 'nominated trustee representative' is not a trustee and may not vote at trustees' meetings or exercise any other rights of the nominated trustee, save that the nominated trustee's representative may speak at trustees' meetings and shall receive notice of all trustees' meetings during his or her appointment.

Article 21 Disqualification, removal or resignation of trustees

21.1. The office of a trustee shall cease immediately if the trustee:

(a) ceases to be a director by virtue of any provision of the Companies Act 2006 or is prohibited from being a director by law;

(b) is disqualified under the Charities Act 1993 or otherwise prohibited by law from acting as a charity trustee;

(c) becomes bankrupt or makes any arrangement or composition with his or her creditors generally;

(d) becomes an employee of the charity;

(e) notification is received by the trustee board from the director that the director is resigning from office, and such resignation has taken effect in accordance with its terms;

(f) receives a written opinion from a registered medical practitioner who is treating that person, and provides to the trustee an opinion that that person has become physically or mentally incapable of acting as a director and may remain so for more than three months;

(g) fails to attend three consecutive meetings of the trustees and in the opinion of the trustees there are no mitigating circumstances for that failure and the trustees therefore resolve that he or she be removed for this reason; or

(h) in accordance with articles 22 or 23 below.

Article 22 Removal of trustees by the board

22.1. The office of a trustee shall be vacated if a majority resolution of no confidence is passed by the trustee board.

(a) The trustee concerned must be given at least 14 clear days' notice in writing that such a resolution is to be proposed and specifying the circumstances alleged to justify removal from office.

(b) The trustee concerned should be afforded a reasonable opportunity of being heard by or making representations in writing to the chair.

(c) For the avoidance of doubt, as regards any trustee who has a conflict of interest, that trustee is not to be counted as participating in the decision-making process for quorum or voting purposes.

(d) If an external trustee or a nominated trustee resigns, is disqualified or is removed from office, an external trustee or a nominated trustee shall be appointed to the vacancy in accordance with articles 21 and 19 respectively.

(e) If a trustee is removed under articles 21 or 22, and that removal would cause the number of trustees to fall below the minimum number fixed by these articles, the purported removal of that trustee shall take effect only upon the appointment or election (as appropriate) of a replacement trust.

Article 23 General meetings

23.1. The charity must hold its first annual general meeting within 18 months after the date of its incorporation. An annual general meeting must be held in each subsequent year and not more than 15 months may elapse between successive annual general meetings.

Article 24 Calling a directors meeting

24.1. The directors may call a general meeting at any time.

Article 25 Notice of general meetings

25.1. The minimum periods of notice required to hold a general meeting of the charity are:

(a) 21 clear days for an annual general meeting or a general meeting called for the passing of a special resolution;

(b) 14 clear days for all other general meetings.

25.2. A general meeting may be called by shorter notice if it is so agreed by a majority in the number of members having a right to attend and vote at the meeting, being a majority who together hold not less than 90 per cent of the total voting rights.

25.3. The notice must specify the date time and place of the meeting and the general nature of the business to be transacted. If the meeting is to be an annual general meeting, the notice must say so. The notice must also contain a statement setting out the right of members to appoint a proxy under section 324 of the Companies Act 2006 and article 30.

25.4. The notice must be given to all the members and to the directors and auditors.

Article 26 Omissions

26.1. The proceedings at a meeting shall not be invalidated because a person who was entitled to receive notice of the meeting did not receive it because of an accidental omission by the charity.

Article 27 Proceedings at general meetings

27.1. No business shall be transacted at any general meeting unless a quorum is present.

27.2. A quorum is:

(a) four members present in person or by proxy and entitled to vote upon the business to be conducted at the meeting; or

(b) one tenth of the total membership at the time, whichever is the greater.

27.3. The authorised representative of a member organisation shall be counted in the quorum.

Article 28 Adjournment

28.1. If a quorum is not present within half an hour from the time appointed for the meeting; or if during a meeting a quorum ceases to be present; the meeting shall be adjourned to such time and place as the directors shall determine.

28.2. The directors must reconvene the meeting and must give at least seven clear days' notice of the reconvened meeting stating the date, time and place of the meeting.

28.3. If no quorum is present at the reconvened meeting within 15 minutes of the time specified for the start of the meeting the members present in person or by proxy at that time shall constitute the quorum for that meeting.

Article 29 Chairing general meetings

29.1. General meetings shall be chaired by the person who has been appointed to chair meetings of the directors.

29.2. If there is no such person or he or she is not present within 15 minutes of the time appointed for the meeting a director nominated by the directors shall chair the meeting.

29.3. If there is only one director present and willing to act, he or she shall chair the meeting.

29.4. If no director is present and willing to chair the meeting within 15 minutes after the time appointed for holding it, the members present in person or by proxy and entitled to vote must choose one of their number to chair the meeting.

Article 30 Reconvening the meeting

30.1. The members present in person or by proxy at a meeting may resolve by ordinary resolution that the meeting shall be adjourned.

30.2. The person who is chairing the meeting must decide the date, time and place at which the meeting is to be reconvened unless those details are specified in the resolution.

30.3. No business shall be conducted at a reconvened meeting unless it could properly have been conducted at the meeting had the adjournment not taken place.

30.4. If a meeting is adjourned by a resolution of the members for more than seven days, at least seven clear days' notice shall be given of the reconvened meeting stating the date, time and place of the meeting.

Article 31 Voting

31.1. Any vote at a meeting shall be decided by a show of hands unless before, or on the declaration of the result of, the show of hands a poll is demanded:

(a) by the person chairing the meeting; or

(b) by at least two members present in person or by proxy and having the right to vote at the meeting; or

(c) by a member or members present in person or by proxy representing not less than one-tenth of the total voting rights of all the members having the right to vote at the meeting.

31.2. The declaration by the person who is chairing the meeting of the result of a vote shall be conclusive unless a poll is demanded.

31.3. The result of the vote must be recorded in the minutes of the charity but the number or proportion of votes cast need not be recorded.

Polls

31.4. A demand for a poll may be withdrawn, before the poll is taken, but only with the consent of the person who is chairing the meeting.

(a) If the demand for a poll is withdrawn the demand shall not invalidate the result of a show of hands declared before the demand was made.

(b) A poll must be taken as the person who is chairing the meeting directs, who may appoint scrutineers (who need not be members) and who may fix a time and place for declaring the results of the poll.

31.5. The result of the poll shall be deemed to be the resolution of the meeting at which the poll is demanded.

(a) A poll demanded on the election of a person to chair a meeting or on a question of adjournment must be taken immediately.

(b) A poll demanded on any other question must be taken either immediately or at such time and place as the person who is chairing the meeting directs.

(c) The poll must be taken within 30 days after it has been demanded.

(d) If the poll is not taken immediately at least seven clear days' notice shall be given specifying the time and place at which the poll is to be taken.

(e) If a poll is demanded the meeting may continue to deal with any other business that may be conducted at the meeting.

Article 32 Content of proxy notices

32.1. Proxies may only validly be appointed by a notice in writing (a 'proxy notice') which:

(a) states the name and address of the member appointing the proxy;

(b) identifies the person appointed to be that member's proxy and the general meeting in relation to which that person is appointed;

(c) is signed by or on behalf of the member appointing the proxy, or is authenticated in such manner as the directors may determine; and

(d) is delivered to the charity in accordance with the articles and any instructions contained in the notice of the general meeting to which they relate.

32.2. The charity may require proxy notices to be delivered in a particular form, and may specify different forms for different purposes.

32.3. Proxy notices may specify how the proxy appointed under them is to vote (or that the proxy is to abstain from voting) on one or more resolutions.

32.4. Unless a proxy notice indicates otherwise, it must be treated as:

(a) allowing the person appointed under it as a proxy discretion as to how to vote on any ancillary or procedural resolutions put to the meeting; and

(b) appointing that person as a proxy in relation to any adjournment of the general meeting to which it relates as well as the meeting itself.

Delivery of proxy notices

32.5. A person who is entitled to attend, speak or vote (either on a show of hands or on a poll) at a general meeting remains so entitled in respect of that meeting or any adjournment of it, even though a valid proxy notice has been delivered to the charity by or on behalf of that person.

32.6. An appointment under a proxy notice may be revoked by delivering to the charity a notice in writing given by or on behalf of the person by whom or on whose behalf the proxy notice was given.

32.7. A notice revoking a proxy appointment only takes effect if it is delivered before the start of the meeting or adjourned meeting to which it relates.

32.8. If a proxy notice is not executed by the person appointing the proxy, it must be accompanied by written evidence of the authority of the person who executed it to execute it on the appointor's behalf.

Article 33 Written resolutions

33.1. A resolution in writing agreed by a simple majority (or in the case of a special resolution by a majority of not less than 75 per cent) of the members who would have been entitled to vote upon it had it been proposed at a general meeting shall be effective provided that:

(a) a copy of the proposed resolution has been sent to every eligible member;

(b) a simple majority (or in the case of a special resolution a majority of not less than 75 per cent) of members has signified its agreement to the resolution; and

(c) it is contained in an authenticated document which has been received at the registered office within the period of 28 days beginning with the circulation date.

33.2. A resolution in writing may comprise several copies to which one or more members have signified their agreement.

33.3. In the case of a member that is an organisation, its authorised representative may signify its agreement.

Article 34 Votes of members

34.1. Subject to article 27, every member, whether an individual or an organisation, shall have one vote.

Article 35 Objections

35.1. Any objection to the qualification of any voter must be raised at the meeting at which the vote is tendered and the decision of the person who is chairing the meeting shall be final.

Article 36 Nominations of representatives

36.1. Any organisation that is a member of the charity may nominate any person to act as its representative at any meeting of the charity.

(a) The organisation must give written notice to the charity of the name of its representative. The representative shall not be entitled to represent the organisation at any meeting unless the notice has been received by the charity. The representative may continue to represent the organisation until written notice to the contrary is received by the charity.

(b) Any notice given to the charity will be conclusive evidence that the representative is entitled to represent the organisation or that his or her authority has been revoked. The charity shall not be required to consider whether the representative has been properly appointed by the organisation.

Article 37 Directors

37.1. Any appointment as director is subject to the Companies Act 2006. A director must be a natural person aged 16 years or older.

(a) No one may be appointed a director if he or she would be disqualified from acting under the provisions of article 41.

Article 38 Number of directors

38.1. The minimum number of directors shall be two but (unless otherwise determined by ordinary resolution) shall not be subject to any maximum.

Article 39 First directors appointed

39.1. The first directors shall be those persons notified to Companies House as the first directors of the charity.

Article 40 Restrictions on alternative directors

40.1. A director may not appoint an alternate director or anyone to act on his or her behalf at meetings of the directors.

Article 41 Powers of directors

41.1. The directors shall manage the business of the charity and may exercise all the powers of the charity unless they are subject to any restrictions imposed by the Companies Acts, the articles or any special resolution.

41.2. No alteration of the articles or any special resolution shall have retrospective effect to invalidate any prior act of the directors.

41.3. Any meeting of directors at which a quorum is present at the time the relevant decision is made may exercise all the powers exercisable by the directors.

Article 42 Retirement of directors

42.1. At the first annual general meeting all the directors must retire from office unless by the close of the meeting the members have failed to elect sufficient directors to hold a quorate meeting of the directors. At each subsequent annual general meeting one-third of the directors or, if their number is not three or a multiple of three, the number nearest to one-third, must retire from office. If there is only one director he or she must retire.

Article 43 Retirement by rotation

43.1. The directors to retire by rotation shall be those who have been longest in office since their last appointment. If any directors became or were appointed directors on the same day those to retire shall (unless they otherwise agree among themselves) be determined by lot.

43.2. If a director is required to retire at an annual general meeting by a provision of the articles the retirement shall take effect upon the conclusion of the meeting.

Article 44 Appointment of directors

44.1. The charity may by ordinary resolution:

(a) appoint a person who is willing to act to be a director; and

(b) determine the rotation in which any additional directors are to retire.

Article 45 Reappointment

45.1. No person other than a director retiring by rotation may be appointed a director at any general meeting unless he or she is recommended for re-election by the directors; or not less than 14 nor more than 35 clear days before the date of the meeting, the charity is given a notice that:

(a) is signed by a member entitled to vote at the meeting;

(b) states the member's intention to propose the appointment of a person as a director;

(c) contains the details that, if the person were to be appointed, the charity would have to file at Companies House; and

(d) is signed by the person who is to be proposed to show his or her willingness to be appointed.

Article 46 Notices

46.1. All members who are entitled to receive notice of a general meeting must be given not less than seven nor more than 28 clear days' notice of any resolution to be put to the meeting to appoint a director other than a director who is to retire by rotation.

Article 47 Appointment by directors

47.1. The directors may appoint a person who is willing to act to be a director.

47.2. A director appointed by a resolution of the other directors must retire at the next annual general meeting and must not be taken into account in determining the directors who are to retire by rotation.

Article 48 Maximum number of directors

48.1. The appointment of a director, whether by the charity in general meeting or by the other directors, must not cause the number of directors to exceed any number fixed as the maximum number of directors.

Article 49 Disqualification and removal of directors

49.1. A director shall cease to hold office if he or she:

(a) ceases to be a director by virtue of any provision in the Companies Acts or is prohibited by law from being a director;

(b) is disqualified from acting as a trustee by virtue of sections 178 and 179 of the Charities Act 2011 (or any statutory re-enactment or modification of those provisions);

(c) ceases to be a member of the charity;

(d) in the written opinion, given to the company, of a registered medical practitioner treating that person, has become physically or mentally incapable of acting as a director and may remain so for more than three months;

(e) resigns as a director by notice to the charity (but only if at least two directors will remain in office when the notice of resignation is to take effect); or

(f) is absent without the permission of the directors from all their meetings held within a period of six consecutive months and the directors resolve that his or her office be vacated.

Article 50 Remuneration of directors

50.1. The directors must not be paid any remuneration unless it is authorised by article 7.

Article 51 Proceedings of directors

51.1. The directors may regulate their proceedings as they think fit, subject to the provisions of the articles.

51.2. Any director may call a meeting of the directors.

51.3. The secretary (if any) must call a meeting of the directors if requested to do so by a director.

51.4. Questions arising at a meeting shall be decided by a majority of votes.

Chair casting vote

51.5. In the case of an equality of votes, the person who is chairing the meeting shall have a second or casting vote.

Communication

51.6. A meeting may be held by suitable electronic means agreed by the directors in which each participant may communicate with all the other participants.

Article 52 Quorum for meetings

52.1. No decision may be made by a meeting of the directors unless a quorum is present at the time the decision is purported to be made.

(a) 'Present' includes being present by suitable electronic means agreed by the directors in which a participant or participants may communicate with all the other participants.

52.2. The quorum shall be two or the number nearest to one-third of the total number of directors, whichever is the greater, or such larger number as may be decided from time to time by the directors.

52.3. A director shall not be counted in the quorum present when any decision is made about a matter upon which that director is not entitled to vote.

Article 53 Election of chair

53.1. If the number of directors is less than the number fixed as the quorum, the continuing directors or director may act only for the purpose of filling vacancies or of calling a general meeting.

Article 54 Appointment

54.1. The directors shall appoint a director to chair their meetings and may at any time revoke such appointment.

54.2. If no-one has been appointed to chair meetings of the directors or if the person appointed is unwilling to preside or is not present within ten minutes after the time appointed for the meeting, the directors present may appoint one of their number to chair that meeting.

54.3. The person appointed to chair meetings of the directors shall have no functions or powers except those conferred by the articles or delegated to him or her by the directors.

Article 55 Resolutions in writing

55.1. A resolution in writing or in electronic form agreed by all of the directors entitled to receive notice of a meeting of the directors and to vote upon the resolution shall be as valid and effectual as if it had been passed at a meeting of the directors duly convened and held.

55.2. The resolution in writing may comprise several documents containing the text of the resolution in like form to each of which one or more directors has signified their agreement.

Article 56 Delegation

56.1. The directors may delegate any of their powers or functions to a committee of two or more directors but the terms of any delegation must be recorded in the minute book.

56.2. The directors may impose conditions when delegating, including the conditions that:

(a) the relevant powers are to be exercised exclusively by the committee to whom they delegate;

(b) no expenditure may be incurred on behalf of the charity except in accordance with a budget previously agreed with the directors.

56.3. The directors may revoke or alter a delegation.

56.4. All acts and proceedings of any committees must be fully and promptly reported to the directors.

Article 57 Validity of directors' decisions

57.1. Subject to article 47(2), all acts done by a meeting of directors, or of a committee of directors, shall be valid notwithstanding the participation in any vote of a director:

(a) who was disqualified from holding office;

(b) who had previously retired or who had been obliged by the constitution to vacate office;

(c) who was not entitled to vote on the matter, whether by reason of a conflict of interests or otherwise;

if without:

(d) the vote of that director; and

(e) that director being counted in the quorum; the decision has been made by a majority of the directors at a quorate meeting.

57.2. Article 47(1) does not permit a director or a connected person to keep any benefit that may be conferred upon him or her by a resolution of the directors or of a committee of directors if, but for article 47(1), the resolution would have been void, or if the director has not complied with article 8.

Article 58 Seal

58.1. If the charity has a seal it must only be used by the authority of the directors or of a committee of directors authorised by the directors. The directors may determine who shall sign any instrument to which the seal is affixed and unless otherwise so determined it shall be signed by a director and by the secretary (if any) or by a second director.

Article 59 Minutes

59.1. The directors must keep minutes of all appointments of officers made by the directors, proceedings at meetings of the charity, meetings of the directors and committees of directors including:

(a) the names of the directors present at the meeting;

(b) the decisions made at the meetings; and

(c) where appropriate the reasons for the decisions.

Article 60 Accounts

60.1. The directors must prepare for each financial year accounts as required by the Companies Acts. The accounts must be prepared to show a true and fair view and follow accounting standards issued or adopted by the Accounting Standards Board or its successors and adhere to the recommendations of applicable Statements of Recommended Practice.

60.2. The directors must keep accounting records as required by the Companies Act.

Article 61 Annual Report and Return and Register of Charities

61.1. The directors must comply with the requirements of the Charities Act 2011 with regard to the:

(a) transmission of a copy of the statements of account to the Commission;

(b) preparation of an Annual Report and the transmission of a copy of it to the Commission;

(c) preparation of an Annual Return and its transmission to the Commission.

61.2. The directors must notify the Commission promptly of any changes to the charity's entry on the Central Register of Charities.

Article 62 Means of communication to be used

62.1. Subject to the articles, anything sent or supplied by or to the charity under the articles may be sent or supplied in any way in which the Companies Act 2006 provides for documents or information which are authorised or required by any provision of that Act to be sent or supplied by or to the charity.

62.2. Subject to the articles, any notice or document to be sent or supplied to a director in connection with the taking of decisions by directors may also be sent or supplied by the means by which that director has asked to be sent or supplied with such notices or documents for the time being.

Article 63 Notices afforded

63.1. Any notice to be given to or by any person pursuant to the articles:

(a) must be in writing; or

(b) must be given in electronic form.

Article 64 Notices methods of communication

64.1. The charity may give any notice to a member either:

(a) personally; or

(b) by sending it by post in a prepaid envelope addressed to the member at his or her address; or

(c) by leaving it at the address of the member; or

(d) by giving it in electronic form to the member's address; or

(e) by placing the notice on a website and providing the person with a notification in writing or in electronic form of the presence of the notice on the website. The notification must state that it concerns a notice of a company meeting and must specify the place, date and time of the meeting.

64.2. A member who does not register an address with the charity or who registers only a postal address that is not within the United Kingdom shall not be entitled to receive any notice from the charity.

Article 65 Notices in person

65.1. A member present in person at any meeting of the charity shall be deemed to have received notice of the meeting and of the purposes for which it was called.

Article 66 Notices proof of delivery

66.1. Proof that an envelope containing a notice was properly addressed, prepaid and posted shall be conclusive evidence that the notice was given.

66.2. Proof that an electronic form of notice was given shall be conclusive where the company can demonstrate that it was properly addressed and sent, in accordance with section 1147 of the Companies Act 2006.

66.3. In accordance with section 1147 of the Companies Act 2006 notice shall be deemed to be given:

(a) 48 hours after the envelope containing it was posted; or

(b) in the case of an electronic form of communication, 48 hours after it was sent.

Article 67 Indemnity

67.1. The charity shall indemnify a relevant director against any liability incurred in that capacity, to the extent permitted by sections 232 to 234 of the Companies Act 2006.

67.2. In this article a 'relevant director' means any director or former director of the charity.

67.3. The charity may indemnify an auditor against any liability incurred by him or her or it:

(a) in defending proceedings (whether civil or criminal) in which judgment is given in his or her or its favour or he or she or it is acquitted; or

(b) in connection with an application under section 1157 of the Companies Act 2006 (power of Court to grant relief in case of honest and reasonable conduct) in which relief is granted to him or her or it by the Court.

Article 68 Rules

68.1. The directors may from time to time make such reasonable and proper rules or bye laws as they may deem necessary or expedient for the proper conduct and management of the charity.

68.2. The bye laws may regulate the following matters but are not restricted to them:

(a) the admission of members of the charity (including the admission of organisations to membership) and the rights and privileges of such members, and the entrance fees, subscriptions and other fees or payments to be made by members;

(b) the conduct of members of the charity in relation to one another, and to the charity's employees and volunteers;

(c) the setting aside of the whole or any part or parts of the charity's premises at any particular time or times or for any particular purpose or purposes;

(d) the procedure at general meetings and meetings of the directors in so far as such procedure is not regulated by the Companies Acts or by the articles;

(e) generally, all such matters as are commonly the subject matter of company rules.

68.3. The charity in general meeting has the power to alter, add to or repeal the rules or bye laws.

68.4. The directors must adopt such means as they think sufficient to bring the rules and bye laws to the notice of members of the charity.

68.5. The rules or bye laws shall be binding on all members of the charity. No rule or bye law shall be inconsistent with, or shall affect or repeal anything contained in, the articles.

Article 69 Disputes

69.1. If a dispute arises between members of the charity about the validity or propriety of anything done by the members of the charity under these articles, and the dispute cannot be resolved by agreement, the parties to the dispute must first try in good faith to settle the dispute by mediation before resorting to litigation.

Article 70 Dissolution

70.1. The members of the charity may at any time before, and in expectation of, its dissolution resolve that any net assets of the charity after all its debts and liabilities have been paid, or provision has been made for them, shall on or before the dissolution of the charity be applied or transferred in any of the following ways:

(a) directly for the objects; or

(b) by transfer to any charity or charities for purposes similar to the objects; or

(c) to any charity or charities for use for particular purposes that fall within the objects.

70.2. Subject to any such resolution of the members of the charity, the directors of the charity may at any time before and in expectation of its dissolution resolve that any net assets of the charity after all its debts and liabilities have been paid, or provision made for them, shall on or before dissolution of the charity be applied or transferred:

(a) directly for the objects; or

(b) by transfer to any charity or charities for purposes similar to the objects; or

(c) to any charity or charities for use for particular purposes that fall within the objects.

70.3. In no circumstances shall the net assets of the charity be paid to or distributed among the members of the charity (except to a member that is itself a charity) and if no resolution in accordance with article 70(1) is passed by the members or the directors the net assets of the charity shall be applied for charitable purposes as directed by the Court or the Commission.

Appendix A

Commencement 1st July 1985

COMPANIES (TABLES A TO F) REGULATIONS 1985, SI 1985/805

TABLE A

Regulations for management of a company limited by shares

INTERPRETATION

1. In these regulations—

"the Act" means the Companies Act 1985 including any statutory modification or re-enactment thereof for the time being in force.

"the articles" means the articles of the company.

"clear days" in relation to the period of a notice means that period excluding the day when the notice is given or deemed to be given and the day for which it is given or on which it is to take effect.

"executed" includes any mode of execution.

"office" means the registered office of the company.

"the holder" in relation to shares means the member whose name is entered in the register of members as the holder of the shares.

"the seal" means the common seal of the company.

"secretary" means the secretary of the company or any other person appointed to perform the duties of the secretary of the company, including a joint, assistant or deputy secretary.

"the United Kingdom" means Great Britain and Northern Ireland.

Unless the context otherwise requires, words or expressions contained in these regulations bear the same meaning as in the Act but excluding any statutory modification thereof not in force when these regulations become binding on the company.

SHARE CAPITAL

2. Subject to the provisions of the Act and without prejudice to any rights attached to any existing shares, any share may be issued with such rights or restrictions as the company may by ordinary resolution determine.

3. Subject to the provisions of the Act, shares may be issued which are to be redeemed or are to be liable to be redeemed at the option of the company or the holder on such terms and in such manner as may be provided by the articles.

4. The company may exercise the powers of paying commissions conferred by the Act. Subject to the provision of the Act, any such commission may be satisfied by the payment of cash or by the allotment of fully or partly paid shares or partly in one way and partly in the other.

5. Except as required by law, no person shall be recognised by the company as holding any share upon any trust and (except as otherwise provided by the articles or by law) the company shall not be bound by or recognise any interest in any share except an absolute right to the entirety thereof in the holder.

SHARE CERTIFICATES

6. Every member, upon becoming the holder of any shares, shall be entitled without payment to one certificate for all the shares of each class held by him (and, upon transferring a part of his holding of shares of any class, to a certificate for the balance of such holding) or several certificates each for one or more of his shares upon payment for every certificate after the first of such reasonable sum as the directors may determine. Every certificate shall be sealed with the seal and shall specify the number, class and distinguishing numbers (if any) of the shares to which it relates and the amount or respective amounts paid up thereon. The company shall not be bound to issue more than one certificate for shares held jointly by several persons and delivery of a certificate to one joint holder shall be a sufficient delivery to all of them.

7. If a share certificate is defaced, worn-out, lost or destroyed, it may be renewed on such terms (if any) as to evidence and indemnity and payment of the expenses reasonably incurred by the company in investigating evidence as the directors may determine but otherwise free of charge, and (in the case of defacement or wearing-out) on delivery up of the old certificate.

LIEN

8. The company shall have a first and paramount lien on every share (not being a fully paid share) for all moneys (whether presently payable or not) payable at a fixed time or called in respect of that share. The directors may at any time declare any share to be wholly or in part exempt from the provisions of this regulation. The company's lien on a share shall extend to any amount payable in respect of it.

9. The company may sell in such manner as the directors determine any shares on which the company has a lien if a sum in respect of which the lien exists is presently payable and is not paid within fourteen clear days after notice has been given to the holder of the share or to the person entitled to it in consequence of the death or bankruptcy of the holder, demanding payment and stating that if the notice is not complied with the shares may be sold.

10. To give effect to a sale the directors may authorise some person to execute an instrument of transfer of the shares sold to, or in accordance with the directions of, the purchaser. The title of the transferee to the shares shall not be affected by any irregularity in or invalidity of the proceedings in reference to the sale.

11. The net proceeds of the sale, after payment of the costs, shall be applied in payment of so much of the sum for which the lien exists as is presently payable, and any residue shall (upon surrender to the company for cancellation of the certificate for the shares sold and subject to a like lien for any moneys not presently payable as existed upon the shares before the sale) be paid to the person entitled to the shares at the date of the sale.

CALLS ON SHARES AND FORFEITURE

12. Subject to the terms of allotment, the directors may make calls upon the members in respect of any moneys unpaid on their shares (whether in respect of nominal value or premium) and each member shall (subject to receiving at least fourteen clear days' notice specifying when and where payment is to be made) pay to the company as required by the notice the amount called on his shares. A call may be required to be paid by instalments. A call may, before receipt by the company of any sum due thereunder, be revoked in whole or part and payment of a call may be postponed in whole or part. A person upon whom a call is made shall remain liable for calls made upon him notwithstanding the subsequent transfer of the shares in respect whereof the call was made.

13. A call shall be deemed to have been made at the time when the resolution of the directors authorising the call was passed.

14. The joint holders of a share shall be jointly and severally liable to pay all calls in respect thereof.

15. If a call remains unpaid after it has become due and payable the person from whom it is due and payable shall pay interest on the amount unpaid from the day it became due and payable until it is paid at the rate fixed by the terms of allotment of the share or in the notice of the call or, if no rate is fixed, at the appropriate rate (as defined by the Act) but the directors may waive payment of the interest wholly or in part.

16. An amount payable in respect of a share on allotment or at any fixed date, whether in respect of nominal value or premium or as an instalment of a call, shall be deemed to be a call and if it is not paid the provisions of the articles shall apply as if that amount had become due and payable by virtue of a call.

17. Subject to the terms of allotment, the directors may make arrangements on the issue of shares for a difference between the holders in the amounts and times of payment of calls on their shares.

18. If a call remains unpaid after it has become due and payable the directors may give to the person from whom it is due not less than fourteen clear days' notice requiring payment of the amount unpaid together with any interest which may have accrued. The notice shall name the place where payment is to be made and shall state that if the notice is not complied with the shares in respect of which the call was made will be liable to be forfeited.

19. If the notice is not complied with any share in respect of which it was given may, before the payment required by the notice has been made, be forfeited by a resolution of the directors and the forfeiture shall include all dividends or other moneys payable in respect of the forfeited shares and not paid before the forfeiture.

20. Subject to the provisions of the Act, a forfeited share may be sold, re-alloted or otherwise disposed of on such terms and in such manner as the directors determine either to the person who was before the forfeiture the holder or to any other person and at any time before sale, re-allotment or other disposition, the forfeiture may be cancelled on such terms as the directors think fit. Where for the purposes of its disposal a forfeited share is to be transferred to any person the directors may authorise some person to execute an instrument of transfer of the share to that person.

21. A person any of whose shares have been forfeited shall cease to be a member in respect of them and shall surrender to the company for cancellation the certificate for the shares forfeited but shall remain liable to the company for all moneys which at the date of forfeiture were presently payable by him to the company in respect of those shares with interest at the rate at which interest was payable on those moneys before the forfeiture or, if no interest was so payable, at the appropriate rate (as defined in the Act) from the date of forfeiture until payment but the directors may waive payment wholly or in part or enforce payment without any allowance for the value of the shares at the time of forfeiture or for any consideration received on their disposal.

22. A statutory declaration by a director or the secretary that a share has been forfeited on a specified date shall be conclusive evidence of the facts stated in it as against all persons claiming to be entitled to the share and the declaration shall (subject to the execution of an instrument of transfer if necessary) constitute a good title to the share and the person to whom the share is disposed of shall not be bound to see to the application of the consideration, if any, nor shall his title to the share be affected by any irregularity in or invalidity of the proceedings in reference to the forfeiture or disposal of the share.

TRANSFER OF SHARES

23. The instrument of transfer of a share may be in any usual form or in any other form which the directors may approve and shall be executed by or on behalf of the transferor and, unless the share is fully paid, by or on behalf of the transferee.

24. The directors may refuse to register the transfer of a share which is not fully paid to a person of whom they do not approve and they may refuse to register the transfer of a share on which the company has a lien. They may also refuse to register a transfer unless—

(a) it is lodged at the office or at such other place as the directors may appoint and is accompanied by the certificate for the shares to which it relates and such other evidence as the directors may reasonably require to show the right of the transferor to make the transfer;

(b) it is in respect of only one class of shares; and

(c) it is in favour of not more than four transferees.

25. If the directors refuse to register a transfer of a share, they shall within two months after the date on which the transfer was lodged with the company send to the transferee notice of the refusal.

26. The registration of transfers of shares or of transfers of any class of shares may be suspended at such times and for such periods (not exceeding thirty days in any year) as the directors may determine.

27. No fee shall be charged for the registration of any instrument of transfer or other document relating to or affecting the title to any share.

28. The company shall be entitled to retain any instrument of transfer which is registered, but any instrument of transfer which the directors refuse to register shall be returned to the person lodging it when notice of the refusal is given.

TRANSMISSION OF SHARES

29. If a member dies the survivor or survivors where he was a joint holder, and his personal representatives where he was a sole holder or the only survivor of joint holders, shall be the only persons recognised by the company as having any title to his interest; but nothing herein contained shall release the estate of a deceased member from any liability in respect of any share which had been jointly held by him.

30. A person becoming entitled to a share in consequence of the death or bankruptcy of a member may, upon such evidence being produced as the directors may properly require, elect either to become the holder of the share or to have some person nominated by him registered as the transferee. If he elects to become the holder he shall give notice to the company to that effect. If he elects to have another person registered he shall execute an instrument of transfer of the share to that person. All the articles relating to the transfer of shares shall apply to the notice or instrument of transfer as if it were an instrument of transfer executed by the member and the death or bankruptcy of the member had not occurred.

31. A person becoming entitled to a share in consequence of the death or bankruptcy of a member shall have the rights to which he would be entitled if he were the holder of the share, except that he shall not, before being registered as the holder of the share, be entitled in respect of it to attend or vote at any meeting of the company or at any separate meeting of the holders of any class of shares in the company.

ALTERATION OF SHARE CAPITAL

32. The company may by ordinary resolution—

(a) increase its share capital by new shares of such amount as the resolution prescribes;

(b) consolidate and divide all or any of its share capital into shares of larger amount than its existing shares;

(c) subject to the provisions of the Act, sub-divide its shares, or any of them, into shares of smaller amount and the resolution may determine that, as between the shares resulting from the sub-division, any of them may have any preference or advantage as compared with the others; and

(d) cancel shares which, at the date of the passing of the resolution, have not been taken or agreed to be taken by any person and diminish the amount of its share capital by the amount of the shares so cancelled.

33. Whenever as a result of a consolidation of shares any members would become entitled to fractions of a share, the directors may, on behalf of those members, sell the shares representing the fractions for the best price reasonably obtainable to any person (including, subject to the provisions of the Act, the company) and distribute the net proceeds of sale in due proportion among those members, and the directors may authorise some person to execute an instrument of transfer of the shares to, or in accordance with the directions of, the purchaser. The transferee shall not be bound to see to the application of the purchase money nor shall his title to the shares be affected by any irregularity in or invalidity of the proceedings in reference to the sale.

34. Subject to the provisions of the Act, the company may by special resolution reduce its share capital, any capital redemption reserve and any share premium account in any way.

PURCHASE OF OWN SHARES

35. Subject to the provisions of the Act, the company may purchase its own shares (including any redeemable shares) and, if it is a private company, make a payment in respect of the redemption or purchase of its own shares otherwise than out of distributable profits of the company or the proceeds of a fresh issue of shares.

GENERAL MEETINGS

36. All general meetings other than annual general meetings shall be called extraordinary general meetings.

37. The directors may call general meetings and, on the requisition of members pursuant to the provisions of the Act, shall forthwith proceed to convene an extraordinary general meeting for a date not later than eight weeks after receipt of the requisition. If there are not within the United Kingdom sufficient directors to call a general meeting, any director or any member of the company may call a general meeting.

NOTICE OF GENERAL MEETINGS

38. An annual general meeting and an extraordinary general meeting called for the passing of a special resolution or a resolution appointing a person as a director shall be called by at least twenty-one clear days' notice. All other extraordinary general meetings shall be called by at least fourteen clear days' notice but a general meeting may be called by shorter notice if it is so agreed—

(a) in the case of an annual general meeting, by all the members entitled to attend and vote thereat; and

(b) in the case of any other meeting by a majority in number of the members having a right to attend and vote being a majority together holding not less than ninety-five per cent. in nominal value of the shares giving that right.

The notice shall specify the time and place of the meeting and the general nature of the business to be transacted and, in the case of an annual general meeting, shall specify the meeting as such.

Subject to the provisions of the articles and to any restrictions imposed on any shares, the notice shall be given to all the members, to all persons entitled to a share in consequence of the death or bankruptcy of a member and to the directors and auditors.

39. The accidental omission to give notice of a meeting to, or the non-receipt of notice of a meeting by, any person entitled to receive notice shall not invalidate the proceedings at that meeting.

PROCEEDINGS AT GENERAL MEETINGS

40. No business shall be transacted at any meeting unless a quorum is present. Two persons entitled to vote upon the business to be transacted, each being a member or a proxy for a member or a duly authorised representative of a corporation, shall be a quorum.

41. If such a quorum is not present within half an hour from the time appointed for the meeting, or if during a meeting such a quorum ceases to be present, the meeting shall stand adjourned to the same day in the next week at the same time and place or such time and place as the directors may determine.

42. The chairman, if any, of the board of directors or in his absence some other director nominated by the directors shall preside as chairman of the meeting, but if neither the chairman nor such other director (if any) be present within fifteen minutes after the time appointed for holding the meeting and willing to act, the directors present shall elect one of their number to be chairman and, if there is only one director present and willing to act, he shall be chairman.

43. If no director is willing to act as chairman, or if no director is present within fifteen minutes after the time appointed for holding the meeting, the members present and entitled to vote shall choose one of their number to be chairman.

44. A director shall, notwithstanding that he is not a member, be entitled to attend and speak at any general meeting and at any separate meeting of the holders of any class of shares in the company.

45. The chairman may, with the consent of a meeting at which a quorum is present (and shall if so directed by the meeting), adjourn the meeting from time to time and from place to place, but no business shall be transacted at an adjourned meeting other than business which might properly have been transacted at the meeting had the adjournment not taken place. When a meeting is adjourned for fourteen days or more, at least seven clear days' notice shall be given specifying the time and place of the adjourned meeting and the general nature of the business to be transacted. Otherwise it shall not be necessary to give any such notice.

46. A resolution put to the vote of a meeting shall be decided on a show of hands unless before or on the declaration of the result of, the show of hands a poll is duly demanded. Subject to the provisions of the Act, a poll may be demanded—

(a) by the chairman; or

(b) by at least two members having the right to vote at the meeting; or

(c) by a member or members representing not less than one-tenth of the total voting rights of all the members having the right to vote at the meeting; or

(d) by a member or members holding shares conferring a right to vote at the meeting being shares on which an aggregate sum has been paid up equal to not less than one-tenth of the total sum paid up on all the shares conferring that right;

and a demand by a person as proxy for a member shall be the same as a demand by the member.

47. Unless a poll is duly demanded a declaration by the chairman that a resolution has been carried or carried unanimously, or by a particular majority, or lost, or not carried by a particular majority and an entry to that effect in the minutes of the meeting shall be conclusive evidence of the fact without proof of the number or proportion of the votes recorded in favour of or against the resolution.

48. The demand for a poll may, before the poll is taken, be withdrawn but only with the consent of the chairman and a demand so withdrawn shall not be taken to have invalidated the result of a show of hands declared before the demand was made.

49. A poll shall be taken as the chairman directs and he may appoint scrutineers (who need not be members) and fix a time and place for declaring the result of the poll. The result of the poll shall be deemed to be the resolution of the meeting at which the poll was demanded.

50. In the case of an equality of votes, whether on a show of hands or on a poll, the chairman shall be entitled to a casting vote in addition to any other vote he may have.

51. A poll demanded on the election of a chairman or on a question of adjournment shall be taken forthwith. A poll demanded on any other question shall be taken either forthwith or at such time and place as the chairman directs not being more than thirty days after the poll is demanded. The demand for a poll shall not prevent the continuance of a meeting for the transaction of any business other than the question on which the poll was demanded. If a poll is demanded before the declaration of the result of a show of hands and the demand is duly withdrawn, the meeting shall continue as if the demand had not been made.

52. No notice need be given of a poll not taken forthwith if the time and place at which it is to be taken are announced at the meeting at which it is demanded. In any other case at least seven clear days' notice shall be given specifying the time and place at which the poll is to be taken.

53. A resolution in writing executed by or on behalf of each member who would have been entitled to vote upon it if it had been proposed at a general meeting at which he was present shall be as effectual as if it had been passed at a general meeting duly convened and held and may consist of several instruments in the like form each executed by or on behalf of one or more members.

VOTES OF MEMBERS

54. Subject to any rights or restrictions attached to any shares, on a show of hands every member who (being an individual) is present in person or (being a corporation) is present by a duly authorised representative, not being himself a member entitled to vote, shall have one vote and on a poll every member shall have one vote for every share of which he is the holder.

55. In the case of joint holders the vote of the senior who tenders a vote, whether in person or by proxy, shall be accepted to the exclusion of the votes of the other joint holders; and seniority shall be determined by the order in which the names of the holders stand in the register of members.

56. A member in respect of whom an order has been made by any court having jurisdiction (whether in the United Kingdom or elsewhere) in matters concerning mental disorder may vote, whether on a show of hands or on a poll, by his receiver, curator bonis or other person authorised in that behalf appointed by that court, and any such receiver, curator bonis or other person may, on a poll, vote by proxy. Evidence to the satisfaction of the directors of the authority of the person claiming to exercise the right to vote shall be deposited at the office, or at such other place as is specified in accordance with the articles for the deposit of instruments of proxy, not less than 48 hours before the time appointed for holding the meeting or adjourned meeting at which the right to vote is to be exercised and in default the right to vote shall not be exercisable.

57. No member shall vote at any general meeting or at any separate meeting of the holders of any class of shares in the company, either in person or by proxy, in respect of any share held by him unless all moneys presently payable by him in respect of that share have been paid.

58. No objection shall be raised to the qualification of any voter except at the meeting or adjourned meeting at which the vote objected to is tendered, and every vote not disallowed at the meeting shall be valid. Any objection made in due time shall be referred to the chairman whose decision shall be final and conclusive.

59. On a poll votes may be given either personally or by proxy. A member may appoint more than one proxy to attend on the same occasion.

60. An instrument appointing a proxy shall be in writing, executed by or on behalf of the appointor and shall be in the following form (or in a form as near thereto as circumstances allow or in any other form which is usual or which the directors may approve)—

" .... PLC/Limited

....

I/We, ..., of ...., being a member/members of the above-named company, hereby appoint .... of ...., or failing him, ... of ...., as my/our proxy tovote in my/our name[s] and on my/our behalf at the annual/extraordinary general meeting of the company to be held on ...... 19 ...., and at any adjournment thereof.

Signed on .... 19 ....".

61. Where it is desired to afford members an opportunity of instructing the proxy how he shall act the instrument appointing a proxy shall be in the following form (or in a form as near thereto as circumstances allow or in any other form which is usual or which the directors may approve)—

> " .... PLC/Limited
>
> ....
>
> I/We, ..., of ...., being a member/members of the above-named company, hereby appoint .... of ...., or failing him .... of ...., as my/our proxy to vote in my/our name[s] and on my/our behalf at the annual/extraordinary general meeting of the company, to be held on .... 19 ...., and at any adjournment thereof.
>
> This form is to be used in respect of the resolutions mentioned below as follows:
>
> Resolution No. 1 *for *against
>
> Resolution No. 2 *for *against.
>
> *Strike out whichever is not desired.
>
> Unless otherwise instructed, the proxy may vote as he thinks fit or abstain from voting.
>
> Signed this .... day of .... 19......".

62. The instrument appointing a proxy and any authority under which it is executed or a copy of such authority certified notarially or in some other way approved by the directors may—

(a) be deposited at the office or at such other place within the United Kingdom as is specified in the notice convening the meeting or in any instrument of proxy sent out by the company in relation to the meeting not less than 48 hours before the time for holding the meeting or adjourned meeting at which the person named in the instrument proposes to vote; or

(b) in the case of a poll taken more than 48 hours after it is demanded, be deposited as aforesaid after the poll has been demanded and not less than 24 hours before the time appointed for the taking of the poll; or

(c) where the poll is not taken forthwith but is taken not more than 48 hours after it was demanded, be delivered at the meeting at which the poll was demanded to the chairman or to the secretary or to any director;

and an instrument of proxy which is not deposited or delivered in a manner so permitted shall be invalid.

63. A vote given or poll demanded by proxy or by the duly authorised representative of a corporation shall be valid notwithstanding the previous determination of the authority of the person voting or demanding a poll unless notice of the determination was received by the company at the office or at such other place at which the instrument of proxy was duly deposited before the commencement of the meeting or adjourned meeting at which the vote is given or the poll demanded or (in the case of a poll taken otherwise than on the same day as the meeting or adjourned meeting) the time appointed for taking the poll.

NUMBER OF DIRECTORS

64. Unless otherwise determined by ordinary resolution, the number of directors (other than alternate directors) shall not be subject to any maximum but shall be not less than two.

ALTERNATE DIRECTORS

65. Any director (other than an alternate director) may appoint any other director, or any other person approved by resolution of the directors and willing to act, to be an alternate director and may remove from office an alternate director so appointed by him.

66. An alternate director shall be entitled to receive notice of all meetings of directors and of all meetings of committees of directors of which his appointor is a member, to attend and vote at any such meeting at which the director appointing him is not personally present, and generally to perform all the functions of his appointor as a director in his absence but shall not be entitled to receive any remuneration from the company for his services as an alternate director. But it shall not be necessary to give notice of such a meeting to an alternate director who is absent from the United Kingdom.

67. An alternate director shall cease to be an alternate director if his appointor ceases to be a director; but, if a director retires by rotation or otherwise but is reappointed or deemed to have been reappointed at the meeting at which he retires, any appointment of an alternate director made by him which was in force immediately prior to his retirement shall continue after his reappointment.

68. Any appointment or removal of an alternate director shall be by notice to the company signed by the director making or revoking the appointment or in any other manner approved by the directors.

69. Save as otherwise provided in the articles, an alternate director shall be deemed for all purposes to be a director and shall alone be responsible for his own acts and defaults and he shall not be deemed to be the agent of the director appointing him.

POWERS OF DIRECTORS

70. Subject to the provisions of the Act, the memorandum and the articles and to any directions given by special resolution, the business of the company shall be managed by the directors who may exercise all the powers of the company. No alteration of the memorandum or articles and no such direction shall invalidate any prior act of the directors which would have been valid if that alteration had not been made or that direction had not been given. The powers given by this regulation shall not be limited by any special power given to the directors by the articles and a meeting of directors at which a quorum is present may exercise all powers exercisable by the directors.

71. The directors may, by power of attorney or otherwise, appoint any person to be the agent of the company for such purposes and on such conditions as they determine, including authority for the agent to delegate all or any of his powers.

DELEGATION OF DIRECTORS' POWERS

72. The directors may delegate any of their powers to any committee consisting of one or more directors. They may also delegate to any managing director or any director holding any other executive office such of their powers as they consider desirable to be exercised by him. Any such delegation may be made subject to any conditions the directors may impose, and either collaterally with or to the exclusion of their own powers and may be revoked or altered. Subject to any such conditions, the proceedings of a committee with two or more members shall be governed by the articles regulating the proceedings of directors so far as they are capable of applying.

APPOINTMENT AND RETIREMENT OF DIRECTORS

73. At the first annual general meeting all the directors shall retire from office, and at every subsequent annual general meeting one-third of the directors who are subject to retirement by rotation or, if their number is not three or a multiple of three, the number nearest to one-third shall retire from office; but, if there is only one director who is subject to retirement by rotation, he shall retire.

74. Subject to the provisions of the Act, the directors to retire by rotation shall be those who have been longest in office since their last appointment or reappointment, but as between persons who became or were last reappointed directors on the same day those to retire shall (unless they otherwise agree among themselves) be determined by lot.

75. If the company, at the meeting at which a director retires by rotation, does not fill the vacancy the retiring director shall, if willing to act, be deemed to have been reappointed unless at the meeting it is resolved not to fill the vacancy or unless a resolution for the reappointment of the director is put to the meeting and lost.

76. No person other than a director retiring by rotation shall be appointed or reappointed a director at any general meeting unless—

(a) he is recommended by the directors; or

(b) not less than fourteen nor more than thirty-five clear days before the date appointed for the meeting, notice executed by a member qualified to vote at the meeting has been given to the company of the intention to propose that person for appointment or reappointment stating the particulars which would, if he were so appointed or reappointed, be required to be included in the company's register of directors together with notice executed by that person of his willingness to be appointed or reappointed.

77. Not less than seven nor more than twenty-eight clear days before the date appointed for holding a general meeting notice shall be given to all who are entitled to receive notice of the meeting of any person (other than a director retiring by rotation at the meeting) who is recommended by the directors for appointment or reappointment as a director at the meeting or in respect of whom notice has been duly given to the company of the intention to propose him at the meeting for appointment or reappointment as a director. The notice shall give the particulars of that person which would, if he were so appointed or reappointed, be required to be included in the company's register of directors.

78. Subject as aforesaid, the company may by ordinary resolution appoint a person who is willing to act to be a director either to fill a vacancy or as an additional director and may also determine the rotation in which any additional directors are to retire.

79. The directors may appoint a person who is willing to act to be a director, either to fill a vacancy or as an additional director, provided that the appointment does not cause the number of directors to exceed any number fixed by or in accordance with the articles as the maximum number of directors. A director so appointed shall hold office only until the next following annual general meeting and shall not be taken into account in determining the directors who are to retire by rotation at the meeting. If not reappointed at such annual general meeting, he shall vacate office at the conclusion thereof.

80. Subject as aforesaid, a director who retires at an annual general meeting may, if willing to act, be reappointed. If he is not reappointed, he shall retain office until the meeting appoints someone in his place, or if it does not do so, until the end of the meeting.

DISQUALIFICATION AND REMOVAL OF DIRECTORS

81. The office of a director shall be vacated if—

(a) he ceases to be a director by virtue of any provision of the Act or he becomes prohibited by law from being a director; or

(b) he becomes bankrupt or makes any arrangement or composition with his creditors generally; or

(c) he is, or may be, suffering from mental disorder and either—

(i) he is admitted to hospital in pursuance of an application for admission for treatment under the Mental Health Act 1983 or, in Scotland, an application for admission under the Mental Health (Scotland) Act 1960, or

(ii) an order is made by a court having jurisdiction (whether in the United Kingdom or elsewhere) in matters concerning mental disorder for his detention or for the appointment of a receiver, curator bonis or other person to exercise powers with respect to his property or affairs; or

(d) he resigns his office by notice to the company; or

(e) he shall for more than six consecutive months have been absent without permission of the directors from meetings of directors held during that period and the directors resolve that his office be vacated.

REMUNERATION OF DIRECTORS

82. The directors shall be entitled to such remuneration as the company may by ordinary resolution determine and, unless the resolution provides otherwise, the remuneration shall be deemed to accrue from day to day.

DIRECTORS' EXPENSES

83. The directors may be paid all travelling, hotel, and other expenses properly incurred by them in connection with their attendance at meetings of directors or committees of directors or general meetings or separate meetings of the holders of any class of shares or of debentures of the company or otherwise in connection with the discharge of their duties.

DIRECTORS' APPOINTMENTS AND INTERESTS

84. Subject to the provisions of the Act, the directors may appoint one or more of their number to the office of managing director or to any other executive office under the company and may enter into an agreement or arrangement with any director for his employment by the company or for the provision by him of any services outside the scope of the ordinary duties of a director. Any such appointment, agreement or arrangement may be made upon such terms as the directors determine and they may remunerate any such director for his services as they think fit. Any appointment of a director to an executive office shall terminate if he ceases to be a director but without prejudice to any claim to damages for breach of the contract of service between the director and the company. A managing director and a director holding any other executive office shall not be subject to retirement by rotation.

85. Subject to the provisions of the Act, and provided that he has disclosed to the directors the nature and extent of any material interest of his, a director notwithstanding his office—

(a) may be a party to, or otherwise interested in, any transaction or arrangement with the company or in which the company is otherwise interested;

(b) may be a director or other officer of, or employed by, or a party to any transaction or arrangement with, or otherwise interested in, any body corporate promoted by the company or in which the company is otherwise interested; and

(c) shall not, by reason of his office, be accountable to the company for any benefit which he derives from any such office or employment or from any such transaction or arrangement or from any interest in any such body corporate and no such transaction or arrangement shall be liable to be avoided on the ground of any such interest or benefit.

86. For the purposes of regulation 85—

(a) a general notice given to the directors that a director is to be regarded as having an interest of the nature and extent specified in the notice in any transaction or arrangement in which a specified person or class of persons is interested shall be deemed to be a disclosure that the director has an interest in any such transaction of the nature and extent so specified; and

(b) an interest of which a director has no knowledge and of which it is unreasonable to expect him to have knowledge shall not be treated as an interest of his.

DIRECTORS' GRATUITIES AND PENSIONS

87. The directors may provide benefits, whether by the payment of gratuities or pensions or by insurance or otherwise, for any director who has held but no longer holds any executive office or employment with the company or with any body corporate which is or has been a subsidiary of the company or a predecessor in business of the company or of any such subsidiary, and for any member of his family (including a spouse and a former spouse) or any person who is or was dependent on him, and may (as well before as after he ceases to hold such office or employment) contribute to any fund and pay premiums for the purchase or provision of any such benefit.

PROCEEDINGS OF DIRECTORS

88. Subject to the provisions of the articles, the directors may regulate their proceedings as they think fit. A director may, and the secretary at the request of a director shall, call a meeting of the directors. It shall not be necessary to give notice of a meeting to a director who is absent from the United Kingdom. Questions arising at a meeting shall be decided by a majority of votes. In the case of an equality of votes, the chairman shall have a second or casting vote. A director who is also an alternate director shall be entitled in the absence of his appointor to a separate vote on behalf of his appointor in addition to his own vote.

89. The quorum for the transaction of the business of the directors may be fixed by the directors and unless so fixed at any other number shall be two. A person who holds office only as an alternate director shall, if his appointor is not present, be counted in the quorum.

90. The continuing directors or a sole continuing director may act notwithstanding any vacancies in their number, but, if the number of directors is less than the number fixed as the quorum, the continuing directors or director may act only for the purpose of filling vacancies or of calling a general meeting.

91. The directors may appoint one of their number to be the chairman of the board of directors and may at any time remove him from that office. Unless he is unwilling to do so, the director so appointed shall preside at every meeting of directors at which he is present. But if there is no director holding that office, or if the director holding it is unwilling to preside or is not present within five minutes after the time appointed for the meeting, the directors present may appoint one of their number to be chairman of the meeting.

92. All acts done by a meeting of directors, or of a committee of directors, or by a person acting as a director shall, notwithstanding that it be afterwards discovered that there was a defect in the appointment of any director or that any of them were disqualified from holding office, or had vacated office, or were not entitled to vote, be as valid as if every such person had been duly appointed and was qualified and had continued to be a director and had been entitled to vote.

93. A resolution in writing signed by all the directors entitled to receive notice of a meeting of directors or of a committee of directors shall be as valid and effectual as if it had been passed at a meeting of directors or (as the case may be) a committee of directors duly convened and held and may consist of several documents in the like form each signed by one or more directors; but a resolution signed by an alternate director need not also be signed by his appointor and, if it is signed by a director who has appointed an alternate director, it need not be signed by the alternate director in that capacity.

94. Save as otherwise provided by the articles, a director shall not vote at a meeting of directors or of a committee of directors on any resolution concerning a matter in which he has, directly or indirectly, an interest or duty which is material and which conflicts or may conflict with the interests of the company unless his interest or duty arises only because the case falls within one or more of the following paragraphs—

(a) the resolution relates to the giving to him of a guarantee, security, or indemnity in respect of money lent to, or an obligation incurred by him for the benefit of, the company or any of its subsidiaries;

(b) the resolution relates to the giving to a third party of a guarantee, security, or indemnity in respect of an obligation of the company or any of its subsidiaries for which the director has assumed reponsibility in whole or part and whether alone or jointly with others under a guarantee or indemnity or by the giving of security;

(c) his interest arises by virtue of his subscribing or agreeing to subscribe for any shares, debentures or other securities of the company or any of its subsidiaries, or by virtue of his being, or intending to become, a participant in the underwriting or sub-underwriting of an offer of any such shares, debentures, or other securities by the company or any of its subsidiaries for subscription, purchase or exchange;

(d) the resolution relates in any way to a retirement benefits scheme which has been approved, or is conditional upon approval, by the Board of Inland Revenue for taxation purposes.

For the purposes of this regulation, an interest of a person who is, for any purpose of the Act (excluding any statutory modification thereof not in force when this regulation becomes binding on the company), connected with a director shall be treated as an interest of the director and, in relation to an alternate director, an interest of his appointor shall be treated as an interest of the alternate director without prejudice to any interest which the alternate director has otherwise.

95. A director shall not be counted in the quorum present at a meeting in relation to a resolution on which he is not entitled to vote.

96. The company may by ordinary resolution suspend or relax to any extent, either generally or in respect of any particular matter, any provision of the articles prohibiting a director from voting at a meeting of directors or of a committee of directors.

97. Where proposals are under consideration concerning the appointment of two or more directors to offices or employments with the company or any body corporate in which the company is interested the proposals may be divided and considered in relation to each director separately and (provided he is not for another reason precluded from voting) each of the directors concerned shall be entitled to vote and be counted in the quorum in respect of each resolution except that concerning his own appointment.

98. If a question arises at a meeting of directors or of a committee of directors as to the right of a director to vote, the question may, before the conclusion of the meeting, be referred to the chairman of the meeting and his ruling in relation to any director other than himself shall be final and conclusive.

SECRETARY

99. Subject to the provisions of the Act, the secretary shall be appointed by the directors for such term, at such remuneration and upon such conditions as they may think fit; and any secretary so appointed may be removed by them.

MINUTES

100. The directors shall cause minutes to be made in books kept for the purpose—

(a) of all appointments of officers made by the directors; and

(b) of all proceedings at meetings of the company, of the holders of any class of shares in the company, and of the directors, and of committees of directors, including the names of the directors present at each such meeting.

THE SEAL

101. The seal shall only be used by the authority of the directors or of a committee of directors authorised by the directors. The directors may determine who shall sign any instrument to which the seal is affixed and unless otherwise so determined it shall be signed by a director and by the secretary or by a second director.

DIVIDENDS

102. Subject to the provisions of the Act, the company may by ordinary resolution declare dividends in accordance with the respective rights of the members, but no dividend shall exceed the amount recommended by the directors.

103. Subject to the provisions of the Act, the directors may pay interim dividends if it appears to them that they are justified by the profits of the company available for distribution. If the share capital is divided into different classes, the directors may pay interim dividends on shares which confer deferred or non-preferred rights with regard to dividend as well as on shares which confer preferential rights with regard to dividend, but no interim dividend shall be paid on shares carrying deferred or non-preferred rights if, at the time of payment, any preferential dividend is in arrear. The directors may also pay at intervals settled by them any dividend payable at a fixed rate if it appears to them that the profits available for distribution justify the payment. Provided the directors act in good faith they shall not incur any liability to the holders of shares conferring preferred rights for any loss they may suffer by the lawful payment of an interim dividend on any shares having deferred or non-preferred rights.

104. Except as otherwise provided by the rights attached to shares, all dividends shall be declared and paid according to the amounts paid up on the shares on which the dividend is paid. All dividends shall be apportioned and paid proportionately to the amounts paid up on the shares during any portion or portions of the period in respect of which the dividend is paid; but, if any share is issued on terms providing that it shall rank for dividend as from a particular date, that share shall rank for dividend accordingly.

105. A general meeting declaring a dividend may, upon the recommendation of the directors, direct that it shall be satisfied wholly or partly by the distribution of assets and, where any difficulty arises in regard to the distribution, the directors may settle the same and in particular may issue fractional certificates and fix the value for distribution of any assets and may determine that cash shall be paid to any member upon the footing of the value so fixed in order to adjust the rights of members and may vest any assets in trustees.

106. Any dividend or other moneys payable in respect of a share may be paid by cheque sent by post to the registered address of the person entitled or, if two or more persons are the holders of the share or are jointly entitled to it by reason of the death or bankruptcy of the holder, to the registered address of that one of those persons who is first named in the register of members or to such person and to such address as the person or persons entitled may in writing direct. Every cheque shall be made payable to the order of the person or persons entitled or to such other person as the person or persons entitled may in writing direct and payment of the cheque shall be a good discharge to the company. Any joint holder or other person jointly entitled to a share as aforesaid may give receipts for any dividend or other moneys payable in respect of the share.

107. No dividend or other moneys payable in respect of a share shall bear interest against the company unless otherwise provided by the rights attached to the share.

108. Any dividend which has remained unclaimed for twelve years from the date when it became due for payment shall, if the directors so resolve, be forfeited and cease to remain owing by the company.

ACCOUNTS

109. No member shall (as such) have any right of inspecting any accounting records or other book or document of the company except as conferred by statute or authorised by the directors or by ordinary resolution of the company.

CAPITALISATION OF PROFITS

110. The directors may with the authority of an ordinary resolution of the company—

(a) subject as hereinafter provided, resolve to capitalise any undivided profits of the company not required for paying any preferential dividend (whether or not they are available for distribution) or any sum standing to the credit of the company's share premium account or capital redemption reserve;

(b) appropriate the sum resolved to be capitalised to the members who would have been entitled to it if it were distributed by way of dividend and in the same proportions and apply such sum on their behalf either in or towards paying up the amounts, if any, for the time being unpaid on any shares held by them respectively, or in paying up in full unissued shares or debentures of the company of a nominal amount equal to that sum, and allot the shares or debentures credited as fully paid to those members, or as they may direct, in those proportions, or partly in one way and partly in the other: but the share premium account, the capital redemption reserve, and any profits which are not available for distribution may, for the purposes of this regulation, only be applied in paying up unissued shares to be allotted to members credited as fully paid;

(c) make such provision by the issue of fractional certificates or by payment in cash or otherwise as they determine in the case of shares or debentures becoming distributable under this regulation in fractions; and

(d) authorise any person to enter on behalf of all the members concerned into an agreement with the company providing for the allotment to them respectively, credited as fully paid, of any shares or debentures to which they are entitled upon such capitalisation, any agreement made under such authority being binding on all such members.

NOTICES

111. Any notice to be given to or by any person pursuant to the articles shall be in writing except that a notice calling a meeting of the directors need not be in writing.

112. The company may give any notice to a member either personally or by sending it by post in a prepaid envelope addressed to the member at his registered address or by leaving it at that address. In the case of joint holders of a share, all notices shall be given to the joint holder whose name stands first in the register of members in respect of the joint holding and notice so given shall be sufficient notice to all the joint holders. A member whose registered address is not within the United Kingdom and who gives to the company an address within the United Kingdom at which notices may be given to him shall be entitled to have notices given to him at that address, but otherwise no such member shall be entitled to receive any notice from the company.

113. A member present, either in person or by proxy, at any meeting of the company or of the holders of any class of shares in the company shall be deemed to have received notice of the meeting and, where requisite, of the purposes for which it was called.

114. Every person who becomes entitled to a share shall be bound by any notice in respect of that share which, before his name is entered in the register of members, has been duly given to a person from whom he derives his title.

115. Proof that an envelope containing a notice was properly addressed, prepaid and posted shall be conclusive evidence that the notice was given. A notice shall, unless the contrary is proved, be deemed to be given at the expiration of 48 hours after the envelope containing it was posted.

116. A notice may be given by the company to the persons entitled to a share in consequence of the death or bankruptcy of a member by sending or delivering it, in any manner authorised by the articles for the giving of notice to a member, addressed to them by name, or by the title of representatives of the deceased, or trustee of the bankrupt or by any like description at the address, if any, within the United Kingdom supplied for that purpose by the persons claiming to be so entitled. Until such an address has been supplied, a notice may be given in any manner in which it might have been given if the death or bankruptcy had not occurred.

WINDING UP

117. If the company is wound up, the liquidator may, with the sanction of an extraordinary resolution of the company and any other sanction required by the Act, divide among the members in specie the whole or any part of the assets of the company and may, for that purpose, value any assets and determine how the division shall be carried out as between the members or different classes of members. The liquidator may, with the like sanction, vest the whole or any part of the assets in trustees upon such trusts for the benefit of the members as he with the like sanction determines, but no member shall be compelled to accept any assets upon which there is a liability.

INDEMNITY

118. Subject to the provisions of the Act but without prejudice to any indemnity to which a director may otherwise be entitled, every director or other officer or auditor of the company shall be indemnified out of the assets of the company against any liability incurred by him in defending any proceedings, whether civil or criminal, in which judgment is given in his favour or in which he is acquitted or in connection with any application in which relief is granted to him by the court from liability for negligence, default, breach of duty or breach of trust in relation to the affairs of the company.

Appendix B The RTM Companies (Model Articles) (England) Regulations 2009, SI 2009/2767

LANDLORD AND TENANT, ENGLAND

Made	*13th October 2009*
Laid before Parliament	*19th October 2009*
Coming into force	*9th November 2009*

The Secretary of State, in exercise of the powers conferred by sections 74(2), (4) and (6) and 178(1) of the Commonhold and Leasehold Reform Act 2002,[1] makes the following Regulations:

Citation, commencement and application

1.—(1) These Regulations may be cited as the RTM Companies (Model Articles) (England) Regulations 2009 and shall come into force on 9th November 2009.

(2) These Regulations apply to RTM companies[2] which exercise the right to manage premises[3] in England.

Form and content of articles of association of RTM companies

2.—(1) The articles of association of a RTM company shall take the form, and include the provisions, set out in the Schedule to these Regulations.

1 2002 c. 15. The "appropriate national authority", in respect of England, is the Secretary of State and, in respect of Wales, is the Welsh Ministers. *See* section 179(1) of the Commonhold and Leasehold Reform Act 2002. By virtue of paragraph 30(2)(c) of Schedule 11 to the Government of Wales Act 2006 (c.32) the functions formerly exercised by the National Assembly for Wales are now exercisable by the Welsh Ministers.

2 For the definition of "RTM company" *see* sections 71(1) and 73 of the 2002 Act.

3 For the premises relevant to RTM companies, *see* section 72 of, and Schedule 6 to, the Commonhold and Leasehold Reform Act 2002.

(2) Subject to regulation 3(2), the provisions referred to in paragraph (1) shall have effect for a RTM company whether or not they are adopted by the company.

Revocation of instrument and transitional provisions

3.—(1) The RTM Companies (Memorandum and Articles of Association) (England) Regulations 2003[4] ("the 2003 Regulations") are revoked.

(2) During the transitional period the 2003 Regulations shall continue to have effect in relation to RTM companies incorporated before 9th November 2009.

(3) The transitional period is the period beginning on 9th November 2009 and ending on 30th September 2010.

Signed by authority of the Secretary of State for Communities and Local Government

Ian Austin
Parliamentary Under Secretary of State
Department for Communities and
Local Government

13th October 2009

SCHEDULE

ARTICLES OF ASSOCIATION OF A RTM COMPANY

Regulation 2

THE COMPANIES ACT 2006

ARTICLES OF ASSOCIATION OF [NAME] RTM COMPANY LIMITED

A COMPANY LIMITED BY GUARANTEE AND NOT HAVING A SHARE CAPITAL

4 S.I. 2003/2120.

PART 1

INTERPRETATION, NAMES AND OBJECTS OF RTM COMPANY AND LIMITATION OF LIABILITY

Defined terms

1.—(1) In the articles, unless the context requires otherwise—

"articles" means the company's articles of association;

"bankruptcy" includes individual insolvency proceedings in a jurisdiction other than England and Wales or Northern Ireland which have an effect similar to that of bankruptcy;

"chairman" has the meaning given in article 17;

"chairman of the meeting" has the meaning given in article 30;

"Companies Acts" means the Companies Acts as defined in section 2 of the Companies Act 2006,[5] in so far as they apply to the company;

"director" means a director of the company, and includes any person occupying the position of director, by whatever name called;

"document" includes, unless otherwise specified, any document sent or supplied in electronic form;

"electronic form" has the meaning given in section 1168 of the Companies Act 2006 ("the 2006 Act");

"immediate landlord" in relation to a unit in the Premises, means the person who—

(a) if the unit is subject to a lease, is the landlord under the lease; or

(b) if the unit is subject to two or more leases, is the landlord under whichever of the leases is inferior to the others;

"member" has the meaning given in section 112 of the 2006 Act;

"ordinary resolution" has the meaning given in section 282 of the 2006 Act;

"participate", in relation to a directors' meeting, has the meaning given in article 15;

5 2006 c. 46.

"the Premises" means [*name and address*];

"proxy notice" has the meaning given in article 36;

"residential unit" means a flat or any other separate set of premises which is constructed or adapted for use for the purposes of a dwelling;

"RTM company" (Right to Manage Company) has the meaning given in section 73 of the Commonhold and Leasehold Reform Act 2002

"special resolution" has the meaning given in section 283 of the 2006 Act;

"subsidiary" has the meaning given in section 1159 of the 2006 Act;

"writing" means the representation or reproduction of words, symbols or other information in a visible form by any method or combination of methods, whether sent or supplied in electronic form or otherwise; and

"2002 Act" means the Commonhold and Leasehold Reform Act 2002.

(2) Unless the context otherwise requires, other words or expressions contained in these articles bear the same meaning as in the Companies Act 2006 as in force on the date when the RTM Companies (Model Articles) (England) Regulations 2009 are made.

NAME AND OBJECTS OF RTM COMPANY

2. The name of the company is

[*name*] ....

RTM Company Limited.

3. The registered office of the company will be situated at

[*address*] ....

4. The objects for which the company is established are to acquire and exercise in accordance with the 2002 Act the right to manage the Premises.

5. These objects shall not be restrictively construed but the widest interpretation shall be given to them. In furtherance of the objects, but not otherwise, the company shall have power to do all such things as may be authorised or required to be done by a RTM company by and under the

2002 Act, and in particular (but without derogation from the generality of the foregoing)—

(a) to prepare, make, pursue or withdraw a claim to acquire the right to manage the Premises;

(b) to exercise management functions under leases of the whole or any part of the Premises in accordance with sections 96 and 97 of the 2002 Act;

(c) to exercise functions in relation to the grant of approvals under long leases of the whole or any part of the Premises in accordance with sections 98 and 99 of the 2002 Act;

(d) in accordance with sections 100 and 101 of the 2002 Act, to monitor, keep under review, report to the landlord, and procure or enforce the performance by any person of the terms of any covenant, undertaking, duty or obligation in any way connected with or affecting the Premises or any of its occupants;

(e) to negotiate for and make applications for the variation of leases pursuant to Part 4 of the Landlord and Tenant Act 1987 ("the 1987 Act");

(f) to do such other things and to perform such other functions in relation to the Premises or any leases of the whole or any part of the Premises as may be agreed from time to time with the landlord or landlords or any other parties to the leases, as the case may be;

(g) to provide and maintain services and amenities of every description in relation to the Premises;

(h) to maintain, redecorate, repair, renew, repaint and clean the Premises; and to cultivate, maintain, landscape and plant any gardens, grounds or land comprised in the Premises;

(i) to enter into contracts with builders, cleaners, contractors, decorators, gardeners, tenants, or any other person;

(j) to consult and retain any professional advisers;

(k) to employ any staff and managing or other agents;

(l) to pay, remunerate or reward in any way any person supplying goods or services to the company;

(m) to make any appropriate or consequential agreements or arrangements for the right to manage the Premises to cease to be exercisable by the company;

(n) to issue and receive any notice, counter-notice, consent or other communication and to enter into any correspondence concerning or in any way affecting the Premises, the management of the Premises, the occupants of the Premises, the company, any of its activities, or any of its members;

(o) to commence, defend, participate in or pursue any application to, or other proceeding before, any court or tribunal of any description;

(p) to insure the Premises or any other property of the company or in which it has an interest up to and including the full cost of rebuilding and reinstating the Premises, including VAT, architects', engineers', solicitors', surveyors', and all other professional persons' fees, the fees payable on any applications for planning permission or other permits or consents that may be required in relation to rebuilding or reinstating the Premises, the cost of preparation of the site including debris removal, demolition, shoring-up, site clearance and any works that may be required by statute, and incidental expenses, subject to such excesses, exclusions or limitations as are usual in the London insurance market. To insure the company and its directors, officers or auditors against public liability and any other risks which it may consider prudent or desirable to insure against;

(q) to collect in or receive monies from any person on account of administration charges, service charges, or other charges in relation to the Premises and, where required by law to do so, to deal with, hold or invest the monies in accordance with the provisions of the 1987 Act and any orders or regulations made under that Act from time to time;

(r) to establish, undertake and execute any trusts which may lawfully be, or which are required by law to be, established, executed or undertaken by the company;

(s) to establish and maintain capital reserves, management funds and any form of sinking fund in order to pay, or contribute towards, all costs, fees, and other expenses incurred in the implementation of the company's objects;

(t) to invest any money of the company in the United Kingdom by depositing it at interest with any financial institution with which a trust fund of service charge contributions might be held in accordance with the 1987 Act; or to invest it in such other manner (including the purchase of securities and other investments) as the company in general meeting may authorise from time to time; and to hold, sell or otherwise dispose of any such investments;

(u) subject to any conditions or limitations imposed by the company in general meeting from time to time, and subject to the provision of adequate security and the payment of interest, to advance and lend money or give credit to any person; to enter into guarantees, contracts of indemnity and surety; to receive money on deposit or loan; and to secure or guarantee the payment of any sum of money or the performance of any obligation by any person;

(v) subject to any limitations or conditions imposed by the company in general meeting from time to time, to borrow and raise money in any manner and to secure the repayment of any money borrowed, raised or owing by mortgage, charge, standard security, lien or other security upon the whole or part of the company's property or assets (whether present or future);

(w) to operate bank accounts and to draw, make, accept, endorse, discount, negotiate, execute and issue cheques, bills of exchange, debentures, promissory notes, and other negotiable or transferable instruments;

(x) to pay all or any expenses incurred in connection with the promotion, formation and incorporation of the company, or to contract with any person to pay such expenses;

(y) to monitor and determine for the purpose of voting, or for any other purpose, the physical dimensions of the Premises and any part or parts of the Premises and to take or obtain any appropriate measurements;

(z) to enter into any agreements or arrangements with any Minister of the Crown, authority (central, municipal, local, or otherwise) that may seem conducive to the attainment of the company's objects, and to obtain from any such Minister of the Crown or authority any charters, decrees, rights, privileges or concessions which the company may think desirable, and to carry out, exercise, and comply with any such charters, decrees, rights, privileges and concessions;

(aa) to do all things specified for the time being in the articles of association of the company;

(bb) to do or procure or arrange for the doing of all or any of the things or matters mentioned above in any part of the world and either as principals, agents, contractors or otherwise, and by or through agents, brokers, sub-contractors or otherwise and either alone or in conjunction with others; and

(cc) to do all such other lawful things as may be incidental or conducive to the pursuit or attainment of the company's objects.

6. The income of the company, from wherever derived, shall be applied solely in promoting the company's objects, and, save on a winding up of the company, no distribution shall be made to its members in cash or otherwise.

LIMITATION OF LIABILITY

Liability of members

7. The liability of each member is limited to £1, being the amount that each member undertakes to contribute to the assets of the company in the event of its being wound up while he is a member or within one year after he ceases to be a member, for—

(a) payment of the company's debts and liabilities contracted before he ceases to be a member,

(b) payment of the costs, charges and expenses of winding up; and

(c) adjustment of the rights of the contributories among themselves.

PART 2

DIRECTORS

DIRECTORS' POWERS AND RESPONSIBILITIES

Directors' general authority

8. Subject to the articles, the directors are responsible for the management of the company's business, for which purpose they may exercise all the powers of the company.

Members' reserve power

9.—(1) The members may, by special resolution, direct the directors to take, or refrain from taking, specified action.

(2) No such special resolution invalidates anything which the directors have done before the passing of the resolution.

Directors may delegate

10.—(1) Subject to the articles, the directors may delegate any of the powers which are conferred on them under the articles—

(a) to such person or committee;

(b) by such means (including by power of attorney);

(c) to such an extent;

(d) in relation to such matters; and

(e) on such terms and conditions;

as they think fit.

(2) If the directors so specify, any such delegation may authorise further delegation of the directors' powers by any person to whom they are delegated.

(3) The directors may revoke any delegation in whole or part, or alter its terms and conditions.

Committees

11.—(1) Committees to which the directors delegate any of their powers must follow procedures which are based, so far as they are applicable, on those provisions of the articles which govern the taking of decisions by directors.

DECISION-MAKING BY DIRECTORS

Directors to take decisions collectively

12.—(1) The general rule about decision-making by directors is that any decision of the directors must be either a majority decision at a meeting or a decision taken in accordance with article 13.

(2) If—

(a) the company only has one director, and

(b) no provision of the articles requires it to have more than one director,

the general rule does not apply, and the director may take decisions without regard to any of the provisions of the articles relating to directors' decision-making.

Unanimous decisions

13.—(1) A decision of the directors is taken in accordance with this article when all eligible directors indicate to each other by any means that they share a common view on a matter.

(2) Such a decision may take the form of a resolution in writing, copies of which have been signed by each eligible director or to which each eligible director has otherwise indicated agreement in writing.

(3) References in this article to eligible directors are to directors who would have been entitled to vote on the matter had it been proposed as a resolution at a directors' meeting.

(4) A decision may not be taken in accordance with this article if the eligible directors would not have formed a quorum at such a meeting.

Calling a directors' meeting

14.—(1) Any director may call a directors' meeting by giving notice of the meeting to the directors or by authorising the company secretary (if any) to give such notice.

(2) Notice of any directors' meeting must indicate—

(a) its proposed date and time;

(b) where it is to take place; and

(c) if it is anticipated that directors participating in the meeting will not be in the same place, how it is proposed that they should communicate with each other during the meeting.

(3) Notice of a directors' meeting must be given to each director, but need not be in writing.

(4) Notice of a directors' meeting need not be given to directors who waive their entitlement to notice of that meeting, by giving notice to that effect to the company not more than 7 days after the date on which the meeting is held. Where such notice is given after the meeting has been held, that does not affect the validity of the meeting, or of any business conducted at it.

Participation in directors' meetings

15.—(1) Subject to the articles, directors participate in a directors' meeting, or part of a directors' meeting, when—

(a) the meeting has been called and takes place in accordance with the articles, and

(b) they can each communicate to the others any information or opinions they have on any particular item of the business of the meeting.

(2) In determining whether directors are participating in a directors' meeting, it is irrelevant where any director is or how they communicate with each other.

(3) If all the directors participating in a meeting are not in the same place, they may decide that the meeting is to be treated as taking place wherever any of them is.

Quorum for directors' meetings

16.—(1) At a directors' meeting, unless a quorum is participating, no proposal is to be voted on, except a proposal to call another meeting.

(2) The quorum for directors' meetings may be fixed from time to time by a decision of the directors, but it must never be less than two, and unless otherwise fixed it is two.

(3) If the total number of directors for the time being is less than the quorum required, the directors must not take any decision other than a decision—

(a) to appoint further directors, or

(b) to call a general meeting so as to enable the members to appoint further directors.

Chairing of directors' meetings

17.—(1) The directors may appoint a director to chair their meetings.

(2) The person so appointed for the time being is known as the chairman.

(3) The directors may terminate the chairman's appointment at any time.

(4) If the chairman is not participating in a directors' meeting within ten minutes of the time at which it was to start, the participating directors must appoint one of themselves to chair it.

Casting vote

18.—(1) If the numbers of votes for and against a proposal are equal, the chairman or other director chairing the meeting has a casting vote.

(2) But this does not apply if, in accordance with the articles, the chairman or other director is not to be counted as participating in the decision-making process for quorum or voting purposes.

Conflicts of interest

19.—(1) If a proposed decision of the directors is concerned with an actual or proposed transaction or arrangement with the company in which a director is interested, that director is not to be counted as participating in the decision-making process for quorum or voting purposes.

(2) But if paragraph (3) applies, a director who is interested in an actual or proposed transaction or arrangement with the company is to be counted as participating in the decision-making process for quorum and voting purposes.

(3) This paragraph applies when—

(a) the company by ordinary resolution disapplies the provision of the articles which would otherwise prevent a director from being counted as participating in the decision-making process;

(b) the director's interest cannot reasonably be regarded as likely to give rise to a conflict of interest; or

(c) the director's conflict of interest arises from a permitted cause.

(4) For the purposes of this article, the following are permitted causes—

(a) a guarantee given, or to be given, by or to a director in respect of an obligation incurred by or on behalf of the company or any of its subsidiaries;

(b) subscription, or an agreement to subscribe, for securities of the company or any of its subsidiaries, or to underwrite, sub-underwrite, or guarantee subscription for any such securities; and

(c) arrangements pursuant to which benefits are made available to employees and directors or former employees and directors of the company or any of its subsidiaries which do not provide special benefits for directors or former directors.

(5) For the purposes of this article, references to proposed decisions and decision-making processes include any directors' meeting or part of a directors' meeting.

(6) Subject to paragraph (7), if a question arises at a meeting of directors or of a committee of directors as to the right of a director to participate in the meeting (or part of the meeting) for voting or quorum purposes, the question may, before the conclusion of the meeting, be referred to the chairman whose ruling in relation to any director other than the chairman is to be final and conclusive.

(7) If any question as to the right to participate in the meeting (or part of the meeting) should arise in respect of the chairman, the question is to be decided by a decision of the directors at that meeting, for which purpose the chairman is not to be counted as participating in the meeting (or that part of the meeting) for voting or quorum purposes.

Records of decisions to be kept

20. The directors must ensure that the company keeps a record, in writing, for at least 10 years from the date of the decision recorded, of every unanimous or majority decision taken by the directors.

Directors' discretion to make further rules

21. Subject to the articles, the directors may make any rule which they think fit about how they take decisions, and about how such rules are to be recorded or communicated to directors.

APPOINTMENT OF DIRECTORS

Methods of appointing directors

22.—(1) Any person who is willing to act as a director, and is permitted by law to do so, may be appointed to be a director—

(a) by ordinary resolution, or

(b) by a decision of the directors.

(2) In any case where, as a result of death, the company has no members and no directors, the personal representatives of the last member to have died have the right, by notice in writing, to appoint a person to be a director.

(3) For the purposes of paragraph (2), where 2 or more members die in circumstances rendering it uncertain who was the last to die, a younger member is deemed to have survived an older member.

Termination of director's appointment

23. A person ceases to be a director as soon as—

(a) that person ceases to be a director by virtue of any provision of the Companies Acts 2006 or is prohibited from being a director by law;

(b) a bankruptcy order is made against that person;

(c) a composition is made with that person's creditors generally in satisfaction of that person's debts;

(d) a registered medical practitioner who is treating that person gives a written opinion to the company stating that that person has become physically or mentally incapable of acting as a director and may remain so for more than three months;

(e) by reason of that person's mental health, a court makes an order which wholly or partly prevents that person from personally exercising any powers or rights which that person would otherwise have;

(f) notification is received by the company from the director that the director is resigning from office, and such resignation has taken effect in accordance with its terms.

Directors' remuneration

24. Except with the consent of the company in general meeting, the directors shall not be entitled to any remuneration. Any resolution giving such consent shall specify the amount of remuneration to be paid to the directors, and unless the resolution provides otherwise, the remuneration shall be deemed to accrue from day to day.

Directors' expenses

25. The company may pay any reasonable expenses which the directors properly incur in connection with their attendance at—

(a) meetings of directors or committees of directors,

(b) general meetings, or

(c) separate meetings of the holders of debentures of the company,

or otherwise in connection with the exercise of their powers and the discharge of their responsibilities in relation to the company.

PART 3

BECOMING AND CEASING TO BE A MEMBER

Becoming a member

26.—(1) Every person who is entitled to be, and who wishes to become, a member of the company shall deliver to the company an application for membership executed by him in the following form (or in a form as near to the following form as circumstances allow or in any other form which is usual or which the directors may approve).

To the Board of [name of company]I, [name]of [address]am a qualifying tenant of [address of flat] and wish to become a member of [name of company] subject to the provisions of the Articles of Association of the company and to any rules made under those Articles. I agree to pay the company an amount of up to £1 if the company is wound up while I am a member or for up to 12 months after I have ceased to become a member. Signed [ ] Dated [ ]

(2) No person shall be admitted to membership of the company unless that person, whether alone or jointly with others, is—

(a) a qualifying tenant of a flat contained in the Premises as specified in section 75 of the 2002 Act; or

(b) from the date upon which the company acquires the right to manage the Premises pursuant to the 2002 Act, a landlord under a lease of the whole or any part of the Premises.

(3) Membership of the company shall not be transferable.

(4) A person who, together with another or others, is to be regarded as jointly being the qualifying tenant of a flat, or as jointly constituting the landlord under a lease of the whole or any part of the Premises, shall, once admitted, be regarded as jointly being a member of the company in respect of that flat or lease (as the case may be).

(5) Applications for membership by persons who are to be regarded as jointly being the qualifying tenant of a flat, or who jointly constitute the landlord under a lease of the whole or any part of the Premises, shall state the names and addresses of all others who are jointly interested with them, and the order in which they wish to appear on the register of members in respect of such flat or lease (as the case may be).

(6) The directors shall, upon being satisfied as to a person's application and entitlement to membership, register such person as a member of the company.

Ceasing to be a member

27.—(1) A member who at any time fails to satisfy the requirements for membership set out in article 26 shall cease to be a member of the company with immediate effect.

(2) If a member (or joint member) dies or becomes bankrupt, his personal representatives or trustee in bankruptcy will be entitled to be registered as a member (or joint member as the case may be) upon notice in writing to the company.

(3) A member may withdraw from the company and thereby cease to be a member by giving at least seven clear days' notice in writing to the company. Any such notice shall not be effective if given in the period beginning with

the date on which the company gives notice of its claim to acquire the right to manage the Premises and ending with the date which is either—

(a) the acquisition date in accordance with section 90 of the 2002 Act; or

(b) the date of withdrawal or deemed withdrawal of that notice in accordance with sections 86 or 87 of that Act.

(4) If, for any reason—

(a) a person who is not a member of the company becomes a qualifying tenant or landlord jointly with persons who are members of the company, but fails to apply for membership within 28 days, or

(b) a member who is a qualifying tenant or landlord jointly with such persons dies or becomes bankrupt and his personal representatives or trustee in bankruptcy do not apply for membership within 56 days, or

(c) a member who is a qualifying tenant or landlord jointly with such persons resigns from membership pursuant to article 27(3),

those persons shall, unless they are otherwise entitled to be members of the company by reason of their interest in some other flat or lease, also cease to be members of the company with immediate effect. All such persons shall, however, be entitled to re-apply for membership in accordance with article 26.

PART 4

DECISION-MAKING BY MEMBERS

ORGANISATION OF GENERAL MEETINGS

Attendance and speaking at general meetings

28.—(1) A person is able to exercise the right to speak at a general meeting when that person is in a position to communicate to all those attending the meeting, during the meeting, any information or opinions which that person has on the business of the meeting.

(2) A person is able to exercise the right to vote at a general meeting when—

(a) that person is able to vote, during the meeting, on resolutions put to the vote at the meeting, and

(b) that person's vote can be taken into account in determining whether or not such resolutions are passed at the same time as the votes of all the other persons attending the meeting.

(3) The directors may make whatever arrangements they consider appropriate to enable those attending a general meeting to exercise their rights to speak or vote at it.

(4) In determining attendance at a general meeting, it is immaterial whether any two or more members attending it are in the same place as each other.

(5) Two or more persons who are not in the same place as each other attend a general meeting if their circumstances are such that if they have (or were to have) rights to speak and vote at that meeting, they are (or would be) able to exercise them.

Quorum for general meetings

29.—(1) No business other than the appointment of the chairman of the meeting is to be transacted at a general meeting if the persons attending it do not constitute a quorum as set out at 29 paragraph (2).

(2) The quorum for the meeting shall be 20 per cent of the members of the company entitled to vote upon the business to be transacted, or two members of the company so entitled (whichever is the greater) present in person or by proxy.

Chairing general meetings

30.—(1) If the directors have appointed a chairman, the chairman shall chair general meetings if present and willing to do so.

(2) If the directors have not appointed a chairman, or if the chairman is unwilling to chair the meeting or is not present within ten minutes of the time at which a meeting was due to start—

(a) the directors present, or

(b) (if no directors are present), the meeting,

must appoint a director or member to chair the meeting, and the appointment of the chairman of the meeting must be the first business of the meeting.

(3) The person chairing a meeting in accordance with this article is referred to as "the chairman of the meeting".

Attendance and speaking by directors and non-members

31.—(1) Directors may attend and speak at general meetings, whether or not they are members.

(2) The chairman of the meeting may permit other persons who are not members of the company to attend and speak at a general meeting.

Adjournment

32.—(1) If the persons attending a general meeting within half an hour of the time at which the meeting was due to start do not constitute a quorum, or if during a meeting a quorum ceases to be present, the chairman of the meeting must adjourn it.

(2) The chairman of the meeting may adjourn a general meeting at which a quorum is present if—

(a) the meeting consents to an adjournment, or

(b) it appears to the chairman of the meeting that an adjournment is necessary to protect the safety of any person attending the meeting or ensure that the business of the meeting is conducted in an orderly manner.

(3) The chairman of the meeting must adjourn a general meeting if directed to do so by the meeting.

(4) When adjourning a general meeting, the chairman of the meeting must—

(a) either specify the time and place to which it is adjourned or state that it is to continue at a time and place to be fixed by the directors, and

(b) have regard to any directions as to the time and place of any adjournment which have been given by the meeting.

(5) If the continuation of an adjourned meeting is to take place more than 14 days after it was adjourned, the company must give at least 7 clear days' notice of it (that is, excluding the day of the adjourned meeting and the day on which the notice is given)—

(a) to the same persons to whom notice of the company's general meetings is required to be given, and

(b) containing the same information which such notice is required to contain.

(6) No business may be transacted at an adjourned general meeting which could not properly have been transacted at the meeting if the adjournment had not taken place.

VOTING AT GENERAL MEETINGS

Voting: general

33.—(1) A resolution put to the vote of a general meeting must be decided on a show of hands unless a poll is duly demanded in accordance with the articles.

(2) If there are no landlords under leases of the whole or any part of the Premises who are members of the company, then one vote shall be available to be cast in respect of each flat in the Premises. The vote shall be cast by the member who is the qualifying tenant of the flat.

(3) At any time at which there are any landlords under leases of the whole or any part of the Premises who are members of the company, the votes available to be cast shall be determined as follows—

(a) there shall first be allocated to each residential unit in the Premises the same number of votes as equals the total number of members of the company who are landlords under leases of the whole or any part of the Premises. Landlords under a lease who are regarded as jointly being a member of the company shall be counted as one member for this purpose;

(b) if at any time the Premises includes any non-residential part, a total number of votes shall be allocated to that part as shall equal the total number of votes allocated to the residential units multiplied by a factor of A/B, where A is the total internal floor area of the non-residential parts and B is the total internal area of all the residential parts. Internal floor area shall be determined in accordance with paragraph 1(4) of Schedule 6 to the 2002 Act. Calculations of the internal floor area shall be measured in square metres, fractions of floor area of less than half a square metre shall be ignored and fractions of floor area in excess of half a square metre shall be counted as a whole square metre;

(c) the votes allocated to each residential unit shall be entitled to be cast by the member who is the qualifying tenant of that unit, or if there is no qualifying tenant of the unit, by the member who is the immediate landlord. The immediate landlord will not be entitled to the vote of a residential unit held by a qualifying tenant who is not a member of the RTM company;

(d) the votes allocated to any non-residential part included in the Premises shall be entitled to be cast by the immediate landlord of that part, or where there is no lease of a non-residential part, by the freeholder. Where there is more than one such person, the total number of votes allocated to the non-residential part shall be divided between them in proportion to the internal floor area of their respective parts. Any resulting entitlement to a fraction of a vote shall be ignored;

(e) if a residential unit is not subject to any lease, no votes shall be entitled to be cast in respect of it;

(f) any person who is a landlord under a lease or leases of the whole or any part of the Premises and who is a member of the company but is not otherwise entitled to any votes, shall be entitled to one vote.

(4) In the case of any persons who are to be regarded as jointly being members of the company, any such person may exercise the voting rights to which such members are jointly entitled, but where more than one such person tenders a vote, whether in person or by proxy, the vote of the senior shall be accepted to the exclusion of the votes of the others, and seniority shall be determined by the order in which the names of such persons appear in the register of members in respect of the flat or lease (as the case may be) in which they are interested.

Errors and disputes

34.—(1) No objection may be raised to the qualification of any person voting at a general meeting except at the meeting or adjourned meeting at which the vote objected to is tendered, and every vote not disallowed at the meeting is valid.

(2) Any such objection must be referred to the chairman of the meeting whose decision is final.

Poll votes

35.—(1) A poll on a resolution may be demanded—

(a) in advance of the general meeting where it is to be put to the vote, or

(b) at a general meeting, either before a show of hands on that resolution or immediately after the result of a show of hands on that resolution is declared.

(2) A poll may be demanded by—

(a) the chairman of the meeting;

(b) the directors;

(c) two or more persons having the right to vote on the resolution; or

(d) a person or persons representing not less than one tenth of the total voting rights of all the members having the right to vote on the resolution.

(3) A demand for a poll may be withdrawn if—

(a) the poll has not yet been taken, and

(b) the chairman of the meeting consents to the withdrawal.

(4) Polls must be taken immediately and in such manner as the chairman of the meeting directs.

Content of proxy notices

36.—(1) Proxies may only validly be appointed by a notice in writing (a "proxy notice") which—

(a) states the name and address of the member appointing the proxy;

(b) identifies the person appointed to be that member's proxy and the general meeting in relation to which that person is appointed;

(c) is signed by or on behalf of the member appointing the proxy, or is authenticated in such manner as the directors may determine; and

(d) is delivered to the company in accordance with the articles and any instructions contained in the notice of the general meeting to which they relate.

(2) The company may require proxy notices to be delivered in a particular form, and may specify different forms for different purposes.

(3) Proxy notices may specify how the proxy appointed under them is to vote (or that the proxy is to abstain from voting) on one or more resolutions.

(4) Unless a proxy notice indicates otherwise, it must be treated as—

(a) allowing the person appointed under it as a proxy discretion as to how to vote on any ancillary or procedural resolutions put to the meeting, and

(b) appointing that person as a proxy in relation to any adjournment of the general meeting to which it relates as well as the meeting itself.

Delivery of proxy notices

37.—(1) A person who is entitled to attend, speak or vote (either on a show of hands or on a poll) at a general meeting remains so entitled in respect of that meeting or any adjournment of it, even though a valid proxy notice has been delivered to the company by or on behalf of that person.

(2) An appointment under a proxy notice may be revoked by delivering to the company a notice in writing given by or on behalf of the person by whom or on whose behalf the proxy notice was given.

(3) A notice revoking a proxy appointment only takes effect if it is delivered before the start of the meeting or adjourned meeting to which it relates.

(4) If a proxy notice is not executed by the person appointing the proxy, it must be accompanied by written evidence of the authority of the person who executed it to execute it on the appointor's behalf.

Amendments to resolutions

38.—(1) An ordinary resolution to be proposed at a general meeting may be amended by ordinary resolution if—

(a) notice of the proposed amendment is given to the company in writing by a person entitled to vote at the general meeting at which it is to be proposed not less than 48 hours before the meeting is to take place (or such later time as the chairman of the meeting may determine), and

(b) the proposed amendment does not, in the reasonable opinion of the chairman of the meeting, materially alter the scope of the resolution.

(2) A special resolution to be proposed at a general meeting may be amended by ordinary resolution, if—

(a) the chairman of the meeting proposes the amendment at the general meeting at which the resolution is to be proposed, and

(b) the amendment does not go beyond what is necessary to correct a grammatical or other non-substantive error in the resolution.

(3) If the chairman of the meeting, acting in good faith, wrongly decides that an amendment to a resolution is out of order, the chairman's error does not invalidate the vote on that resolution.

PART 5

ADMINISTRATIVE ARRANGEMENTS

Means of communication to be used

39.—(1) Subject to the articles, anything sent or supplied by or to the company under the articles may be sent or supplied in any way in which the Companies

Acts provides for documents or information which are authorised or required by any provision of those Acts to be sent or supplied by or to the company.

(2) Subject to the articles, any notice or document to be sent or supplied to a director in connection with the taking of decisions by directors may also be sent or supplied by the means by which that director has asked to be sent or supplied with such notices or documents for the time being.

(3) A director may agree with the company that notices or documents sent to that director in a particular way are to be deemed to have been received within a specified time of their being sent, and for the specified time to be less than 48 hours.

Company seals

40.—(1) Any common seal may only be used by the authority of the directors.

(2) The directors may decide by what means and in what form any common seal is to be used.

(3) Unless otherwise decided by the directors, if the company has a common seal and it is affixed to a document, the document must also be signed by at least one authorised person in the presence of a witness who attests the signature.

(4) For the purposes of this article, an authorised person is—

(a) any director of the company;

(b) the company secretary (if any); or

(c) any person authorised by the directors for the purpose of signing documents to which the common seal is applied.

Inspection and copying of accounts and other records

41.—(1) In addition to, and without derogation from, any right conferred by statute, any member shall have the right, on reasonable notice, at such time and place as shall be convenient to the company, to inspect, and to be provided with a copy of, any book, minute, document or accounting record of the company, upon payment of any reasonable charge for copying. Such rights shall be subject to any resolution of the company in general meeting.

(2) In the case of any book, minute, document or accounting record which the directors reasonably consider contains confidential material, the disclosure of which would be contrary to the interests of the company, to the exclusion or

excision of such confidential material (the fact of such exclusion or excision being disclosed to the member), and to any other reasonable conditions that the directors may impose.

Provision for employees on cessation of business

42. The directors may decide to make provision for the benefit of persons employed or formerly employed by the company or any of its subsidiaries (other than a director or former director or shadow director) in connection with the cessation or transfer to any person of the whole or part of the undertaking of the company or that subsidiary.

PART 6

DIRECTORS' INDEMNITY AND INSURANCE

Indemnity

43.—(1) Subject to paragraph (2), a relevant director of the company or an associated company may be indemnified out of the company's assets against—

(a) any liability incurred by that director in connection with any negligence, default, breach of duty or breach of trust in relation to the company or an associated company,

(b) any liability incurred by that director in connection with the activities of the company or an associated company in its capacity as a trustee of an occupational pension scheme (as defined in section 235(6) of the Companies Act 2006),

(c) any other liability incurred by that director as an officer of the company or an associated company.

(2) This article does not authorise any indemnity which would be prohibited or rendered void by any provision of the Companies Acts or by any other provision of law.

(3) In this article—

(a) companies are associated if one is a subsidiary of the other or both are subsidiaries of the same body corporate, and

(b) a "relevant director" means any director or former director of the company or an associated company.

Insurance

44.—(1) The directors may decide to purchase and maintain insurance, at the expense of the company, for the benefit of any relevant director in respect of any relevant loss.

(2) In this article—

(a) a "relevant director" means any director or former director of the company or an associated company,

(b) a "relevant loss" means any loss or liability which has been or may be incurred by a relevant director in connection with that director's duties or powers in relation to the company, any associated company or any pension fund or employees' share scheme of the company or associated company, and

(c) companies are associated if one is a subsidiary of the other or both are subsidiaries of the same body corporate.

EXPLANATORY NOTE

(This note is not part of the Regulations)

In accordance with Chapter 1 of Part 2 of the Commonhold and Leasehold Reform Act 2002 ("the 2002 Act"), a company, referred to in that Chapter as a RTM company, may acquire and exercise rights in relation to the management of premises. Section 73(2) of the 2002 Act provides that a company is a RTM company in relation to premises if it is a private company limited by guarantee and its articles of association state that its object, or one of its objects, is the acquisition and exercise of the right to manage those premises. Subsections (3) to (5) of that section describe companies that are not RTM companies and the circumstances in which a RTM company ceases to be a company of that description. Section 74(2) of the 2002 Act provides that "the appropriate national authority" shall make regulations about the content and form of articles of association of RTM companies. Section 179(1) of the 2002 Act provides for the Secretary of State to be "the appropriate national authority" as respects England.

These Regulations, which apply in England, prescribe, by reference to the Schedule to the Regulations, the form and content of the articles of association of RTM companies. They include provision, authorised by section 74(4) of the 2002 Act, to the effect that the articles have effect for a RTM company whether or not the company adopts the articles set out in the Schedule.

The Regulations revoke the RTM Companies (Memorandum and Articles of Association) (England) Regulations 2003, subject to transitional provisions. RTM companies incorporated before 9th November 2009 can continue to operate under their existing constitutions until 30th September 2010. Alternatively, such companies can choose to adopt the articles of association prescribed by these Regulations.

A full impact assessment of the effect that this instrument will have on business and the voluntary sector is available from the Department for Communities and Local Government, Leasehold and Park Homes Policy Team, Eland House, Bressenden Place, London SW1E 5DU and is annexed to the Explanatory Memorandum which is available alongside the instrument on the OPSI website at www.opsi.gov.uk/stat.htm.

Printed and published in the UK by The Stationery Office Limited under the authority and superintendence of Carol Tullo, Controller of Her Majesty's Stationery Office and Queen's Printer of Acts of Parliament.

Appendix C The Community Interest Company Regulations 2005, SI 2005/1788, Schedule 1

PROVISIONS PRESCRIBED FOR THE MEMORANDUM OR ARTICLES OF A COMMUNITY INTEREST COMPANY LIMITED BY GUARANTEE WITHOUT A SHARE CAPITAL

Regulation 7

1.—(1) The company shall not transfer any of its assets other than for full consideration.

(2) Provided the conditions in sub-paragraph (3) are satisfied, sub-paragraph (1) shall not apply to—

(a) the transfer of assets to any specified asset-locked body, or (with the consent of the Regulator) to any other asset-locked body; and

(b) the transfer of assets made for the benefit of the community other than by way of a transfer of assets to an asset-locked body.

(3) The conditions are that the transfer of assets must comply with any restrictions on the transfer of assets for less than full consideration which may be set out elsewhere in the memorandum or articles of the company.

(4) In this paragraph—

(a) "asset-locked body" means—

  (i) a community interest company, charity or Scottish charity; or

  (ii) a body established outside the United Kingdom that is equivalent to any of those persons;

(b) "community" is to be construed in accordance with section 35(5) of the Companies (Audit, Investigations and Community Enterprise) Act 2004;

(c) "charity" (except in the phrase "Scottish charity") has the meaning given by section 96(1) of the Charities Act 1993;[1]

(d) "the Regulator" means the Regulator of Community Interest Companies;

(e) "Scottish charity" has the meaning given by section 1(7) of the Law Reform (Miscellaneous Provisions) (Scotland) Act 1990;[2]

(f) "specified" means specified in the memorandum or articles of association of the company for the purposes of this paragraph; and

(g) "transfer" includes every description of disposition, payment, release or distribution, and the creation or extinction of an estate or interest in, or a right over, any property.

2.—(1) The subscribers to the memorandum are the first members of the company.

(2) Such other persons as are admitted to membership in accordance with the articles shall be members of the company.

(3) No person shall be admitted a member of the company unless he is approved by the directors.

(4) Every person who wishes to become a member shall deliver to the company an application for membership in such form (and containing such information) as the directors require and executed by him.

(5) Membership is not transferable to anyone else.

(6) Membership is terminated if:

(a) the member dies or ceases to exist; or

(b) otherwise in accordance with the articles.

3.—(1) A person who is not a member of the company shall not have any right to vote at a general meeting of the company; but this is without prejudice to any right to vote on a resolution affecting the rights attached to a class of the company's debentures.

(2) No powers to appoint directors of the company may be given to persons who are not members of the company which immediately after their exercise could result in the majority of the directors of the company having been appointed by persons who are not members of the company.

1 1993 c. 10.
2 1990 c. 40.

(3) No powers to remove directors of the company may be given to persons who are not members of the company which immediately after their exercise could result in either—

(a) the majority of the remaining directors of the company having been appointed by persons who are not members of the company; or

(b) the number of directors removed during the current financial year of the company by persons who are not members of the company exceeding the number of the remaining directors of the company.

(4) However, sub-paragraphs (2) and (3) shall not prevent a director from appointing, or subsequently removing, an alternate director, if permitted to do so by the articles.

(5) In this paragraph, "financial year" has the meaning given in section 223 of the Companies Act 1985.[3]

4.—(1) Questions arising at a meeting of directors shall be decided by a majority of votes; in case of an equality of votes, the chairman shall have a second or casting vote.

(2) A director who is also an alternate director shall be entitled in the absence of his appointer to a separate vote on behalf of his appointer in addition to his own vote.

(3) Except as provided by sub-paragraphs (1) and (2) in all proceedings of directors each director must not have more than one vote.

3 Section 223 of the 1985 Act was inserted by section 3 of the Companies Act 1989.

Appendix D The Community Interest Company Regulations 2005, SI 2005/1788, Schedule 2

PROVISIONS PRESCRIBED FOR THE MEMORANDUM OR ARTICLES OF A COMMUNITY INTEREST COMPANY LIMITED BY SHARES, OR LIMITED BY GUARANTEE WITH A SHARE CAPITAL

Regulation 8(a)

1.—(1) The company shall not transfer any of its assets other than for full consideration.

(2) Provided the conditions in sub-paragraph (3) are satisfied, sub-paragraph (1) shall not apply to—

(a) the transfer of assets to any specified asset-locked body, or (with the consent of the Regulator) to any other asset-locked body; and

(b) the transfer of assets made for the benefit of the community other than by way of a transfer of assets to an asset-locked body.

(3) The conditions are that the transfer of assets must comply with any restrictions on the transfer of assets for less than full consideration which may be set out elsewhere in the memorandum or articles of the company.

(4) In this paragraph—

(a) "asset-locked body" means—

  (i) a community interest company, charity or Scottish charity; or

  (ii) a body established outside Great Britain that is equivalent to any of those persons;

(b) "community" is to be construed in accordance with section 35(5) of the Companies (Audit, Investigations and Community Enterprise) Act 2004;

(c) "charity" (except in the phrase "Scottish charity") has the meaning given by section 96 of the Charities Act 1993;

(d) "the Regulator" means the Regulator of Community Interest Companies;

(e) "Scottish charity" has the meaning given by section 1(7) of the Law Reform (Miscellaneous Provisions) (Scotland) Act 1990;

(f) "specified" means specified in the memorandum or articles of association of the company for the purposes of this paragraph; and

(g) "transfer" includes every description of disposition, payment, release or distribution, and the creation or extinction of an estate or interest in, or a right over, any property.

2.—(1) The directors may refuse to register the transfer of a share to a person of whom they do not approve.

(2) They may also refuse to register the transfer unless it is lodged at the registered office of the company or at such other place as the directors may appoint and is accompanied by such evidence as the directors may reasonably require to show the right of the transferor to make the transfer, and by such other information as they may reasonably require.

(3) If the directors refuse to register such a transfer, they shall within two months after the date on which the transfer was lodged with the company send to the transferee notice of the refusal.

(4) The provisions of this paragraph apply in addition to any restrictions on the transfer of a share which may be set out elsewhere in the memorandum or articles of the company.

3.—(1) A person who is not a member of the company shall not have any right to vote at a general meeting of the company; but this is without prejudice to any right to vote on a resolution affecting the rights attached to a class of the company's debentures.

(2) No powers to appoint directors of the company may be given to persons who are not members of the company which immediately after their exercise could result in the majority of the directors of the company having been appointed by persons who are not members of the company.

(3) No powers to remove directors of the company may be given to persons who are not members of the company which immediately after their exercise could result in either—

(a) the majority of the remaining directors of the company having been appointed by persons who are not members of the company; or

(b) the number of directors removed during the current financial year of the company by persons who are not members of the company exceeding the number of the remaining directors of the company.

(4) However, sub-paragraphs (2) and (3) shall not prevent a director from appointing, or subsequently removing, an alternate director, if permitted to do so by the articles.

(5) In this paragraph, "financial year" has the meaning given in section 223 of the Companies Act 1985.

4.—(1) Questions arising at a meeting of directors shall be decided by a majority of votes; in case of an equality of votes, the chairman shall have a second or casting vote.

(2) A director who is also an alternate director shall be entitled in the absence of his appointer to a separate vote on behalf of his appointer in addition to his own vote.

(3) Except as provided by sub-paragraphs (1) and (2) in all proceedings of directors each director must not have more than one vote.

Appendix E The Community Interest Company Regulations 2005, SI 2005/1788, Schedule 3

ALTERNATIVE PROVISIONS PRESCRIBED FOR THE MEMORANDUM OR ARTICLES OF A COMMUNITY INTEREST COMPANY LIMITED BY SHARES, OR LIMITED BY GUARANTEE WITH A SHARE CAPITAL

Regulation 8(b)

1.—(1) The company shall not transfer any of its assets other than for full consideration.

(2) Provided the conditions in sub-paragraph (3) are satisfied, sub-paragraph (1) shall not apply to—

(a) the transfer of assets to any specified asset-locked body, or (with the consent of the Regulator) to any other asset-locked body;

(b) the transfer of assets made for the benefit of the community other than by way of a transfer of assets to an asset-locked body;

(c) the payment of dividends in respect of shares in the company;

(d) the distribution of assets on a winding up;

(e) payments on the redemption or purchase of the company's own shares;

(f) payments on the reduction of share capital; and

(g) the extinguishing or reduction of the liability of members in respect of share capital not paid up on the reduction of share capital.

(3) The conditions are that the transfer of assets—

(a) must comply with any restrictions on the transfer of assets for less than full consideration which may be set out elsewhere in the memorandum or articles of the company; and

(b) must not exceed any limits imposed by, or by virtue of, Part 2 of the Companies (Audit, Investigations and Community Enterprise) Act 2004.

(4) In this paragraph—

(a) "asset-locked body" means—

  (i) a community interest company, charity or Scottish charity; or

  (ii) a body established outside Great Britain that is equivalent to any of those persons;

(b) "community" is to be construed in accordance with section 35(5) of the Companies (Audit, Investigations and Community Enterprise) Act 2004;

(c) "charity" (except in the phrase "Scottish charity") has the meaning given by section 96 of the Charities Act 1993;

(d) "the Regulator" means the Regulator of Community Interest Companies;

(e) "Scottish charity" has the meaning given by section 1(7) of the Law Reform (Miscellaneous Provisions) (Scotland) Act 1990;

(f) "specified" means specified in the memorandum or articles of association of the company for the purposes of this paragraph; and

(g) "transfer" includes every description of disposition, payment, release or distribution, and the creation or extinction of an estate or interest in, or a right over, any property.

2.—(1) The directors may refuse to register the transfer of a share to a person of whom they do not approve.

(2) They may also refuse to register the transfer unless it is lodged at the registered office of the company or at such other place as the directors may appoint and is accompanied by such evidence as the directors may reasonably require to show the right of the transferor to make the transfer, and by such other information as they may reasonably require.

(3) If the directors refuse to register such a transfer, they shall within two months after the date on which the transfer was lodged with the company send to the transferee notice of the refusal.

(4) The provisions of this paragraph apply in addition to any restrictions on the transfer of a share which may be set out elsewhere in the memorandum or articles of the company.

3.—(1) A person who is not a member of the company shall not have any right to vote at a general meeting of the company; but this is without prejudice to any right to vote on a resolution affecting the rights attached to a class of the company's debentures.

(2) No powers to appoint directors of the company may be given to persons who are not members of the company which immediately after their exercise could result in the majority of the directors of the company having been appointed by persons who are not members of the company.

(3) No powers to remove directors of the company may be given to persons who are not members of the company which immediately after their exercise could result in either—

(a) the majority of the remaining directors of the company having been appointed by persons who are not members of the company; or

(b) the number of directors removed during the current financial year of the company by persons who are not members of the company exceeding the number of the remaining directors of the company.

(4) However, sub-paragraphs (2) and (3) shall not prevent a director from appointing, or subsequently removing, an alternate director, if permitted to do so by the articles.

(5) In this paragraph "financial year" has the meaning given in section 223 of the Companies Act 1985.

4.—(1) Questions arising at a meeting of directors shall be decided by a majority of votes; in case of an equality of votes, the chairman shall have a second or casting vote.

(2) A director who is also an alternate director shall be entitled in the absence of his appointer to a separate vote on behalf of his appointer in addition to his own vote.

(3) Except as provided by sub-paragraphs (1) and (2) in all proceedings of directors each director must not have more than one vote.

Index

[*All references are to paragraph numbers*]